W9-AZL-600

The Economics of Social Responsibility

This book offers a rethinking of the burgeoning research on not-for-profit organizations and socially responsible economics. Adopting a comparative approach, the chapters explore and reinterpret the impact of social enterprises on the provision of general-interest services, work integration, microfinance, and fair trade, and show how these enterprises form the hub of an emerging economy of social responsibility. The book provides a new interpretation of social enterprises as entrepreneurial organizations that pursue social objectives and are successful due to the non-self-seeking motives of their members.

As the current financial crisis highlights, social enterprises often have the capacity to tackle social and economic problems more effectively and efficiently than public agencies and for-profit enterprises. The contributors argue that social enterprises are able to create value in socially responsible and environmentally sustainable ways due to their competitive advantages in providing goods and services that meet the needs of their clients and the communities in which they operate. By focusing on the main features, incentive structures, and governance models of these enterprises, the book moves beyond the traditional conception of non-profits and paves the way for the development of a more comprehensive theory of the firm.

A key finding of the book is that social enterprises constitute a viable form of entrepreneurship that complements the activities of public authorities and for-profit firms. Against this background, productive initiatives with explicit social goals should not be considered 'against the market', but rather seen as successful mechanisms for reconciling equity and efficiency on the one hand with the creation of economic and social value on the other.

This book will be of interest to postgraduate students, professionals working in the not-for-profit sector, and scholars interested in socially responsible economics. It is particularly suitable for seminars and workshops focusing on the management of not-for-profit organizations, sustainable development, and globalization.

Leonardo Becchetti is Professor of Economics at the University of Roma 'Tor Vergata', Italy. **Carlo Borzaga** is Professor of Economics at the University of Trento, Italy, and President of the European Research Institute on Cooperative and Social Enterprises (Euricse).

Routledge advances in social economics
Edited by John B. Davis
Marquette University

This series presents new advances and developments in social economics think-ing on a variety of subjects that concern the link between social values and eco-nomics. Need, justice and equity, gender, cooperation, work poverty, the environment, class, institutions, public policy, and methodology are some of the most important themes. Among the orientations of the authors are social econo-mist, institutionalist, humanist, solidarist, cooperatist, radical and Marxist, fem-inist, post-Keynesian, behaviouralist, and environmentalist. The series offers new contributions from today's foremost thinkers on the social character of the economy.

Published in conjunction with the Association of Social Economics.
Previous books published in the series include:

1 **Social Economics**
   Premises, findings and policies
   Edited by Edward J. O'Boyle

2 **The Environmental Consequences of Growth**
   Steady-state economics as an alternative to ecological decline
   Douglas Booth

3 **The Human Firm**
   A socio-economic analysis of its behaviour and potential in a new economic age
   John Tomer

4 **Economics for the Common Good**
   Two centuries of economic thought in the humanist tradition
   Mark A. Lutz

5 **Working Time**
   International trends, theory and policy perspectives
   Edited by Lonnie Golden and Deborah M. Figart

The Economics of Social Responsibility

The world of social enterprises

Edited by Leonardo Becchetti and
Carlo Borzaga

 Routledge
Taylor & Francis Group

LONDON AND NEW YORK

First published 2010
by Routledge
2 Park Square, Milton Park, Abingdon, Oxon OX14 4RN

Simultaneously published in the USA and Canada
by Routledge
270 Madison Avenue, New York, NY 10016

Routledge is an imprint of the Taylor & Francis Group, an informa business

Typeset in Times by Wearset Ltd, Boldon, Tyne and Wear
Printed and bound in Great Britain by TJI Digital, Padstow, Cornwall

British Library Cataloguing in Publication Data
A catalogue record for this book is available from the British Library

Library of Congress Cataloging in Publication Data
The economics of social responsibility: the world of social enterprises/
edited by Leonardo Becchetti and Carlo Borzaga.
p. cm.
Includes bibliographical references and index.

Nonprofit organizations. 2. Entrepreneurship. 3. Social responsibility of
business. I. Becchetti, Leonardo. II. Borzaga, Carlo.

HD62.6.E37 2010
338.7–dc22

2009047910

ISBN13: 978-0-415-46576-2 (hbk)
ISBN13: 978-0-203-85102-9 (ebk)

Contents

viii *Contents*

Illustrations

Figures

Tables

Contributors

Leonardo Becchetti is Professor of Economics at the University of Roma 'Tor Vergata'. He has coordinated several impact studies on microfinance and fair trade, and has around 300 scientific publications.

Carlo Borzaga is Professor of Economics at the University of Trento, Italy, and the President of Euricse. He has coordinated many European projects on social cooperatives and non-profit organizations.

Rocco Ciciretti is Assistant Professor of Economic Policy at the University of Roma 'Tor Vergata'. His research interests include corporate finance, financial markets and institutions, and applied financial econometrics.

Marco Costantino is a postgraduate student in the Department of Economic Geography at the University of Bari. He has an MA in International Cooperation and Development Economics and has conducted impact studies of fair trade in Kenya, Peru, and Thailand.

Sara Depedri is a researcher in the Department of Economics at the University of Trento. She has a PhD in Law and Economics and her research focuses on the motivations and satisfaction of workers in social cooperatives and non-profit organizations.

Luca Fazzi is Associate Professor of Sociology at the University of Trento. His research interests include comparative social policy, third-sector activities, and voluntary action.

Giulia Galera is the Research Area Coordinator of Euricse. She has a PhD in International Studies from the University of Trento and has conducted comparative research on social enterprises in Eastern Europe.

Giuseppe Mastromatteo is Professor of Economics at the Catholic University of Milano. His current research interests include globalization and labour economics, and he is a member of the steering committee of EconomEtica.

Ermanno Tortia is a researcher in the Department of Economics at the University of Trento. His research interests include the theory of the firm and labour economics, cooperative and social enterprises, human resources management, and local economic development.

Abbreviations and acronyms

CDFI	Community Development Finance Institution
CIC	Community Interest Company (UK)
CNP	Johns Hopkins Comparative Nonprofit Sector Project
COPAVIC	Cooperativa de producciòn artesanal de vidrio Cantel
CSR	corporate social responsibility
EU	European Union
FLO	Fairtrade Labelling Organizations International
GDP	gross domestic product
GMM	generalized method of moments
ICA	International Cooperative Alliance
ICT	information and communication technology
IMF	International Monetary Fund
KLD400	FTSE KLD400 Social Index
MCCH	Maquita Cushunchic Comercializando como Hermanos
MFI	microfinance institution
NGO	non-governmental organization
OECD	Organisation for Economic Co-operation and Development
ROSCA	rotating savings and credit association
UNDP	United Nations Development Programme
WFTO	World Fair Trade Organization (until 2009, International Fair Trade Association)
WTO	World Trade Organization

Introduction

Leonardo Becchetti and Carlo Borzaga

In many developed countries, the sustainability of employment, welfare, and development policies has been increasingly challenged by anaemic rates of economic growth, the complexity of society, and growing demands for services. The capacity of general-interest services to satisfy the needs of citizens has declined as the demand for these services—especially social, health, educational, and environmental services—has increased. The appearance of new needs and the increasing differentiation of existing ones have made demands by citizens more wide-ranging and complex. In addition to the difficulties generated by fiscal crises, the public supply of standardized services has proved incapable of satisfying users with differentiated needs.

Labour and employment policies have often failed to maintain low unemployment rates and critics have complained that some of these policies provide disincentives for the unemployed to accept job offers. Clearly, these policies have failed to tackle long-term unemployment and underemployment by the disadvantaged. The inability of labour and employment policies to ensure that all workers can find jobs that allow them to benefit from their capabilities has resulted in widespread and persistent exclusion of individuals and groups from the labour market.

Development policies managed by international institutions and national governments have increasingly proved to be insufficient and ineffective. The amount of public expenditure committed to development issues has decreased over recent decades, and aid programmes have been unable to support balanced economic development at regional and international levels. Moreover, preferences by governments for top-down initiatives have often prevented the empowerment of beneficiaries and, as a result, spawned initiatives that have frequently proved to be unsustainable.

Several innovations have been introduced by national governments to improve the effectiveness of these policies. Reforms have strongly reshaped the range, organization, and delivery of welfare and general-interest services, including the roles played by public and private actors. Private managerial models have increasingly been adopted by public institutions, and many services have been privatized, mainly through the transfer of production to private providers with public funding. In some cases, public commitment to funding such services has been curtailed. The reforms that have been introduced have often failed to achieve satisfactory outcomes, and indeed they have contributed to a growing imbalance between the demand and supply of general-interest services, especially in the key areas of health, social services, and education.

Labour and employment policies have also been reformed in many respects. The main driver of these reforms has been the shift from passive to active employment policies. Unemployment subsidies have been shortened in duration and the rate of substitution has been reduced. New welfare-to-work policies—involving training schemes, employment services, and employment subsidies—have been introduced with the aim of reducing unemployment spells. The labour market has been deregulated in order to increase the level of employment, often by creating temporary and low-paid jobs. Public employment services have been privatized in most countries and forced to compete directly with the remaining public services. These reforms have had mixed effects, with some of them—particularly active labour market policies—contributing to increases in employment, though the rate of unemployment has not declined as expected. Many of the new jobs created are short term, and these have contributed to a broadening sense of precariousness. Long-term unemployment has not been curbed and tends to be concentrated among certain groups.

Development policies have strengthened the 'trade not aid' strategy that considers international trade the main driver of economic growth. This strategy has been supported by the process of globalization and used to justify reductions in aid programmes. Increased trade has achieved positive results for some countries, but has failed in others, leaving more than one billion of the world's population living in poverty. Increased trade has proved to be ineffective in sustaining economic development and job creation, especially in countries where underdevelopment can be considered a consequence of poorly functioning markets. Moreover, trade liberalization has not always reflected the concerns of developing countries and generally not involved agriculture, which is the economic activity most capable of supporting broad-based and balanced development.

Many scholars have analysed the impact and shortcomings of reforms upon providers, users, and funders.[1] Most of these analyses, however, have not taken into account the extent and vigour of voluntary responses to these issues by individuals and groups, and how these responses differ from those of both for-profit enterprises and public institutions. Particularly noteworthy has been the development of private not-for-profit economic activities that have given rise to innovative organizations that are motivated by preferences that are not self-seeking. These bottom-up initiatives can be interpreted as concrete expressions of an increasing sense of social responsibility on the part of citizens and as an 'endogenous response' to their discontent about the shortcomings of public policies.

This emerging economy of social responsibility has entailed an enlargement of existing actors and activities. By stimulating responsible economic behaviour, these initiatives have had a strong impact upon the well-being of society and supported the institutionalization of collective participatory practices. These initiatives have also called into question conventional economic paradigms and paved the way for new theoretical explanations of economic behaviour.

This surge in responsible behaviour has entailed four distinct, albeit interdependent, trends: the reinforcement and globalization of advocacy initiatives and movements, the adoption of socially responsible behaviour by individuals, the direct production of general-interest services by groups of citizens, and the adoption of corporate social-responsibility practices by conventional enterprises.

The first trend consists of a wave of advocacy movements that have mobilized around not only traditional socio-economic concerns but also environmental, feminist, and globalization issues and spawned a rapid increase in the number of organizations and participants. Collective action by these movements (protests, petitions, boycotts, and demonstrations) has increasingly transcended the boundaries of national policies and started to pressure corporations to adhere to international environmental and social standards (Schmitter and Trechsel 2004). In effect, advocacy organizations perform regulatory functions in lieu of national governments and international institutions, which have often failed to perform this task. Accordingly, the frame of reference within which the behaviour of corporations is regulated has grown increasingly complex, as it is both regulated by the conventions of international organizations and subjected to pressures by the new international advocacy organizations. In some cases, advocacy movements have succeeded in forcing enterprises to change their behaviour and to improve their ecological and social standards.

The effectiveness of these advocacy organizations is partly due to reductions in communication costs associated with the media revolution. Intensive use of the Internet, for example, has not only exacerbated the negative effects of globalization, but also facilitated worldwide cooperation among consumer and advocacy organizations in ways that are consistent with the transnational character of the issues that they address.

The second trend entails citizens becoming increasingly aware of the impact that individual behaviour and action can have in the economic sphere. One important development of the last two decades has been an upsurge of interest in bottom-up mobilization that seeks to influence corporate behaviour. Individual citizens have learned to 'vote with their pocketbooks', thereby increasing their degree of active participation in political and economic life by becoming responsible consumers and savers. This proactive response by citizens embraces everyday behaviour and choices, ranging from daily consumption to ethical tourism.

The most innovative feature of responsible consumption, however, is that it takes into account not simply the quantitative and qualitative characteristics of products (as orthodox economic theory assumes), but also the process and conditions under which goods and services are produced. Moreover, responsible consumption also entails an explicit decision to support a more fair distribution of resources between consumers and producers. Responsible shopping involves 'green consumption' (eco-labelling), 'sustainable consumption' (the organic food movement), and behaviour in line with the current 'ethics and responsibility' agenda (fair trade and ethical products and services).

Similarly, responsible saving has gathered pace in recent years as people increasingly demand to know what use is being made of their savings. A growing number of people consider it unacceptable that their savings are used for questionably ethical investments, and they choose to use their savings to support specifically ethical activities, even when this may involve lower returns. Socially responsible savings and investments recognize the importance of ethics in the functioning of modern market economies.

The third trend involves groups of citizens voluntarily initiating new economic activities with the goal of providing services to the community and the disadvantaged who are often neglected by conventional private and public actors. Some of these activities also help ensure the sustainability of initiatives promoted by ethical consumption and investment. These activities have developed into new types of enterprises that challenge the main assumptions of conventional economic theory about the predominance of self-seeking agents and the conceptualization of enterprises as profit-maximizing mechanisms. These initiatives were initially established on a voluntary basis, but they have evolved into stable organizations that provide continuous and often innovative services.

The fourth trend consists of a gradual change in behaviour by conventional for-profit firms that have adopted practices known as corporate social responsibility. This has occurred due to demands by concerned consumers and investors that firms take responsibility for the social and environmental sustainability of their activities. Some firms have responded by ameliorating the negative consequences of their activities and by generating positive external effects. The emergence of these practices has stimulated research and debate on the definition and sustainability of corporate social responsibility and the adoption of a range of inclusive governance models and accountability systems.

It is noteworthy that all these actions by individuals, groups, and firms result from an increasing tendency to take into account the social consequences of economic activities. This new form of thinking and behaviour has been spreading and growing—from local phenomena into global trends, from informal actions into institutionalized initiatives, and from spontaneous initiatives into regulated activities.

Interestingly, these four trends have become intertwined and mutually supportive. Voluntary and advocacy organizations have transformed into institutionalized entities that promote in practical ways the social rights of disadvantaged groups and communities. Through the provision of work-integration services, the new not-for-profit enterprises have been effective advocates for the rights of people excluded by the labour market. Responsible consumption has stimulated the creation of enterprises engaged in the production and sale of fair-trade products, while the not-for-profit enterprises promoting fair trade have encouraged the development of pro-social behaviour by consumers.

Of the four trends, the most far-reaching and innovative has been the emergence and consolidation of autonomous and sustainable bottom-up initiatives engaged in the direct provision of general-interest services. This development has also been the most interesting from social and economic points of view. Whereas the enlargement of activities such as advocacy is consistent with conventional approaches that presuppose enterprises are either public or for-profit, the upsurge of the new not-for-profits—or, as they are often called, *social enterprises*—challenges the validity of these approaches.

An important feature of these productive not-for-profit organizations is their capacity to overcome the traditional separation between the creation and redistribution of economic value. In classical economic theory, self-seeking agents create value and distribute it according to the rules of the market, which is indifferent to satisfying the needs of those unable to pay. These agents can act being confident that the 'invisible hand' of the market will reconcile self-interested motives with socially desirable results, while the state compensates for social and environmental unbalances generated by corporate actions. The emergence of social enterprises, however, has been prompted by the incapacity of the market–state model to reconcile economic development with social and environmental sustainability due to the limits both of the invisible hand and of state institutions ridden by conflicts of interests, problems of misrepresentation, and lack of resources.

Social enterprises provide an alternative to for-profit firms and public agencies by creating economic value in socially and environmentally sustainable ways. From this perspective, two important threads are developed in this book: the feasibility of doing business differently and the complementary role played by social enterprises with respect to public and for-profit actors. Against this background, the creation of productive initiatives with an explicit social goal are not 'against the market'; quite the contrary, they are an important innovation that can enhance the capacity of the market to reconcile equity and efficiency on the one hand with the creation of economic and social value on the other. Markets themselves are often unable to create such intangible values as trust, responsibility, and social capital that are the essential conditions for their functioning, particularly following financial and economic crises. Social enterprises not only produce economic value but also crucial intangibles, thereby performing an essential role in modern economies (Becchetti and Huybrechts 2008).

Given these premises, this book concentrates on the emergence and spread of social enterprises. This focus provides a useful perspective from which to understand the four major trends that have been highlighted. The novelty introduced by social enterprises has been their capacity to simultaneously support advocacy activities and pro-social behaviour. It is clear that the dual-pole paradigm of state and market must be transformed into a three-pole paradigm with the third actor reconciling redistributive aims with productive activities and nourishing a broad spectrum of socially responsible behaviour.

Social enterprises have a direct impact upon the production of goods and services of general interest, which cover a wide range of activities that strongly affect the well-being and quality of life enjoyed by communities. Given their not-for-profit aims and their specific proprietary and governance structures, social enterprises supply services that have a beneficial impact upon society by favouring the allocation of resources to the most vulnerable parts of the population and by contributing to economic growth and employment.

To date, research on social enterprises has generally been fragmented and descriptive. Most studies focus on specific countries, fields of activity, and types of behaviour, and this approach has hindered the development of a comprehensive account. This book aims to consolidate existing knowledge and provide a general account of the emergence of social enterprises, which are regarded as the impetus for the creation of an economy of social responsibility. The contributions are both theoretical and empirical, and they examine conceptual, historical, sociological, legal, and economic issues. Before introducing the specific topics addressed by each chapter, it is helpful to clarify some of the key concepts that are used in the book.

A working definition of *social enterprises*

The increase in socially responsible behaviour and its institutionalization have prompted efforts both to conceptualize the innovative practices of citizens and organizations and to develop a theoretical framework that can explain the rise of economic institutions pursuing explicit social goals. Various definitions have been proposed for characterizing the new institutions, both as single organizations and as an ensemble. Each definition emphasizes specific aspects, such as the non-profit distribution constraint or the social mission, and embraces specific organizational typologies, depending upon the prevailing tradition and national context. These definitions include the *non-profit* or *not-for-profit sector*, the *third sector*, and the *social economy* (Borzaga and Defourny 2001).

The term *non-profit sector* was initially used during the late 1970s in the US (Salamon *et al.* 1999), and it has developed into a framework emphasizing that organizations in this sector are strictly bounded to the non-profit distribution constraint in that they cannot distribute profits to either managers or owners. The non-profit sector includes associations, foundations, and voluntary organizations depending upon the specific legal and fiscal context.

In contrast to the term *non-profit*, *not-for-profit* refers to a larger group of organizations pursuing goals other than profit maximization. It also includes organizations that are not necessarily subject to the non-profit distribution constraint, such as cooperatives and mutual aid societies.

The term *third sector* emphasizes the intermediary nature of the belonging organizations, which are neither public nor for-profit. Like the term *not-for-profit*, *third sector* refers to a wide variety of organizations, but it traditionally excludes cooperatives. However, recent definitions tend to include also mutual aid societies and cooperatives (HM Treasury and Cabinet Office 2007).

The *social economy* approach stresses the mission of the belonging organizations, which aim to benefit either their members or the larger community. It also focuses on the primacy of workers over capital and on the implementation of democratic management models (Borzaga and Defourny 2001).

These concepts are all broad, since they bring together various types of organizations that reflect specific aspects of socially responsible behaviour, including redistribution and advocacy in addition to productive activities. However, all these definitions fail to highlight entrepreneurial dynamics within the sector. Consequently, there is a need for more precise definitions that emphasize entrepreneurial aspects: two such terms—*social entrepreneurship* and *social enterprise*—have increasingly been used in the literature (Defourny and Nyssens 2008). The term *social entrepreneurship* is quite broad and covers a range of activities and initiatives that do not necessarily involve the production of goods and may vary over time; this term does not necessarily imply a dedicated organization with all the characteristics of an enterprise. The organizations referred to under the rubric of social entrepreneurship range along a continuum that includes social initiatives occurring in profit-seeking businesses; institutionalized entities explicitly pursuing goals, relations, and practices that yield social benefits; and entrepreneurial trends in non-profit organizations, including innovative practices developed within the public sector (Johnson 2000; Roper and Cheney 2005; Mair and Martí 2006).

By contrast, the term *social enterprise* is used mainly to refer to institutionalized entrepreneurial actors that pursue social goals. Despite the lack of a common usage of the term *social enterprise* in the international literature, a growing convergence in meaning has emerged in Europe, where the concept of *social enterprise* is used to identify a 'different way' of doing business that occurs when institutional structures are created to pursue specifically social goals.[2] Following the European tradition, social enterprises are conceptualized as private autonomous institutions that supply merit or general-interest goods and services. The specific character of social enterprises stems from the type of goods and services they supply and from the production and allocation processes they provide for vulnerable groups. Social enterprises are characterized by goals, profit distributions, ownership rights, and control power that differentiate them from other types of institutions and provide competitive advantages. Given the types of goods produced and the social goals pursued, social enterprises do not maximize profit. They observe a distribution constraint, which can be either total or partial, but is in all cases substantive.[3] Finally, ownership rights and control in social enterprises are often assigned to stakeholders other than investors. Depending upon the type of social enterprise under consideration, ownership rights and control can be assigned to a single category of stakeholders—such as users, employees, or donors—or to more than one category—in other words, a multi-stakeholder organization (Borzaga and Mittone 1997).

For the purpose of this book, social enterprises are defined as autonomous not-for-profit organizations providing goods or services that explicitly aim to benefit the community. Due to a total or partial non-profit distribution constraint, social enterprises are obliged to invest all or at least a significant part of their profits in the enterprise. The non-profit distribution constraint discourages owners from selling these enterprises, and thus tends to turn them into common access resources. To achieve their aims, social enterprises often adopt innovative governance structures involving various types of stakeholders.

The reasons for adopting this conceptualization are twofold: first, it has come to be widely accepted at an institutional level; second, unlike *social entrepreneurship*, the term *social enterprise* focuses on a specific institutional mechanism.

Our definition of *social enterprise* excludes several other types of organizations with social aims: third-sector associations that do not carry out entrepreneurial activities and mainly perform advocacy or redistributive functions, public agencies, for-profit firms engaged in social projects, and revenue-generating activities operated by non-profit organizations to support their social aims.

It should be emphasized that social enterprises are *not-for-profit*, but they are not necessarily *non-profit* since they may be allowed to distribute part of their surpluses to their owners. For purposes of clarity, the term *not-for-profit* is used throughout the book to refer both to these innovative forms of enterprise and to traditional non-profits. The term *non-profit* is used to refer to those organizations that operate under a total non-profit distribution constraint.

The evolution of social enterprises

Social enterprises emerged during the 1980s when the limitations of traditional public welfare provision were becoming evident, the process of privatization was accelerating, and traditional aid programmes were increasingly failing to support economic development. In this context, the emergence and consolidation of various forms of solidarity and new initiatives producing general-interest services or managing economic activities like fair trade stimulated the search for alternative institutional arrangements. In Europe, the reaction of groups of citizens dissatisfied by both the public supply and market provision of services has contributed to shaping the evolution of social enterprises as a specific institutional arrangement that facilitates the balancing of demand for these services with the supply of them. The growth and spread of social enterprises has been especially impressive in countries where the provision of welfare services was underdeveloped, such as in Italy, and in countries where the process of privatization was more marked, such as the UK. In countries where private non-profit organizations were already involved in the provision of social services, the prevailing trend has been a shift towards a more entrepreneurial stance and transformation into self-sustainable enterprises that are less dependent on public funding (Bacchiega and Borzaga 2003).

The development of social enterprises as economic actors has entailed several organizational innovations that involve the transformation of not-for-profit organizational forms, including cooperatives, voluntary organizations, and associations. In some countries, cooperatives have gradually started to move beyond their traditional goals of serving members to embrace more general-interest goals; in other words, the new cooperatives—often called *social cooperatives*—do not simply promote the interests of a specific category of stakeholders, but support the interests of the community as a whole or of specific disadvantaged groups. In 1995, this evolution was acknowledged by the International Cooperative Alliance (ICA) through the introduction of the principle 'Concern for the Community'. At the same time, some voluntary organizations and associations have strengthened their involvement in the provision of services by adopting an increasingly entrepreneurial approach. Thus, traditional cooperative and associative models have begun to merge, with associations becoming more entrepreneurial and cooperatives less member-oriented. The consequence has been the evolution of new organizational forms that combine associative governance models with entrepreneurial activities and often involve direct participation by a plurality of stakeholders.

Initially, social enterprises developed to provide social services and to facilitate the work integration of disadvantaged people. Over time, this range of activities has broadened to include the provision of microfinance services, the production and commercialization of fair-trade products, and the promotion of educational, cultural, and environmental services. This broadening of activities demonstrates that social enterprises tend to develop general-interest services and products in different contexts according to the specific needs arising at the local level; this diversity is observable across and within countries and is due to a range of economic, social, and political factors.

The enlargement of their range of activities has contributed to making social enterprises the leading social actor in the economy of social responsibility.

Political recognition and legal evolution

The adoption of public schemes at both national and EU levels has contributed to the political recognition of social enterprises. In the first phase of their emergence, social enterprises were established mainly by utilizing pre-existing legislation. They were organized as associations in France and Belgium, as cooperatives in Italy, and as companies limited by guarantee in the UK.

From the 1990s onwards, specific legal frameworks for social enterprises have been introduced into the national legislation of some European countries. These initiatives have been designed to encourage the development of entrepreneurial dynamics to achieve social goals, and they recognize that social enterprises constitute a distinctive form of entrepreneurship that adds to the overall capacity of enterprises to meet a range of economic and social needs.

Two trends can be identified: the adoption of specific legal frameworks through the adaptation of existing legislation; and, more recently, the introduction of new legal frameworks imposing clear social aims (e.g. interest of the community) and specific constraints to established social enterprises (e.g. a total or partial non-profit distribution constraint and limitations on fields of activity). The first trend was initiated by the Italian Parliament, which in 1991 approved Law 381 that created the *Cooperativa Sociale* as a specific legal category. This approach has subsequently been adopted by several countries in and outside Europe, including Spain, Portugal, Poland, and South Korea. The second trend involves the introduction of broader legal frameworks in which social enterprises can operate. This trend was initiated by Belgium and followed more recently by the UK and Italy, which exemplifies both trends. To date, Italy and the UK have the most comprehensive legislation, with laws that allow for a plurality of organizations to qualify as social enterprises and for the enlargement of the fields of activity in which social enterprises can operate.

In 2005, legislation in the UK established Community Interest Companies (CICs) as limited companies that commit to pursuing community interests. CICs are conceived as complements to government services that function in areas such as childcare provision, social housing, community transport, and leisure. The CIC framework was primarily envisaged for productive non-profit organizations, but it can also be utilized by other organizations that deliver community benefits (Regulator of CICs 2007). No restrictions exist regarding the fields of economic activity: CICs can engage in any lawful trade activity or enterprise, provided they pass the Community Interest Test,[4] comply with the asset lock, and submit an annual Community Interest Report.

In Italy, Law 159 of 2005 on *Impresa Sociale* allows a wider range of legal forms to be classified as social enterprises and defines the types of general-interest services that can be supplied: welfare, health, education, culture, environmental protection, and work integration. According to this law, a social enterprise is defined as a non-profit private organization that permanently and principally carries out economic activities aimed at the production and commercialization of socially beneficial goods and services and pursues general-interest goals.

To conclude, the development and expansion of legislation in Europe has led to social enterprises becoming increasingly recognized and institutionalized.

Organization of the book

From the perspective of orthodox economics, the emergence and rapid spread of social enterprises is difficult to interpret. Moreover, several objections have been raised about the viability and effectiveness of social enterprises. The main criticism is that tensions between their financial and social goals will inevitably make social enterprises unsustainable and force them to rely on public funding in order to survive. A further criticism is that social enterprises will tend to undermine labour conditions not only for those who are directly employed by the enterprises themselves, but also more broadly for those who work in the industries in which they operate. A third strand of criticism is that the commercialization inherent in social enterprises will weaken, if not completely undermine the commitment of non-profit organizations to their original social goals (Weisbrod 1998).

Some of these criticisms have a degree of empirical support, though this is often partial and certainly not definitive. Furthermore, the arguments that are usually advanced to support these criticisms are both grounded in and strongly linked to conventional interpretative models that are inconsistent with the nature of social enterprises.

This book seeks to contribute to the development of a systematic account of the upsurge of social enterprises. The first part subjects the criticisms that have been raised about viability to theoretical analysis and proposes alternative frameworks that clarify the economic rationale of social enterprises.

In Chapter 1, Carlo Borzaga and Ermanno Tortia examine the economic nature of social enterprises. They start by analysing the shortcomings of orthodox theories of the firm that focus on profit maximization and on self-interested preferences as the only possible drivers of entrepreneurial behaviour. The authors propose a general framework that encompasses organizations characterized by social objectives and non-self-seeking preferences. They argue that entrepreneurial organizations can be interpreted as coordination mechanisms that pursue production objectives that are not necessarily private, while economic actors can be driven by intrinsic motivations and other-regarding preferences.

In Chapter 2, Sara Depedri examines the competitive advantages of social enterprises. She argues that the non-profit distribution constraint does not provide a sufficient account of the advantages enjoyed by social enterprises that produce general-interest services. The main features of these enterprises that explain their efficiency and effectiveness are their democratic and participative forms of organization, their ability to transmit their mission and mobilize resources, and their capacity to develop trustworthy and cooperative behaviour among all stakeholders.

In Chapter 3, Ermanno Tortia analyses how social enterprises socialize resources and involve all the main stakeholders in their management and strategic decision making. Using a dynamic approach, this chapter demonstrates that social enterprises make a direct contribution to the increase of output since they provide services that would not otherwise exist. Consequently, social enterprises have a direct impact on employment in general and especially on creating employment opportunities for the disadvantaged. Social enterprises also contribute to reducing poverty and marginalization since some of them allocate part of their resources to people who lack the ability to pay and are not supported by public schemes.

In Chapter 4, Leonardo Becchetti and Giuseppe Mastromatteo examine the orthodox literature on economic growth and show that social enterprises are an important innovation for achieving socially and environmentally sustainable development. Against the background of the distributional challenge posed by the global integration of labour and product markets, the authors assert that a new generation of pioneering social enterprises that promote fair trade and microfinance can contribute to reducing the wage gap and supporting the rapid improvement of economic conditions in developing countries.

The second part of the book investigates the main areas of activity in which social enterprises initially established a foothold and have since become consolidated as leading economic actors: general-interest services, work integration, fair trade, and microfinance.

In Chapter 5, Luca Fazzi describes the roles played by social enterprises and other productive not-for-profit organizations in providing general-interest services. He analyses international variations in the distribution and activities of social enterprises, focusing on Europe and North America. He then examines how political, economic, and cultural factors influence the development and spread of these enterprises. The final part of this chapter identifies the main difficulties and challenges faced by the further expansion and consolidation of social enterprises providing general-interest services.

In Chapter 6, Giulia Galera examines the role, development, and potential of social enterprises created specifically to foster employment among disadvantaged workers. After a brief survey of the difficulties faced by these workers in the labour market, she analyses the strengths and weaknesses of conventional policies. The chapter then focuses on new employment initiatives with special regard to the development of not-for-profit organizations that integrate disadvantaged people into work and society through productive activities. The chapter then provides an overview of the main characteristics, resources, target groups, and legal structures of work-integration social enterprises in four representative European countries.

In Chapter 7, Leonardo Becchetti provides an overview of fair trade, which promotes the inclusion of marginalized producers in the South who lack sufficient market access and suffer from low bargaining power vis-à-vis monopolistic transportation intermediaries. Fair trade provides these producers with an alternative trade channel, capacity building and export services, and opportunities for financing and investment in local public goods. Furthermore, fair trade publicizes the social value incorporated in the final products in order to match marginalized producers with 'concerned' consumers who are willing to pay for it. The chapter then examines the main critiques of fair trade, demonstrating that it is fully compatible with market principles and has the capacity to address both market failures and the inadequacies of local antitrust institutions.

In Chapter 8, Leonardo Becchetti and Marco Costantino argue that since the social and environmental value of fair-trade products cannot be directly verified by consumers, fair-trade impact studies have important implications for policy. They discuss the main methodological issues of these studies and argue that it is crucial to disentangle the direct fair-trade effect from the selection bias that would arise if producers who are more skilled affiliate with fair-trade organizations in greater numbers than those who are less skilled. If this occurs, the observed advantages of fair trade could be attributable to ex ante heterogeneity between affiliated and non-affiliated producers rather than to the effects of fair trade itself. The authors examine solutions to this problem and discuss the empirical findings that show that length of affiliation tends to increase productivity and reduce producers' risk by diversifying their sales channels and product portfolios.

In Chapter 9, Leonardo Becchetti considers microfinance institutions as pioneering social enterprises in the field of finance. Animated by the social goal of easing credit access for the 'unbankable' (those who do not have enough wealth to collateralize bank loans), microfinance simultaneously promotes economic development and equal opportunities. Paradoxically, microfinance has the capacity to reconcile outreach (loans for the poorest) with an impressively low ratio of write-offs (irrecoverable loans). The chapter examines the reasons for the success of microfinance by focusing on technical solutions such as group lending with joint liability and individual progressive loans. Equally important, however, is the role played by immaterial factors such as self-esteem and social approval that contribute to explaining borrowers' performance.

In Chapter 10, Leonardo Becchetti and Rocco Ciciretti argue that corporate social responsibility can be conceived of as the endogenous reaction by profit-maximizing corporations to the growing number and influence of ethically motivated consumers and investors. The issue for large corporations that are usually constrained by profit maximization due to their governance structure is whether social responsibility is compatible with survival in highly competitive international markets. This issue is examined by identifying two potential benefits—employee motivation and the socially responsible consumer effect—that can potentially offset the cost of being more socially responsible and, therefore, more sensitive to the needs of stakeholders. The findings show that both of these benefits are needed to counterbalance the higher costs. For this reason, the effects of the decision to strengthen a corporation's social responsibility stance is less rewarding for firms selling intermediate products that do not entail direct contacts with final consumers.

This book cannot possibly highlight all the activities that have so far been undertaken by social enterprises, let alone point to all the social problems that they could potentially engage. Social enterprises are active in other fields such as housing and the environment and many opportunities for expansion certainly exist, particularly in the context of the current economic crisis.

The authors of this volume hope that their contributions will help convince readers that much can be achieved when individuals consume and invest ethically and support or join enterprises that have explicit social goals.

The ideas set out in this book are the result of joint reflection and discussion with colleagues from the Università di Trento, Università di 'Tor Vergata' Roma, ISSAN (Institute for the Development of Non-profit Organizations), EconomEtica (the Inter-university Center for Economic Ethics and Corporate Social Responsibility), the EMES European Research Network, and Euricse (European Research Institute on Cooperative and Social Enterprises).[5] Some of these colleagues have been contributors to this book, while others include Ash Amin, Michele Bagella, Kaushik Basu, Luigi Bonatti, Jacques Defourny, Raffaello Durante, Robert Lensink, Luigi Mittone, Marco Musella, Luigi Paganetto, Victor Pestoff, Fabio Pisani, Lorenzo Sacconi, Stefania Sambataro, Felice Scalvini, Roger Spear, Roger Sugden, Paola Villa, Stefano Zamagni, and Flaviano Zandonai.

We are particularly grateful to Mark Beittel for persistently managing and rigorously editing the text, Giulia Galera for coordinating the authors and contributing to this introduction, and Thomas Sutton and his colleagues at Routledge for their patience and production expertise.

Notes

1 See, for example, Le Grand and Bartlett (1993), Esping-Andersen (1999), and Ferrera and Rhodes (2000) for welfare and general-interest services; Kaushal and Kaestner (2001), Kluve (2006), Freud (2007), and Davies (2008) for labour and employment; and Stiglitz (2002), Rodrik (2004), and Page (2006) for development.
2 The term *social enterprise* has been conceptualized by the EMES European Research

Network, which developed a common approach to the study of European social enter-prises that has proven to be capable of encompassing national differences (Borzaga and Defourny 2001).
3 Profit caps, for example, allow for the partial distribution of profits up to a predefined amount for each share.
4 'An organization satisfies the community interest test if a reasonable person might con-sider that it carries on its activities for the benefit of the community or a section of the community' (Regulator of CICs 2007: 4).
5 Evolving from ISSAN and established in 2008, Euricse aims to strengthen the research focus on social and cooperative enterprises from an international perspective.

1 The economics of social enterprises

An interpretative framework

Carlo Borzaga and Ermanno Tortia

During the last decade, entrepreneurial non-profit organizations and social enterprises have rapidly expanded and become a focus of research in Europe, the US, and many other countries (Anheier and Salamon 1992; Borzaga and Defourny 2001; Anheier and Ben-Ner 2003; Borzaga and Spear 2004; Nyssens 2006; United Nations Development Programme 2008). The process of defining the key features of social enterprises has been advanced by legislation introduced in the UK during 2004 and in Italy during 2005.[1] Given these important developments in the social and legal domains, a coherent theoretical framework is needed to account for the economic nature and effects of social enterprises.

This framework cannot ignore the history of producers' associations, cooperatives, and not-for-profit organizations with an entrepreneurial character, since social activism has played an important role in creating entrepreneurial ventures with social goals (Stryjan 2004; Borzaga and Ianes 2006; Ianes and Tortia forthcoming). For example, worker cooperatives have often been created with the aim of reducing unemployment through the open door and of improving job stability through employment protection. Better working conditions and a more inclusive organizational model can also favour the moral development of the membership through closer, non-hierarchical, and more transparent relations between the main patrons of the organization—workers, users/clients, and managers. In a similar fashion, non-profit organizations have been developed in order to alleviate social problems that for-profit firms and public agencies are unable to manage.

Furthermore, over the last decades cooperatives and non-profits have spread in systems characterized by high levels of social capital based on trust and embeddedness. In these contexts, a process of cumulative causation has occurred as social ties have been reinforced through the influence of organizations in which private and self-seeking objectives are weaker, and intrinsic and other-regarding motivations assume a prominent role (Jones and Kato 2007). This exemplifies the way in which culture and institutions co-evolve, since social ties based on trust and personal relations favour the establishment social enterprises, while the operations of social enterprises reinforce the process of accumulating social capital (Borzaga *et al.* forthcoming).

Our framework draws upon recent developments in the theories of the firm, institutional evolution, and motivational complexity to explain the crucial changes in ownership rights and governance rules that have been necessary both to implement the new entrepreneurial form of the social enterprise and to meet the needs and motivations expressed by the actors involved. As a first step, a satisfactory theory needs to overcome the limitations imposed by the conventional conception of the firm. These limitations consist of an inability to adequately account for institutional and organizational variety, mainly because of orthodox assumptions about self-interested motivations and profit-maximization on the one hand and of a static approach to institutional and cultural changes on the other (Borzaga and Tortia 2007). This problem is equally true for both the neo-classical and the new institutionalist schools of thought.

Second, to explain the economic nature of social enterprises it is necessary to assume that individuals are characterized by motivational complexity. Self-interested preferences interact with relational, procedural, and intrinsic aspects of human behaviour (Ben-Ner and Putterman 1998). A realistic portrayal of human agency starts from the analysis of predispositions and habits in a manner similar to the classical institutionalist and evolutionary schools (Hodgson 2006). Third, it is necessary to move beyond a conception of economic systems as divided into two main sectors: for-profit firms and public agencies. The intermediate area between these two sectors is often labelled the 'third sector' and is populated mainly by not-for-profit organizations, a growing variety of which have an entrepreneurial character (Weisbrod 1977, 1988; Hansmann 1996). Finally, the conventional assumption that investor-owned firms are universally the most efficient is untenable, since at least in some industries non-investor-owned organizations have become widespread.[2] During the last two decades, entrepreneurial non-profits have increasingly provided services with a quasi-public and meritorious character.

Starting from these observations, an adequate theoretical account of social enterprises requires an innovative conception of the firm in which profit maximization is no longer an essential condition. While altruism and social objectives have conventionally been studied outside the realm of production carried out by firms, an alternative approach is to consider firms as complex organizations that must coordinate different actors in the economic pursuit of production through the implementation of suitable governance structures. According to this approach, the economic and institutional nature of firms does not necessarily entail the private appropriation of net surpluses. A new account of the firm can help explain the existence of entrepreneurial organizations that conventional economics views as altruistic, but not productive.

This chapter begins by identifying the limitations of the new institutionalist and orthodox approaches for understanding cooperatives and not-for-profit enterprises. It argues that the behavioural approach to the study of economics, which focuses on individual habits and motivations (Nelson and Winter 1982), and the evolutionary approach, which focuses on organizational routines and institutional change (Hodgson 1993, 2006), offer a better basis for understanding the emergence and role of social enterprises. The chapter proposes a simple framework for understanding the tendency of social enterprises to satisfy needs rather than to pursue purely economic objectives.

In the second part of the chapter, an examination of non-traditional entrepreneurial forms, mainly cooperative firms[3] and non-profit organizations, highlights the features that they have in common with social enterprises in terms of their limited profit motive and forms of governance. Starting from a critical understanding of the history and theory of cooperatives and non-profits, a systematic framework is then defined and elaborated. It builds upon an analysis of the institutional factors and organizational routines shaping the evolution of social enterprises and argues that this institutional evolution has been driven mainly by social objectives rather than production efficiency, with economic and monetary factors playing an instrumental role in the overall production process. Investor-owned firms, by contrast, seek to achieve the economic objectives of maximizing their surplus and increasing their market value.

The orthodox approach

The orthodox approach focuses exclusively on cooperative firms. It was initiated by Ward (1958), who studied how cooperatives react to market stimuli by comparing worker-run with for-profit enterprises, and it was further developed by Furubotn and Pejovich (1970), who examined the issue of undercapitalization from an intertemporal perspective. This approach starts from the assumption that workers in self-managed firms maximize in the short run the average income per head net of operating costs. It predicts perverse supply behaviour in equilibrium since worker-members will equate average and marginal income. These optimality conditions imply an incentive to lay off part of the membership in good economic conditions, when prices increase, and the existence of a negatively sloped supply curve.

This claim of perverse supply behaviour did not withstand empirical tests (Bonin *et al.* 1987, 1993), though some results do show that cooperatives are characterized by a more rigid supply curve than for-profit firms[4] due to their tendency to protect the stability of jobs by considering labour fixed in the short run. Hence, employment in cooperatives responds more weakly to variations in the demand for products than in profit-maximizing firms.[5] Another important finding is that undercapitalization tends to occur in cooperative firms due to their inefficient allocation of self-financed capital funds.[6]

The orthodox approach has several limitations. First, it focuses exclusively on worker cooperatives, disregarding the existence of other forms of cooperative enterprises. Second, the hypothesis of the maximization of per-member income in cooperatives versus the maximization of total profits in investor-owned firms oversimplifies the behaviour of cooperatives because it excludes other important factors influencing the degree of *x*-efficiency (Leibenstein 1966). In particular, it neglects non-monetary objectives, the importance of job stability, the possibility of satisfying common and collective needs,[7] and the involvement and self-realization of members. A second set of factors neglected by the orthodox approach is the ability of cooperatives to increase employment, output, and wages in the presence of market imperfections, such as the welfare losses caused by monopoly in the output market and monopsony in the input market. The historical record shows that cooperative firms tend to be formed in contexts characterized by a market power concentration. Cooperatives of producers, consumers, workers, and borrowers can be interpreted as institutional responses to market concentration, since they all increase supply and input prices while reducing output prices.

The orthodox approach concludes that cooperatives are less efficient than investor-owned firms, both in their static and in their dynamic (intertemporal) behaviour. This conclusion, however, relies upon the faulty procedure of evaluating cooperative firms exclusively based on their ability to maximize average income per member. Several studies have argued that this approach is reductionist due to its methodological individualism and its narrow focus on the institutional features of investor-owned firms. Consequently, this approach disregards the specific features of cooperative institutions that can support efficiency through participation and non-self-interested motivations, rather than through hierarchy and monetary incentives (Borzaga and Tortia 2005; Zamagni 2005).

The new institutionalist approach

Hansmann (1988, 1996) explains the existence of non-profit organizations and cooperative firms based on their relative ability to reduce transaction costs in the presence of market and contract failures. Hansmann's model represents a new synthesis and a complement to many previous findings concerning cooperatives and non-profits since it fosters an understanding of the process of creation and diffusion of all ownership forms—investor-owned, cooperative, and non-profit—in market economies. Organizations that survive in the market are those able to minimize the sum total of costs connected with their operation. Costs are divided into two categories: contract costs, which concern all actors entering into contractual relation with the organization without controlling it, and ownership costs, which are born by the organization's patrons. Control is assigned to the stakeholder (or *patron*, in Hansmann's terminology) that has the most strategic role in making firm-specific investments. In other words, the owners risk the greatest economic loss deriving from market exchanges in cases of negative economic results or of morally hazardous (opportunistic) behaviour by the other classes of patrons. The costs of the operation of the market derive from market power ex ante (monopoly and monopsony), market power ex post (lock-in), and asymmetric information, while the costs of ownership are due to agency relations that induce costs of controlling employees and managers, decision-making processes, and risk taking by entrepreneurs. Given N different classes of patrons interacting with the firm, it is efficient to assign ownership[8] to the class that is able to minimize the sum total of costs:

$$ CP_j + \sum_{i=1}^{j-1} CC_i , $$

where *CP* is the ownership costs for the j class of patrons, and CC_i is the contractual costs undergone by all the other classes of stakeholders. Competitive pressure on the market will make the minimization hypothesis effective.

According to this model, cooperatives can be more efficient than investor-owned firms in three cases. First, when capital is not the strategic factor of production, i.e. when other patrons such as producers, workers, or borrowers make the most specific investments and incur the highest risk of losing the value of the invested resources. Professional partnerships are a useful example, since they are characterized by highly specialized competences, while the physical capital utilized is usually general purpose. Second, cooperatives are more efficient when market power is concentrated in both the factor and output markets. Third, and for Hansmann the most crucial, cooperatives are more efficient when their memberships have homogeneous preferences, since the similarity of interests and objectives favours the implementation of organizational forms based on participation and mutuality, and decreases control costs. In this case, cooperative firms are often more efficient than investor-owned organizations, since they are better able to reduce agency costs of managers and workers and to increase organizational x-efficiency. Conversely, a crucial limitation is the higher collective decision-making costs of cooperatives when their memberships are heterogeneous. This usually occurs when a cooperative grows larger and its members become more differentiated with unequal endowments in terms of financial wealth or human capital, and they thus develop different objectives. This is true even if the division of labour and economies of scale allow the reduction of costs, since the crucial aspect is the higher decision-making costs incurred by cooperatives relative to investor-owned firms. Not all cooperatives suffer from this limitation in the same way, but the problem potentially exists whenever members' interests are not highly aligned with one other.

In Hansmann's model, non-profit firms originate in the context of asymmetric information when none of the stakeholders is able to minimize costs. Since control by a specific group of agents would entail the possibility of exploiting asymmetric information and other contractual imperfections, ownership is entirely excluded, positive residuals are devoted to the development of the firm's activities, and the organization is managed by professionals who operate according to a statutory social mission. However, insofar as they cannot be sold and do not maximize profits, non-profit organizations are less efficient than investor-owned firms because they lack the necessary incentives to reduce costs in order to maximize efficiency. Like cooperatives, non-profit organizations are seen as an effective solution to severe market failures, but they will inevitably disappear when markets are perfected, i.e. when competition increases and regulation improves. Hence, non-profits are considered by Hansmann to be transitional organizational forms that spread mainly during the initial stages of market development, when imperfections are too pronounced to allow competition to deliver its beneficial effects.[9]

Hansmann's model obscures three important aspects of non-profits: the public benefits and meritorious nature of their activities, the high relational intensity that characterizes their operation, and the quasi-public nature of the services they deliver. These three attributes locate non-profits in an intermediate position between the public and for-profit sectors and are linked to the non-profits' social rather than private objectives, which justify the imposition of the non-profit distribution constraint. Consequently, non-profits serve a different role in the economy than for-profit firms and cannot be compared with them solely on the grounds of efficiency. This issue has been underlined by Weisbrod (1977, 1988), who argues that non-profits emerge as a response to government failures to satisfy the demand for niche public goods or as a result of binding budgetary constraints. Hence, the public-benefit nature of their objectives is fundamental for their creation, and government failures are more prominent than market and contract failures.

In contrast to Hansmann's model, the framework developed in this chapter compares the production of public benefit goods and services by different typologies of private organizations and considers the supply of meritorious goods and services by ideological entrepreneurs (Young 1983; James 1983; Rose-Ackerman 1996). Hence, it considers the role played by supply-side—and not merely demand-driven—factors that have led to the emergence and spread of non-profit organizations.

The new institutionalist model has provided important insights into the emergence and operation of non-investor-owned organizations operating in non-competitive markets characterized by the concentration of power, asymmetric information, and contract incompleteness. Indeed, these are among the main elements that historically triggered the creation of non-investor-owned organizations. The new institutionalist model, however, has important limitations: it does not adequately examine the specific features of non-profit-making firms ranging from property rights and governance to the nature of the goods and services produced. Public benefit objectives, instead of private appropriation, are not explicitly taken into consideration as the driving force of production activities, since the entire approach is based upon transaction cost minimization. Consequently, the model cannot explain the continuous increase in the incidence of socially oriented organizations in modern economies. The interpretive limitations of new institutionalism result in misleading interpretations of the economic nature of social enterprises in four respects. First, it only explains one typology of non-profit organization—donative foundations—where the main patrons—donors—would incur higher costs if the organization were controlled by some other category of patrons. On the other hand, donors cannot control the organization, since they are usually widely dispersed and numerous. Mori (2007) argues that this position excludes ex ante the possibility that one or more groups of stakeholders could control the organization in a way that is functional to its social objectives under the non-profit distribution constraint. Ideological entrepreneurs are a case in point, since they create and control their organizations but have aims other than profit (Young 1983; Rose-Ackerman 1996). At the same time, the existence of the non-profit distribution constraint does not deny the entrepreneurial nature of the venture, even if it requires different coordination mechanisms—for example, in terms of governance—that are functional to inclusion more than to private appropriation (Bacchiega and Borzaga 2001, 2003).

Second, new institutionalism underestimates the role of institutional change in fixing the problems generating higher ownership costs. For example, the enforcement of discretionary managerial decisions in cooperatives can simplify and make effective governance procedures even when the membership is heterogeneous. This kind of solution can help cooperatives to limit the inflation of costs and conflicts linked to preference heterogeneity.[10] Consequently, institutional change and the refinement of rules are not alien to non-investor-owned organizations and need to be taken into consideration in the explanatory framework (Borzaga and Tortia 2005). Conversely, new institutionalism overestimates the potential of market regulation and competition. Even if regulation and competition can reduce market failures, effectiveness in service delivery may not be satisfactory for all sectors of activity that are usually populated by social enterprises. Where tacit knowledge (Polanyi 1958), private information, and personal relations are crucial in determining the strategic orientation of the organization, regulation and competition may not be adequate tools for maximizing expected efficiency.

Third, the new institutionalist perspective endorses the main assumptions of the neoclassical school concerning the behaviour of firms and individuals. According to this approach, the operation of the firm is based on cost minimization and individuals are exclusively self-interested; a more realistic account of motivational complexity is not provided. Closer scrutiny of the behaviour of non-profit organizations, however, offers important insights into this complexity. The main limitation of non-profits identified by Hansmann is their inability to provide efficient economic incentives due to the high degree of control bestowed upon patrons other than investors. However, Leete (2000) and Benz (2005) observe that the principal actors in non-profits are not motivated primarily by monetary considerations since their main objectives are not pecuniary. Without resorting to high-powered monetary incentives, non-profits are able to motivate their key stakeholders through relational and other non-material incentives. This pattern cannot be explained by conventional economic theories, while it can be accounted for by behavioural economics (Borzaga and Mittone 1997). In many countries, not-for-profits are the organizational forms best suited for producing services such as education and health care (Weisbrod 1998). Furthermore, as shown in other chapters of this volume, goods and services such as work integration for the disadvantaged and fair trade can *only* be delivered economically by not-for-profit organizations, since both the state and for-profit firms are unable to operate with comparable degrees of effectiveness. Hence, not-for-profits create and sustain new markets with what Gui and Sugden (2005) call a 'relation character'. These markets might not exist at all or be severely curtailed if not-for-profits were absent.

Fourth, new institutionalism neglects the social aspects of the institutional structure of firms. This is problematic, as the studies on corporate social responsibility demonstrate with regards to for-profit firms.[11] Corporate social responsibility is fundamental for the operation of social enterprises given their public-benefit vocation, tendency to socialize resources, and governance based on stakeholder involvement. Most of these enterprises aim to solve specific social problems and devote all or most of their resources to doing so. As will be shown below, economic and financial aspects are likely to be merely instrumental to the pursuit of these goals.

The conception of the firm in new institutionalism is largely based on the minimization of transaction costs, while the study of the multifaceted complexity of behavioural predispositions and organizational routines emphasizes that different organizational forms can generate, other things equal, varying amounts of economic and social surpluses (Hodgson 2006). These variations also entail different cost structures, and not-for-profit organizations can reduce at least some categories of costs, above all labour costs. Lower salaries are often paid to employees of some types of not-for-profits relative to the public sector and sometimes to for-profit firms (Mosca *et al.* 2007) without reducing job satisfaction and loyalty to the organization (Borzaga and Depedri 2005; Borzaga and Tortia 2006; Tortia 2008).[12] However, a simple comparison between costs and revenues is not sufficient to evaluate the action of these organizations, since they often rely upon unpaid work by volunteers and partial work donations by employees.[13] For example, many administrators of social enterprises either serve as volunteers or receive only symbolic remuneration. Consequently, social enterprises are able to produce greater surpluses and distribute resources beyond what is indicated by their balance sheets.[14]

To summarize the criticisms of new institutionalism, cost minimization cannot be taken as the sole relevant efficiency criterion for social enterprises. Other criteria must be considered, including those linked to the production of surpluses in monetary terms, the quality and effectiveness of service delivery, and the satisfaction of social needs. Simple balance sheet data on revenues and value added may not be a good approximation of the quality of services delivered. Given the public-benefit nature of their activities, social enterprises are able to produce surpluses in non-traditional ways, and their impact needs to be assessed comprehensively (see Chapter 3 of this volume). A deeper analysis of governance is necessary as well, since the structure of decision making is where actors' motivations and organizational objectives meet. These issues are best examined by adopting the evolutionary and behavioural approaches, which focus on organizational routines, behavioural responses, and changes in both over time.

A behavioural and evolutionary framework

An alternative approach should emphasize the impact of social enterprises on the formation and dissemination of more inclusive governance forms, the valorization and the spread of non-monetary motivations, the accumulation of social capital, and a more equitable distribution of resources. Though the new institutionalist and neoclassical schools have provided useful insights into non-investor-owned organizations, their shortcomings cannot be overcome starting from the same assumptions.

Behavioural and evolutionary economists have recently made important theoretical and empirical contributions that can be extended to the study of non-investor-owned organizations. They have introduced more realistic hypotheses and flexible methodologies showing that human behaviour cannot be described exclusively in self-interested terms (Fehr and Gächter 2000; Fehr and Schmidt 2001) and that a theory of entrepreneurial organization does not need to be based upon an assumption of profit maximization.

Behavioural economics stresses that human behaviour should be understood as complex, and the presence of self-interested—economic and monetary—motivations can coexist and co-evolve with non-self-interested motivations and behaviours (Sen 1977; Sugden 1991; Ben-Ner and Putterman 1998). The self-interest assumption inevitably leads to restrictive and unrealistic conclusions that tend to cripple the interpretive power of economic models. It may be a useful basis for describing the behaviour of actors in for-profit firms, given their focus on financial performance, hierarchical control, and monetary incentives, but it becomes unrealistic and misleading when applied to social enterprises due to the social and non-instrumental component of their operation, which requires and supports the fulfilment of non-self-interested preferences. Finally, the characterization of human behaviour as exclusively driven by self-interest, which is implicit to methodological individualism, is questionable at the ontological level, since it proposes an unwarranted and reductionist metaphysical description of the human essence that is not supported by empirical evidence (Screpanti and Zamagni 2004).

While behavioural economics has deepened scientific knowledge of individual behaviour and motivations, the evolutionary school has provided insights into the institutional architecture of organizations and its interaction with individual motivations. Modern evolutionism in the study of the economy was initiated by Penrose (1959) and is based upon the idea that organizational routines in the social world serve a similar function to genetic material in the biotic world (Nelson and Winter 1982). Organizational routines serve as codes (replicators) transmitting instructions that support the behavioural propensities of the organization, which can be interpreted as interlocking equilibria of individual habits (Hodgson 1993, 2006). These routines can be renewed through organizational innovation and transmitted by imitation, and they define the potential for adaptation and survival in the socio-economic environment. According to evolutionary theory, institutions take the form of organizational routines in terms of property rights, governance structures, and organizational models. Preferences are clearly endogenous since cultural contexts and institutions have varying impacts on individual behaviour even when the social problems to be solved are similar (Bowles 1998, 2004). Consider the importance of interacting in an environment where decision processes are transparent. This situation is common to all organizational environments, but different ownership and organizational forms generate different perceptions of fairness by their stakeholders, and these in turn induce different preferences and behaviours. Hence, individual behaviour cannot be understood solely ex ante based on general criteria or axioms, but has to be assessed empirically by examining the interaction among individuals, institutions, and organizations. This interaction can be also modified along with social demands, since both needs and the ability to satisfy these needs evolve and create new organizational solutions in response to new demands.

The evolutionary framework has never been applied systematically to the study of non-investor-owned enterprises. In order to do so, firms cannot be conceived as mere maximizers of the net returns accruing to their investment programmes and operating in competitive markets; rather, they must be interpreted as coordinating devices operating in imperfect markets where the production of value added, and not the maximization of profit, is the best predictor of firm survival and expansion. Firms organize production for the satisfaction of needs that can be private and material, but also collective, social, relational, and psychological (Dopfer 2005). When individual activities are not capable of effectively or efficiently achieving expected results, organizational routines evolve that allow people to come together and arrange production on a collective basis. The common objective of this process is the enjoyment of the results (the surplus) deriving from the activity, but the social function is the satisfaction of needs, and the enjoyment of the results must involve all stakeholders and not simply investors. Social goals can be pursued thanks to the implementation of specific organizational routines, such as the socialization of a firm's capital and stakeholder involvement in decision making.

The evolutionary and behavioural approaches help overcome the shortcomings of new institutionalism since they do not require individuals within organizations to be solely and fully motivated by self-interest, and the social aspects of enterprises can be interpreted as co-evolving with organizational objectives. Indeed, theoretical and empirical studies of group selection clearly show that altruism and pro-social attitudes can help to increase the reproductive success of individuals, organizations, communities, and society by boosting sympathy, cooperation, trust, and a sense of community (Hodgson 1993; Bowles 2004; Gowdy and Seidl 2004). Motivational complexity also encourages the implementation of a suitable institutional environment in which non-self-regarding motivations interact with self-interested ones and are supported by conformism to shared rules of behaviour and common values (Grimalda and Sacconi 2005; Sacchetti and Sugden 2009). Relational and other-regarding preferences along with an interest in fair procedures play a crucial role in advancing the well-being of the actors involved (Helliwell and Huang 2005; Tortia 2008). One important implication is that higher monetary remuneration may not be a good substitute for shortcomings in the social side of production since the two aspects play different roles in the overall well-being of the actors (Borzaga and Depedri 2005). Economic and monetary objectives need to cohere with the relational and social aspects of firm operation. Substitution between the two aspects (monetary and non-monetary) is possible but limited. For example, in the case of employed workers, higher wages can purchase the acceptance of an unpleasant work environment only to a limited extent, and this is an inefficient solution insofar as costs are increased. The following section argues instead that the main aim of social enterprises is the satisfaction of social needs, which require the valorization of intrinsic and pro-social motivations, while economic and monetary objectives are merely instrumental to the pursuit of social goals.

An interpretive model of social enterprises

Within the evolutionary and behavioural frameworks, it is feasible to assess the importance of non-profit entrepreneurship by examining non-instrumental aspects of economic behaviour. This approach is consistent with the main institutional feature of social enterprises: the strong social component underlying their creation and development.

The satisfaction of needs and the pursuit of collective and social objectives can be sufficient to motivate entrepreneurial ventures even in the absence of high-powered incentives like the profit motive; in such ventures, financial and economic objectives may be limited to instrumental roles. Financial equilibrium, economic sustainability, and an adequate level of productive efficiency are necessary conditions for the pursuit of the objectives of all firms, including social enterprises, but they need not constitute the final aim, which can instead be the satisfaction of needs and the creation of individual and collective well-being mainly by means of the valorization of intrinsic and pro-social motivations.

Specific property rights and objectives have important consequences in terms of governance; for example, they may influence how information circulates, knowledge is created and used, and competences and human capital are accumulated and retained. In non-investor-owned organizations, reduced hierarchy and control favour the circulation of information that sustains the creation and spread of non-codified and tacit knowledge. This alternative system of knowledge production supports the development of more informal and horizontal models of governance where trust and personal interaction play a more fundamental role than in other organizational forms (Frey and Osterloh 1999). Eventually, inclusive and participatory governance can help the organization to retain its management and workforce without intensive recourse to career advancement and wage increases, but rather through the valorization of non-monetary motivations and pro-social attitudes.

Social enterprises also differ from for-profit firms in terms of the role they can play in local development and the provision of welfare. Social enterprises usually exhibit a high degree of embeddedness (Granovetter 1985), since in the vast majority of cases they are created and run by local actors who develop and utilize personal ties with public authorities, other firms, and civil society organizations. Embeddedness generates local knowledge and resources with a personal and relational character that represent an important component of the enterprise's productive capabilities. These traits are particularly important for the provision of communal services, since social enterprises often aim to satisfy localized needs, which have idiosyncratic features linked to a specific community that may not be satisfied in the same way in other contexts. For example, where the negative effects of de-industrialization, such as alcoholism and unemployment, spread in particular communities, social services are best delivered by those who have deep personal knowledge of the people affected and a local understanding of the issues and resources. The potential for the reduction of negative spillover and for the reinforcement of social capital are substantial. The inclusiveness of the governance structure in social enterprises supports these aims since the motivations of the actors involved interact proactively with the public-benefit objectives. In this way, social enterprises can be active promoters of local development, since objectives are defined endogenously by the same actor that will benefit from the outcomes of the process (Borzaga and Tortia 2009).

Our conceptual framework classifies typologies of firms in terms of their main objectives. It encompasses not only not-for-profit enterprises but also for-profit firms, which are characterized by the prevalence of economic and financial objectives that aim to obtain the highest possible value of the organization on the market. Consequently, for for-profit firms, the satisfaction of needs and the pursuit of social objectives is instrumental for maximizing economic results (Bonatti *et al.* 2001).

The model presented in Figure 1.1 summarizes the approach. All entrepreneurial ventures need to fulfil two conditions: the satisfaction of socially defined needs and the economic sustainability of the venture. The latter does not require the maximization of profits, but only breaking even in the medium run. These two conditions can be satisfied in varying degrees by different types of enterprises.

In order to clarify this model, enterprise types can be located on a continuum where at one pole economic and financial objectives predominate and at the other pole social objectives predominate. In the former, the satisfaction of needs is instrumental and represented by the satisfaction of a market demand for goods and services. This economic condition is best expressed, for example, by the functioning of regulated financial markets that publicly price the value of stocks based on expected future returns.[15] Indeed, the same principle is often dominant in non-publicly quoted enterprises where the pursuit of economic objectives is a necessary condition for the sale of the firm at the highest possible price. This

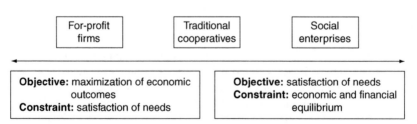

Figure 1.1 Organizational objectives and the satisfaction of needs.

pole of the continuum represents the classical model of the for-profit firm presented in microeconomic textbooks.

This pole, however, represents only one possible rationale for the creation of entrepreneurial ventures and does not necessarily apply to other types of enterprises. At the opposite pole of the continuum, the satisfaction of social needs predominates and is the main objective of the organization, while economic and financial constraints need to be fulfilled to guarantee the sustainability of the venture in the medium and long run. This pole is exemplified by those social enterprises that can be defined as 'pure' insofar as their activity is completely devoted to public-benefit objectives, while financial and economic equilibrium is merely instrumental for this aim. Between the two poles, there exists a wide variety of intermediate firm types. For example, traditional cooperative firms are primarily committed to the satisfaction of their members' private needs, such as the stability of employment in worker cooperatives, a better quality of products in consumer cooperatives, and access to credit for small producers in credit cooperatives. These types of cooperative are characterized by a high degree of membership involvement and a commitment to mutualism, which has a range of collective implications such as the sharing of democratic rules and reciprocal aid. If economic objectives are predominant, cooperatives come closer to for-profit firms and usually pursue the maximization of per-member income—i.e., as Ward (1958) assumes, they intensively pursue the private benefit of their members. To the extent that cooperatives do operate in this way, they occupy a position in the continuum near for-profit firms.[16] However, when they do not distribute positive residuals to their members, socialize resources through indivisible reserves ('locked assets'), and pursue non-mutualistic aims, they are closer to social enterprises. Cooperatives are the most flexible organizational type and, in principle, can be found in any position on the continuum.

The proposed framework is useful for positioning traditional cooperative firms relative to social enterprises. Cooperatives are created to promote the welfare of their members, controlled by stakeholders other than investors, and managed according to democratic principles. They solve the problem of horizontal coordination of non-investor stakeholders. Social enterprises add to this picture the dominant role of a public-benefit objective. The pursuit of the actors' welfare inside these enterprises needs to be reconciled with this aim and is only part of the broader social milieu in which the firm operates. A balance between these two aspects must be struck in order obtain the best possible satisfaction of both private and social needs. The two aspects may indeed be complementary more than substitutive since the presence of other-regarding preferences means that satisfying social needs positively influences the well-being of the actors actively involved in the firm.

The basic ideas that underpin this approach to entrepreneurial forms can now be clarified. While the conventional conception of the firm specifies the primacy of economic objectives and considers social objectives mainly as a constraint on firm operation, in the case of social enterprises the satisfaction of needs is no longer a constraint but rather the core of firm operation—the aim around which all the main organizational variables develop. The main implication in evolutionary terms is that the urge to satisfy needs becomes the active basis of the formation of all the organizational processes, which in turn allow the enterprise to pursue its objectives.

Furthermore, this approach highlights the deep interconnection between institutional and motivational factors as the basis of organizational behaviour. On the one hand, the institutional nature of different organizational and ownership forms favours the emergence, strengthening, and enforcement of different kinds of behaviour inside the organization. In this sense, preferences are endogenous (Bowles 1998, 2004), since institutions are able to influence the behaviour of economic agents through a process of downward reconstructive causation (Hodgson 2006). The process of preference evolution occurs as the organizational structure modifies initial propensities and behaviours over time. For example, the non-profit distribution constraint, inclusive governance, and the social objectives of social enterprises are likely to favour the creation of trust relations and horizontal control while limiting the effectiveness of traditional governance schemes, which are mainly based on economic incentives, hierarchy, and control. Intrinsic motivations, trust, and horizontal coordination can be sufficient to guarantee an adequate degree of efficiency even when monetary incentives and control are weak. Indeed, organizational models that are able to implement non-monetary incentive schemes based on trust and personal knowledge can result in increased x-efficiency thanks to a reduction of agency costs.

Conversely, economic actors do not join organizations as *tabulae rasae*, devoid of motivational content and complexity; clearly, people self-select into different types of organizations based on the idiosyncratic features of their motivational drives. Processes of self-selection are present in all entrepreneurial typologies, but they become strikingly evident in the case of social enterprises (Tortia 2008). People motivated mainly by economic and monetary rewards are likely to eschew employment in enterprises with social goals as they become dissatisfied due to inadequate monetary incentives and career prospects. On the other hand, people motivated by intrinsic, relational, and other-regarding preferences will tend to choose organizations that have social objectives.

The proposed framework can thus be interpreted in two different ways: institutions mould individual behaviour while individuals driven by different motivations self-select into different types of organizations. The former case can be interpreted as a static depiction of the behavioural variety already existing in the system, since the distribution of the organizational forms provides a good approximation of the prevailing attitudes driving the economic agents. This is so because of the top-down process of downward reconstructive causation envisaged by the evolutionary approach (Hodgson 2006): existing institutions enable and constrain individual preferences and choices. In the latter case, a bottom-up evolutionary approach[17] is envisaged whereby actors driven by different motivations flow into different organizational forms. This process determines a dynamic perspective that encompasses change in the distribution of the existing organizational forms and may favour the modifications of the institutional architecture due to the influence of the motivational drives, needs, and demands coming from actors as they strive to modify organizational processes in ways that better fit with their desired outcomes.

While the framework can account for general trends in the various organizational types, specific organizations can move nearer to, or even cross over into, other organizational types. Various factors can cause horizontal movements. For example, by adopting criteria of corporate social responsibility such as self-regulation, ethical codes, or social accounting, for-profit firms can move rightwards by improving their social standing. Similarly, for-profit entrepreneurs that put greater weight on the nature of the goods and services produced rather than on purely financial objectives can push their organizations rightward. In contrast, social enterprises are usually located at the right-hand pole of the continuum due to the statutory imposition of public-benefit aims, but the intensive utilization of commercial activities can push them leftward. As Figure 1.1 illustrates, cooperatives are positioned between the two poles, but changes in their ownership, control, and governance rules may move them closer to either the for-profit or social enterprise poles.

The position of different organizational forms can shift on the continuum over time due to reforms of the legal system or of general cultural changes. For example, during the 1980s and 1990s cooperatives in most European countries underwent a process of financial evolution that led to the introduction of new instruments, such as cooperative shares and bonds, bringing their behaviour nearer to investor-owned firms on the left-hand side of the continuum.[18] Following these reforms and cultural trends, cooperatives were interpreted as organizations that maximize the returns on the investments made by members, with weak reference to the social nature of their institutional set-up.

Other reforms and regulatory decisions have tended to push cooperative firms in the opposite direction, toward increased attention to social problems. Cases in point are the introduction during the last two decades of laws on social cooperatives, firstly in Italy and later in many other countries,[19] and the adoption in 1995 of the seventh principle of the International Cooperative Alliance (ICA), which requires cooperatives to contribute to the development of the communities in which they operate.

The continuum in this framework may have empty areas where no organizational form currently exists. In such cases, new typologies of social ventures may emerge to fill the existing gap. This phenomenon has been observed many times in the past; for example, the creation of cooperatives and non-profit organizations has compensated for shortfalls in the public and for-profit supply of goods or services caused by the concentration of power in the market or the inability of the government to intervene in the production of public goods. A more recent instance of this process has been the creation of social cooperatives in many European countries to complement and substitute the public provision of social services. Other examples involving the social nature of goods and services include the development of micro-credit, ethical finance, and fair-trade organizations, which have helped to alleviate severe social problems and improved the social criteria used by banks to evaluate investment programmes. The process of establishing entre-preneurial ventures with a social character has been reinforced by the legal recog-nition of the communitarian role of enterprises in some countries: in 2005, for example, the Community Interest Company Regulation was adopted in the UK and Law 155 on the *Impresa Sociale* in Italy.[20]

A general consequence of these processes is that all organizational and own-ership typologies have tended to shift rightwards on the continuum because of the stress put by the new laws on the public-benefit objectives of social enter-prises. In the UK and Italy, social enterprises can be constituted as non-profit organizations, cooperatives, community interest companies, and investor-owned firms. The introduction of a suitable legal framework may persuade many com-panies, including some that are investor owned, either to adopt the new legal status or to imitate social enterprises by pursuing social goals more intensively than they otherwise might. Legal reforms and cultural change are the basic drivers of a re-orientation in the objectives of a growing share of productive activities.

Finally, the complex picture that emerges can be interpreted in terms of insti-tutional complementarities (Pagano 1992; Aoki 2001; Gagliardi 2008). Diverse institutions can be complementary in the sense that the presence or effectiveness of one mechanism is reinforced either directly or indirectly by the presence of other arrangements denoting the same or an embedding institutional domain. In the case of social enterprises, institutional complementarity refers to the relation-ship among different coordination mechanisms, since social enterprises can be functional for the growth of for-profit firms by supplying collective services or by improving their social standing. On the other hand, social enterprises are not likely to be a viable organizational form for conducting traditional commercial activities and producing private goods.

Conclusions

Starting from the theoretical premises of behavioural and institutional economics, this chapter has proposed a new interpretive framework that explains why social enterprises are spreading in many countries, widening the supply of public and meritorious goods, and complementing the public and for-profit sectors. Social enterprises also produce positive spillovers mainly at the local level in terms of accumulation of social capital. Given their similarities with earlier forms of coop-erative and non-profit organizations, social enterprises were initially examined by considering established theories and approaches. Theoretical speculation and the historical record show that the satisfaction of collective and social needs has always been crucial in the creation and growth of not-for-profit organizations and cooperatives. However, their entrepreneurial character differentiates social enter-prises from non-profit organizations, while their public-benefit objectives repre-sent a step forward relative to traditional cooperative firms.

To highlight these important differences, our framework goes beyond exist-ing theories by examining the way in which social enterprises combine both social and economic components in their activities. The framework focuses on the entrepreneurial character of these organizations and explains how social enterprises have introduced innovation into the routines and institutional architecture of the existing forms of enterprises. Moreover, it sheds light on the patterns of institutional evolution leading to the development of new entrepreneurial forms.

The economic analysis of this process is important for sustaining the feedback loop of cumulative causation that goes from the establishment of social enterprises to their spread throughout the system at large, since the new organizational routines need to satisfy economic sustainability in the medium and long run. Given their social nature, social enterprises have gone through an intense process of adaptation of their internal equilibria that has led to the establishment of new governance solutions and allocative mechanisms.[21] When new solutions prove feasible and sustainable, they are reinforced and tend to spread by imitation. The recent growth of organizational forms with a social character—not necessarily in contexts where specific legislation exists—demonstrates the viability of this evolutionary pattern. The theoretical framework developed in this chapter suggests that social enterprises will become increasingly important producers of economic and social welfare in a variety of socio-economic contexts.

Notes

1 In the UK, social enterprises were established under the Companies (Audit, Investigations and Community Enterprise) Act of 2004 and the UK Community Interest Companies Regulation of 2005; in Italy, social enterprises are regulated by Italian Law 118/2005 on the *Impresa Sociale* and Ministerial Decree 155/2006.
2 Non-investor-owned organizations are not controlled by investors and include non-profits and cooperatives. In contrast, not-for-profit organizations do not have profit as their main objective and include non-profit organizations, social enterprises, and social cooperatives. Traditional cooperatives—such as worker, consumer, and producer cooperatives—are classified as either non-profit or for-profit depending upon the author and the context.
3 Starting from their initial appearance in Rochdale, Lancashire, in 1844, cooperative firms aimed to solve social problems, as observed by such well-known economists as John Stuart Mill (1848), Leon Walras (1865), and Alfred Marshall (1890, 1919). The objectives of these organizations were diverse, but in addition to increasing the incomes and security of their members, they included the moral elevation of marginalized social groups. Thus, these organizations were not simply created to maximize the economic returns of their members. Most economists, however, have located cooperative firms in a straight neoclassical methodological milieu; see Ward (1958), Domar (1966), Vanek (1970, 1977), Furubotn and Pejovich (1970), Furubotn (1976), Bonin *et al.* (1993), and Dow (1986, 2003).
4 In most traditional microeconomic models of firm behaviour, investor-owned firms have a more elastic supply curve because profit maximization requires them to equate marginal costs and marginal revenues. Hence, these firms adapt the amount of labour they utilize to price variations.
5 Increased rigidity of the supply curve implies a smaller dimension of worker cooperatives in the short run when profits are positive. This, in turn, implies lower barriers to entry and increased competition (Vanek 1970; Bonin *et al.* 1987).
6 Furubotn and Pejovich (1970) and Vanek (1970) show that when positive residuals are re-invested in indivisible capital funds, worker cooperatives will tend to misallocate

investment funds due to the members' truncated temporal horizon of permanence in the firm. Since members know that they will leave the organization at some future point in time, they will finance only those projects in which the initial value will be recouped before the departure of the median member. Consequently, they will require returns on investments higher than the opportunity cost, i.e. the market interest rate on loans. This behaviour is inefficient and tends to lead worker cooperatives to underinvest relative to the optimality condition (equality of marginal returns and marginal cost of capital). For-profit firms, by contrast, tend to satisfy this condition. Podivinsky and Steward (2006) show that the problem of undercapitalization is real, and various solutions have been proposed to compensate for it (Tortia 2003, 2006).

7 Common goods are rivalrous, but not excludable (Ben-Ner and Van Hoomissen 1991). They are relevant to the operation of all typologies of non-investor-owned organizations since their surplus is rivalrous, but it may be non-excludable—for example, when members decide jointly about its destination. Collective goods are non-rivalrous, but excludable. They are often relevant in the operation of non-profit organizations, cooperatives, and social enterprises since many typologies of quasi-public services—for example, in culture, education, health care and environmental protection—show a low degree of rivalry, but can be excludable.

8 Ownership rights consist of residual rights of control and the right of appropriation of the residual (Hansmann 1988).

9 This is illustrated by Hansmann's claim (2000) that non-profits in advanced and mature industries should be converted into organizations that operate in new and unregulated fields. In Hansmann's view, mature sectors such as health care and education should be left to competition among for-profit providers, even if these sectors have traditionally been populated by non-profit organizations.

10 For example, the well-known group of cooperatives in Mondragon in the Basque Region seem to have found appropriate solutions to the technical and governance problems that have traditionally affected financial growth, organization coordination, and membership expectations in this form of enterprise.

11 See Freeman (1984), Sacconi (2000), and Chapter 10 of this volume.

12 The potential efficiency on the cost side is often found in conjunction with a reduced ability to pay due to economic and financial constraints. The limited financial resources devoted by public authorities to the support of social enterprises further demonstrate that many services with a social character would not be delivered in their absence.

13 Partial work donations take place when employees accept wages under the market equilibrium rate or do unpaid overtime.

14 This is also true because public tenders tend to equalize the price paid for services irrespective of the quality delivered.

15 However, recent financial crises demonstrate that the process of pricing stocks in financial markets undergoes severe imperfections leading to anomalous fluctuations and speculative movements in stock prices, which can become weakly connected with the real value of economic activities.

16 These remarks apply only to some categories of cooperatives: those in which members' involvement is reduced to the minimum and any form of socialization of resources is excluded. This may occur, for example, when involvement consists solely of the ratification by the membership of the annual balance sheet without any real involvement in strategic decision making or in situations in which positive results are completely appropriated by members without any collective involvement in the management of resources.

17 Top-down evolutionary processes are understood here as the influences exerted by institutions and organizations on individuals. Conversely, bottom-up evolutionary processes refer to the influences exerted by individual motivations and behaviour on institutional variety and organizational change.

18 In Italy, cooperative shares without voting rights and financial members with minority voting rights were introduced by Law no. 59 in 1992.
19 By 2009, at least 14 European and North American countries have approved laws on social cooperatives, as have Japan and South Korea.
20 Social enterprises have been spreading in the UK mainly because they support local development and pursue other social aims; to date, about 2,700 have been officially recorded. The new Italian law on the *Impresa Sociale* became applicable only in 2009; hence, it is too soon to assess its impact.
21 The impact of these mechanisms on output and welfare is examined in Chapter 3 of this volume.

2 The competitive advantages of social enterprises

Sara Depedri

The emergence of non-profit organizations and social enterprises has been explained mainly by their ability to overcome market and government failures in providing general-interest services, especially in the areas of social welfare, health, and education. The quality of services provided by for-profit firms tends to be low, and public agencies are exposed to the failures of the electoral system in that services tend to be supplied in response to the preferences of the median voter. Not-for-profit organizations—both traditional donative non-profits and social enterprises—help diversify the supply and increase the quality of services, improving the overall well-being of the population.

The literature has identified the non-profit distribution constraint as the main mechanism for reducing asymmetric information between parties and attracting free resources like donations and volunteers. Indeed, this constraint helps to ensure that resources are employed for the interests of stakeholders other than the owners of the organization and not for individual opportunistic purposes. Moreover, the distribution constraint encourages greater investment in the quality of services, limiting the opportunism of organizations and reducing asymmetric information about quality. The overall advantage of the non-profit distribution constraint is that it fosters fiduciary relationships, especially between organizations and stakeholders exposed to problems of information asymmetry (Hansmann 1996).

Less attention has been devoted to other competitive advantages of not-for-profit organizations. Some authors have recognized the contribution these organizations make by increasing the quantity of services provided, but they have focused on generating donations (Weisbrod 1988) or involving consumers (Ben-Ner and Van Hoomissen 1991). Some studies have emphasized the net increase in employment generated by not-for-profits and the opportunities created for people who are difficult to employ (see Chapters 3 and 6 of this volume). However, empirical analyses have rarely investigated the ability of not-for-profits to guarantee x-efficiency and gather resources other than donations, especially through market exchanges. In addition, some empirical studies of specific areas of activity have shown that not-for-profits perform better than public agencies and for-profit firms.[1]

Researchers have generally not recognized the advantages that not-for-profits derive from their ability to manage human resources. Indeed, some researchers have seen the growth of not-for-profits as a way to curb the cost of labour, with a consequent decline in employees' well-being as surplus is transferred to the organizations themselves, their clients, or their contracting agencies.

These limitations in the interpretation of the role of not-for-profits make existing analyses insufficient, especially given the assumption of productive goals by some of these organizations and the legal recognition of social enterprises in many European countries. These developments call for a more in-depth study of the competitive advantages that non-profits and social enterprises enjoy in comparison with public agencies and for-profit firms. Particular attention should be devoted to the capacity of not-for-profits to identify the specific demands for general-interest services, to provide innovative services to meet new social needs, and to manage the organization of production processes efficiently.

This chapter examines the broad range of advantages that social enterprises have in order to overcome some of the weaknesses in existing studies.[2] In doing so, this contribution provides both an input-savings analysis, which assesses whether social enterprises utilize their human and financial resources differently from other types of organizations and hence incur lower costs to achieve the same performance, and an output-increasing analysis, which aims to determine whether social enterprises supply higher quantities of services with the same amount of resources. Some advantages seem to have a direct impact on organizations' x-efficiency or on transaction costs with their main stakeholders. The chapter shows how social enterprises can overcome the shortcomings that plague other types of organizations, especially failures that involve increased transaction costs in exchanges not only with clients, donors, employees, and volunteers, but also with the local community and the market.

The first two sections of the chapter identify salient features of the general-interest services industry and of social enterprises. The third section illustrates the most analysed issue in the provision of social services: information asymmetry with clients and donors. The fourth section examines the advantages that social enterprises have over for-profit firms, public agencies, and other types of non-profits in attracting resources at lower costs. It shows that social enterprises are able to collect donations and voluntary labour, but also to accumulate risk capital and to recur to the debt market. The fifth section examines employment relationships in social enterprises, since competitive advantages of these enterprises are rarely studied and are very important given the labour-intensive nature of the productive activities involved. Based on behavioural theory, this section shows that social enterprises tend to substitute economic benefits with intrinsic incentives and to select employees who are intrinsically motivated and altruistic. The sixth section provides empirical support for the arguments by analysing data collected by two surveys of social cooperatives in Italy during 1998 and 2006.

General-interest services

Most not-for-profit organizations, including social enterprises, operate in the general-interest services industry.[3] Economists have largely concentrated their attention on the problems of asymmetric information that characterize this industry: on the one hand, donors cannot control how managers (more generally, shareholders) use financial resources to achieve the declared aims of these organizations; on the other, clients and providers cannot be ensured of the quality of the services supplied. However, the problems of asymmetric information with stakeholders and several related issues have frequently been underestimated, and they must be examined in order to understand the competitive advantages of social enterprises in providing general-interest services.

First, there is a contradiction between the role of the industry in improving the well-being of the population and the shortage of private and public resources available to satisfy the demand for services. Private demand is characterized by the fact that part of the population does not have sufficient resources to purchase general-interest services on the market. Financial limitations increasingly constrain the ability of public agencies to provide these services, and externalization to private for-profit providers has not solved the problem of resource shortages.

Second, the productivity of the general services industry tends to be stagnant, especially when compared with other industries. Furthermore, average salaries paid to employees tend to increase without corresponding increases in productivity, resulting in what Baumol (1993) calls the 'costs disease'. This problem has been exacerbated by the retention of direct control over many activities by public authorities, since this has tended to increase wages and salaries over the level offered by for-profit firms.

Third, asymmetric information involves not only clients and donors, but also employment relationships. Organizations incur costs by controlling managers' and employees' behaviour and effort. The multitasking dimension of providing general services implies a trade-off between quantity and quality.[4] As demonstrated by public services in many countries, a risk of failure exists in the provision of incentives for employees, which can lead to inefficiencies in the production process and to low-quality services. These problems can cause client dissatisfaction, the misuse of resources in favour of employees rather than clients, and inefficient planning (for example, concerning decisions to open or close specific services).

Fourth, the general services industry supplies services that have a high social impact and are important for the intrinsically motivated and altruistic members and employees who deliver them. Moreover, relationships among the parties within the industry are emotionally intense, especially those between clients and organizations and between organizations and employees. Consequently, a comprehensive analysis needs to focus on the ability of providers of general-interest services to produce intrinsic and non-self-regarding incentives in contracts with employees and managers. This analysis must consider the various needs of employees and the factors that enter into their utility function, including relational goods, participation, autonomy, and procedural fairness.[5]

Finally, it must be noted that relationships between organizations and stakeholders are dynamic and have long-run consequences for the behaviour of both parties. Strong sets of interrelations among different parties increase opportunities to learn from others' behaviour and to conform to emerging social norms. When people inside working groups behave opportunistically, self-interested behaviour tends to prevail, and when people behave altruistically, cooperation tends to develop. The general services industry has a social function that may be valorized differently by each organization involved in the provision of services due to prevailing behaviours and internal social norms. Organizations can be more-or-less attentive to promoting a corporate culture and internal social norms to which other parties should converge, and this aspect provides social enterprises with several comparative advantages that are analysed in the following section.

Social enterprises from a comparative perspective

An analysis of the comparative advantages and limitations of social enterprises illustrates what distinguishes these enterprises from other organizations. Traditions and, where they exist, specific legal rules frame social enterprises as an institutional solution that adopts selective features of both donative non-profits and for-profit firms. Social enterprises are characterized by non-investor ownership, social goals, and productive activities. Nevertheless, social enterprises are not simply hybrid institutions, but rather have a unique set of features that offer competitive advantages.

The main advantage that social enterprises have over traditional non-profit organizations is their governance structure. While traditional non-profits are usually defined as non-proprietary organizations (Hansmann 1996), social enterprises are effectively controlled by stakeholders. Social enterprises often have a multi-stakeholder membership, while property rights are shared among several stakeholders, including clients, donors, other public and private organizations, and above all employees and volunteers. The assignment of property rights to clients or representatives of their interests both safeguards these stakeholders and reinforces the non-profit aims of the organization (Ben-Ner and Van Hoomissen 1991). It also explains why the non-profit distribution constraint, typically identified as the main characteristic of non-profits, is weakened in social enterprises, allowing them to accumulate financial resources, increase their capital, and improve their economic stability.

The main factor that distinguishes social enterprises from for-profit firms is their explicit social aim. Although for-profit firms are engaged in production of general-interest or welfare services, social enterprises are more constrained— both by law and by the kind of services provided—to serve the general interests of the community and of people in need. Furthermore, social enterprises are often embedded in the local community and share common aims with their stakeholders more than other organizational types usually do. The strength of the relationships with their stakeholders offers social enterprises several advantages in the management of exchanges with their constituent parties, as will be shown in the following sections. Furthermore, social enterprises tend to reduce self-regarding preferences and opportunistic behaviour by their various stakeholders, with positive consequences both for clients and for the overall management of the organization. Relationships with the local community strengthen fairness principles, collective actions, and altruistic behaviour. Founders are usually motivated by social interests, altruism, and philanthropy, while stakeholders share with them knowledge and principles. Work teams as well as groups of decision makers cooperate and share internal norms. At the same time, deviant behaviour can be sanctioned materially and normatively not only by the organization, but also by other stakeholders. Therefore, adherence to general community ideals produces an internal network of overlapping social norms that control the behaviour of all parties, and in particular of employees who are directly responsible for providing services.

Social enterprises and public agencies are expected to pursue the sole interests of their clients, maximize social well-being, behave according to altruistic preferences, and communicate with and involve the local community. In public agencies, however, decision making by bureaucrats and the opportunistic behaviour of civil servants can increase problems of asymmetric information. Furthermore, public agencies are often characterized by a rigidity and standardization in the supply of services: they respond mainly to the needs of the 'median voter' and do not provide for the needs of all citizens. Consequently, citizens may not trust public agencies and feel dissatisfied. Again, social enterprises enjoy competitive advantages in their relationships with stakeholders.

Advantages in exchanges with clients and in achieving quality

The first set of advantages enjoyed by social enterprises involves exchanges with clients. As already noted, the literature generally assumes that the non-profit distribution constraint is the main mechanism for ensuring appropriate behaviour by organizations. However, some social services are exempt from several problems of asymmetric information, while in other cases, thanks to the technology and the increasing verifiability of the quality of services supplied, asymmetries seem to have been reduced (Ben-Ner 2002). Limitations on profit distribution alone cannot fully explain the advantages of social enterprises.

The extended membership and the democracy of decision-making processes that typically characterize social enterprises, together with their clear communication of organizational behaviour and aims, offer the first advantage: the ability of these enterprises to improve the sense of trust and reputation among their various stakeholders. Clients, for example, choose their service suppliers by comparing the characteristics of the organizations and information available. Consequently, social enterprises must build their reputations through fair communication, social accounting, and stakeholder participation. Communication, participation, and fairness are the key principles of social enterprises.

The second advantage is an overlapping of organizational aims with their clients' interests, and this feature guarantees a better alignment between the supply of and demand for services, with positive consequences for both clients and organizations. For clients, this alignment means a better satisfaction of needs. The provision of services by social enterprises increases both the quantity and quality of services consumed and reduces organizational inefficiencies and opportunistic behaviour.[6] The result is superior production, which means that at each level of resources employed social enterprises tend to produce more and perform better.

For the organization, the individuation of demand and clients' needs means lower costs and less waste of resources. Social enterprises can enjoy the direct and voluntary involvement of the local community and of clients in decisions concerning production (Hansmann 1996). Their embeddedness in the local community increases the exchange of information (with cheap talk[7] or lower transaction costs) and the internalization of the clients' well-being in individual and organizational goals. Participation by stakeholders allows social enterprises to collect information on the characteristics of services required. Multilayered membership and participation by diverse stakeholders in decision-making processes allow for the identification of clients' needs, diminishing both transaction costs and failures in the satisfaction of demand.

In comparison with other organizational types, social enterprises also enjoy a higher degree of innovation and elasticity of supply. Innovation derives from the capacity of these organizations to acquire both financial and human resources. The accumulation of profits due to asset locks means that social enterprises can accumulate capital to invest in new projects, while the presence of human resources characterized by intrinsic motivations and abilities other than technical knowledge (e.g. relational abilities and altruistic behaviour) increases information flows, the specialization of work, and innovation. Flexibility is ensured by low levels of bureaucracy (especially in comparison with public agencies), small size (compared with public agencies and for-profit firms), and multiple and flexible goals (compared to the profit-maximizing aims of for-profit firms and the rigid management of public agencies).

The final advantage is the ability of social enterprises to organize economically sustainable production even when, with homogeneous prices, revenues do not cover costs. Social enterprises can induce clients to accept discriminating prices, i.e. they attract clients who accept they will pay heterogeneous prices for their services. Discrimination in prices can be used by social enterprises in opposition to the equal prices that characterize the competitive market. Social enterprises seem to involve their clients in their redistributive aims and to make it possible to accept payments that are sometimes higher than for other clients. The development of a perception of fairness among different clients helps to overcome the comparison with others' payments and to evaluate the social usefulness of price discrimination. From a self-regarding perspective, clients only evaluate their well-being by comparing the price paid and the service received, but from an altruistic perspective they become happier when other people are better off.

With regards to relations between organizations and clients, it seems reasonable to claim that social enterprises enjoy several advantages over other organizational types. Social enterprises have lower costs, are better able to align their supply of services to clients' needs, and avoid the inefficiencies of other organizational types, especially public agencies, since they are less bureaucratic and more flexible.

Competitive advantages in gathering resources

Trust, reputation, participation in decision-making processes, and good communication are all factors that assist social enterprises in gathering financial and free resources from the local community that might otherwise not be employed to improve the provision of general-interest services.

Social enterprises often enjoy good relationships with both volunteers, who contribute free human capital (i.e. working hours), and donors, who contribute free financial capital. Most studies consider volunteers as pure altruistic employees (e.g. Andreoni 1989, 1990). Nevertheless, participation by volunteers is not only driven by altruism. Volunteers are frequently interested in other non-monetary aspects of their activities, such as relationships and social recognition, and in extrinsic (or monetary) aspects, such as preparation for better job opportunities, on-the-job training, and tangible economic benefits. Social enterprises tend to satisfy some of these expectations. Compared with other types of not-for-profit organizations (especially donative non-profits) and public agencies, social enterprises offer their volunteers more opportunities to become remunerated employees over time. Compared with for-profit firms, social enterprises are able to attract people who are purely altruistic or socially conscious. The opportunity to employ non-remunerated workers not only is a source of direct advantages, but also allows these enterprises to utilize people who have the abilities and motivations to introduce innovations in the provision of services.

Another source of free resources is donors, who clearly have a variety of motivations that include social preferences, pure altruism, and—to varying degrees—self-regarding preferences. Social enterprises can satisfy this range of motivations by offering a mix of reasons for deciding to donate: pure other-regarding benefits (in terms of the social utility generated by donations), self-regarding intrinsic motivations (e.g. social recognition, visibility in the community, and participation in decision-making processes), and extrinsic incentives (e.g. tax relief). Moreover, social enterprises interact with donors based on voluntary exchange, while public agencies tend to decrease the intrinsic and altruistic motivations of people due to their authoritarian character. In contrast, the perception of for-profit firms as egoistic organizations excludes donations.

A final advantage of social enterprises is that they can gather significant shares of capital through the market and by using profits to create and increase asset locks. By operating in the financial market, social enterprises ensure that some financial resources are channelled from other uses to the production of general-interest services. When social enterprises are absent from the market, fewer human and financial resources will be employed to produce these services, even when unsatisfied demand exists. Furthermore, social enterprises accumulate most or all of their profits as asset locks. This is a sort of long-term donation from members, who renounce their financial benefits and rights in order to increase the enterprise's capital, stability, and opportunities to innovate and grow.

Efficiency in managing human resources

The competitive advantages of social enterprises are also evident in the management of human resources. Several studies have shown that three main features distinguish not-for-profits from other organizational types: the ability to select altruistic and intrinsically motivated employees; the provision of incentives different from standard economic rewards; and the presence of managers who internalize the social aim of the organization (Leete 2000; Borzaga and Depedri 2005; Benz 2005).

The advantages of employing intrinsically motivated employees can best be understood by analysing preferences from the perspective of behavioural economics. According to this approach, employees are motivated by a range of preferences in addition to self-interest. For example, employees are interested in non-wage incentives, and job satisfaction entails a complex process of evaluating incentives received on the job and in light of preferences and expectations (Locke 1969). Employees evaluate not only economic rewards, but also extrinsic incentives—such as job security, flexible working hours, and career opportunities—and intrinsic incentives—such as the desire to work for personal interests and individual satisfaction (De Charms 1968; Deci 1975). Some scholars (e.g. Frey 1997) emphasize the importance of the 'crowding-out effect'—the possibility that an excess of extrinsic incentives (e.g. high wages) reduces intrinsic motivations (e.g. personal interest and self-esteem), leaving work commitment unchanged or even diminished.[8] Moreover, according to Ben-Ner and Putterman (1998), individuals are simultaneously motivated by self-regarding egoistical motivations, other-regarding social preferences, and process-regarding motivations linked to how an organization manages its human resources.

The debate over employee motivations can be simplified by including extrinsic and intrinsic motivations in self-regarding preferences, which are those preferences that can be satisfied either by monetary rewards—mainly economic incentives—or by non-monetary rewards. Included in the latter category are opportunities to express creativity, establish new relationships, and enjoy satisfying work relationships with colleagues, managers, and clients (Gui and Sugden 2005; Borzaga and Depedri 2005). Other-regarding preferences are closely connected with social preferences through altruism and conformism.[9] These preferences induce employees to evaluate the consequences of their activity on others' well-being. Finally, process-regarding preferences involve both perceived distribution, the satisfaction employees get when the wage structure is seen as equitable, and procedural fairness, employees' positive evaluation of organizational processes, career paths, information transmittal, and work organization.

The range of approaches to employee motivation and job incentives shows the multidimensionality of preferences and incentives that organizations can supply. Considering the various alternatives provides a clearer portrayal of the comparative advantages of social enterprises. The assumption is that motivations differ according to the characteristics of each individual, but also according to the peculiarities of the industry and of the organization in which the person is employed, since organizations differ in how they manage incentives and shape the working environment.

The first source of evidence supporting the claims of this approach is that not-for-profits often pay their managers and other employees below the average for the industry,[10] but without negative consequences on their job satisfaction and effort. A possible explanation is that social enterprises are able to attract people who are intrinsically motivated and interested in the social dimension of the job (Handy and Katz 1998). Moreover, employees of not-for-profits are intrinsically attracted by the organization in itself (Goddeeris 1988; Borzaga and Depedri 2005), interested in the activity performed (Weisbrod 1983), and have stronger intrinsic and social preferences than do employees in other organizational types (Mirvis 1992; Tortia 2008). Furthermore, the characteristics of the job (mainly its social usefulness), the working environment (relationships with colleagues and internal social norms), and the employees (mainly intrinsically motivated) tend to reduce opportunistic and self-regarding behaviour, while cooperation is improved by a 'sense of group' linked to the social dimension of the activity, thus reducing turnover (Almond and Kendall 2001). The employees of not-for-profits are also willing to donate part of their effort (Preston 1989), and altruism positively influences employees' loyalty to the organization (Almond and Kendall 2001). The advantages for social enterprises are a reduction in the costs of control and an increase of productivity at each wage level.

The process of selecting intrinsically motivated employees is facilitated by the specific mix of incentives supplied by social enterprises to their employees. The monetary benefits provided can include flexibility, job stability, on-the-job training, and fringe benefits (Steinberg 1990). The most important non-monetary incentives are participation in decision making (Michie and Sheehan 1999), low stress, perceived autonomy, and creativity (Mirvis and Hackett 1983). The relevance of these process-regarding factors is supported by the governance and organizational system of social enterprises. Consultation and direct participation by employees in decision-making processes are often high, the work offers autonomy and personal relationships, the climate is collaborative, and the level of control is low. Moreover, incentives seem to be supplied to employees in a fair way. This is why job satisfaction is significantly influenced by the perception of both distributive fairness (Levine 1991; Mirvis 1992) and procedural fairness, which involves the transparency and appropriateness of organizational procedures, information transmission, and career management (Benz 2005; Tortia 2008). Job satisfaction is also strengthened by the democratic management of human resources, which entails the participation by employees in decision-making processes (Leete 2000).

Relationships between organizations and managers in social enterprises have several specific characteristics. Empirical analyses by Leete (2000) and others show that not-for-profits tend to select managers with ideals aligned to those of the organization, and this helps overcome problems of asymmetric information and opportunistic behaviour. Only managers that are not solely motivated by self-interest can ensure the long-term aims of non-profit and social enterprises.

Moreover, effective managers provide leadership for their organizations. They not only shape expectations and social norms, but also provide models of behaviour that may be reciprocated by employees. Consequently, when managers are excessively controlling, then employees may become less intrinsically motivated and behave unkindly, but when managers are intrinsically motivated and participate in the mission or their organization and their co-workers, they will be better able to transmit these principles to their subordinates. Moreover, policies of human resources management become fairer and information and control are less costly.

To sum up, the main inefficiency that characterizes employment relationships in the provison of general-interest services is asymmetric information, which can cause opportunistic behaviour, weak work performance, costly forms of control, and higher economic rewards. Inefficiencies can only be overcome by means of trust, cooperation, participation, and consultation. All these factors seem more likely to be prevalent in social enterprises that in other organizational types.

Another competitive advantage of social enterprises is their ability to provide incentive policies that satisfy employees and develop loyalty to the organization. This supports the hypothesis that the efficiency of human resources policies depends not only on the individual characteristics of employees, but also on the organization's efficiency in selecting employees and in providing adequate incentives. The ability of social enterprises to align employee behaviour with organizational goals is key, since it ensures both the quality of work performance and the efficiency of management. The selection process helps to achieve a sorting equilibrium between employees' motivations and an organization's aims.

Consequently, employees and managers in social enterprises tend to behave kindly, exert more effort, balance the quantity and quality of their performance, and to develop abilities (in terms of both technical knowledge and cognitive abilities) that encourage the promotion of new ideas and innovation. In addition, the advantages of social enterprises in production and efficiency are achieved at low costs, since no extra economic incentives are needed.

Empirical findings on Italian social enterprises

A significant number of empirical investigations have studied the advantages of not-for-profits, but with several limitations. First, they do not distinguish among different types of not-for-profits and tend to underestimate the prevalence of those with an explicit productive function. Second, the effectiveness of not-for-profits has been studied separately from their efficiency, analysing either the qualitative or the quantitative dimensions. Third, attention has been devoted to the management of human resources in non-profit organizations, but generally not to the advantages linked to employment relationships.

The empirical analysis of this chapter draws upon surveys conducted in Italy during 1998 (Fivol-Feo) and 2006 (ICSI2007).[11] The 1998 survey investigated

228 organizations delivering social services (54 public agencies, 17 for-profit firms, and 157 not-for-profits, 74 of which were social cooperatives) and 2,066 paid employees (588 in social cooperatives). It compared the characteristics of social cooperatives with other organizational types. The 2006 survey focused exclusively on social cooperatives[12] and detailed information was collected on 310 enterprises, 285 managers, and 4,134 remunerated employees.[13] The 2006 survey reflected the distribution of Italian social cooperatives along three dimensions: type (with social cooperatives divided by law into social cooperatives providing social services and those fostering work integration), location (the sample was geographically representative), and size (organizations with fewer than 15 employees, from 15 to 50 employees, and more than 50 employees).

The quality of services and the social aim

In the 2006 survey, the quality of services was evaluated by asking the representatives of social cooperatives to self-assess the level of attention that the organization devoted to clients and to the quality of their services.[14] The study found that the principal aims of the surveyed cooperatives were to provide high-quality services (29 per cent) and to respond to the general interests of the community (32 per cent). The non-profit distribution constraint was perceived as only one of the components of the cooperative's identity (16.8 per cent identified the non-profit distribution constraint as an organizational goal).

Quality was systematically monitored by 58 per cent of social cooperatives, against 11.6 per cent that did not monitor quality or clients' satisfaction; 90 per cent of the respondents claimed that the quality of services had increased over the previous two years. The outcome seems to be the provision of high-quality services (as self-assessed by 72 per cent of cooperatives) and the satisfaction of clients' needs (claimed by all cooperatives). Furthermore, about 80 per cent of social cooperatives claimed that the quality of their services was higher than that offered by other types of organizations.

As proposed in the theoretical sections above, there seem to be five factors that are crucial for improving the quality of services provided: reputation, stakeholder participation, trust, effective communication, and community involvement. The 2006 survey provides insights into how social cooperatives perceive each of these factors.

Reputations are an important strategy for improving relationships, increasing involvement in the local community, and improving performance. Social cooperatives claimed that they had a good reputation among all major actors: clients (average score of 5.7 on a scale from 1 to 7), private organizations and public agencies (5.6 for both), and the local community (5.5).

Social cooperatives reported that they had multi-stakeholder memberships, although only 9.8 per cent of them had clients as members. Nevertheless, social cooperatives usually claimed to have open access to their stakeholders, and all of them accepted their employees as members, 90 per cent accepted volunteers, 46.6 per cent also accepted clients, and frequently they were open to other stakeholders—such as supporters and financial contributors—becoming members. Even though clients were a small component of overall membership, social cooperatives consider themselves public-interest organizations that aim to solve the problems of all their clients (and not only of their members).

Social cooperatives reported that trust was important especially in relationships with clients (average scores of 6.3 on a scale from 1 to 7) and with public agencies (5.9).

Effective communication and accountability involve formal documentation of an organization's activities. Certificates of quality were used by 53 per cent of social cooperatives. Accountability instruments (such as the statute, balance sheet, and social balance) were used to self-evaluate organizational performance (average score of 5.6 on a scale of 1 to 7), involve employees and members in the organization's mission (4.9), spread information (4.6), and improve relationships with stakeholders (4.3).

The development of good relationships with the local population has positive consequences on the development of social capital. The well-being of the local community was a primary aim for 57.4 per cent of social cooperatives. Social enterprises claimed that their activities offered important services that were not otherwise provided by other organizational types or by governmental agencies (average score of 4.9 on a scale from 1 to 7). They also claimed to provide high-quality services (5.0) and to create new employment opportunities (4.6). Half of the respondents reported that they were more able than other organizations to collect human and material resources from the local community, and another 40 per cent agreed at least in part.

The acquisition and use of resources

One of the hypothesized advantages of social enterprises is their ability to mobilize volunteers. The 2006 survey demonstrated the importance of volunteers, and 66 per cent of cooperatives utilized them. Only 9 per cent of organizations had registered a decline in the number of volunteers in the three years prior to the survey, while 24.6 per cent of them had registered increases; there was no variation in the number for about half of them. This labour donation averaged 40 hours a week per cooperative. Furthermore, the quality of the volunteers' performance was good, since organizations declared themselves quite satisfied with both volunteers' motivations and skills (on both aspects, 60 per cent assigned a 7 on a scale from 1 to 10). Nevertheless, the 1998 survey found that voluntary work was less important for social cooperatives than for other types of non-profits, which utilized more volunteers. The 2006 survey found that 34 per cent of social cooperatives had no volunteers, and that in some other cooperatives volunteers were only formally involved in the organization as members, without actively participating in the daily work.

There is little evidence that social cooperatives have an advantage in collecting donations. Generally, donations contributed little to the revenue of social cooperatives: 85.7 per cent of social cooperatives received no contributions from private entities and citizens, and more than 50 per cent of them supplied their services through arrangements with public authorities. Nevertheless, private market sales were acquiring growing importance and a trade-off seemed to exist between donations on the one hand and public and market revenue on the other.

Social enterprises are able to accumulate assets and to access financial markets. In 2006, 32 per cent of organizations achieved the break-even point, and when profits were made, they were mostly accumulated as asset locks (on average 83.4 per cent of the amount of profits). On average, asset locks amounted to €130,000 per organization and capital to €37,000, for a total of €167,000. Moreover, the demand for external (mainly debt) financial resources was quite high and important especially for supporting the current activities and investments. The 2006 data show that debts amounted to an average of €749,000 per organization, and this value was quite high considering that social cooperatives had a value of production that was about double their debts (€1.5 million on average, with 53.6 per cent of social cooperatives having production valued over €600,000). For about 40 per cent of social enterprises, debts and investments significantly increased from 2003 to 2005, which demonstrates the vitality of social cooperatives.

These data collectively reflect the ability of social cooperatives to accumulate capital and sustain the hypothesis that social cooperatives are increasingly stable, efficient, and investment-driven.

Cost savings and benefits in employment relationships

The analysis of employment relationships shows some possible cost savings which social enterprises can achieve in managing their human capital. In 1998, employees in social cooperatives were paid less than in other comparable organizations: full-time employees earned about €770 per month (after tax) compared to about €900 in public agencies and about €800 in for-profit firms. There were similar differences in hourly wages. In 2006, wages in social cooperatives remained quite low, amounting on average to €1,000 a month for full-time and €630 for part-time employees.

Moreover, supplementary hours were frequently not remunerated nor recuperated by employees, and these data imply a further reduction in labour costs: the 2006 data show that about 30 per cent of employees interviewed donated supplementary hours, while in 1998 the percentage of unpaid overtime was also higher and significantly over the levels registered in public agencies and for-profit firms.

Lower costs were also achieved in the monitoring of employee performance, which is usually not bureaucratized by formal procedures and is directly conducted by superiors (as asserted by 63 per cent of employees in 2006). Managers were considered by employees as important mediators in the transmission of organizational goals and information. In addition, the cost of the selection process was low, since candidates were frequently chosen because they were directly known by the organization or had experience in the same area in which the cooperative operates.

The cost savings achieved by the management of employment relationships and the low economic compensation received do not seem to have influenced employees' satisfaction or effort. Overall job satisfaction was quite high (5.5 on average on a scale from 1 to 7), although employees were generally not satisfied with their wages (average score of 3.8, which was the lowest response in the survey). On the other hand, high levels of satisfaction were reported by employees about other on-the-job incentives, including relationships with managers and co-workers (average scores over 6 on a scale from 1 to 7), the usefulness of the job (5.9), the variety and creativity of the job (6.1), the working hours (5.4), job security and the working environment (both 5.3), and autonomy and social recognition (both 4.9).

Employees' effort also seems quite high, since employees of social cooperatives reported having a high degree of engagement with their jobs. Furthermore, they claimed that the effort they provide is above the level that employees in general expend for the given wage (5.5 on a scale from 1 to 7, where 4 expresses a 'normal' level of effort). Employees' commitment is further confirmed by the high proportion of employees who reported that they intended to stay in the organization. In 1998, 65.1 per cent of employees of social cooperatives wanted to stay in the organization at least for some years (47 per cent as long as possible and 18.1 per cent for some years). Although this percentage is not that high and is roughly similar to what employees of for-profit firms report, it is significantly higher than for public agencies (where 50 per cent of employees reported their willingness to stay at least for some years). Furthermore, the degree of loyalty in social cooperatives seemed to have greatly increased in 2006: the percentage of people who expressed their willingness to stay was about 90 per cent.

The high levels of satisfaction, effort, and loyalty reported by employees of social cooperatives can be explained by the characteristics of both employees and human resource management practices. One important factor is that employees of social cooperatives seem to be intrinsically motivated, as both surveys clearly indicate. Before they entered social cooperatives, the respondents had been searching for jobs offering mainly non-monetary incentives, such as personal growth and awareness, good work relationships, and the satisfaction of social needs (as asserted by more than 80 per cent of the respondents).[15] When asked to judge the most important aspects of a job, respondents ranked relationships and social usefulness first (average scores of 9.5 on a scale from 1 to 12), followed by job stability (9.4), and the sharing of ideals (8.7). Wage and other economic incentives came in only sixth, followed by other extrinsic aspects. Among the specific factors that employees identified as having influenced their decision to accept a job in a cooperative, social usefulness was high (average score of 5.5 on a scale from 1 to 7), followed by shared ideals (4.7), collective projects with other people (4.5), and enjoying good relationships (4.6). However, employees were also attracted by the extrinsic aspect of expected professional development (5.4). A small proportion (17.1 per cent) reported that they had no job alternative.

The contribution of employee motivation to good organizational outcomes was also recognized by social cooperatives. The presence of intrinsically motivated employees was considered by 75 per cent of organizations as the most important factor in determining the achievement of both organizational goals and effective performance.[16] In the self-identification of the advantages enjoyed in comparison with other organizational types, social cooperatives asserted that employees are the main contributors to the quality and effectiveness of the services provided. More than 40 per cent claimed to take advantage of the cooperative climate and the trustworthiness among co-employees, while 31 per cent identified the intrinsic motivation of employees. Furthermore, social cooperatives believe that the quality achieved mainly depends upon employee motivation (average score of 6.5 on a scale from 1 to 7), employee effort (6.4), and only secondarily on organizational characteristics (5.7 for organizational forms and 5.4 for organizational structure). The Italian survey data therefore support the thesis that employment relationships are the main sources of comparative advantages.

The second explanation of employees' satisfaction is based on the mix of incentives supplied by social cooperatives. This mix seems to satisfy most employees' needs, except those regarding economic benefits. Specifically, although wages and salaries are low, other extrinsic and intrinsic aspects are supplied by social cooperatives. Professional development is guaranteed through training opportunities (reportedly offered to more than 70 per cent of their employees during the three-year period prior to the study) and by cooperation with managers (as asserted by all workers interviewed). Flexibility in working hours is frequently offered to employees: 34.3 per cent of them had chosen part-time work and 70.2 per cent claimed that their cooperatives were attentive to satisfying their needs for flexible schedules. Finally, job stability was reflected not only by the low percentage of employees with temporary contracts (17.7 per cent), but also by the perception of employees with temporary contracts that their jobs were relatively secure.

Furthermore, non-monetary benefits are more important than monetary incentives in explaining employment relationships in social cooperatives. Employees claimed they had a good degree of autonomy on the job (average score of 4.7 on a scale from 1 to 7), friendly relationships with managers (5.5), and experienced altruism and cooperation in team work (4.9). Thus, employees perceive that social cooperatives frequently use a combination of both extrinsic (working hours, job stability, careers, and other economic incentives) and intrinsic incentives (relationships and participation) to increase their effort.

Another factor that contributes to employee satisfaction and loyalty is the perceived fairness of procedures. Both surveys corroborate the hypothesis of high procedural fairness in social enterprises. Employees perceived that they were adequately informed of organizational aims and received satisfactory information for improving their performance (average level of agreement of 5.2 on a scale from 1 to 7), reported that promises to employees were always respected (5.7), and believed that they were treated without discrimination (5.2). Distributive fairness was also perceived as high: employees reported they received a fair wage when compared with that of their co-workers (average score of distributive fairness of 4.4 on a scale from 1 to 7 where 4 indicates 'fairness') and especially with their supervisors (4.9).

These findings are confirmed by data collected from managers, who seem to be intrinsically motivated and willing to donate part of their labour by serving as volunteers or working additional hours for free. They claimed to be very satisfied with their job and with many intrinsic aspects of it. Most of them reported their intention to stay in the organization as long as possible (82.4 per cent). Furthermore, managers claimed to have extensive experience either inside or outside the organization: 50.2 per cent of them had been members of the social cooperative, or presidents or members of the board of directors; 52.2 per cent had been remunerated or voluntary employees inside the same organization; 83.3 per cent had experiences as volunteers in other organizations; and 25.3 per cent worked previously in a for-profit firm or public agency. Finally, managers seem to be the key mediators of organizational principles and the guarantors of transparency and fairness procedures. They are highly involved in decision-making processes (average level of influence on decisions was reported as 5.4 on a scale from 1 to 7), enjoy great autonomy (average score of 5.5), and tend to manage the organization in order to ensure distributive and procedural fairness (the average score for attention to fairness of wages within the cooperative was 6.3 and to communication and career processes was 6.1) and to satisfying their employees' needs (average score of 6.2).

The main problem that seems to exist for managing employment relationships is the risk of exit by young, educated employees.[17] Multinomial models demonstrate that age and level of education are negatively correlated with job satisfaction and willingness to stay. These models also identify possible reasons for leaving: the expectations of young educated people, especially with regard to economic incentives (salary, stability, and career); the low intrinsic motivation of newly employed people, which may be caused by the selection of people mainly interested in monetary recognition; and the risk that low wages threaten loyalty to the organization due to the inability to cover economic needs, notwithstanding general job satisfaction (Borzaga and Depedri 2009).

Organizational efficiency in comparison with other organizational types

In 1998, social cooperatives were found to be generally more efficient than other organizational types and tended to be more attentive to their clients and to the development of high-quality services. In terms of efficiency, social cooperatives met costs with revenues (although revenues frequently depended upon contracts with public administrations), showed a great dynamism (being on average more involved than other organizational types in processes of growth), and were more efficient, especially in the production of services and in the management of human resources. In the three years prior to the survey, revenues were reported to have increased by 66 per cent, the number of clients by 78 per cent, and the number of employees by 100 per cent. These percentages are all higher than those reported by for-profit firms and public agencies. Overall, social cooperatives were better able to meet new clients' needs with their own resources and to increase the supply of services.

As regards the quality of services, in 1998 social cooperatives (together with religious non-profit organizations) were the only organizational types to frequently involve their clients in decision-making processes and in membership (33 per cent of cases). Furthermore, social cooperatives protected clients more than in other organizational types thanks to consultancies in formal meetings and the periodical monitoring of quality of services (carried out in 38 per cent of social cooperatives against 27.6 per cent in all other organizational forms).[18]

The 2006 survey provides additional insights into the competitive advantages that social cooperatives identify as important. Social cooperatives claimed to be more cost effective than other organizational types in managing human resources: specifically, 50 per cent asserted that they had lower costs in involving employees in decision-making processes and in ensuring stimulating working environments, 36 per cent in providing incentives other than wages, and 23 per cent in collecting information on employees' behaviour and controlling managers' activities.

However, social cooperatives do not perceive that they have economic advantages in managing decision-making processes, since they assert that they expend greater amounts of resources than other organizational types on consulting with citizens (claimed to be higher by 56 per cent of social cooperatives), decision-making processes (higher by 30 per cent), and the development of trust relationships with stakeholders (higher by 48 per cent). These data sustain the hypothesis that not-for-profit organizations bear transaction costs with regard to their governance (Hansmann 1996). Nonetheless, the data may also reflect the general engagement of social cooperatives in innovative and less standardized services. Indeed, social cooperatives claim to have developed good methods for satisfying local demand for services, thanks mainly to their involvement in local communities (considered as very important by 93 per cent of social cooperatives) and trust relationships with other organizations (considered important by 35 per cent of the cooperatives).

Finally, it should be noted that the comparative advantages that have been identified do not necessarily apply to every social cooperative, since organizations with different characteristics perform in different ways. For example, small-sized cooperatives are more likely to suffer from problems of capitalization, competition, and meeting costs. The biggest organizations seem to be less advantageously positioned for promoting an efficient mix of incentives for their employees.

Summary and conclusions

Social enterprises are an innovative and competitive form of organization that has internalized the specificities of providing general-interest services and reduced many of the inefficiencies, transaction costs, waste of resources, and limitations of public agencies and for-profit firms. The main problems in providing these services are linked to the opportunistic motivation and the non-verifiability of behaviour by stakeholders on the one hand, and bureaucracy and difficulties in evaluating the real needs and expectations of clients and employees on the other. While these problems can lead to a reduction of the social well-being of all parties involved and a waste of resources, they have also created space for innovative institutional forms to achieve competitive advantages by developing alternative mechanisms of coordination and participation. By briefly summing up the advantages described in both the theoretical and empirical sections above, several competitive advantages emerge as crucial for the efficiency of social enterprises since they provide increases in output and savings in inputs.

There are three main sources of increasing output. First, the services produced by social enterprises tend to be more flexible and innovative, especially when compared with public services. Consequently, they can satisfy a greater number of clients and a larger proportion of local needs. Second, employees of social enterprises exert more effort and ensure the stability of production, despite the lower salaries that they are often paid. The satisfaction of employees' expectations and needs (i.e. the good level of job satisfaction among employees of social enterprises) increases loyalty and reduces the cost of turnover. Consequently, the production of services is more stable both in terms of quantity, due to the specialization of employees, and in terms of quality, since when reciprocal knowledge increases, people tend to improve the quality of relationships and become more trusting. Third, the mobilization of local resources and the transmission of social norms to the community (specifically, to agents belonging to the community) create a virtuous cycle: they enlarge relationships, increase cooperation and trust, diffuse knowledge and ideals, and reduce the opportunism of the people involved.

Social enterprises have four main advantages in achieving input savings by reducing costs. First, they benefit from free resources and enjoy some advantages in collecting financial resources in the market. The gathering of free resources is significant when social enterprises are compared with public agencies and for-profit firms; while compared to traditional donative non-profits social enterprises usually receive fewer donations. On the other hand, social enterprises enjoy an advantage in the financial market, since their entrepreneurial character and stable delivery of services allow them to cover debts and to offer a guarantee in recourse to debt funding. However, the main advantage of social enterprises in collecting resources comes from the balance between their social and economic aims. Organizational goals—together with transparency of communication, participation by various stakeholders, good relationships with local actors, and the community itself—develop a sense of trust and strategically increase opportunities to gather both financial and human capital locally.[19]

A second advantage is that social enterprises enjoy lower transaction costs (e.g. in the collection and transmission of information) and less waste of resources (e.g. due to less bureaucracy and high flexibility). Inefficiencies are reduced by overcoming asymmetric information among the various parties. The relationships of social enterprises with the community and stakeholders improve the exchange of information, make relationships easier, and guarantee a high level of involvement. These competitive advantages are reinforced by implicit contracts stipulated with clients and other parties, especially if they are formalized through accountability systems. Consequently, control over the behaviour of social enterprises is exercised by various stakeholders, verifiable by other parties, and less costly for external individuals due to the transparency of communication. Purchasers and clients can also better verify the appropriateness and effectiveness of innovations in services. Moreover, the provision of services frequently takes place not through contractual or market mechanisms, but through partnerships, agreements, and participation. These arrangements save on the costs of bargaining, increase the distribution of resources in favour of different classes of clients, and overcome contractual incompleteness and market failures.

A third advantage of social enterprises is that they incur lower costs in controlling the performances of managers and employees by utilizing mechanisms of control and punishment differently from other organizational types. A crucial actor in the planning of these policies is managers. Their involvement in defining organizational aims and their ability to develop fair procedures strengthen their relationships with employees, who consequently perceive themselves more as collaborators than as subordinates. Furthermore, managers tend to act less as controllers, avoiding crowding-out effects on employees' motivations, decreasing the costs of monitoring, and increasing employees' commitment to organizational goals. Moreover, the selection of altruistic employees decreases the risk of opportunistic behaviour, while direct participation by employees in decision-making processes reduces the problems and costs of controlling employee behaviour. Morality and the internalization of social norms become self-controlling routines and are a cost-free source of controlling individual behaviour. Finally, whilst in other organizational types the power of control is assigned to managers, in social enterprises a range of stakeholders—members, the local community, other employees—share control. Therefore, alternative and low-cost mechanisms of monitoring are characteristic of social enterprises, and these mechanisms reduce opportunism and increase the adhesion to common social norms and rules of behaviour.

A fourth advantage of social enterprises is that the mix of incentives that they provide to their employees is less costly than for other organizational types. The research literature and data collected in the 1998 survey show that social enterprises have low labour costs, which can be achieved both through the provision of salaries at below-market averages or overtime provided by workers for free. This implies that each hour of work costs less, given the same level and quality of performance by employees. Social enterprises can also provide intrinsic incentives to their employees that are less costly than other rewards and than the incentive schemes of other organizations, since intrinsic incentives emerge naturally from the internal characteristics of social enterprises. For example, employees of social enterprises enjoy opportunities for membership, personal and professional growth, good relationships with superiors and colleagues, and autonomy in the management of daily activities. Working for social enterprises is characterized by frequent contacts with clients and by the internalization of social norms, ideals, and social preferences. All these considerations suggest that social enterprises have greater opportunities to provide intrinsic incentives at a lower cost than do other organizational types. In comparison, for-profit firms and public agencies (especially those of large size) are able to offer more extrinsic incentives (such as economic rewards and job stability) that are less burdensome on these organizations' economic resources. Consequently, social enterprises enjoy comparative advantages by supplying employees a differentiated mix of incentives at lower costs.

In conclusion, there are several advantages enjoyed by social cooperatives in comparison to other organizational types, and the non-profit distribution constraint is only one of them. These competitive advantages tend to improve both the efficiency and the effectiveness of production. Indeed, the ability to select motivated employees and to provide effective incentives enhances the quality of services and leads to increases in output and savings in inputs. Efficiency and effectiveness in social enterprises seem to be complements rather than substitutes. Nevertheless, the opportunity to achieve good results and to simultaneously increase redistributive effects and produce social capital depends upon the ability of social enterprises to involve all stakeholders and to develop trusting and transparent relationships, above all with employees.

Notes

1 See Cutler and Berndt (2001) for the medical care industry and Krueger and Malečková (2003) on education.
2 Obviously, an analysis of the advantages of social enterprises does not preclude that these organizations have limitations and incur costs. Some data on these issues will be considered in the empirical section.
3 See Chapter 5 of this volume for a detailed analysis of this industry.
4 As defined in Bacchiega and Borzaga (2001), general services are characterized by multidimensionality in the sense that they consist of various quantitative and qualitative dimensions that can be differently evaluated by clients. A failure to provide multitasking services emerges when one or more of these dimensions are not measurable, and both organizations and employees under-invest in one dimension and over-invest in another. Employees are necessarily involved in multitasking activities, since their aim is not simply—or even mainly—to increase productivity, but also to improve relationships with clients and other intrinsic dimensions of their activities.
5 For example, relationships are experienced on the job, and therefore enter into the employees' utility function as intrinsic factors (Gui and Sugden 2005). Similarly, on-the-job autonomy offers opportunities for personal as well as professional growth. Moreover, the services provided have positive and observable consequences for clients' well-being, and this element provides incentives for employees, especially if they have strong other-regarding preferences.
6 The reduction of opportunistic behaviour in social enterprises increases the investment in quality that enhances clients' well-being and decreases failures in the provision of services. Consequently, social enterprises not only improve quality for clients, but also are more efficient than other organizational types.
7 Cheap talk is an informal and colloquial modality of transmitting information, and it implies low transaction costs.

8 This distinction suggests that the wage enters the individual's choice function not solely as a positive determinant, but also as a negative influence mediated by possible distorting effects on other motivations.

9 This gives rise to disinterested behaviour in response to the behaviour of colleagues or to decisions by the organization that are deemed correct.

10 Most empirical analyses show that average wages in not-for-profits are lower than those offered by public agencies and for-profit firms. There are, however, some exceptions: Mocan and Viola (1997) find that public agencies do not pay better than non-profits, and Anheier (1991), Almond and Kendall (2001), and Mirvis and Hackett (1983) show that non-profits pay higher wages than do for-profit firms, especially in industries where non-profits are more widespread.

11 The 1998 Fivol-Feo survey was financed by the Fondazione Italiana Volontariato and the Fondazione Europa Occupazione and was conducted by a network of Italian universities coordinated by the Università di Trento. The findings of this survey have been extensively reported and analysed in Borzaga and Musella (2003), Borzaga and Depedri (2005), Borzaga and Tortia (2006), and Mosca *et al.* (2007). The ICSI2007 (Investigation of Italian Social Cooperatives) survey was conducted between 2006 and 2007 by universities in Trento, Brescia, Naples, Milan, and Reggio Calabria. The findings of this survey have been less extensively analysed and reported, so the analysis in this chapter draws mainly on this survey and refers to the earlier one for information on organizational types and for comparative purposes.

12 The empirical analysis covers only social cooperatives, which are a particular form of social enterprises. The decision to focus exclusively on social cooperatives was made because social cooperatives are the most diffused types of social enterprises in Italy and the survey occurred before the law regulating social enterprises had been enacted.

13 Employees of social cooperatives are mostly females (74 per cent) and highly educated (about 35 per cent have a secondary school diploma and 30 per cent a university degree). Only 18.5 per cent of these employees have temporary contracts, while 45 per cent work part-time.

14 Neither of the surveys included interviews with clients of the organizations, and consequently data about clients were collected only indirectly through the questionnaires administered to the organizations.

15 Nevertheless, less than half of them were initially interested in working for a social cooperative.

16 Among other important aspects identified were the involvement of members (identified as important by 62 per cent of social cooperatives), cooperative values (54 per cent), and the multitasking nature and social relevance of services provided (both 46 per cent). The non-profit distribution constraint was least important (23 per cent).

17 The percentage of employees intending to quit the organization is higher among young people with a degree, and the level of satisfaction of these employees is lower.

18 In the 2006 survey, 87 per cent of social cooperatives claimed to monitor the satisfaction of their clients and about 60 per cent had quality certification of their services.

19 A clear relationship emerges between the involvement of social enterprises in the community and the mobilization of local resources, donations, abilities, and voluntary work.

3 The impact of social enterprises on output, employment, and welfare

Ermanno Tortia

Social enterprises are able to undertake productive activities when for-profit firms and public agencies are either ineffective or unable to operate. Based on their innovative property rights and forms of governance, social enterprises produce public and quasi-public—i.e. common and collective—goods and services that are meritorious and beneficial for the public. They are typically more efficient, innovative, and productive than public agencies and for-profit firms when market and contract imperfections are prevalent due to asymmetric information (Hansmann 1996), contract incompleteness (Bacchiega and Borzaga 2001, 2003; Borzaga 2003), or high relational intensity in the production of goods (Gui and Sugden 2005).

Social enterprises have wide-ranging potential for the development of modern economic systems and encompass activities well beyond the industries traditionally populated by not-for-profit organizations. Social enterprises not only have expanded the supply and range of services in traditional fields of not-for-profit activity such as welfare and social services, but also have been important sources of innovation by creating jobs for disadvantaged workers and by promoting fair trade, microfinance, cultural activities, and environmental protection. In these areas, for-profit firms are in general not effective due to low levels of profitability and the public nature of the services provided. This new productive potential has involved a shift from profit maximization to the satisfaction of social needs (Borzaga and Tortia 2007, 2009), and it has been facilitated by innovative forms of inclusive governance that support the expression of intrinsic and pro-social motivations (Valentinov 2007, 2008).

The goal of social enterprises is to produce public benefit goods with a meritorious character. This type of production can be observed in market economies not only by public agencies, but also by private organizations, including at times for-profit firms. Hence, it is not necessarily carried out by organizations that fall within a strict legal definition of social enterprises. It should be noted that even when firms are investor-owned, they may share some important features with the definitions of social enterprises introduced in path-breaking legislation in the UK during 2005 and in Italy during 2006. In these new legal definitions, social enterprises do not pursue profit as their main objective and explicitly identify social aims in their statutes and organizational protocols. In so doing, they usually seek to reinforce trust relations with all their main patrons, including clients, volunteers, employees, borrowers, and sub-contractors.

Social enterprises have similarities with traditional non-profit organizations, but also important differences. They are often understood as entrepreneurial ventures that engage in sustained commercial activity. While commercial activity and its relation to the mission of non-profits is problematic (Weisbrod 1998), social enterprises engage in commercial activities as a matter of course, though these activities must be instrumental for the accomplishment of social aims and conducted in an economically sustainable manner. In other words, economic objectives represent constraints to be satisfied and not final aims to be pursued (see Chapter 1 of this volume).

This chapter highlights the welfare effects of social enterprises by examining their impact on employment and output. It begins by identifying three crucial institutional characteristics—objectives, control rights, and governance—of social enterprises. First, the public-benefit objective has important implications for the ability of social enterprises to attract resources, motivate workers and managers, and distribute surpluses not only by means of market exchanges, but also by allocating their products and services under the cost level to weak social groups. Second, the socialization of capital due to the non-profit distribution constraint and to the accumulation of indivisible reserves of capital increases the amount of resources devoted to the social objectives of these enterprises. Third, participatory governance is functional to the accumulation and distribution of socialized resources since it is not designed to pursue the narrow interests of one party, but rather to accommodate the interests of all the parties involved in the venture, including those who are usually marginalized and excluded. Thanks to these features, social enterprises are able to employ non-market inputs like volunteer labour and donations, devote extensive resources to the pursuit of social goals, and satisfy non-paying demand.

One claim of this chapter is that the allocative and distributive mechanisms that characterize social enterprises are unique and well adapted to increasing the production of socially beneficial goods and reducing poverty. While these effects have often been downplayed and simply considered positive externalities, this interpretation is unsatisfactory since the most important public benefits of social enterprises are not unintended, but rather stem from deliberate choices and strategies informed by intrinsic, social, and other-regarding motivations.

The motivational drivers steering the behaviour of actors inside social enterprises are crucial since these actors do not pursue uniquely private, self-regarding objectives (Valentinov 2007, 2008). Hence, the assumption of purely self-interested economic agents that can be found in the literature on not-for-profit organizations (Glaeser and Shleifer 2001) needs to be substituted by an empirically and experimentally informed study of the interplay between self-seeking and other-regarding preferences on the one hand and between intrinsic and extrinsic motivations on the other (Ben-Ner and Putterman 1998). Furthermore, conformity and not hierarchy is the main force driving compliance with the objectives of the organization (Grimalda and Sacconi 2005), and a sense of common identity underpins interactions between the main patrons of the organization (Akerlof and Kranton 2000). For example, the strength of non-self-seeking preferences in not-for-profit organizations can help explain why social entrepreneurs and employees appear less reactive to monetary and extrinsic incentives than workers in public and for-profit firms (Young 1983; James 1983; Rose-Ackerman 1996; Borzaga and Depedri 2005; Borzaga and Tortia 2006). Entrepreneurs, managers, and employees of not-for-profits may enjoy greater self-fulfilment of their intrinsic and pro-social aspirations and prefer non-monetary incentives, such as better on-the-job relations and increased autonomy. Similarly, financial donations and volunteering are strictly linked to the social aim of the organization.

In this context, the accusation of social dumping sometimes made against social enterprises due to their low levels of wages appears misplaced since it does not consider the organizational and motivational specificities that differentiate these enterprises from other organizational forms. Thanks to these specificities, the supply of socially oriented and meritorious goods would decrease together with social welfare in the absence of social enterprises. When worker well-being is considered in a comprehensive way, social enterprises are more effective than public agencies and for-profit employers at improving their employees' sense of satisfaction and perceptions of fairness (Tortia 2008). The best explanation for this phenomenon is that a social—rather than a profit—objective supports a more integrated and participatory interaction between employees, managers, and the organization as a whole by means of more equitable and transparent procedures.

These behavioural predispositions underpin the claim that social enterprises are able to increase the supply of meritorious goods,[1] augment employment, and lower prices. These outcomes depend upon a lower exploitation of market power, which entails fixing lower prices and utilizing non-market resources such as voluntary labour. As a result, social enterprises are able to shift the socio-economic system from Pareto inferior to Pareto superior outcomes by increasing the welfare of beneficiaries and users.

This chapter is organized as follows: the next section identifies the features of social enterprises that support their ability to allocate and distribute resources by bypassing market exchanges and helping poor and marginalized social groups. The subsequent sections provide a closer analysis of social enterprises' allocative and distributive mechanisms and of their impact on output, employment, and welfare. The final section offers concluding remarks and considers policy implications.

The institutional framework and its effects

The organizational routines of social enterprises influence the recruitment of resources and the allocation and distribution of the surplus produced; these routines allow social enterprises to increase the supply of quasi-public and meritorious goods and services. This result is achieved by overcoming the strict observance of the rule of equivalence that characterizes market exchanges since social enterprises are able to employ non-market resources and distribute goods and services free of charge or under the cost level to disadvantaged social groups.

Figure 3.1 illustrates how the institutional set-up of social enterprises increases social welfare. At the top of the diagram, the non-profit distribution constraint coupled with the requirement of a public-benefit objective are the fundamental institutional features that limit ownership rights by preventing controlling stakeholders from appropriating the surplus and by favouring the satisfaction of social needs through the production of public goods and services. The exclusion of the profit motive reinforces trust relations with all patrons and reduces the incentive to exploit information advantages by the strongest contractual party (Hansmann 1996). This exclusion also encourages the implementation of less hierarchical organizational models due to the augmented opportunities for involvement by all the main patrons of the organization (Borzaga and Mittone 1997). Inclusion of stakeholders can be accomplished through democratic rules, as in traditional cooperative firms where the 'one member, one vote' rule means that member stakeholders have the formal right to participate in defining the organization's objectives. However, inclusion can also be an informal characteristic of the governance structure due to flat organizational protocols embracing both production and strategic decisions, and encouraging the expression of non-monetary and intrinsic motivations by the actors involved. To be successful, participatory governance requires the implementation of proper organizational routines regulating the interaction between employees and their superiors in managing production and defining objectives. It also requires an adequate mix in which monetary and non-monetary incentives are appropriately conjugated. The evidence for this interpretation is that incentive mixes in social enterprises are usually quite different from those in public agencies and for-profit firms, where extrinsic and monetary incentives appear more prominent (Borzaga and Tortia 2006).

Since profit is not the guiding motive, the needs, motivations, and objectives of non-investor stakeholders shape the development of social enterprises and may have a broader social impact. Participation by a range of actors both within the organization itself and in the broader community is a necessary condition for defining public-benefit objectives. Indeed, when investors cannot freely impose their own objectives, decision making can be undertaken by other patrons based on shared objectives, rules, values, and perceptions. Furthermore, the combined effect of the non-profit distribution constraint and of multi-stakeholder governance can result in increased service quality since involvement helps to improve information flows and accumulate firm-specific knowledge.

Given its role in coordinating actors driven by diverse motivations and objectives, multi-stakeholder governance should be considered a defining characteristic of social enterprises. While limiting some of the most severe negative external effects linked to contractual failures, pluralist governance ensures that the embedded social parties have a voice in the definition of development objectives. Hence, the modus operandi of public agencies and for-profit firms is

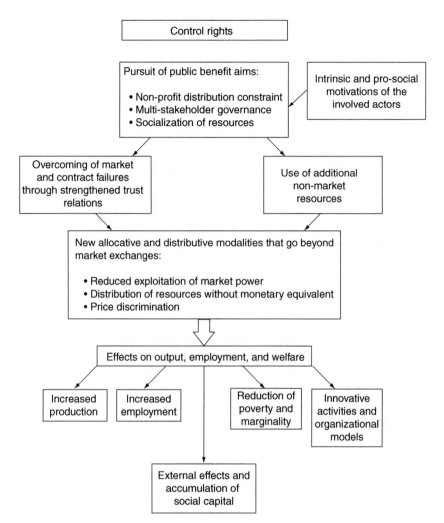

Figure 3.1 The impact of social enterprises on output, employment, and welfare.

superseded by innovative institutions that facilitate the private provision of public goods by motivated economic actors, thanks mainly to the reduction of transaction costs, the reinforcement of trust, and the creation of new knowledge (Besley and Ghatak 2005). The innovative routines of social enterprises mean that production is obtained by overcoming the invisible hand of the market. Even when coordination costs are significant, the net benefit of involvement and of the creation of new knowledge can be positive, at least in some specific areas of activity. In these instances, participatory governance guarantees greater efficiency than organizational models based on hierarchy and control.

In addition, the high degree of socialization of resources that characterizes social enterprises is functional to the development of their activities since non-distributed surpluses and financial donations are socialized by means of the accumulation of non-divisible reserves ('locked assets'). In this way, social enterprises are able to increase the stock of socialized capital at the disposal of the community for development purposes. The accumulation of indivisible reserves supports the private supply of public goods by alleviating the difficulties that social enterprises encounter in gathering financial support from the market in the absence of tradable shares and investor control. Social enterprises are therefore in the position to alleviate failures of public supply, such as the over- and under-provision of public goods and services.

Public provision can be characterized by the overproduction of public goods when it is concentrated in a few areas of activity. For example, the exclusive focus on health-care services in residential hospitals can reduce the supply of nursing care at home for the non-self-sufficient elderly.[2] On the other hand, the public sector is often unable to deliver an adequate variety of services for several reasons, including median voter preferences, a lack of resources, and inefficient production (Weisbrod 1977, 1988; Ben-Ner and Van Hoomissen 1991). Since social enterprises represent a more flexible expenditure channel, they can compensate for these failures of the public sector and reduce costs. Furthermore, socialized resources and governance based on involvement allow flexible prices to be charged for different clients based on their ability and willingness to pay, thus reducing financial dependence on public resources.

Two important consequences of these basic institutional features are indicated in Figure 3.1 below the list of public benefit aims pursued by social enterprises. The first of these is that when strong competition and regulated markets exist, standardized goods and services are delivered efficiently by profit-making firms. However, when asymmetric information and contract incompleteness become severe, particularly in cases where services are non-standardized and have a high relational intensity (Gui and Sugden 2005), the profit motivation can easily be used to favour the stronger contractual party (Ben-Ner and Van Hoomissen 1991). The weaker party in the transaction is often unable to control the quality of the services, and quality may be reduced in order to increase profits. In this context, non-profit ownership acts as a signalling device (Hansmann 1980) that allows fiduciary, not purely instrumental, relations to develop both between managers and workers and between the organization and the public—i.e. users, clients, and the local community. Trustworthiness also generates a positive spill-over in terms of accumulation of social capital.

A second crucial effect of excluding the profit motive, introducing multi-stakeholder governance, and pursuing public-benefit objectives is that social enterprises can utilize additional non-market resources such as financial donations and voluntary work. While donating and volunteering are not compatible with private appropriation, they can be justified in social enterprises by the meritorious character of the services produced. The purpose of the non-profit distribution constraint is not only or even primarily to limit the appropriation of the surplus; rather, it is a facilitating, or empowering, institutional tool that aims to substitute the dominance of monetary and extrinsic motivations with intrinsic and pro-social motivations (Valentinov 2007, 2008). Hence, the co-evolution of pro-social motivations and of the meritorious character of the services delivered is not accidental, and the economic and social impact of this process can be observed and studied. In contexts where non-market resources are utilized, the commercial activities of social enterprises play only an instrumental role in the pursuit of social objectives, while intrinsic and pro-social motivations become the core elements in the development of the activity.[3] The social responsibility of the organization is therefore enhanced. Social enterprises are evaluated by donors and volunteers based on their ability to generate social surpluses that make donations effective. At the same time, the additional resources together with the socialization of the firm assets contribute to overcoming the problem of free riding since they provide common pools of resources that can be used to solve social problems.

These are the main preconditions for assessing the impact of social enterprises. In the following sections, it is argued that the introduction of social enterprises transforms the static conception of the economic system, where enterprises compete for increasing their share of a given level of attainable production, into a dynamic perspective, where new organizational forms produce differently than older ones and create new opportunities for increased output and employment. It is first necessary, however, to examine the allocative and distributive mechanisms that distinguish social enterprises from other organizational forms.

Allocation mechanisms

The main objective of social enterprises is to satisfy socially relevant needs under the constraints of economic sustainability. This can be done by analysing the cost structure of the organization, which is closely connected with its social objectives. The same is true for the way in which social enterprises produce their surpluses.[4] The implications of the cost structure and of the way in which the value added is produced and distributed are important for the allocation of resources and output, particularly when competition does not define prices univocally, i.e. in situations of imperfect competition, the usual context in which social enterprises operate.

Among the multiplicity of the causes of imperfect competition, some are particularly important for the operation of social enterprises. First, in situations where some degree of monopoly or monopsony power or of asymmetric information exists, imperfect competition allows the appropriation of quasi-rents. In this case, for-profit firms are usually induced to increase prices and profits as much as possible, thereby reducing supply. Second, the goods and services produced by social enterprises often exhibit collective features, i.e. non-rivalry and non-excludability. Non-rivalry implies the impossibility of fixing variable prices without revealing clients' private information. The revelation of private information can be also indirect, as in the case of second-degree price discrimination; examples are theatre performances and different types of educational curricula. However, the existence of asymmetric information coupled with the private appropriation of the surplus can limit the indirect disclosure of information as well. Since for-profit firms can use private information to increase profits and reduce clients' surplus, unsatisfied clients will often revert to not-for-profit suppliers. Hence, these suppliers can more easily determine the clients' reserve prices (Ben-Ner and Van Hoomissen 1991; Ben-Ner 1994). Non-excludability, on the other hand, requires that services also be delivered to users who are unable to pay the market price. The employment of non-market resources like voluntary and partially remunerated labour, and the socialization of resources allow social enterprises to meet this objective as well.

While in orthodox economics the presence of market power necessarily leads to increased prices and lower supply, these implications do not necessarily follow in the case of social enterprises since these organizations show a lower tendency to exploit their positional advantage than for-profit firms do. The conclusions of orthodox economics would also be relevant in the case of not-for-profit organizations if individuals were exclusively self-seeking, but the existence of pro-social motivations and the involvement of different stakeholders in the governance of the organization can shift organizational objectives towards the satisfaction of socially relevant needs and the maximization of output. If prices are increased and quality reduced, opportunism would be perceived and trust relations with users and other local actors would be damaged since relations would be seen as instrumental to the pursuit of private ends. Hence, the formal and informal controls exerted by non-investor stakeholders over the organizations can induce more desirable social outcomes.

These behavioural features provide important advantages to social enterprises relative to for-profit firms (see Chapter 2 of this volume). For-profit firms have no interest in intervening with the same allocative and distributive modalities since, in the general case, they are forced to increase profits as much as possible in order to avoid weakening their competitive position and reducing their market value. This focus on private appropriation can also exacerbate conflicting interests and asymmetric information since self-seeking behaviour by firm owners is perceived as a threat to the objectives and motivations of the other classes of patrons. Hence, for-profit firms are not likely to enter the same sectors of activity as social enterprises. One reason for this is that profitability in these sectors is low, and a high degree of socialization of resources and the involvement of non-investor stakeholders are often required. Furthermore, because of the focus on private appropriation, for-profit firms do not enjoy financial donations and volunteer work, even if they produce services with a meritorious character. For the same reasons, for-profit firms are also less likely to receive government support. When the services provided are meritorious, under-provision by for-profit firms becomes a serious problem and creates the space for the introduction of social enterprises.

In addition to the lower tendency to exploit positional advantages in the market, a second possible allocation mechanism is to distribute resources without the equivalent of the equilibrium price. The pursuit of social aims may require the delivery of goods and services to persons unable to pay for them, as in the case of meritorious goods. Hence, social aims need an appropriate institutional structure in order to be fulfilled. The public-benefit objective, the use of non-market resources, the socialization of capital, and multi-stakeholder governance all serve to assure that social enterprises take into consideration the needs of patrons such as users and beneficiaries. All these elements favour the expansion of production due to the demands made by different 'publics' involved in the operation of the organization (Sacchetti and Sugden 2009). This is true even if many users are not able to pay for the services produced by the firm when the factors of production are not fully remunerated for the surplus that they have produced. In these cases, the rule of equivalence that characterizes market trans-actions can be bypassed by decisions taken within the organization's boundaries.

However, the distribution of resources to weak social groups under the cost level is not a necessary consequence of the institutional structure of social enter-prises. It is instead to be understood as a potentiality, the accomplishment of which is favoured by specific organizational routines. In order to be realized, crucial conditions such as appropriate motivational drivers and adequate eco-nomic results need to be satisfied. One implication is that some organizations may have a strong commitment to distributing resources to weak social groups, even if they do not actually distribute them due to a lack of sufficient resources. A second implication is that some social enterprises do not fulfil their social aims because the appropriate motivational drivers are absent.[5] This said, the empirical evidence seems to confirm a marked tendency for social enterprises to distribute a substantial part of their value added to social purposes (Borzaga *et al.* forthcoming).

A third possible allocation mechanism that characterizes social enterprises and, more generally, not-for-profit organizations is price discrimination. Two common problems in the provision of many quasi-public goods are high fixed costs and low variable costs. These problems lead to under-provision by for-profit firms when the high fixed costs cannot be recouped through market trans-actions. For example, when break-even is not possible with homogeneous prices because the demand curve lies above the curve of average costs, price discrimi-nation becomes the only allocative technique able to guarantee private produc-tion: clients characterized by higher willingness to pay (reserve prices) need to be charged higher prices. The fixing of variable prices is feasible when different clients perceive the same characteristics and quality of the good in different ways, even when their ability to pay is similar. By setting actual prices equal to clients' reserve prices, revenues can meet costs and production becomes sustain-able. For this to happen, clients may be required to disclose private information concerning their reserve evaluation of the purchased services. In this case, they are prepared to sacrifice part or all of their surplus in order to have the service delivered (Grillo 1992). Contrary to what is observed in competitive markets, in the absence of the private appropriation of net surpluses, prices for goods and services delivered by not-for-profit firms may show significant variation in equilibrium since profit is not appropriated by anybody and users can show markedly different preferences.[6]

In order to facilitate the disclosure of private information and make price discrimination possible, direct participation by clients in the governance of the organization and in decision making concerning the fixing of prices may be needed. This is so because strengthened inclusion and control over financial variables increases clients' willingness to reveal their real ability to pay, even when the prices paid by other clients with similar economic possibilities are different.[7] When revenues generated by charging reserve prices are just sufficient to meet costs, the consumer surplus is nil, but the allocation is Pareto efficient, similar to the case of a perfectly discriminating monopoly. However, unlike a private monopoly, revenues do not generate the private appropriation of the net surplus.

A second case in which price discrimination becomes a useful allocation mechanism relates to the meritorious character of the produced services, which leads the firm to redistribute resources in favour of weak social groups. The presence of intrinsic and pro-social motivations by the actors involved is again a central element of these behavioural patterns and organizational outcomes. The firm can decide to use its surplus to increase production in favour of non-paying demand, even if in principle the users unable to pay can be excluded. The example of health care is paradigmatic, because this kind of service is supposed to be available for the whole population. The same is true for education, since the children of poor families must be provided access to schools. In these instances, price discrimination serves a redistributive function (Weisbrod 1977, 1988) since the organization decides to reduce private appropriation to satisfy non-paying demand. In a similar fashion, a redistributive pattern is endogenously defined whereby consumers characterized by high reserve prices subsidize those characterized by lower reserve prices.

Historically, the problem of extending production of meritorious goods to subjects who are unable to pay the cost level has been managed through charitable interventions by non-profit organizations and through the redistributive interventions of governments. Social enterprises open up new possibilities due to their public-benefit objective and to their governance mechanisms based on involvement and trust among different stakeholders. Price discrimination should not be interpreted in this case as a device used to increase profits, but as a complex problem-solving process based on personal interaction and participation. When social enterprises perform a redistributive role, the main aim of price setting is to maximize production and the satisfaction of needs. The value-laden and meritorious nature of the activity is a powerful justification for the redistribution of resources and does not exclude subsidization by public authorities. In contrast, when price discrimination is used as a technique for increasing profits, as usually happens in for-profit firms, it is not compatible with the disclosure of private information about consumers' reserve prices since this kind of disclosure would allow producers to reap part or all of the consumers' surplus (Ben-Ner and Van Hoomissen 1991).

The impact of social enterprises on welfare

Thus far, this chapter has identified the preconditions for, and analysed the allocative and distributive features of, social enterprises. The impact of these features on production, employment, and welfare are visualized at the bottom of Figure 3.1 and examined in this section.

Efficiency of production

Given their vocation of public benefit, social enterprises often constitute an alternative to public provision. Two well-known shortcomings of public welfare systems are found first at the micro level in the costs due to severe difficulties in efficiently managing entrepreneurial (non-bureaucratic) production processes and in motivating employees. Higher costs and a slower pace of innovation activity tend to hinder the dynamic potential of the public sector. Second, external constraints often occur at the macro level due to the limits imposed on public expenditure by binding financial constraints. Consequently, it is not surprising that externalization, decentralization, and private provision are increasing tendencies in the production of quasi-public goods (Pestoff 2004). Social enterprises may suffer less from the bureaucratization and procedural inefficiencies that undermine the efficiency of public agencies.

Labour costs provide an important example. The higher wages observed in most countries in the public sector relative to not-for-profit organizations imply that social enterprises will have lower costs and higher efficiency. The lower labour costs of social enterprises can underwrite increased production and employment when both public agencies and for-profit firms are unable to do so. Interestingly, this lower wage bill cannot be explained simply by lower skills since social enterprises tend to employ more educated and skilled workers (Handy and Katz 1998; Ruhm and Borkoski 2003). Rather, a more complex set of factors must be considered. Employees in social enterprises have higher overall job satisfaction than do those employed by public agencies (Borzaga and Tortia 2006) and are more satisfied than employees in for-profit firms (Benz 2005). They also perceive that they enjoy higher degrees of distributive and procedural fairness compared to those who work for both public agencies and for-profit firms (Tortia 2008). In addition, wage dispersion is lower in social enterprises mainly due to lower managerial and clerical compensation, and this tends to increase internal cohesion and productivity by strengthening distributive fairness (Leete 2000). These findings suggest that higher salaries do not necessarily correspond to improved well-being, since well-being is also determined by non-monetary factors.[8] Moreover, in addition to the positive influences exerted on workers' well-being, robust trust relations in social enterprises favour a reduction in ownership costs since they allow decisions to be taken more smoothly, information to circulate informally, control over the operation of managers and workers to be less intense and costly, and firm-specific knowledge to be accumulated.

This counter-intuitive evidence can be explained by observing that jobs in non-profit-seeking organizations are characterized by stronger participatory mechanisms. Hence, lower wage levels are supported by the more extensive presence of non-monetary—intrinsic and pro-social—motivations, which means that social enterprises less often need to revert to costly monetary incentives, and as a result are more efficient. Workers driven by non-self-seeking and pro-social motivations prefer meaningful jobs and organizational models that create room for autonomy and creativity rather than higher monetary remuneration. A sorting process can be identified whereby intrinsically motivated workers self-select themselves into socially oriented firms even if they will receive lower salaries (Handy and Katz 1998), while those workers driven mainly by extrinsic preferences tend to prefer public employment and for-profit firms. Monetary remuneration represents only one component of a more complex incentive mix. It works as a threshold that can induce workers to accept or refuse employment (the participation constraint), while above this threshold monetary remuneration is widely ineffective in influencing well-being (Borzaga and Depedri 2005). Consequently, monetary remuneration is not a good proxy for worker ability and skills, at least in social enterprises. Greater effectiveness in implementing non-monetary incentives can compensate for lower monetary remuneration and make social enterprises more desirable employers for intrinsically motivated workers.

The combined effect of these factors encompasses both labour relations and reduced bureaucratization. It reduces conflicts and impasses and makes organizational mechanisms less burdensome and costly, thereby enhancing the efficiency and efficacy of production. Contrary to most predictions inherited from orthodox and new-institutionalist economics, not-for-profit firms are characterized by considerable potential for efficiency enhancement and cost reduction, which contribute to making social enterprises a more efficient solution in many fields of activity traditionally populated by public providers.

Innovations in organization and production

The entrepreneurial aspect of social enterprises is designed to encourage innovation in the organizational and production domains in terms of both new services and new organizational solutions. Contrary to what is observed in the public sector, the innovative potential of social enterprises is linked to competitive pressures and the freedom to start new entrepreneurial ventures. However, innovation in social enterprises is also linked to governance mechanisms based on involvement, since they are more likely to support autonomy and creativity in the performance of work tasks. Moreover, entrepreneurial initiatives and the introduction of innovative products and services are conducive to the accumulation of firm-specific human capital and knowledge (Hodgson 1998, 2006). At the organizational level, improved circulation of information, increased trust, and intensified interaction among intrinsically motivated stakeholders are all likely to enhance innovation by strengthening incentives to cooperate in implementing new projects and organizational schemes. Product quality is the main by-product of the ability to innovate and accumulate firm-specific knowledge. In addition to increasing economic returns, these factors shield the organization from competitive pressures and support the long-term sustainability of investment projects.

Non-monetary motivations again come under the spotlight since excessive emphasis on hierarchy and monetary remuneration tends to crowd out the potential for creativity and innovation (Frey 1997; Sacchetti and Sugden 2009). The valorization of intrinsic motivations and the cost-inflating features of participatory governance need to be carefully balanced since what distinguishes social enterprises from other ownership forms, most notably from public agencies, is the *possibility* of implementing innovative activities thanks to a governance structure based on involvement. This objective, however, can only be achieved if costs are kept under control, effective organizational routines are implemented, and patrons are adequately motivated. The necessity of coordinating the activities of workers in the pursuit of collective objectives may require the organization of workers into teams and the introduction of enforcement mechanisms that alter incentives and thereby limit worker autonomy. Organizational routines need to grow in a way that balances autonomy and compliance with collective decision making. This is especially true in organizations such as social enterprises where individual activity is characterized by high control costs and trust is necessary to make coordination mechanisms effective. Since hierarchy is difficult to implement due to the high degree of contract incompleteness, the complementarity of workers' autonomy with coordination mechanisms poses a conundrum that influences these organizations' prospects for survival, growth, and innovation. When this interaction has positive effects, the absence of hierarchy and autonomy can provide important competitive advantages. For example, the empirical evidence strongly suggests that many innovations by social enterprises stem from the availability of free resources such as volunteer workers and entrepreneurs driven by pro-social and ideological motivations (Rose-Ackerman 1996; Young 1983). Given their lack of contractual remuneration, volunteers are often in a position to pursue their own objectives and initiate innovative activities that, in other types of organizations, might be hindered by bureaucratic procedures, hierarchy, and objectives that diverge with those of owners.

Increases in production and employment

In static conceptions of the economic system, increased production by social enterprises would simply reduce the supply provided by the public and for-profit sectors. This conception is based on the assumption that economic systems are always in equilibrium: for each product, demand equals supply and the needs compatible with the equilibrium price are satisfied. However, when the existence of unsatisfied needs is considered, the specific institutional and behavioural responses of social enterprises become relevant since it is possible to demonstrate that their ability to produce quasi-public goods economically—either by increasing the produced surplus or by reducing costs—increases the efficiency of the system, reduces under-provision, and increases employment because public agencies and for-profit firms cannot intervene in the same way.

Hence, the sum of the game for the economy as a whole is non-zero because social enterprises are able to utilize resources that would otherwise remain unused. Intrinsic and pro-social motivations again play a crucial role since they contribute to increased production even in the absence of hierarchy and high-powered incentives. In this way, social enterprises can create paying demand and employment. Furthermore, they can increase production and employment indirectly by reducing the negative consequences of the under-provision of collective and general-interest services, such as social services. This is so because the production of quasi-public goods, besides increasing production and employment directly, supports the development of other economic activities since, for example, the delivery of child and elderly care improves the productive potential of other industries. Finally, the socialization of resources helps to increase production and employment since it increases the stock of productive assets and reduces capital costs, thereby reducing also the risks of fluctuations in wages and employment during economic downturns. Consequently, the communitarian and collective features of social enterprises linked to trust relations and the embeddedness of the actors involved help to stabilize and reinforce growth and development at the local level.

Employment in social enterprises can also increase through the work integration of disadvantaged people. In terms of the argument developed above, the ability to recoup productive potential and employ otherwise unemployable people increases the efficiency and effectiveness of the system as a whole, alleviating the negative external effects connected with social marginality, such as in the case of drug addiction and crime (see Chapter 6 of this volume). Given the social nature of the services produced and the increased attention paid to the needs of their workers, who are often active stakeholders endowed with formal decision-making power, social enterprises also tend to employ weaker components of the labour force, such as women with family responsibilities and young people with little work experience.

Reduction of poverty and marginality

The claim that non-profit organizations can reduce poverty and redistribute resources is controversial since there is no conclusive empirical evidence supporting it. Indeed, traditional non-profits have been reported to serve mainly the socio-economic groups supplying financial support, with limited spillover for the less well-off when public subsidies are absent (Clotfelter 1992; Ben-Ner 1994). This finding may depend upon the types of goods and services produced since, for example, some services such as art exhibitions and cultural performances are not usually utilized by the poor. Thus, the extension of the supply to non-paying subjects does not necessarily benefit marginalized social groups. In this respect, improved results can be expected under the new definitions of social enterprise provided by legislation in the UK and Italy. Unlike traditional non-profit organizations, social enterprises are constrained by the nature of the goods and services supplied, which is better suited for satisfying the needs of poor and marginalized groups than for distributing value added to the wealthy. Extended distribution to social groups unable to pay is required by the public-benefit aim of the enterprise when the meritorious character of the delivered services calls for inclusion of all the groups present in society. The reduction of poverty and exclusion becomes possible when the allocative and distributive mechanisms highlighted in the previous sections are conjugated with community development and other social objectives. Micro-credit in developing countries is a clear example of the potential for poverty reduction triggered by adopting social objectives and implementing non-traditional allocative mechanisms. In Italy, there is accumulating evidence that social enterprises engage extensively in distributive activities that bypass market exchanges (Nyssens 2006; Borzaga *et al.* forthcoming). The greatest impact is again at the local level, where social enterprises show a peculiar ability to interact with embedded actors and the surrounding economic environment.

Positive externalities and the accumulation of social capital

The effects of social enterprises are not linked exclusively to deliberate choices embedded in the social character of their institutional set-up. Positive externalities and other unintended consequences can also be envisaged, leading to the accumulation of new social capital in the form of strengthened trust relations and networks of co-interested actors developing productive programmes that support socio-economic development (Sacchetti and Sugden 2003). Hansmann (1996) has demonstrated the functional relevance of trust linked to the absence of the profit motive in allowing non-profits to overcome market and contract failures where other organizational types have been unable to do so. It should be noted that the spread of positive external effects linked to the meritorious character of the services delivered requires and fosters trust relations since organizations would not be able to overcome market and contract failures in the absence of trust. When the market fails, social enterprises can substitute contractual relations with integrated governance based on reinforced trust, thereby fostering the development of personal ties and embeddedness mainly at the local level.

This is true also when the interaction between the organization and other social actors is considered. Networking based on mutual dependence, trust, and horizontal monitoring reduces the costs of asymmetric information and the expected costs deriving from adverse selection and moral hazard in firm-to-firm and other micro- and meso-level interactions (Sacchetti and Sugden 2003). Consequently, networks of co-interested and co-motivated actors driven by pro-social motivations nurture patterns of socio-economic development. Both through the production of positive external effects and through the creation of networks, social enterprises contribute to the accumulation of social capital and to the development of civil society (Zamagni 2005).

The highlighted linkages between the operation of social enterprises and the accumulation of social capital are a case in which microeconomic institutional mechanisms are responsible for influencing the existing stock of relational capital and trust that derive from involvement and networking. Given the paucity of studies that have rigorously analysed social capital beyond its alleged positive effects on economic growth and other social outcomes (Putnam 1993; Helliwell and Putnam 2000; Durlauf and Fafchamps 2005), the development of social enterprises should be considered a case in which the determinants of social capital are made explicit and investigated. In light of this research, it will then be feasible to formulate policy recommendations informed by new knowledge about the sources of growth of social capital.

Conclusions

Social enterprises are an innovative organizational solution that has the potential to spread well beyond those industries where not-for-profit organizations have traditionally operated. The public-benefit and not-for-profit rationales of social enterprises, together with stakeholder involvement and the accumulation of socialized assets, have been shown to support new allocative and distributive modalities as well as to have an important impact on welfare in terms both of increased production and employment and of reduced poverty and marginality.

The cross-ownership character of social enterprises means that this innovative entrepreneurial form can be used flexibly to make important improvements in the efficiency and effectiveness of producing public-benefit goods and services. These improvements can be expected mainly in comparison with public agencies since for-profit firms are rarely engaged in the production of public-benefit services due to their profit orientation and stress on self-seeking motivations. Heightened involvement by diverse stakeholders supports the internalization of external effects linked to contractual incompleteness (Kreps 1990) and a more equitable distribution of resources towards marginalized people and other subjects lacking adequate economic means. Innovative activities, a larger supply of services, and utilization of non-market resources can contribute to increasing the economic and social surplus generated by social enterprises. Moreover, welfare can be increased through the development of trust relations, the production of positive externalities, and the accumulation of social capital.

The arguments developed in this chapter demonstrate that social enterprises cannot spread and valorize their pro-social motivations without preserving and developing their distinctive institutional and organizational features. For this to happen, two conditions are necessary: the development of suitable and coherent legislation on the one hand, and adequate policies of financial and political support on the other. These conditions are being realized to date only in pioneering national and local contexts, such as the UK, while in other countries they are still in initial stages or await the most basic forms of recognition and regulation. Indeed, legal regulation also needs to be improved in the pioneering countries with regards to, for example, opportunities for participation by all patrons, particularly users and employees, in organizational and governance issues. No conclusive agreement has yet been reached in the UK or Italy on these issues, and participatory mechanisms remain undefined and weak. In addition, improvements need to be made in the regulation of the accumulation of socialized assets and in the mechanisms designed to protect collective ownership in social enterprises. Effective regulation is necessary to ensure that social enterprises reach their full potential for contributing to community development.

Following the legislative initiatives that have occurred in the UK and in Italy, other countries are evaluating whether to augment the institutional and organizational variety in their economies by introducing the new entrepreneurial form of social enterprises. Increasingly, this innovation is being seen as a necessary step for overcoming the out-of-date dichotomy between the private for-profit and the public sectors and in order to reform publicly based models of welfare.

Notes

1 Goods are meritorious if they produce positive external effects whose social value is not adequately mirrored by the market price. Given the public good nature of positive externalities, private production is likely to lead to the under-provision of meritorious goods. This form of under-provision can be relieved by social enterprises thanks to their not-for-profit nature and their ability to use non-market resources and socialize positive surpluses.

2 This may be due to a preference in the public sector for residential nursing given the risk of asymmetric information and contractual failures when nursing is delivered at home. Social enterprises may be better positioned to offer the elderly home nursing due to their ability to reduce the negative effects of asymmetric information and contractual failures.

3 As shown in Chapter 1 of this volume, there is a tendency for extrinsic motivations to become dominant in investor-owned firms.

4 Social enterprises are often labour-intensive firms, and the achievement of economic sustainability in the medium and long run is often tantamount to their ability to meet labour costs. These costs can be reduced when workers characterized by pro-social and other-regarding motivations are prepared to make partial work donations.

5 When the distribution of resources in favour of weak social groups occurs, financial data on social enterprises need to be interpreted with caution since conventional accounting techniques may not be tailored to show the surplus of resources distributed without the equivalence of the market price.

6 Price discrimination may not be necessary even if prices are only sufficient to meet variable costs when other financial resources are used to meet high fixed costs. These resources may be generated by contracts signed with public authorities, public tenders, subsidies, tax advantages, or donative interventions by private institutions.

7 Involvement can be linked to other forms of information disclosure that help the organization to discriminate on prices while meeting its financial obligations. For example, users can be required to disclose information concerning their income levels when the organization delivers meritorious goods that are characterized by non-excludability (Provasi 2004).

8 Some kinds of monetary incentives such as profit sharing, however, have been found to enhance worker satisfaction (Frey and Osterloh 1999; Green and Heywood 2008), while inappropriate incentives linked to pay-for-performance can crowd out intrinsic motivations (Frey 1997). These findings are not incompatible with the distributive patterns found in social enterprises since in some types of social enterprises, such as social cooperatives, employees can appropriate part of the net residuals accruing to the operation of the firm.

4 From economic growth to sustainable development[1]

Leonardo Becchetti and Giuseppe Mastromatteo

The focus on growth by economists may not be easy to understand for those outside the profession. It has been argued, not without justification, that this seemingly narrow focus does not coincide with generally accepted definitions of human well-being, such as those measured by various socio-economic development indicators and, ultimately, with individual happiness. Clearly, well-being does not depend solely upon monetary considerations, and empirical studies of self-reported happiness show that the main determinants of well-being are—in addition to (relative more than absolute) income—health, education, and the quality of relational goods, while adverse aggregate shocks such as inflation and unemployment have a significant negative impact on it (Alesina *et al.* 2001; Easterlin 2001, 2005; Frey and Stutzer 2000; Di Tella *et al.* 2001). In spite of the inevitable cultural and interview biases that must be taken into account when dealing with self-reported happiness, medical studies document a strong and significant link between the same variables and personal health, supporting the reliability claims of the studies based on self-reporting (Pavot *et al.* 1991; Ekman *et al.* 1990; Shedler *et al.* 1993; Koivumaa-Honkanen *et al.* 2000). The empirical happiness literature suggests that economic growth is a fundamental *intermediate* target, but that the maximization of individual well-being should be pursued by looking at broader goals that include non-monetary variables whose significant and positive relationship with self-reported happiness have been documented.

In the last decade, the findings of the happiness literature have gradually been incorporated into political economy. For example, the *World Development Report 2003* (World Bank 2003) proposed that the traditional consumption–output channel fuelling individual welfare should be complemented by other channels where the direct enjoyment of human, social, and environmental resources is independent from productive considerations. The happiness literature has contributed to a paradigm shift that has been accelerated by the global financial crisis. In 2008, French President Nicholas Sarkozy appointed a commission of prominent economists to investigate the limitations of GDP as a measure of economic performance and social progress and to elaborate new indicators of well-being (Stiglitz *et al.* 2009).

A deeper inspection of the close relationships between these non-immediately productive dimensions of individual well-being and personal income clearly reveals that economic growth, or the creation of economic value at the aggregate level, provides the resources needed to invest in education, health, leisure, and the preservation of the environment. Hence, economic growth remains a crucial factor for the development of the non-monetary dimensions of individual happiness. This is why research into the drivers of economic growth is one of the important ways that economists can contribute to pursuing the desirable goals of poverty eradication and life satisfaction.

This chapter first illustrates recent advances in the growth literature and then outlines some new perspectives that implicitly integrate broader indicators of human well-being.

Three fundamental sources of value creation

The stylized model adopted by economists to analyse economic growth is based upon a (production) function that maps the contribution of inputs into physical production. In reality, what matters for value creation in a given country is the volume of goods and services sold—not just produced!—in a given time interval. Hence, a first critical point is that the creation of value entails a matching process between decisions over physical production and consumer tastes. An examination of the contributions of different inputs to economic growth shows that this is a non-trivial issue.

The first critical input in the production function is labour. This is something different from the *economically active population*, which is conventionally defined as people between 15 and 65 years of age. Only a share of the active population is willing to participate in the labour market, and this share is highly variable and far below 100 per cent, especially for the category of women with children. Moreover, since aggregate and individual working times are highly variable, the labour input is not adequately represented by the number of active workers but rather by the total number of hours worked.

In the initial neoclassical growth model (Solow 1956), the labour input is combined with the second critical input of physical capital and with a labour-augmenting residual component that captures all additional factors moving up the production frontier. The model demonstrates that, in equilibrium, per capita growth of GDP may be generated only from the growth of this residual component. According to this model, divisions among countries are bound to persist only in the case of enduring structural differences in physical capital accumulation, tax systems, population growth, and rates of growth of the residual component. If this were not the case, a general process of convergence in per capita GDP should occur.

Even in this simple model, it is evident that *conditional convergence* is a key concept in the growth literature. The term *convergence* indicates that countries that lag behind in economic development may catch up by growing at a rate that is higher than that of the more industrialized countries. The term *conditional* specifies that this can occur only if such countries satisfy some side conditions, i.e. if they level out differences in terms of endowment of crucial factors, such as physical capital and all other determinants affecting the residual that augments the productivity of labour. In the post-Solow growth literature, most if not all intellectual efforts have been dedicated to investigating the contents of the 'residual black box' with the goal of identifying the additional factors that determine economic growth.

A fundamental contribution has been the identification of the importance of human capital investment—the investment in education that increases working skills and productivity, and thereby shifts upward the production function for a given number of worked hours (Lucas 1988; Romer 1990). Education is modelled as a capital input in which the stock of accumulated knowledge in a given period depends upon inflows (investment) and outflows (depreciation). The impact of education on GDP growth is supported by abundant empirical evidence at the micro level. This evidence documents the existence of returns to schooling, i.e. significant increases in the wage earned on average for every additional year of education achieved after controlling for the effects of all other determinants.[2] Since wages roughly correspond to individual productivity, this evidence does not contradict the hypothesis that education raises productivity and, therefore, the contribution of the labour input to production.

In the case of education, the correspondence between the intermediate goal of economic growth and the broader one of human development and individual happiness is clear: a more educated workforce spurs economic growth. At the same time, more educated individuals enjoy a higher level of knowledge assets, which may increase their capabilities and functionalities (i.e. through a higher capacity to appreciate and enjoy cultural goods), thereby directly contributing to human well-being without passing through the output channel.

A fascinating historical perspective on the increasing influence of human capital on growth and its consequences in terms of the relationship between growth and inequality is provided by Galor and Moav (2004). They argue that the process of economic development may be divided into two successive stages. During the first stage, physical capital accumulation predominates and inequality is beneficial for growth since accumulation can only be due to the high savings rates of the rich. During the second stage, in which we now live, the physical capital and financial assets needed for investment are abundant at the world level. The crucial factor that can spur creation of value is a country's capacity to develop the potential of individuals by investing in their education and by easing access to the financial resources needed for investment. Hence, a more equal distribution of income turns out to be beneficial for growth, since it ensures equal opportunities and reduces financial constraints to human and physical capital investment.

The role of education creates a first important challenge to the standard textbook (Solow-type) models of economic growth. The existence of a strong negative relationship between female education and fertility is an empirically established stylized fact (Barro and Becker 1989; Becker *et al.* 1990).[3] Women who are more educated invest more time in themselves and their careers, and they therefore tend to have fewer children. This is a problem for the standard Solow model since it is evident that the growth of the labour force can no longer be taken as exogenous when an input of the production function (human capital) significantly affects the dynamics of another input (labour). A first important consequence of the augmented-growth models of human capital in terms of policy advice is that promoting education, especially of women, has positive effects on per capita GDP that increase the nominator and reduce the denominator of this ratio. This explains the strong emphasis placed on this issue by international institutions and the United Nation's Millennium Development Goals. Enthusiasm about the contribution of human capital in understanding economic growth must be tempered, however, by noting that education requires complementary factors in order to increase workers' productivity. Two such factors are adequate training and a willingness to translate higher human capital into entrepreneurial ideas. Murphy *et al.* (1991) argue that social rewards may play a crucial role in affecting the direction in which talents are invested. They use this argument to explain why the industrial revolution did not occur in China centuries before it did in England, even though China enjoyed the institutional stability, large market, and scientific knowledge necessary to realize the required technological innovations. They explain the puzzle by arguing that at that time in China greater social prestige was attached more to the rent-seeking professions than to entrepreneurship. Whenever this is the case, it is highly unlikely that human talent and capital will be invested in the creation of wealth, and consequently their contribution to economic growth is reduced.

Institutional, cultural, and religious determinants of growth

In the current literature, the quality of institutions ranks highly as a determinant of growth. In increasingly integrated labour, product, and financial markets, production inputs are always more mobile and abundant at the world level. Consequently, the link between the creation of domestic value and domestic inputs is always weaker. This means that domestic economic growth depends to a declining degree upon the domestic labour force, domestic savings,[4] or domestic human capital. The higher mobility of production inputs is such that, if a country can create local conditions that attract investment from other countries, it can prosper even in the absence of a relative strength in their domestic inputs. The US during the 1990s is a perfect illustration of this point, since it was striving to create the best local environment for attracting financial resources, promising students, and highly skilled workers, and the country achieved leadership in economic growth despite the negative saving rates of its citizens.

The increasing importance of creating a 'friendly' environment for attracting production inputs from all over the world demonstrates the importance of the *quality of institutions*. According to the *Economic Freedom of the World Index* (Gwartney and Lawson 2003), institutional quality depends upon three factors: the independence, impartiality, and capacity of the legal system; monetary policies that promote price stability through an independent central bank with an anti-inflationary mandate; and the proper regulation of credit, labour, and business.

The prominent role of rules and institutions (Barro and Sala-i-Martin 1992; Rodrik 2000)—more specifically, financial institutions (King and Levine 1993; Pagano 1997)—is widely acknowledged in the recent literature. Among the wide range of theoretical and empirical contributions that analyse the role of institutional quality on growth, the most important and representative are Rodrik (1999, 2002) and Frankel (2002), who argue that market-based economies can only be successful if they have institutions capable of protecting property rights, fighting corruption, supporting macroeconomic stabilization, and promoting social cohesion. Klein and Luu (2003) find that technical efficiency is positively related to policies supporting *laissez-faire* and political structures that promote policy stability, while Esfahani and Ramírez (2003) argue that good institutions support the creation of the infrastructure needed to promote growth. Other specific facets of institutional quality that have been examined are the roles of the public sector (Hall and Jones 1997), social and political stability (Alesina and Perotti 1994), and corruption (Mauro 1995). The impact of institutions on growth, with specific reference to transition countries, has been tested by, among others, de Melo *et al.* (1996), Fischer *et al.* (1996), and Becchetti *et al.* (2008). Finally, in a direct comparison of the relative significance of various factors at an empirical level, Sala-i-Martin (2002) finds that institutional quality is one of the most robust.

The focus on institutions foregrounds the role of cultural and religious factors, thereby highlighting the fascinating relationship between economic growth and 'deep fundamentals' (such as cultural *ethos* or religious beliefs) that have an impact on growth not only directly, but also by shaping and ordering the set of values that shape individual behaviour, institution building, and the 'wealth of nations'. A synthesis of this literature suggests that the deepest roots of success or failure in economic growth relies on the relationship between the system of cultural values promoted by a given religion on the one hand and the formation of quality institutions that can promote growth on the other. It is important to remember that such a relationship does not require a high share of active religious participation today to have had an influence. What matters is the role of religion in shaping the cultural background in the past and that this cultural background is persistent.

A well-known starting point in this literature is the Weberian hypothesis on the positive relationship between Protestantism and economic growth. Delacroix (1995) summarizes Weber's argument by saying that 'the worldview propagated by Protestantism broke with traditional psychological orientations through its emphasis on personal diligence, frugality, and thrift, on individual responsibility, and through the moral approval it granted to risk-taking and to financial self-improvement'.[5]

This hypothesis has been widely criticized at least with regard to Catholicism. Trevor-Roper (1969), for example, demonstrates that prosperity and accumulation started in Italian Catholic municipalities (such as Florence) well before the Protestant Reformation and that economic leadership passed to Protestant countries such as the Netherlands only after increased tax pressure associated with the reaction to the Reformation led many merchants living in Italian cities to shift the focus of their economic activities to Flanders.

In the last two decades, several empirical studies have focused on specific facets of religious culture in relation to institutions and economic growth. Stultz and Williamson (2003) investigated whether religious beliefs significantly affect financial institutions by controlling for the effects of language, trade openness, and the origin of the country's legal system. They find that creditors' rights are significantly less protected in Catholic than in Protestant countries. Becchetti *et al.* (2005) show that the cultural background generated by the prohibition of the payment or receipt of any predetermined, guaranteed rate of return (*riba*; *Sura* II, v. 279), which is the basis for the rejection of the concept of interest in Islamic finance (Iqbal 2001), is associated with weaker financial institutions in Muslim countries.

Regional integration and the quality of institutions

If institutions are important for economic growth, then which policies most effectively strengthen their overall quality? Even if it is broadly understood how to build good institutions and create local conditions for attracting inputs, the experience of many countries is that it is hard to put this knowledge into practice because of limits in the domestic capacity to create consensus on reforms (i.e. for the lobbying activity of rent seekers against reforms). In such cases, an external anchor (or constraint) may help to remove obstacles to domestic consensus and encourage institutional reforms. One of the most valuable devices for triggering institutional reform may be the desire to enter a club of wealthier countries or to integrate more closely with them.

Recent empirical research strongly supports this hypothesis. It shows that the desire to be admitted to negotiations for admission to the EU stimulated institutional change with positive effects on growth for transition candidates (Becchetti *et al.* 2008; De Grauwe and Schnabl 2008). This research also shows that the process of convergence towards the European Monetary Union significantly improved institutional quality and reduced real effective exchange rate volatility in Eurozone countries, with positive effects on growth (Bagella *et al.* 2004). These findings highlight a potential path for developing countries and suggest that the policy of EU integration with Turkey and the southern Mediterranean countries might have significant effects on the development of the Middle East and North Africa.

The role of the ICT revolution

A recent and influential strand of the literature on economic growth focuses on the impact of technological innovation and, specifically, of the so-called information and communication technology (ICT) revolution. From a general point of view, if discoveries and technological innovation rapidly become public knowledge, they can be equally adopted by everyone and therefore should not be important in explaining differences in the levels and growth of GDP across countries. On the other hand, access to innovation (and the capacity to exploit existing knowledge) is not the same everywhere. Therefore, it is inappropriate to neglect these variations by capturing the effect of innovation as a uniform constant variable, such as Mankiw *et al.* (1992) do, or as a country specific, but time-invariant, fixed-effect variable, as Islam (1995) does.

In this respect, the occurrence of the ICT revolution is both a challenge and an opportunity that may help to identify the country-specific time-varying effects of access to knowledge on economic growth. The difficulty in evaluating ICT effects stems from the complexity of this development, which includes high quality physical capital (computers and other hardware), telecommunication infrastructure that dramatically reduces the transportation costs of weightless products and eases access to information and knowledge, and new ways of storing and reproducing such knowledge (such as software and databases). The various strands of ICT components are closely linked since hardware is necessary to exploit the telecommunication infrastructure by using software and databases to process and transfer voice, images, and data.

How does ICT affect growth? As mentioned above, an important aspect of ICT is that weightless, expandable, and infinitely reproducible *knowledge products* (software and databases) create value by increasing the productivity of labour or by adding value to traditional physical products and services. Knowledge products are similar to public goods in that expandability and infinite reproducibility make them non-rivalrous, while copyright (rather than patent) protection makes them much less excludable than other types of innovation such as new drugs (Quah 1999).

If ICT consisted solely of knowledge products, then it would be almost immediately available everywhere, no matter where it originated. This does not occur, however, since the immediate diffusion and availability of knowledge products is prevented by bottlenecks such as the incapacity of the network to carry the largest amount of knowledge products in the shortest time, lack of universal access by individuals to the network in which knowledge products are immaterially transported and exchanged, and the limited power and availability of the terminals that process, implement, and exchange knowledge products over the internet (Becchetti and Di Giacomo 2004; Becchetti and Adriani 2005). These bottlenecks are responsible for the so-called digital divide, which is an additional factor that has conditioned convergence of per capita GDP.

Even though the role of ICT on growth seems clear from a theoretical perspective, the first vintage of empirical research produced ambiguous results. In the 1980s and early 1990s, several studies found irrelevant or negligible productivity effects associated with ICT investment (Bender 1986; Roach 1991; Strassmann 1990). This research concluded that there was no statistically significant association between ICT investment and productivity at various levels of analysis. However, with the availability of additional data and the application of innovative methodologies, more recent investigations have found evidence that in the second half of the 1990s ICT investment did contribute to improvements in productivity, to intermediate measures, and to economic growth (Brynjolfsson and Hitt 1996, 2000; Sichel 1997; Lehr and Licthenberg 1999; Jorgenson and Stiroh 2000). Oliner and Sichel (2002) and Jorgenson *et al.* (2002) also found evidence of this link in 2001, despite the recession that began in March of that year and the downward revisions in the US GDP and investment in software.

A typical interpretation of the discrepancies in the findings of these two vintages of empirical research is David's (1990) argument, based on his studies of the effects of electrification on growth, that any breakthrough innovation requires both time and a reorganization of the productive process to measurably influence productivity. Brynjolfsson and Hitt (2000) shed further light on the ICT–productivity paradox by noting that ICT represents a crucial but small part of a wider system of tangible and intangible assets. They argue that the potential contribution of ICT to productivity can only be fully exploited by reorganizing the firm and the conditions under which this occurs. The problem is that this relationship is much easier to investigate at firm than at the aggregate level, as Brynjolfsson and Hitt recognize. Based on their evidence, however, it seems that the conditions which ease firm restructuring include flexibility in the creation and destruction of jobs and businesses on the one hand and an institutional system that properly rewards human capital on the other.[6]

The role of geography and natural resources

Other factors have been found to affect conditional convergence. In a comprehensive survey of four decades of research, Durlauf and Quah (1999) identified 87 different potential determinants whose impact on growth had been empirically tested. A somewhat surprising finding is that latitude (measured as the distance from the equator) is strongly significant in growth estimates after controlling for the impact of more traditional regressors such as human and physical capital, the quality of institutions, and technological innovation.

This finding is puzzling and harks back to the 'climate theories' of the ancient Greek philosophers such as Polybius. Even innovations that are expected to reduce the impact of climate on productivity, such as air conditioning, do not seem to have weakened the link between geography and growth. A more recent and intriguing historical explanation of the geographical puzzle comes from Acemoglu *et al.* (2001), who argue that the climate effect is determined by colonizers' choices to settle (and therefore invest in local infrastructure) only in colonies with temperate climates, while simply extracting resources and importing raw materials from tropical or subtropical colonies.

This interpretation helps to shed light on another seemingly surprising result in the growth literature: the so-called 'curse of natural resources' (Sachs and Warner 2001). It might be expected that those countries endowed with natural resources would be leading the development race. The actual situation, however, is exactly the contrary, since the availability of the resources needed to start production has so far been much less important than controlling the process of value creation. This has occurred as (corporations from) countries that have relatively poor endowments of natural resources have developed more political and military (market) power and, therefore, been able to control the international process of value creation in many industries in which final products are created and manufactured by using imported raw materials. In parallel to this development, an abundance of natural resources seems to attract corruption, civil unrest, and inefficient governments, thereby explaining how, all other things being equal, abundance of natural resources tends to affect economic growth negatively.

Theoretical and empirical frontiers

The achievements in the literature summarized above still need to be further investigated and scrutinized to overcome the methodological weaknesses that almost inevitably arise when measuring determinants of economic growth. Some of the most important of these innovations are summarized in this section, with a minimum of technical detail.

One problem that needs to be tackled is endogeneity and reverse causation. A careful reader will have noted that almost all the factors described in previous sections are both the causes and consequences of economic growth. A more educated workforce is more productive but, at the same time, higher per capita income positively affects investment in education. Corruption may hinder economic growth but, at the same time, low per capita income and poorly paid government officials may be more prone to corruption. These bi-directional links make it difficult to disentangle causes and effects in order to move beyond simple correlations between economic growth and its determinants. Proposed solutions to this problem are inevitably partial and imperfect, and consist of instrumental variable techniques and more sophisticated first-differenced or system GMM (generalized method of moments) estimates (Blundell and Bond 1998; Bond *et al.* 2001). The aim of these techniques is to identify lagged factors that are correlated with the recent determinants of economic growth under investigation (and under risk of endogeneity and reverse causation) and that cannot be caused by current growth itself, either due to their intrinsic characteristics or because they are sufficiently distant in time. Research with these instruments ranges from the simple recipe of adopting lagged values of the regressors to the use of different 'exogenous' variables that are valid instruments correlated with these regressors. The selection of appropriate instruments is arduous given that per capita GDP is highly persistent and exhibits significant autocorrelation even at distant lags. Consequently, it is always possible that economic development in the past (which is strictly correlated with current economic development) is the cause and not the consequence of the determinants of growth that are observed.

The general conclusion of the research conducted along these lines is that it is highly likely that for many variables the causality nexus functions in both directions. The implication is that growth determinants exist, but that they may be overstated if direct and reverse causation are not disentangled.

Another important issue on the research agenda is the impact of non-linearities and heterogeneity on the relationship between growth and its determinants. The mainstream approach usually starts from the restrictive assumption that the sensitivity of economic growth to a given factor is similar regardless of the level of that factor and the context. However, this would imply that, for instance, the effect of an additional year of schooling on growth is the same in Ghana and in the US. Attempts to overcome the untenable consequences stemming from this assumption have included the development of semiparametric mixture models, which do not uniformly make estimates for all countries but rather for subsets of countries that have homogeneous characteristics, and the identification of threshold effects, where the impact of a variable is significant only after it reaches a given threshold (Durlauf and Johnson 1995; Masanjala and Papageorgiou 2004).

The semiparametric mixture approach has the advantage of being very parsimonious since, after estimating a general model valid for all countries, it identifies a finite number of random components on a chosen set of model coefficients and identifies homogeneous subgroups in which the impact of regressors on the dependent variable is significantly different from that of the general model. The random component has the advantage of capturing the effects of all the latent variables that cannot be measured (or are purposely not included in the estimate). Empirical studies have shown that subgroup deviations from the average impact of human-capital and technological progress are well explained by latent factors such as institutional quality, geography, and culture (Liu and Stengos 1999; Kalaitzidakis *et al.* 2001; Masanjala and Papageorgiou 2004).

Another promising innovation has been the incorporation into growth models of the effects of geographical externalities. Recent empirical work in this field shows that these externalities are significant and, if not considered, risk producing biased impacts of traditional variables on conditional convergence and growth leading to faulty policy suggestions (Anselin 1998; Fingleton 2000, 2001).

To sum up, recent advancements in empirical techniques for estimating the determinants of growth and conditional convergence have led to the identification of strict correlations among the most important growth determinants and threshold effects. These effects, geographical externalities, and the need for a coordinated improvement in many growth determinants explain the clustering of countries into growth clubs. These clubs remain distinct if within-group differences tend to decrease while between-group differences persist over time, with the consequence that poor countries become trapped in a club from which they cannot escape. The main challenge for the future is to develop comprehensive and coordinated strategies that can overcome these poverty traps.

The governance problem

Although the methodological problems described in the previous section make it difficult to calculate with precision the magnitude of the causal link between economic growth and each of its potential determinants, it is quite clear which policies should be adopted in order to enhance world economic development and prosperity. At the same time, it is also apparent that at the current stage of economic development, equal opportunities are beneficial for growth (Galor and Moav 2004) and that the fight against poverty is an important goal to pursue, not only per se but also for the purpose of fostering overall economic development.

The question is why these recipes are so difficult to apply. The easy answer is that there is a lack of willingness to apply them or, from the perspective of economists, there is neither a 'global planner' nor appropriate international institutions capable of fostering sustainable development. Globalization has clearly been more rapid than the capacity to create global rules to govern the process, and the various existing domestic and international institutions that have the mission of fostering economic development are riddled with conflicts of interest. In this context, society and the private sector are beginning to fill some of these governance gaps with bottom-up initiatives. It is very important to interpret such actions not as a demonstration of the uselessness of governance and rules, but rather as complementary actions that create awareness of the need for more equitable rules.

This bottom-up mobilization of society has given rise to the large number of social enterprises and not-for-profit organizations that are increasingly called upon to address market failures and contribute to solving the dual problems of the insufficient production of public goods and government budget constraints (Borzaga and Defourny 2001). These enterprises have an important role to play and are strongly competitive since they are more efficient and can better pursue stakeholders' interests than can public agencies or for-profit firms.[7] Two promising avenues in which social enterprises and not-for-profit organizations have been influential are *microfinance* and *fair trade*.

Bottom-up mobilization and financial markets: microfinance

The Aghion *et al.* (1999) inquiry into growth and inequality and insights from the Galor and Moav (2004) model show that access to education and credit are two fundamental channels by which a society may create equal opportunities and the potential for social and economic development for all individuals, regardless of unequal economic endowments.

Equal opportunities have never been as important for sustainable development as they are in today's globalized world. The integration of labour, product, and financial markets has significantly increased returns to talent and education, and economic activities are becoming increasingly intensive in terms of human capital and knowledge. In this context, the socio-economic potential of each country is the sum of the talents and skills that have been developed by its citizens during their lives. This is the reason why access to credit and education are fundamental, and equal opportunities and sustainable development go hand in hand. Microfinance plays the crucial role of easing access to credit to uncollateralized borrowers who cannot obtain loans from the conventional banking system.

The diffusion and coverage of microfinance in the world today is impressive and growing. The Microcredit Summit Campaign has documented that at end

December 2007, 3,552 microcredit institutions served more than 154 million clients, 106 million of whom were among the poorest when they took their first loans (Daley-Harris 2009).

The key issue that microfinance has to solve is how the problems of moral hazard, adverse selection, and the risk of strategic default (due to ex post hidden information) can be managed while lending to uncollateralized borrowers. Microfinance institutions have generally provided successful solutions for these problems through dynamic incentives of progressive loans, group-lending schemes with or without joint liability, and innovative mechanisms for monitoring borrowers. Among these success factors, group lending has been identified as an optimal feature of lending contracts when information asymmetry is more severe between lenders and borrowers than it is among borrowers themselves (Morduch 1999; Ghatak and Guinnane 1999).

As in any industry, not all experiences have been successful and several reasons for the heterogeneous performance of microfinance institutions have been identified: the uneven capacity of local microfinance institutions to monitor groups of lenders, differences in competitive and geographic scenarios which may affect alternative credit choices and the incentive to repay (Buckley 1996), and variations in the levels of 'peer pressure' and 'social capital' that determine the level of deterrence exerted over borrowers who violate their debt obligations (Armendáriz de Aghion 1999; Ghatak and Guinnane 1999).

Empirical studies of microfinance around the world have shown that some crucial issues need to be tackled in order to increase its effectiveness. Microfinance schemes are particularly vulnerable to aggregate shocks that reduce diversification gains from group lending. Joint liability has the advantage of significantly reducing the insolvency risk for banks (when groupmate projects are negatively correlated and diversification gains exist) at the cost of reducing borrowers' welfare with respect to individual lending (group lending poses an extra burden on the solvent borrower who is obliged to repay the debt of an insolvent groupmate). Furthermore, the administrative costs of monitoring small loans are extremely high and often lead to exorbitant real interest rates.

Several innovative loan schemes have been utilized to cope with these problems. One microfinance pioneer, the Grameen Bank, has taken a step beyond group lending by showing that it is possible to maintain the incentive to repay with a progressive loan scheme in which groupmates are not liable for a member's insolvency (Armendáriz de Aghion and Morduch 2005). Individual lending schemes have been devised in which the absence of collateral with market value is compensated by 'notional collateral', which consists of assets that are worthless on the market but are of high value for the borrower. High administrative costs have been circumvented in some innovative schemes developed in India in which borrowers are given credit lines and credit cards that allow them to choose when and how much to borrow up to a given threshold without additional transaction costs. Self-help groups have been created in which women borrowers become shareholders of the bank with a limited amount of forced savings and are made responsible for preparing loan applications that are supervised by the bank.

These solutions show that microfinance innovation involves two important processes: the replacement of the standard collateral of the individual borrower with new forms of collateral (joint liability, borrower monitoring, notional collateral, dynamic incentives in a progressive loan scheme) and the reduction of fixed administrative costs that may be exorbitant given the small scale of loans and the absence of standard guarantees.

Another crucial issue in microfinance concerns the use of subsidies. Armendáriz de Aghion and Morduch (2005) argue that most of the discussion about the role of subsidies is based on static cost–benefit analyses that miss the dynamic contribution subsidies may provide to borrowers' capacity building and its consequences on economic development. The authors conclude that the evaluation of the welfare effects of microfinance subsidies depends upon several assumptions. Specifically, theoretical models generally find that subsidies are beneficial when assuming a non-flat distribution of social weights, a demand of credit that is elastic to interest rates, adverse selection effects that entail a non-positive impact of interest rates on project returns, and positive spillovers of microfinance credit to other lenders. This approach provides a rationale against offering subsidies that is similar to the traditional 'infant industry' critique, which suggests subsidies undermine the efficiency of microfinance institutions.

These recent advancements in microfinance studies show that bottom-up actions by society can successfully promote equal opportunities, thereby increasing the potential for economic growth and individual happiness.

Fair trade and the role of corporate social responsibility

Fair trade is a product chain created by zero-profit importers, distributors, and retailers of food and textile products that have been manufactured partially or wholly by poor rural communities in developing countries according to specific social and environmental criteria.[8] This initiative represents another promising direction of bottom-up mobilization and of grassroots welfare initiatives that focus on socially responsible saving and consumption and aim to develop important processes of inclusion and development.

The best-known characteristic of fair trade is the payment of a 'fair price' that is higher than the market price paid for primary products by local intermediaries or transnationals in the food industry. The payment of a fair price does not necessarily represent a violation of market principles for two reasons. First, buyers of primary products are usually highly concentrated and exploit their market power to conclude transactions at prices that are far below the value of primary producers' marginal product.[9] Second, fair-trade products can be more properly considered a new variety of product that is a bundle of traditional characteristics and social responsibility features, and therefore cannot be compared with standard non-social responsibility products. From this point of view, the introduction of fair-trade products may be seen as reducing market incompleteness and increasing the welfare of consumers with social preferences (or inequity aversion) and who previously lacked the opportunity to purchase such products. Over time, it has become evident that the fair-trade contribution consists of a package of additional initiatives that go beyond the fair price. These initiatives include the provision of both pre-financing opportunities, which allow fair traders to compete with monopolistic local moneylenders and reduce the impact of credit rationing, and price stabilization mechanisms, which are countercyclical mark-ups on commodity market prices that insulate risk-averse primary product producers from the high volatility of such prices. These two initiatives significantly contribute to reducing producers' financial risk.

In addition, the fair-trade package includes important initiatives that aim to improve the position of producers in the real economy. These initiatives include improvements in working conditions and the amelioration of factors leading to child labour, not through a ban on products incorporating child labour but rather through the monetary integration of the incomes of poor households[10] and the preferential inclusion in the fair-trade distribution chain of projects reinvesting part of the surplus arising from the fair price in local public goods, such as health and education. Finally, fair trade contributes to the environmental sustainability of production processes in two ways: by providing full information on how the price is determined through the various passages in the value chain and by creating long-run relationships between importers and producers, including the provision of the export services that are essential for the penetration of fair-trade products in foreign markets.

A final 'hidden effect' of fair trade is its capacity to encourage and foster imitation in social responsibility by traditional producers. Becchetti and Gianfreda (2007) demonstrate that the entry of fair-trade producers triggers social responsibility imitation in incumbents under reasonable parametric conditions on consumers' social preferences. Social responsibility imitation by the non-social responsibility incumbent is only partial, but higher in dynamic frameworks in which the incumbent's goal is to reduce the formation of socially responsible consumer habits (Becchetti *et al.* 2005).

Consistent with predictions from the theoretical models mentioned above, the diffusion of forms of socially responsible consumption such as fair trade is accompanied by a wide range of imitation strategies by traditional producers. Many more companies are starting to advertise not only price and quality, but also their socially responsible actions.[11] In 2005, KPMG Global Sustainability Services (2005) found that 52 per cent of the world's largest corporations published corporate social responsibility reports. Social labelling and corporate responsibility is gradually becoming an important competitive feature in real and financial markets.

Today fair trade benefits around 1.5 million poor families with an average market share that is far below its potential.[12] In addition to this direct contribution, the indirect impact from imitation practices of conventional producers needs to be added. These developments suggest that it would be potentially beneficial for international institutions to act as low-cost catalysts for the promotion of fair-trade products. Supporting and monitoring bottom-up initiatives may be an economically efficient application of the subsidiarity principle and an example of the potential synergies that can arise from cooperation between international institutions and civil society in the pursuit of sustainable development.

Conclusions

The traditional theoretical and empirical growth literature has done a tremendous job in identifying the most important factors that impact economic growth and conditional convergence on aggregate. Recent refinements and developments on the empirical side are contributing to the incorporation into standard conditional convergence analyses of the effect of geographical externalities, the presence of threshold effects, and the heterogeneity of the impact of standard variables on growth. At the same time, a new consensus is emerging on the importance of institutional quality and of access to education, credit, and ICT technologies, all of which are crucial to transforming talents into economic outcomes in spite of the inequality of their initial endowments.

In this new framework, it is becoming increasingly clear that in order to avoid the paradox of generating 'frustrated achievers', economic growth should be considered an intermediate target that can be placed into a broader framework of socio-economic well-being. Along this path, an increasingly important role is being played by those bottom-up initiatives—microfinance and socially responsible consumption—that promote inclusion of the poor and remove barriers to credit. Such initiatives complement the actions of institutions and will help achieve the goals of sustainable development and individual happiness.

Beyond their current coverage and success, bottom-up policies in support of economic development signal a promising principle for the future evolution of economic systems. These policies illustrate that the goals of poverty alleviation, economic development, and human well-being cannot be achieved if responsibility for them is entirely delegated to global planners and international institutions. These goals will be much easier to achieve if the societies of developed countries with socially responsible consumption and savings act in cooperation with the societies of developing countries and complement the efforts of governments and international institutions in creating new rules for global governance.

Notes

1 The ideas developed in this chapter have greatly benefited from several presentations of research papers on economic growth, microfinance, and consumer social responsibility. This chapter has been adapted from Becchetti and Mastromatteo (2006) with the permission of the journal *Economia Internazionale*.
2 Microeconomic empirical research suggests that each additional year of schooling is associated with significantly higher earnings (between 5 and 15 per cent) in a wide range of countries (Card 1999; Psacharopoulos 1994).
3 Women's education is expected to reduce family size for a series of reasons. First, educated women may have higher aspirations for their children and this may reduce their desired family size, given the quantity–quality trade-off between the number of children and the time available for each child. Second, education increases the opportunity cost of women's time and is positively related to the use of contraception and

to the adoption of less pro-fertility social norms. From a similar, but slightly different perspective, the higher initial stock of human capital may lead to lower fertility rates because people shift from saving in the form of children to saving in the form of physical and human capital (Barro and Becker 1989; Becker *et al.* 1990).

4 See the seminal contribution by Feldstein and Horioka (1980).

5 The existence of a link between capitalism and the Protestant Reformation is implicitly in the entry on 'capitalism' in the *Encyclopedia Britannica* (2009): 'The development of capitalism was spearheaded by the growth of the English cloth industry during the sixteenth, seventeenth, and eighteenth centuries. The feature of this development that distinguished capitalism from previous systems was the use of the excess of production over consumption to enlarge productive capacity rather than to invest in economically unproductive enterprises, such as pyramids and cathedrals. This characteristic was encouraged by several historical events. In the ethic encouraged by the Protestant Reformation of the sixteenth century, traditional disdain for acquisitive effort was diminished, while hard work and frugality were given a stronger religious sanction. Economic inequality was justified on the grounds that the wealthy were also the virtuous.'

6 This is clearly illustrated by the authors' 'Macromed' case study, where 'eventually the management concluded that the best approach was to introduce the new equipment in a "greenfield" site with a handpicked set of young employees who were relatively unencumbered by knowledge of the old practices' given that old 'line workers still retained many elements of the now obsolete old work practices' (Brynjolfsson and Hitt 2000: 43).

7 See Chapter 2 of this volume for a discussion of the competitive advantages of social enterprises.

8 For the theoretical debate over the role and impact of fair trade at the micro and aggregate levels, see Maseland and de Vaal (2002), LeClair (2002), Moore (2004), and Hayes (2006).

9 Support for the existence of monopsonistic labour markets for unskilled workers, not just in least developed countries but also in developed countries, is provided by Manning (2003) and Card and Krueger (2000).

10 The child labour literature clearly shows that the most effective strategy for reducing child labour is to raise the incomes of poor households. Several empirical studies demonstrate that the decision to send children to school is taken when household income rises above a given threshold (Basu 1999; Basu and Van 1998).

11 On 7 October 2000, the BBC announced that 'Nestlé has launched a fair-trade instant coffee as it looks to tap into growing demand among consumers'. The BBC commented that 'ethical shopping is an increasing trend in the UK, as consumers pay more to ensure poor farmers get a better deal'. In 2003, Procter & Gamble announced that it would also begin to offer fair-trade certified coffee through one of its speciality brands. Following Procter & Gamble's decision, another coffee giant, Kraft Foods, expressed its commitment to purchase sustainably grown coffee. The growth in corporate social responsibility seems to be strongly driven by bottom-up pressures. When a sample of companies was asked about reasons for their socially responsible behaviour, 90 per cent responded that it was corporate perception by consumers (Globescan 2007).

12 Empirical research on consumers' willingness to pay for the social and environmental features of products shows that in many countries the share of positive responses is between 20 and 30 per cent. These preferences, however, do not translate into an equivalent market share due to information asymmetries on the ethical content of fair-trade products and distribution bottlenecks.

5 The provision of welfare and general-interest services

Luca Fazzi

An overall evaluation of the role performed by social enterprises in supplying general-interest services is hampered by national and international accounting systems, which mainly measure the size and economic contribution of the for-profit and public sectors. These systems tend to perpetuate what Monzon and Chaves (2008: 549) call the 'institutional invisibility' of social enterprises. Moreover, findings vary greatly according to the definition of social enterprise adopted (Bouchard *et al.* 2006). National censuses are particularly susceptible to this problem of classification. In Sweden, for example, Wijkström *et al.* (2004) studied the language used in the central government's budget to describe third-sector organizations and found that more that 110 different collective nouns were applied to 27 different areas of expenditure.

A wide variety of terms is also used to refer to the concept of *social enterprise* in the scientific literature. In a recent study, Kerlin (2006) highlights differences in terminology between European and North American researchers, while in Europe itself diverse traditions and legal systems pose obstacles for a shared definition (Defourny and Nyssens 2008). Consequently, organizations may be classified as social enterprises according to researchers' interests, the characteristics of organizations, or other criteria of convenience. Even in countries where explicit legal definitions exist, some organizations that function as social enterprises may still not be counted as such for administrative reasons.

A description of social enterprises providing general-interest services is therefore fraught with contradictions and information gaps. Given these difficulties, this chapter overviews a broad range of organizations from traditional non-profits to forms of social cooperatives that may partially distribute their profits. Further research based on more rigorous concepts and methods is clearly needed to fill in the details.

Against this backdrop, the chapter is organized as follows. The first section defines *general-interest services* and describes the role played by not-for-profit organizations generally and social enterprises specifically in the production of these services. This section then analyses differences in the distribution and role of social enterprises across countries, highlighting the main patterns from a comparative perspective. The second section analyses the factors that have influenced the development and spread of social enterprises. The third section identifies the main difficulties and challenges faced by the further expansion and consolidation of social enterprises providing general-interest services.

Social enterprises in the provision of general-interest services

The term *general-interest services* covers a wide range of activities that strongly affect the well-being and quality of life enjoyed by the population of a given community. These services are a pillar of society and an important component of citizenship, since their provision is a prerequisite for the enjoyment of funda-mental rights. General-interest services include energy, telecommunications, transport, water supply, waste management, broadcasting, postal services, edu-cation, health, and social services. All of these services contribute to sustainable economic and social development in terms of the satisfaction of basic needs, social inclusion, employment, integration of marginalized groups, economic growth, and environmental quality. In particular, health care, social services, employment creation, and public housing form a specific and crucial dimension of modern welfare societies (Blakemore 2003). Since many of these services have a public character, they cannot be supplied solely according to market rules. Their provision relies heavily on governments, local authorities, and often on not-for-profits.

The reasons for the emergence and spread of social enterprises in the provi-sion of general interest services have been closely linked to crises in welfare systems (Evers and Laville 2004). Government failures have been most exten-sive when, amid greatly increased demand, the expansion of public services has been hindered by excessive bureaucracy, organizational rigidity, shortages of funds, and reluctance by governments to make unpopular decisions (Salamon *et al.* 2000). The Johns Hopkins Comparative Nonprofit Sector Project (CNP) has collected comparative data that show that the majority of non-profit growth between 1990 and 1995 took place in social services. A notable exception was the US, where growth in the sector was greater in the field of health (Salomon *et al.* 1999; Independent Sector 2005; OECD 2008). The number of social-service practitioners in 2001 amounts to about a quarter of all employees in the non-profit sector, where social enterprises have often expanded due to their lower start-up and management costs (Wing *et al.* 2008). Services like home care for the elderly or day nurseries require low investments in facilities and capital. Consequently, they are not characterized by particularly significant barriers to entry in terms of economic and financial investment.

A second important area of activity by social enterprises is health services. Local medical centres, dental clinics, and facilities providing care for the men-tally ill, disabled, or non-self-sufficient elderly are widespread in many coun-tries. Fewer not-for-profit organizations are involved in the management of hospitals, except in the US, where 42 per cent of all paid workers in non-profit organizations in 2001 were employed in health services, and specifically in non-profit hospitals (Independent Sector 2005). In Europe, not-for-profit organiza-tions manage hospital health-care delivery (partly through religious bodies) almost exclusively in the Netherlands, and to lesser degrees in Germany, France, and the UK.

A third important area of activity by social enterprises is in the provision of educational and cultural services. According to data collected by the CNP, between 1990 and the 1995 education and culture accounted for 17 per cent of non-profit job growth. The US occupied the dominant position with 22 per cent of all workers in the non-profit sector engaged in the delivery of education. While many US universities and colleges are operated as non-profit organizations, in Europe the public character of primary, secondary, and tertiary education has limited the involvement of social enterprises. The only significant exception is the Netherlands, where 27.1 per cent of employees in not-for-profit organizations work in education and research (Burger and Dekker 2001). In Europe, after-school educational services, training schemes, and educational support for the disabled are widespread. In recent years, a growing number of organizations have begun to provide assistance for the linguistic and social integration of immigrants.

Finally, social enterprises also furnish general-interest services such as transport, electricity, and water. In the US, the non-profit sector has a long tradition of supplying these types of services, and there are as well important schemes in other English-speaking countries and in the French-speaking parts of Canada.

Patterns of international variation

The contribution of social enterprises to the production of general-interest services is difficult to estimate at the level of individual countries because the datasets are highly heterogeneous and do not distinguish between the various types of providers. Nevertheless, the available data indicate broad differences at the international level. Some studies have identified ideal-typical models for analysing the diffusion of social enterprises and not-for-profit organizations by using a comparative approach (Salamon and Anheier 1998; Freise and Zimmer 2004; Conférence permanente des coordinations associatives 2008). The results differ according to the number of countries and the variables considered: for example, the earliest studies excluded the countries of eastern Europe, while more recent surveys not only include some countries in eastern Europe but also in Latin America, Africa, and Asia (McCabe and Hahn 2006; Mori and Fulgence 2009; Zhao *et al.* 2009). The current state of empirical knowledge enables the range of analysis to be extended so that the phenomenon can be depicted more extensively.

To date, the US has one of the largest and most productive not-for-profit sectors. Low public spending on welfare has fostered the growth of a commercial system of social and health services in which not-for-profit organizations play a major role. The principle of self-organization to deal with collective problems is an integral part of American culture, and the wide variety of ethnic, religious, and cultural groups in the country, together with geographical distance, have favoured the bottom-up growth of community-based and not-for-profit organizations furnishing highly diversified general-interest services. No comprehensive data are available on social enterprises in the US, but social enterprises can be found in many sectors of activity including social and health services, community development, biomedicine, alternative trade and development, education, media and communications, and culture (Kerlin 2006).

Canada also has an established tradition of not-for-profit organizations providing general-interest services. No comprehensive data on social enterprises are available, but as a proportion of the overall economy Canada's not-for-profit sector surpasses that of the US. At the turn of the century, extrapolated data suggest that more than 18 million Canadians are involved in the not-for-profit and voluntary sector, which involves more than 160,000 organizations, employs about two million people, and generates $75 billion in annual revenue (Statistics Canada 2004).

In Western Europe, the development of the not-for-profit sector and the involvement of social enterprises in the provision of general-interest services are more recent and heterogeneous phenomena (Kerlin 2006). The 'old' European countries have a 50-year tradition of public provision of general-interest services. Consequently, the development of the not-for-profit sector has been less extensive in these countries, and the growth of social enterprises is ongoing but still largely restricted to welfare services.

The literature identifies four kinds of welfare regimes in European countries: the social democratic, the corporativist, the Mediterranean, and the liberal (Esping-Andersen 1999). The role and size of social enterprises and more generally of the not-for-profit sector in each of the four welfare regimes is different.

The social democratic regimes include the Scandinavian and Nordic countries. In these countries, social enterprises do not play a major role in providing general-interest services, since public authorities are responsible for doing so. The not-for-profit sector consists mainly of voluntary organizations engaged in advocacy and policy formulation rather than service provision (Stryjan and Wijkström 1996). Social enterprises have emerged only recently, and the main sector in which they operate is social services. In Denmark, the principal area of intervention is assistance to the elderly and the disabled, while in Sweden and Finland, day nursery services are extensively provided by cooperatives with the involvement of parents. The situation in Norway is similar, with only 6 per cent of paid employment in the welfare sector provided by not-for-profit organizations (Sivesind *et al.* 2002). In Scandinavia, there is close integration between the public and third sectors, and social enterprises often rely on public support and publicly subsidized staff. The tasks undertaken by not-for-profits in Scandinavia are frequently the same as those carried out by the public welfare state (Hulgård 2006). Although forms of social enterprise have emerged in recent years, the state still predominates in the delivery of general-interest services.

A second group of countries consists of the so-called 'corporative' Europe: Germany, Austria, Belgium, France, and the Netherlands. In these countries, not-for-profits have a much more consolidated tradition, and there is greater involvement by social enterprises in the provision of general-interest services.

However, social enterprises do not deliver welfare services on their own, since in the Netherlands and Germany not-for-profits are tightly integrated into the public sector. In the Netherlands, for example, not-for-profits are a central pillar of the national educational and health systems and provide extensive social services and public housing. Constituting over 12 per cent of the labour force, the Dutch not-for-profit sector is in relative terms the largest in the world (Burger and Dekker 2001). In France, Belgium, and Austria, social enterprises also provide welfare services, although their legal status varies greatly: there are specific provisions for them in Belgium and France, while in Austria they have no special legal status.

In Germany, not-for-profit organizations frequently provide residential and domiciliary care for the elderly and disabled and assistance to minors through the management of day centres and residential facilities (Pfenning and Bahle 2002). In France, so-called 'proximity services'—for example, family day nurseries—have developed (Laville 2001), while in Austria services for families and young children are provided (Trukeschitz 2004).

In 'corporative' Europe, social enterprises are largely financed by the state, either directly or through reimbursements to purchasers (Conférence permanente des coordinations associatives 2008). These countries have a corporative system that assigns not-for-profit organizations a role based on historical processes of mutual adjustment and integration with the state (Burger and Veldheer 2001; Zimmer *et al.* 2005). Since the 1990s, there have been increasing pressures to commercialize these services due to the worsening of the economy (Hupe and Meijs 2000). In recent years, the environmentalism that is deeply rooted in German-speaking countries has bred a new generation of not-for-profit organizations engaged in environmental awareness and education campaigns. Social enterprises have also been involved in a limited and uneven way in the provision of traditional general-interest services such as water distribution, renewable energy, and transportation. For example, Switzerland and Germany introduced the first car-sharing schemes managed by social enterprises in Europe (Beutler and Brackmann 1999).

A third group of countries comprises those of southern (or Mediterranean) Europe: Portugal, Italy, Spain, and Greece. In these countries, not-for-profit organizations played a major role in providing social services before the advent of the welfare state, but since the beginning of the twentieth century the growing role of the state has stunted their development. Nevertheless, since the 1990s social enterprises have proliferated and today provide a significant proportion of social services. In Spain, 'social economy enterprises' increasingly deliver residential and domiciliary services for the elderly and disabled (Ruiz Olabuénaga 2000). In Portugal, social enterprises provide services for vulnerable children, the elderly, and the disabled and disadvantaged (Campos Franco 2005). In Italy, 60 per cent of municipal social services are delivered by social cooperatives and almost 80 per cent by social enterprises of various kinds (Montemurro 2008). The state performs an important function in the financing of such enterprises in Italy and Portugal, while in Spain the role of the state and local authorities is less important. Owing to the fragmentary nature of national welfare systems, social enterprises have often moved into areas in which public intervention is intermittent or non-existent. Particularly in their initial phases of development, social enterprises have played an innovative role by offering services to people not otherwise served by the public welfare system. In Italy, the bulk of social services for the disabled, children, and the disadvantaged have been developed through the initiatives of social enterprises (Borzaga and Santuari 2001). In Spain, social enterprises have filled the gaps left by the withdrawal of public services. Greece is an exception to the Mediterranean welfare pattern. The not-for-profit tradition is weak there, and social enterprises have only recently appeared. Although with some variations, in recent years the Mediterranean countries have enjoyed a certain dynamism in developing innovative industries such as social tourism or social agriculture. These are areas where production costs are only partly covered by public funds, and income from private sources is the economic engine driving the growth of social enterprises.

A fourth welfare model in Europe is that of the UK, which like the US has a strong tradition of not-for-profit organizations but has a more comprehensive public welfare system. In the UK, the reforms of the 1990s and the fiscal crisis have revived interest in private providers of welfare services and now exhibit a great dynamism (Haugh and Kitson 2007). According to recent surveys, not-for-profit organizations in 2004 employed a paid workforce varying between 475,000 and 608,000 people (from 1.6 to 2.0 per cent of the total workforce) and utilized around 300,000 volunteers (IFF Research 2005; Wilding *et al.* 2006). In 2004, an estimated 15,000 social enterprises produced an economic value of £27 billion, which was more than 1 per cent of GDP (IFF Research 2005).

In the UK, social enterprises have developed into a culture that supports mutual responsibility as a 'third way' between the free market and state control (Amin *et al.* 2002). This trend was reinforced in 2004 when the government introduced legislation creating Community Interest Companies, which are a form of social enterprise that must operate in the interest of the community and use their profits and assets for the public good. Since 2000, there has been a boom of services for the elderly and the disabled furnished by social enterprises (Folbre 2008). The government is clearly committed to developing social enterprises in health care and in January 2007 introduced 25 experimental projects to encourage innovation in this industry.

Social enterprises in the UK are active in a broad range of activities other than traditional welfare, including public transport and energy distribution. Half of all social enterprises are located in deprived areas, which illustrates the important role that social enterprises play in community regeneration.

Explaining international variations

There are marked differences among countries in the diffusion and features of social enterprises engaged in the production of general-interest goods and services. The principal reasons for this are the roles played by the state and by for-profit providers, funding strategies, culture and values, and the composition of the social structure. A brief analysis of these factors follows.

The role of the state

The state clearly plays an important role in shaping the involvement of social enterprises in the production and delivery of general-interest goods and services. In countries where the state has supplied welfare and general-interest services historically and successfully, little scope has been left for the development of social enterprises. In Denmark, Sweden, Finland, and Norway, for example, social enterprises are of only minor importance, because the Scandinavian welfare-state model has successfully been able to reconcile high levels of social spending with a strong reduction of social inequalities, and there is broad public satisfaction with welfare services. Social enterprises are more widespread where the state has historically been less involved in delivering these services or when it has fallen behind in doing so (Weisbrod 1988).

Failures by the state to deliver welfare services can take various forms. In Italy, for example, the development of social cooperatives began in the 1970s as a response to a highly centralized and bureaucratic welfare system based mainly on cash benefits that were unable to satisfy the needs of a society undergoing great changes. In the UK, the development of an entrepreneurial approach by not-for-profit organizations occurred at the end of the 1990s, mainly due to the rationalization of social protection systems managed by the public authorities and to pressures to intensify efforts for the work integration of disadvantaged people (Knapp 2002). In general, during the past 15 years the withdrawal of the state due to economic crisis and the need to curb public spending have fostered political preferences for privatization and the development of a social market for welfare services (Kendall 2000).

By contrast, not-for-profit organizations have performed a greater role in countries where public intervention has been more limited; in the US, for example, spending on welfare in relationship to GDP has been much lower than in the countries of old Europe. In the US, welfare is by tradition largely financed by private individuals and agencies, and this has facilitated the supply of non-public services to broad sections of the population.

For-profit providers

A second factor influencing the diffusion of social enterprises is the role played by for-profit firms in the production and delivery of general-interest services. The role of these firms is more important in some countries than in others, and it varies depending upon the type of general-interest goods and services. For example, the privatization of services such as transport and communications in many European countries has benefited for-profit firms. These firms also exert a strong influence on the development of the personal services industry. In countries such as Germany, Austria, and Italy, strong barriers against entry into the social services market have always existed, and not-for-profit enterprises are able to operate in a semi-protected market with limited competition from for-profit firms. In other countries, competition between for-profit and social enterprises is a key component of government strategies for reorganizing the provision of welfare. The paradigmatic case is that of the health sector in the US, where for-profit and non-profit hospitals directly compete with each other.

Competition between for-profit firms and social enterprises is generally increasing, and where it intensifies conditions may become more hostile to the development of social enterprises. In the UK, reforms made in the early 1990s to residential services for the elderly fostered rapid growth in the for-profit supply of these services, and within a few years significantly reduced the role of not-for-profits in the industry. A similar phenomenon has occurred in Spain, and increasing pressures on the supply of services has occurred in Germany since the introduction of long-term care insurance. In those countries with extensive public provision of social services, opening up the market to for-profit firms has created an obstacle for the growth of not-for-profit enterprises. In Sweden, for example, between 1994 and 2004 privatization caused a large increase in employment in the for-profit social services industry and a corresponding decrease in the not-for-profit sector. In the US, studies have shown that since the late 1980s competitive pressures in the health sector have forced many non-profit hospitals to convert into for-profit firms (Salamon 1990). In countries where the not-for-profit sector has enjoyed favourable legislative regulation due to the social goals pursued, not-for-profit organizations have often become more bureaucratic. 'Free welfare associations' in Germany, for example, have become much more bureaucratic due to closer public regulation; this situation contrasts with that of social cooperatives in Italy (Thamm 1995; Fazzi 1996).

Funding strategies

The development of social enterprises is also conditioned by the ways in which services are funded and by their access to risk and debt capital. Financing models differ according to the history and legislation of each country. The state-financed model of social services is mainly regulated by contract.[1] The contracting-out process may come about directly without competition or be based on competitive bidding. Historically, contracting-out without competition was characteristic of the period before the mid-1990s, when public administrations directly allocated services to a single provider. Since the mid-1990s, governments at all levels have expanded the range of services they finance through competitive forms of contracting-out (Savas 2000; Ascoli and Ranci 2002; Lamothe and Lamothe 2009).

This increased formalization of contractual arrangements has significantly influenced the autonomy and organization of social enterprises, since formalization promotes specialization and bureaucratization to the detriment of other features such as reliance on voluntary workers, a focus on innovation, and strong relationships with the community (Brown *et al.* 2007). A similar effect has been exerted by the introduction of so-called quasi-markets, which are financing mechanisms that involve a direct relationship between purchaser and provider to promote efficiency (Le Grand 1991). In this arrangement, the state functions as a regulator, defining the criteria for entitlement to particular services and leaving citizens broad margins of choice in their selection of service providers (Kodner 2003; Glendinning and Kemp 2006). Quasi-markets have been introduced in many countries including the UK, Holland, France, Germany, Denmark, Sweden, and more recently Italy (Vick *et al.* 2006).

The introduction of quasi-markets does not free suppliers from public control, but does subject them to precise rules about how services are delivered. In Germany, for example, long-term care insurance specifies the average amount of time to be devoted to individual care activities, and thus places strong pressures on providers to furnish care rapidly and according to defined standards (Blinkert and Klie 1999). A further effect of these financing models is that the budgets for purchasing services depend upon the availability of public resources. If these resources are reduced, the capacity of suppliers to develop may be blocked.

The development of social enterprises is favoured by financing systems that mobilize private resources. This is the case in the US, where social enterprises have access to innovative programmes (for example, in the field of community development), financial instruments, and large pools of capital.

In recent years, new financing instruments designed to support investment in social enterprises have appeared in Europe as well. 'Social finance', 'ethical investment', and 'community-based investment' are some of the terms used to describe these emerging activities (Nicholls 2008). Financial institutions devoted to the development of not-for-profit organizations and social enterprises have been established, including Finansol in France, the International Association of Investors in the Social Economy (INAISE), the Féderation Européenne des Banques Ethiques et Alternatives (FEBEA), and Fineurosol, the network of solidarity financial institutions in Europe that was launched in 2005 by the European Commission (Mendell and Nogales 2009). The UK has invested most extensively in innovative instruments for financing risk capital for social enterprises.

Culture and values

Another important factor explaining the expansion and growth of social enterprises is culture—that is, the set of collective values, norms, and beliefs through which institutions and social groups attribute meaning and value to reality. The development of social enterprises has been shaped by both the crisis of modern welfare systems and the political and cultural movements of the 1970s. The cultural ferment and the emancipatory pressures of those years engendered strong social dynamism and grass-roots participation, which provided the impetus for the early development of social enterprises in several countries. In Italy, for example, the first social cooperatives arose out of the movement campaigning for closure of asylums for the mentally ill (Borzaga and Ianes 2006), while in

France financing by the Maisons de la culture and of the Maisons des Jeunes et de la culture aimed to enhance the role of culture in social renewal (Archambault 2001). During the 1990s, privatization was encouraged by such ideologies as New Public Management and Management by Objectives, and since 2000 neo-liberal ideologies have directed the attention of governments to the entrepreneurial promotion of not-for-profit organizations.

While the cultural representation of not-for-profit organizations as producers of general-interest goods and services is an essential prerequisite for the development of social enterprises, culture also contributes in other ways to the evolution of such organizations by, for example, contributing to social legitimization. In the countries of southern and central Europe, the influence exerted by Catholicism has helped create high social and institutional approval for the not-for-profit sector. Catholic doctrine has provided a distinctive anti-socialist and anti-liberal rationale for public social policies, and the political parties inspired by this doctrine have historically favoured the growth of a network of not-for-profit organizations over increases in public welfare services. Not-for-profits have certainly benefited from this support both directly and indirectly through their enhanced ability to apply pressure on national and local governments.

Culture has also contributed to the development of social enterprises in the 'new Europe'. In these countries, social enterprises are still underdeveloped compared with potential demand for their services and the entrepreneurial spirit of their citizens (UNDP 2008). Moreover, social enterprises tend to be considered stopgap measures rather than long-term welfare and economic actors (Leś and Jeliazkova 2007). Several cultural factors account for the weak legal and socio-economic institutionalization in these countries.

Ideological legacies can lead to political distrust in certain organizational models such as cooperatives, which in some countries are still regarded as relics of communism. Consequently, the potential of not-for-profit organizations as service providers has been underestimated, as has the role of cooperatives in the economic development of localities and industries hard hit by economic transition. Moreover, the general distrust of cooperatives and not-for-profit organizations has been exacerbated by the corrupt practices of some of these organizations and their leaders during the early years of transition.

Cultural elements have also influenced the attitudes of not-for-profit organizations towards undertaking functions typical of for-profit firms. The boom in not-for-profit industries in the former East Germany since the mid-1990s has been almost entirely financed by public subsidies. This has been the consequence of the economic depression that existed when the Berlin Wall collapsed and a legacy of policies that have tended to suffocate entrepreneurial activities.

Social structure

Variation in the provision of general-interest services by social enterprises is also influenced by differences in social structure. Increased social diversity has certainly undermined the sense of national solidarity that led to the formation of modern welfare systems (Alesina and Glaeser 2004). In countries with values of national solidarity, there is a substantially greater willingness to pay taxes and support welfare (Taylor-Gooby 1996). Moreover, social diversity is a factor that can be exploited by political parties to gain support during elections. For example, Monsma and Soper (1997) argue that social, and especially religious, heterogeneity accounts for the greater economic and occupational success of not-for-profit organizations in the Netherlands, a country characterized by the presence of religious and ethnic groups that have hindered the growth of a unitary welfare state. Each group has consequently self-organized based on its specific needs, resulting in the 'pillarization' of welfare services from education to social work.

Social differences have also disrupted the bases on which the universalist welfare state was founded by creating a widening gap between basic social welfare services and more individualistic demands and needs. Greater heterogeneity of demand has favoured the development of diversified responses and, according to some authors, this explains the growth of not-for-profit organizations (Weisbrod 1988). Kendall and Anheier (2001) emphasize in particular the ability of social enterprises to augment the problem-solving capacity of contemporary societies.

Social enterprises can help to alleviate social exclusion. They are often the most efficient producers of general-interest services in marginal areas with specific needs and demands. This is the case for rural areas of the UK and Ireland that have high levels of social exclusion and only limited access to public services due to problems of scale and distance from urban centres.

The universalist welfare model also encounters great obstacles in responding to the needs of urban inhabitants that reside in highly diversified communities in terms of lifestyles, cultural and religious customs, levels of income, and economic and social needs. The development of urban and metropolitan areas, with consequent increases in social heterogeneity and complexity, is therefore an important factor that tends to promote the growth of social enterprises in terms not only of providing basic social services but also of meeting cultural, leisure, and educational needs.

Unlike during the period when the modern welfare state was established, the social and economic evolution of many countries today has increased the differences among individuals and social groups, so that the model of equal responses to similar needs has been largely superseded.

Social enterprises and public policies

Another important factor in the development of not-for-profit organizations is the role performed by national and local governments (Gidron *et al.* 1992; Salamon *et al.* 1999). Mendell and Nogales (2009) distinguish four main types of state intervention to promote the development of social enterprises: tax policies, loan guarantees, direct legislation, and injections of funds.

Tax policy has proved to be an important instrument for the development of social enterprises, and it has long been an influential mechanism for encouraging innovations in not-for-profit organizations (Dehne *et al.* 2008). Many countries have introduced tax rebates on donations to encourage the solicitation of funds from private donors. In other cases, governments exempt from taxes the purchase of services from social enterprises or reduce taxation on profits in order to encourage innovation and the assumption of business risk. Fiscal policy can also foster capital investment in social programmes. The UK has followed the example of the US, where the 1977 Community Investment Act and the 2000 New Markets Tax Credit Program created tax incentives for private individuals investing in social and community-based enterprises.

Governments can also favour the development of social enterprises by means of loan guarantees. Social enterprises usually have scant capital of their own and must resort to banks to finance their investments. Access to credit may be difficult for these enterprises, especially those of smaller size. The availability of guaranteed public loans is an important factor in sustaining development and innovation.

Legislation also influences the development of social enterprises. In the US, for example, there is a minimal welfare state, but social enterprises have access to capital that banks are obliged to allocate to social activity and community development. The 2000 New Markets Tax Credit Program is expected to yield resources for social investments amounting to $19.5 billion in 2008. In European countries, recognition of the role of social enterprises has often been precarious during their early phases of development because of prejudices and concerns about their abilities to pursue the public interest in a professional and universalistic manner. The enactment of specific legislation and regulations has usually triggered the spread, and not simply the legal recognition, of social enterprises. In Italy, legislation in 1990 empowered local administrations to contract-out service delivery to social cooperatives, so that what had been hitherto a limited and sporadic practice became routine. In the UK, the watershed in the development of social enterprises came with the election of the Blair government and the success of the so-called 'third way', which emphasised the ethical role of the private sector in providing and supporting public services as a solution to state and market failures. In general, the enactment of laws allowing social enterprises to perform functions recognized as being in the public interest marks the beginning of an institutional process of legitimization that rescues such organizations from the limbo of informality and gives them the status of agents appointed to undertake economic functions in the public interest.

Finally, a significant role in the development of social enterprises has been performed by financing that is disbursed by governments directly from their own funds and indirectly from supranational sources such as the European Structural Fund. For example, in the past six years, European Equal Initiative funds distributed at country level have provided an important impetus for developing social entrepreneurship.

Current trends and future challenges

What is the future of social enterprises providing general-interest services? Are they likely to continue their growth of the past 20 years? And what are the factors that may facilitate or hamper such growth?

There has been growing political interest in not-for-profits and social enterprises. Recent policies to promote social enterprises in the UK are indicative of this interest (Hombach 2000). Ethical products and forms of social entrepreneurship are increasingly attracting public support. In the UK, the US, and the Nordic countries, the market for ethical products is steadily expanding.[2]

Moreover, the figures on employment in the OECD countries show that the greatest increase in job creation is taking place in social and health services, an area in which the presence of social enterprises is most important and which seems likely to grow further in the near future.

Despite these successes, social enterprises are an emerging but not yet consolidated phenomenon. There is still a gap between the rhetoric about the inevitable development of social enterprises as solutions for state and market failures and the empirical reality in which these enterprises actually operate.

One obstacle for the development of social enterprises is that research has not yet reached consensus on the real advantages these enterprises may provide in delivering general-interest services. Advantages identified as crucial by some studies are contradicted by others, and the impact of social enterprises is difficult to measure. For example, the supply of services by social enterprises is deemed preferable in conditions of information asymmetry to avoid the opportunism typical of for-profit firms (Hansmann 1980). Because they are not primarily profit-oriented, social enterprises can also be expected to deliver higher quality and greater equity in service provision (James and Rose-Ackerman 1985; Weisbrod 1989). One feature associated with the reduction of information asymmetries and the risks of opportunism is the democratic governance of social enterprises (Pestoff 1992). Organizational ideologies can contribute to the efficiency of social enterprises by motivating workers to put in greater effort (Rose-Ackerman 1996). According to recent studies, the motivation of workers in social enterprises is also encouraged by the horizontal nature of decision making and by greater opportunities to participate in the governance of the organization (Borzaga and Tortia 2006; see also Chapter 2 of this volume). Contributions by unpaid workers are a factor that further enhances the capacity of social enterprises to produce value (Badelt and Weiss 1990). Moreover, social enterprises are regarded as flexible organizations that are particularly suited to meeting the needs of small groups of individuals who for geographical, cultural, or material reasons require assistance that the state is unable to provide (Weisbrod 1988).

However, current research highlights that none of these characteristics is typical of all social enterprises, which can take heterogeneous forms in different countries and change over time. Social enterprises may have problems in assuming investment risks not only because of the difficulty of calculating their economic returns but also due to the collective ownership that often distinguishes such organizations (Young 2005). While the risk of opportunism is lower when the non-profit distribution constraint is operative, social enterprises are susceptible to the problem of particularism, which may lead them to underestimate the real distribution of needs and focus exclusively on solving problems deemed ideologically important (Salamon 1987). Moreover, democracy is not necessarily a central component of governance in social enterprises. Today, many of these organizations continue to be characterized by charismatic leaderships, coalitions of interests, and monocratic cultures that may promote the organizations' ideologies but risk curtailing the exercise of democracy (Elstub 2006). In addition, motivational factors that instil commitment by workers are malleable and strongly context-dependent. Many social enterprises, for example, complain about a marked decline of ideological motivation by young workers, who value job security over organizational ideologies. In other cases, social enterprises themselves change their goals, replacing their initial principles with professional and occupational interests. Similar considerations apply to volunteers, whose participation tends to be inversely proportional to specialization and commercialization. Moreover, the advantages and drawbacks of social enterprises and the nature of their mission are closely associated with existing policies and regulatory systems (Frumkin and Andrè-Clark 2000). It has been shown, for example, that cuts in public funding are often associated with an increase in mercantile behaviour (Young 2005), that the codification of contracts is a major cause of increased bureaucratization (Kramer 1981), and that dependence on scarce resources gives rise to organizational isomorphism (DiMaggio and Powell 1988). A further analytical problem is underestimation of the new forms of large-sized social enterprises that do not utilize voluntary workers (Bennet *et al.* 2003).

Several scholars maintain that due to the ambivalence of the current debate and research findings, there is still inadequate empirical knowledge about the advantages and disadvantages of social enterprises (Jones and Keogh 2006; Thompson and Doherty 2006). Consequently, there is the risk of a debate developing parallel to the scientific one that is characterized by ideologies and stereotypes that will hamper support for policies that are consistent with the needs and potential of social enterprises.

A second problem concerns the existence and extent of markets that are able to support the development of social enterprises. Because social enterprises in many countries are still dependent on public funding, their evolution must come to terms with strong pressures to curb and rationalize costs. This is a general tendency, and its intensity differs from country to country. Social enterprises have reacted to these pressures to rationalize and curb spending in various ways. In the absence of specific legislation, less structured organizations are subject to increasing pressure, and they find it difficult to resist the drive for rationalization. As the pool of public support that averts the risk of failure for less efficient organizations shrinks, the likelihood of being forced out of the market increases. Numerous projects in new areas of intervention have been financed out of public funds, but when this support is reduced, the organizations struggle to continue with private funds. The drive to curb spending by public authorities also reduces the profit margins of social enterprises that depend substantially on public financing. This phenomenon may greatly reduce their capacity to invest in innovation, exacerbating the investment-risk aversion typical of organizations with collective ownership structures.

In addition, dependence upon public authorities has exposed social enterprises to the problems of bureaucratization and specialization due to the tighter controls and contractual conditions dictated by public authorities (Ascoli and Ranci 2002; Bahle 2003). Especially in a period of strong pressures to curb and rationalize spending, there is an increasing risk of what Wolch (1990) has called the 'shadow state'. These observations highlight the need for social enterprises to modify their financing models and seek access to new markets and new capital.

However, especially in countries with large and consolidated welfare systems, the main obstacle for changing the financing models of social enterprises is the weak private demand for welfare and general-interest services. The high level of taxation necessary to finance the public provision of services limits the opportunities for citizens to purchase alternative services directly. This is especially the case in periods of financial crisis, and consequently the current crisis does not favour the expansion of private demand. The reforms necessary to finance the future growth of social enterprises with private resources have been slow, and frequent changes of government have tended to impede this process further. Moreover, although demand for welfare services and 'ethical' products is growing rapidly, it is still subject to what Cowe and Williams (2000: 37) call the '30:3 phenomenon': the paradox whereby the willingness of citizens to purchase ethical products and services (personal or of other kinds) is higher in expressed intent than in actual behaviour.

A second obstacle is the development of markets for social enterprises is hindered by difficulties in accessing financial markets. As Hebb *et al.* (2006) observe, some services, especially in the health sector, require a critical mass of capital that is not yet in place. At present, only in the UK and the US is there any significant concern about improving the landscape of social finance (Mendell and Nogales 2009). The likely consequence is a 'blockage' in the evolutionary process that often confines the activities of these enterprises to small market niches.

A third obstacle for the development of markets for social enterprises is stakeholders' limited access to good quality information through adequate mechanisms of accountability. If markets are to function, they must have accessible and comparable information. However, tools with which to measure the performance of social enterprises are still inadequate. Only in the US and, more recently, in the UK is the monitoring of social enterprises relatively well developed. The technology for defining standards of performance and information transparency in the provision of general-interest services still seem to be in an early stage, especially with regards the social impact of initiatives (Flynn and Hodgkinson 2001). Surveys on the performance of social enterprises are often conditioned by pressures applied by external agents (state and market) that use tools and techniques unsuited for furnishing accurate assessment of the social impact and the distinctive activities of social enterprises (Paton 2003). Moreover, indicators of economic performance cannot measure overall efficiency in the provision of health and social services (Herman and Renz 2008). Given this lack of clarity, investors are often discouraged from mobilizing resources in a market where results are difficult to evaluate.

A final obstacle to the development of social enterprises is competition. The tendency is for social enterprises to decreasingly provide goods and services to monopolistic markets, but rather for them to compete with other social enterprises and for-profit firms. This competition may distort both the aims and the practices of social enterprises (Foster and Bradach 2005). The case of the conversion of many US non-profit hospitals into for-profit firms has been widely cited as exemplifying the risks of marketization (Salamon 1993). Some authors have emphasized that increased competition with for-profits forces not-for-profits to make mission-related compromises—such as raising prices or retrenching unprofitable services—that will adversely affect the selection of beneficiaries and reduce the ability of not-for-profits to devote resources to their traditional public-service missions (Gray and Schlesinger 2002). The US government has expressed concern about this trend, and some states such as Illinois have introduced legislation requiring non-profits to spend 8 per cent of their annual operating costs on charitable services. Also in areas like education, increased competition with for-profits has produced detrimental effects, such as escalating costs, the commercialization of research, and a decline in concern for poorer students (Stewart *et al.* 2002).

To a lesser extent, competition between not-for-profits and for-profits in Europe has increased significantly. In the health-care industry, for example, reforms have led to a much greater increase in the number of for-profit hospitals compared with not-for-profit ones, even in the traditionally corporative countries. For example, in Germany between 1990 and 2002 the number of hospital beds managed by for-profit companies increased by 84 per cent, while the number in not-for-profit hospitals decreased by 8 per cent (Busse and Riesberg 2004). Moreover, social enterprises providing social services have increasingly found themselves in direct competition with for-profit firms (Ascoli and Ranci 2002). One area in which competition is particularly fierce is in the provision of services to the elderly, which have been subject to major capital investments by for-profit companies such as Blackstone in the UK and Medica France in France. The ageing of the population has increased the potentially paying population, and the market of services to the elderly has reached a level of profitability that attracts the interest of large for-profit providers. In Germany, the introduction of long-term social care insurance has promoted competition for the management of ambulatory care services, thus breaking the 30-year monopoly over social services exercised by large not-for-profit organizations (Boessenecker and Trube 2000).

Social enterprises have adopted various strategies in response to this increased competition. At the political level, the action of both national and local lobbies has intensified. There are highly influential third-sector representation organizations in the UK, Spain, Italy, the Netherlands, and Germany. However, the lobbies for not-for-profit organizations are less powerful than they were in the past, and in order to counter growing competition social enterprises have become increasingly specialized and professionalized to an extent that may be detrimental to several of their distinctive characteristics, including participation by volunteers, democratic governance, and a focus on social problems (Ascoli and Ranci 2002). Brandsen *et al.* (2005) refer to the 'hybrid' nature of social enterprises, since they must interact with the state and the market in a context in which their social recognition and legitimization are still to be consolidated.

Conclusions

The recent expansion of social enterprises is a novel feature in the provision of welfare and general-interest services. The extent of the economic influence of not-for-profit organizations generally and of social enterprises specifically in supplying such services is visible in numerous countries, and an economic alternative to the public sector and the market seems to be taking shape amid ongoing innovations in welfare systems. Even greater interest in these enterprises is foreseeable in the future. However, expansion of social enterprises is not driven solely by ideals or convictions. International experience demonstrates the need to conduct quantitative and qualitative research that allows for a better understanding of the rationale and roles of these enterprises. This in turn will contribute to greater public recognition and to the adoption of policies that will be decisive over the medium-to-long term in sustaining the development of social enterprises.

Notes

1 Contracting has weakened the grants culture that characterized the relationship between the state and not-for-profit organizations up to the 1980s. The introduction of contracting has been based upon the premise that the increased role of not-for-profit organizations in supplying services requires closer regulation by the state. Contracting has therefore become the means to define the public purchaser's requirements and to restrict the autonomy of not-for-profit organizations and social enterprises with regard to the objectives of central and local governments.
2 See Chapters 7 and 8 of this volume for a discussion of ethical products and fair trade.

6 Social enterprises and the integration of disadvantaged workers

Giulia Galera

Among the host of activities supported by social enterprises, the integration of disadvantaged workers is the most widespread, and not only in places where unemployment is high or during times of economic crisis (Davister *et al.* 2004). Participation in the labour market is a crucial form of social integration through which individuals affirm their identities (Schmid 1998). As a defining feature of human existence, work is crucial to the welfare of families and to the stability of societies. Nevertheless, not all human beings have the same opportunities to work. Within the labour market, there are always individuals and groups whose characteristics—physical, social, or demographic—influence the extent to which they are able to participate (Smith and Twomey 2002). As such, exclusion from the labour market can be considered as one of the most important causes of social exclusion. In addition to criticism from an ethical and civic point of view, the failure to integrate all potentially productive workers is a source of inefficiency, since it wastes resources and generates additional costs (Borzaga *et al.* 2001). Against this background, there has been a growing recognition by governments and organizations of the economic burden placed on others by people excluded from the labour market (Yeo and Moore 2003).

Given the goal of equal treatment in the labour force, specific policies have been adopted to ensure employment opportunities for disadvantaged workers. Despite their evolution over time, these policies have not proved to be satisfactory (Borzaga *et al.* 2001). Starting in the 1980s, new productive initiatives—defined as social enterprises—have developed bottom-up with the goal of supporting the full integration of disadvantaged workers into the labour market. The effectiveness of social enterprises stems from their capacity to provide an institutional response to the labour market's incapacity to adequately allocate the available labour force. As such, *a work integration social enterprise* is an institutional mechanism of supported employment that favours workers discriminated against by conventional enterprises and provides them with appropriate on-the-job training to help them overcome their disadvantages (Borzaga 2007). The pioneering role of these enterprises is demonstrated by their early successes in implementing active labour market policies bottom-up before these policies became institutionalized and started to be adopted by public authorities (Defourny and Nyssens 2008).

The aim of this chapter is, first, to provide an overview of the role, development, and potential of social enterprises that have been created specifically to foster employment growth among disadvantaged workers and, second, to link these initiatives to other policy measures that aim to support these workers. The chapter is organized as follows: after a brief description of the difficulties faced by disadvantaged workers in the labour market, it analyses the strengths and weaknesses of the policies that have traditionally been used to address this issue. The chapter then focuses on the upsurge of new initiatives in the field of employment with special regard to those organizations that integrate disadvantaged people into work and society through productive activity and offer a more effective allocation of society's human resources. The chapter then provides an overview of the main characteristics, resources, target groups, and legal structures of work integration social enterprises, and illustrates the development of these enterprises in several representative European countries.

Disadvantaged people in the labour market

Unlike the standard assumption of neoclassical theoretical models, the labour market is far from being perfect. Labour markets are characterized by information imperfections, asymmetries, and constraints that sharply reduce employment opportunities for some categories of workers (Borzaga *et al.* 2001). Factors affecting the demand for and supply of labour differ for various categories of workers. Thus, both demand- and supply-side factors explain the relatively weak position of disabled workers in the labour market when compared to their counterparts without disabilities. Factors influencing an individual's ability to supply his or her labour include the severity of the disability or disadvantage, access to and within a potential workplace, the likelihood of facing discrimination or the availability of suitable jobs, and the trade-off between employment income and benefit receipt. Factors affecting demand include whether the requirements of a job can be fulfilled by a disadvantaged worker and whether any additional costs of hiring a disabled worker—such as the purchase of special equipment—is borne by the employer (Smith and Twomey 2002). Conventional enterprises normally lack information on the abilities, skills, and productivity levels of workers.

An enterprise that decides to hire a new worker has to bear both the costs and risks of recruitment. More specifically, the employer incurs both *selection costs* in identifying the applicant who has the most suitable profile for the job and *training costs* in preparing the worker to adequately carry out the tasks assigned. As a general rule, there is a trade-off between the two: the higher the selection costs, the lower the training costs (Borzaga *et al.* 2001). Employers are often unable to screen workers effectively and may lack the internal structures and resources necessary to train the selected workers with the basic skills they need to perform the tasks assigned (Deavers and Hattiangadi 1998).

In order to simplify the employee selection process, enterprises tend to recruit only those workers who bear positive signals—i.e. those applicants who can show that they have the right competences. Workers who are characterized by negative signals—for example, a physical or mental disability—tend to be excluded regardless of their productivity. Indicators are based on previous experience, prejudices, and evaluations provided by an imperfect labour market. While signals allow for considerable savings for employers, they also result in the exclusion of those applicants who are characterized by average productivity levels but at the same time are bearers of negative signals (Borzaga 2006). In short, selection and training processes favour more qualified and trained applicants and exclude those applicants who suffer from various types of disadvantages. As a result, there tends to be a widening gap between those workers who are regarded as less productive or risky and those who have more favourable characteristics (Borzaga *et al.* 2001). Consequently, the labour market assumes a dualistic character with, on the one hand, skilled workers benefiting from on-the-job training and enjoying career prospects with real possibilities of improvement in wage levels, and, on the other, those workers who bear a number of negative signals and are at risk of labour market exclusion (Borzaga 2006).

Disability is one of the main sources of negative signals that engender substantial wage and participation differences (Kidd *et al.* 2000). As emphasized by Jones (2008), disability has negative effects on labour market outcomes, regardless of the data source or time period. Similarly, the rate of employment for the disabled is about half of that for the non-disabled (Jones 2006).

Workers qualify as disadvantaged with respect to the labour market not only if they are disabled, but also if they are considered less productive due to other specific characteristics, including lack of skills or low educational levels. It should be noted, however, that the effects of such limitations are in most cases difficult to unravel and depend upon the particular skills required in specific jobs (Kidd *et al.* 2000). Accordingly, the meaning of disadvantage with respect to work should not be considered in absolute terms, but rather in specific organizational contexts. Having said this, limitations do not necessarily reduce the real or potential productivity level that can be achieved by workers in performing specific tasks, nor do they prevent their professional valorization. A number of limitations can be overcome through the adaptation of the working place, an adequate training programme, or the identification of a job that is adapted to a worker's specific characteristics (Borzaga *et al.* 2001). Furthermore, the disadvantage can also be limited or overcome when the integration of a disadvantaged worker is adequately supported by individualized training.

Over the last two decades, the conditions that generate what is considered disadvantage have gone through an evolution, with a broadening of the categories of disadvantaged workers. The traditional definition refers to disabled people, while the more recent definition is reflected in European Commission Regulation no. 2204/2002, which identifies 'disadvantaged workers' as those who have difficulties entering the labour market without assistance according to the following specific criteria:

- any person who is under 25 or is within two years after completing full-time education and who has not previously obtained his or her first regular paid employment;
- any migrant worker who moves or has moved within the Community or becomes resident in the Community to take up work;
- any person who is a member of an ethnic minority within a Member State and who requires development of his or her linguistic, vocational training or work experience profile to enhance prospects of gaining access to stable employment;
- any person who wishes to enter or to re-enter working life and who has been absent from both work and from education for at least two years, and particularly any person who gave up work on account of the difficulty of reconciling his or her working life and family life;
- any person living as a single adult looking after a child or children;
- any person who has not attained an upper secondary educational qualification or its equivalent, who does not have a job or who is losing his or her job;
- any person older that 50, who does not have a job or who is losing his or her job;
- any long-term unemployed person, i.e. any person who has been unemployed for 12 of the previous 16 months, or six of the previous eight months in the case of persons under 25.[1]

It is important to note that this regulation embodies a fundamental shift in the conception of disability: whereas for centuries people with disabilities were defined by their physical conditions, it is now recognized that disabilities are relative and result from the interaction between an individual's functional capacities and their surrounding environment, both social and physical (Savedoff 2006). As such, the status of disability becomes a social rather than an individual problem. This re-conceptualization presupposes an important shift from a view that people with disabilities are passive beneficiaries who need charity towards a view that considers them participants and actors who can make their own contributions and must be fully included in society (Savedoff 2006). Accordingly, issues like the right to full inclusion and participation have come to the fore and have paved the way for more active policies that help ensure that disabled people can take part in the everyday life of their communities on an equal basis with others.

To conclude, the more recent and comprehensive concept of *disadvantage* includes people who are 'disabled' as well as those who face systematic limitations preventing them from performing jobs according to accepted standards (Borzaga *et al.* 2001). Important and continuing barriers to employment include a lack of formal education, low skills and cognitive abilities, physical and mental problems, drug and alcohol use, and unstable housing arrangements (Deavers and Hattiangadi 1998).

Labour policies

Labour policies have been adopted by modern welfare states to tackle employment issues. These include policies that aim to facilitate the work integration of people who cannot achieve standard productivity levels unless they are offered specialized training programmes or are allowed to perform specific jobs.

Numerous conventions, laws, and other instruments have been adopted with the goal of removing the barriers of exclusion and stimulating the work integration of disabled workers. Interest in vocational training and employment opportunities for people with disabilities emerged during the Second World War in response to the number of people disabled by the war and the need to find workers capable of filling the jobs left vacant by mobilized workers (O'Reilly 2003). The European Community has attempted to tackle unemployment in general and unemployment of disadvantaged workers in particular, although in a fragmented manner. In the 1980s, for example, structural funds were directed to the most vulnerable categories in the labour market.

The goal of employment and labour policies is to contribute to an effective allocation of the labour force. Employment policies have a role in ensuring that all workers can find suitable jobs that allow them to make adequate use of their capabilities and to acquire any missing abilities that may boost their competitiveness. During the last 50 years, many policies designed to sustain disadvantaged workers have been implemented. These policies can be classified as regulatory, compensation, and substitutive (Borzaga *et al.* 2001).

Regulatory policies consist of the adoption of quota systems that oblige enterprises to hire a minimum percentage of disadvantaged workers. However, there are national variations with respect to quotas, other specific requirements, and the nature and effectiveness of sanctions in cases where an employer fails to meet the requirement (O'Reilly 2003).

Compensation policies encourage enterprises to employ disadvantaged workers by compensating firms for the lower productivity of disadvantaged workers employed or for the hiring and training costs involved. These policies may include training and vocational guidance before recruitment and economic incentives for recruitment (Borzaga *et al.* 2001).

Substitutive policies aim to create 'out of the market' demand, often called a 'substitutive labour market', where work integration of disadvantaged workers is promoted in the public sector, in public sheltered workshops, and in enterprises that are created ad hoc. Many countries operate some form of sheltered employment, even if a shared concept of sheltered employment does not exist (O'Reilly 2003).

The overall impact of these measures has been controversial and several shortcomings can be identified. Failures are due mainly to circumstances that make these policies difficult to enforce. An additional problem that jeopardizes the effectiveness and efficiency of these policies is the emergence of new forms of disadvantage and social exclusion that cannot easily be covered by measures that were initially tailored to disabled people. Moreover, the sustainability of these policies has been hampered by increasing costs.

Each of the three types of policies has specific issues. Quota systems often fail to achieve their targets due to an embedded rationale that presupposes protected workers are uncompetitive; this rationale has encouraged employers to evade their obligations to employ such workers (O'Reilly 2003).

The main difficulty with compensatory policies is assessing the required compensation. These measures tend to be tailored to the characteristics of the disadvantaged workers involved and result in the exclusion of workers who have severe disadvantages. Furthermore, they tend to have a 'stigma effect',[2] which prevents the full empowerment of beneficiaries.

Negative side effects of substitutive policies are their low levels of productivity, dependency upon public agencies, and incapacity to ensure the full work integration of the disadvantaged workers employed, also owing to a lack of employment contracts and poor pay (O'Reilly 2003). While improving transition to the regular labour market is the stated policy of sheltered employment in most countries, transition rates appear to be rather low, ranging from about 1 to 5 per cent. Furthermore, the high percentage of disadvantaged workers employed often results in the creation of ghettos. The philosophy of sheltered employment has been harshly debated in recent years and other employment measures that are more oriented to empowering disadvantaged workers have come into favour (Borzaga *et al.* 2001).

In brief, instead of encouraging the professional and social integration of beneficiaries, these measures tend to confine disadvantaged workers into a ghetto, including those workers who are potentially capable of performing active roles in conventional enterprises (Borzaga 2006).

Employment policies that integrate disadvantaged workers have shown increasing signs of success following the shift from passive (income transfer) to active labour market policies (Borzaga 2007). An increased focus on active policies has also been prompted by other policy changes, including the de-institutionalization of social care (for the mentally ill and disabled) and new initiatives that aim to move people from welfare to work (Spear and Bidet 2005).

Accordingly, recent initiatives have emphasized the activation of labour market policy through measures that discourage welfare dependency; mainstream employment and vocational training services for people with disabilities; introduce incentives to participate in educational, training, and work initiatives; strengthen workers' involvement; improve employment support services; implement anti-discrimination legislation; and enforce existing quota scheme provisions. Furthermore, combining a variety of policies has become more popular; for example, the obligation to hire a certain proportion of disadvantaged workers is coupled with the adoption of specific training programmes. However, while the scope for shifting the balance may appear to be significant, passive measures continue to consume a greater proportion of public resources than active labour market measures (O'Reilly 2003).

The development of supported employment as a mix of policies has become increasingly popular. Supported employment is an innovative policy measure that intervenes directly to support the selection and training costs of enterprises.

It can be provided in a variety of ways, including individual placement, enclaves, mobile work crews, and small business arrangements. However, these kinds of measures appear to require high levels of support at every stage of the business operation and are not widespread (O'Reilly 2003). Given the high costs and degree of complexity generated, these measures have been implemented mainly by public enterprises or non-profit organizations (Borzaga *et al.* 2001).

To conclude, considerable variations exist in the types and mixes of policies depending upon the interplay of a number of factors, including culture and tradition, social and labour market conditions, welfare benefits systems, and the influence of civil society organizations, such as associations of disabled people (O'Reilly 2003). Interestingly, the shift towards active policies was anticipated in the late 1970s by the emergence of innovative bottom-up initiatives that aimed to fully integrate people excluded from the labour market. These initiatives have been intertwined with the new labour policies.

The emergence of new initiatives

Notwithstanding the range and number of measures implemented, disadvantaged people throughout the world continue to be subjected to violations of their human rights. People with disabilities are the most deprived and neglected human beings in the world (Sen 2006). The available statistics indicate that unemployment rates among workers with disabilities tend to be twice or three times that of other workers, with the highest levels being among those who are mentally ill (O'Reilly 2003). Furthermore, globalization and changes to the division of labour have negatively affected employment opportunities and labour markets. While raising the level of unemployment and making work more precarious, these trends have also increased the conditions for social exclusion of disadvantaged workers in the labour market (Spear and Bidet 2005). At the same time, following a decrease in employment opportunities and an increasingly selective demand for labour, traditional employment policies designed to support disadvantaged workers—including combinations of various measures—have become less effective (Borzaga *et al.* 2001). Clearly, labour market failures have been compounded by policy failures. One of the most important trends has been an increasing recognition that many programmes have failed to make the necessary connections between training and employment (Spear and Bidet 2005). These failures have opened the way to new initiatives for the most disadvantaged, albeit on a relatively small scale (Aiken and Spear 2005).

One such initiative has been the bottom-up development of autonomous organizations that specialize in facilitating the work integration of disadvantaged people. The philosophy of these organizations, which emerged in the 1980s, was to empower and integrate excluded people. Against this background, disadvantaged workers have been encouraged to participate in social enterprises that offer them an opportunity both to reassess the role of work in their lives and to gain control over their own personal projects. This conception implies assisting disadvantaged workers not only to develop an occupation but also to acquire specific values through democratic management structures (Borzaga *et al.* 2008).

Innovative initiatives in the field of work integration can be found in many European countries. Attempts made so far to identify these organizations suggest that traditional and innovative initiatives exist side-by-side.[3] A recent effort to systematically identify the main patterns of work integration was conducted by the EMES European Research Network,[4] which covers ten European countries (Nyssens 2006). Thirty-nine different types of initiatives were identified and categorized into four main modes of integration: transitional occupation, creation of permanent self-financed jobs, professional integration with permanent subsidies, and socialization through productive activities. This classification includes both traditional and innovative initiatives, and it seems to be more oriented towards the (re)socialization of disadvantaged groups rather than towards work integration. The joint consideration of both types of initiatives has two problems: it does not sufficiently valorize the added value of those experiences that have proved to be more self-sustainable and effective in empowering disadvantaged workers, and it runs the risk of reproducing the problems of traditional policies such as dependency upon public agencies, high costs, and the failure to empower beneficiaries.

Unlike traditional initiatives, work integration social enterprises are distinguished by their entrepreneurial orientation and their aim of supporting the permanent and full work integration of the disadvantaged. These enterprises integrate the disadvantaged into work and society through productive activity and facilitate the effective and efficient allocation of human resources, including those people who are characterized by specific disadvantages with respect to the labour market (Borzaga *et al.* 2001). Work integration social enterprises have developed two strategies for doing this: first, to create transitional occupations that provide work experience and on-the-job training with a view to supporting the integration of the target group into the open labour market; second, to create permanent self-financed jobs that are sustainable alternatives for workers disadvantaged in the open labour market.

Work integration social enterprises

Work integration social enterprises are usually promoted and supported bottom-up by groups of citizens and disadvantaged workers and are directly oriented to providing goods and services to consumers, enterprises, and local authorities. Differences can be noticed between a more inclusive model, which aims to provide permanent positions within the enterprise for disadvantaged workers, and a more transitory model, which favours fixed-term contracts that assist participants in developing the work and professional skills that are required to enter the open labour market. Notwithstanding national and local specificities, these initiatives share a number of innovative characteristics that help overcome the problems of traditional policies.

Main characteristics

Work integration social enterprises differ from sheltered employment work-shops by devoting attention to market dynamics and paying disadvantaged employees an income equal to, or at least comparable with that of other workers (Nyssens 2006). By contrast, sheltered workshops simply offer starting job ini-tiatives, without paying a market salary and creating protected markets. In work integration social enterprises, the integration of disadvantaged workers is achieved either through productive activity with tailored follow-up or through on-the-job training. Work integration is pursued through the production of goods and services in a stable and continuous way. Against this background, varying proportions of disadvantaged workers are employed, but these are invariably lower than for sheltered workshops. Several studies have shown that work integration social enterprises are more successful at motivating disadvan-taged workers than are sheltered workshops (Bracci 2009). Work integration social enterprises are also more successful in helping disadvantaged workers to gain control over their own lives.

In contrast to other policy measures, work integration social enterprises are new initiatives explicitly created for training and employing disadvantaged workers directly, either in stable or temporary ways. These enterprises have an entrepreneurial character that empowers disadvantaged workers and stimulates their productivity, at least with regards to covering their labour costs. Work inte-gration social enterprises should be considered mechanisms of supported employment that operate in contexts specializing in the integration of disadvan-taged workers (Borzaga 2006).

Unlike for-profit firms, work integration social enterprises produce two types of output simultaneously: on the one hand, goods and services that are sold to private or public clients according to market and contractual logics; on the other, work integration services that stimulate the development of skills and compe-tences that render disadvantaged workers competitive in the open labour market. Consequently, work integration social enterprises should be conceived of as 'double-output' enterprises that produce not only marketable goods and services, but also work integration for the disadvantaged.

The competitive advantage of work integration social enterprises stems from their expertise accumulated by working in a stable and continuous way with spe-cific types of disadvantaged workers. While acquiring specialized knowledge with respect to certain disadvantages and their impact upon various types of work activities, work integration social enterprises develop appropriate organ-izational processes that contribute to strengthening their efficiency and managing specific failures of the labour market. Given their expertise and experience, work integration social enterprises are able to select disadvantaged workers and train them at lower costs compared to conventional enterprises, and they are more capable of identifying the most suitable job according to the type of disadvan-tage a worker has (Borzaga *et al.* 2001). Furthermore, work integration social enterprises are effective at integrating training and employment components, thus helping individuals to break the cycle of training schemes leading to temporary employment followed by unemployment (Spear and Bidet 2005).

Finally, owing to their social motivations and democratic governance systems, work integration social enterprises are seen as trusting organizations by communities, public institutions, trade unions, and for-profit firms.[5] Hence, these enterprises have the capacity to gather additional resources, such as voluntary work, free of charge (Borzaga 2006).

Target groups

Whereas sheltered workshops tend to focus mainly on people who are either physically or mentally disabled, work integration social enterprises also support the integration of more diversified categories of disadvantaged workers. Moreover, work integration social enterprises may work with more than one target group at a time, depending upon the specific characteristics of the local labour market. Beneficiaries of work integration social enterprises include jobseekers with serious social problems resulting from a lack of qualifications and professional inactivity that renders reintegration into the labour market difficult. Additional beneficiaries may include people who suffer persistent social stigmatization due to alcoholism, psychiatric disabilities, drug use, or their status as ex-prisoners or parolees. Another subgroup is hard-to-place jobseekers who have been inactive in the labour market for several years by choice or due to a lack of opportunities. Work integration social enterprises may also assist jobseekers who are young and have few qualifications, belong to disadvantaged minorities, or are disadvantaged in the labour market due to their gender or sexual preferences (Davister *et al.* 2004).

Resources

Work integration social enterprises provide a number of positive externalities for the community, including improvements in the quality of life for beneficiaries and consequent reductions in the demand for health-care services, but these enterprises usually entail higher production costs than for-profit firms. These higher costs are mainly related to the training and supervision of beneficiaries (Borzaga *et al.* 2001).

Given their higher costs, work integration social enterprises have to rely on a plurality of public and private resources in addition to those generated by the mainstream economy (commercial incomes or public funding or both). Monetary resources originate from sales of goods or services in the open market or under contract to private entrepreneurs and public authorities, while non-market monetary resources are derived from public subsidies or indirect governmental support and from donations received from members, other individuals, or organizations. The recognition by public authorities of the importance of work integration usually provides social enterprises with access to public subsidies. Public funding, however, can influence the objectives of social enterprises over time through a process of institutionalization (Defourny and Nyssens 2008).

As far as non-monetary resources are concerned, some social enterprises receive support from people who offer their services as a voluntary contribution. Volunteers can be found at various levels, including board members, trainers, and guidance staff; contributions of specific professional skills may also be made (Davister *et al.* 2004). The importance of additional resources with respect to mainstream sources of income depends upon the degree of 'disadvantage' taken on by the social enterprise and the degree of financial support provided by traditional funding sources. Similarly, the extent of participation by stakeholders required for the efficient and effective management of social enterprises varies by the type of goods and services supplied. Depending upon the industry in which they are involved, work integration social enterprises will engage to greater or lesser degrees with other similar organizations, public authorities, and commercial organizations.

Legal structures

Work integration social enterprises in Europe vary in terms of the legislation in which they operate, and in some countries they are not regulated by specific legislation. Social enterprises established during the 1980s and 1990s were based on a wide variety of legal forms that gradually converged into two main types—associations and cooperatives. Over the last decade, new laws specifically aimed at recognizing social enterprises have been introduced in some European countries such as Italy and Finland. These laws specify work integration as an activity that can be—or in some cases, must be—provided by social enterprises. The most widespread legal form for work integration social enterprises is the social cooperative.

Thus, in some countries work integration social enterprises have a specific legal framework that applies to them and focuses on work integration (in Italy, for example, these are 'type B' social cooperatives); in other countries, work integration social enterprises operate under various legal arrangements that also apply to other types of organizations (Spear and Bidet 2005). Some national differences can be observed with regards to profit distribution, which in most cases is not allowed; the prescribed threshold of disadvantaged workers as a proportion of the total labour force, which ranges from 30 to 80 per cent; and the type of governance system envisaged.

The diffusion of work integration social enterprises in Europe

Several factors play a key role in defining the growth of work integration social enterprises: the legal framework in which work integration activities are organized, the clarity of the goal pursued, the types of services supplied, the compulsory minimum proportion of disadvantaged employees, the typology of workers integrated, the relationships established with public agencies and for-profit firms, the legal regulation of profit distribution, and the governance systems implemented. Against this background, the existing models of work integration social enterprises show a mix of innovative and standard features. So far, it has not been possible to identify successful patterns of development, but an analysis of several representative cases—Italy, Finland, Portugal, and Poland—indicate a number of enabling and hampering factors that seem to impact the development of work integration social enterprises. These factors are identified below and summarized in Table 6.1.

Italy

The first work integration initiatives developed during the 1980s following the deinstitutionalization of social care for people with severe mental illnesses and in conjunction with various initiatives designed to supply social services. Thus, the original aim of 'integrated labour cooperatives' was the social integration of former patients of mental hospitals closed after the introduction of Law 180 in 1978. The development of these new types of enterprises in the field of work integration was triggered by the emergence of new demands for the support of disabled people, who had previously, but generally unsuccessfully, participated in educational and training programmes. Furthermore, the shortcomings of the existing quota systems provided for by Law 482/68—including excessively high compulsory quotas and the exclusion of sizeable groups such as drug addicts and people affected by mental disabilities—played an important role in the development of innovative initiatives (Loss 2003).

During the 1980s, autonomous groups of activists organized cooperative enterprises that aimed to provide disadvantaged workers with remunerated and stable jobs. Unlike traditional cooperatives that promote the interests of their owners, however, these new types of cooperatives promoted the interests of disadvantaged people who were not necessarily members. Initially, some cooperatives carried out a combination of social and work integration activities. Law 381 of 1991 recognized social cooperatives and separated them into two typologies: those that deliver social, health, and educational services (known as 'type A') and those that provide work integration for the disadvantaged (known as 'type B'). The latter are allowed to produce any kind of goods or services except those provided by type A social cooperatives. Italian law provides for a clear-cut distinction between social services and other types of services delivered by work integration social enterprises. Unlike in some other European countries (e.g. Portugal), in Italy this distinction between activities has contributed to the success of work integration social enterprises. The delivery of social services by enterprises integrating disadvantaged workers has proved to be problematic, owing to the complexity created by simultaneously pursuing two different goals. Type B social cooperatives have to ensure remunerated jobs for a proportion of disadvantaged workers amounting to at least 30 per cent of the total labour force and are exempted from social security contributions for the disadvantaged workers employed. Type B social cooperatives are currently the only type of social enterprises that are specifically designed to integrate disadvantaged workers.

In Italy, work integration social enterprises have gradually become effective labour policy tools. In 2005, there were 2,419 work integration social enterprises employing 62,691 workers, of which 55 per cent were categorized as disadvantaged. Most work integration social enterprises have been set up as type B social cooperatives, but Legislative Decree 155/2006 provides for their establishment also as investor-owned firms, associations, and foundations (Borzaga 2007).

Portugal

Due to their entrepreneurial approach, 'insertion companies' are the only work integration social enterprises operating in Portugal. Their emergence was closely related to several favourable contextual factors, including the recognition given to third-sector organizations by the Portuguese system of social security and the public policy priorities established by the national strategy to fight poverty and social exclusion (Perista and Nogueira 2006). Against this background, the programme of insertion companies was launched in 1998 with the goal of tackling crucial social and economic problems affecting a wide range of disadvantaged people through the creation of jobs and economic activities addressing unmet social needs (Perista and Nogueira 2002). Unlike Italian type B social cooperatives, insertion companies pursue a plurality of goals simultaneously. Professional integration or reintegration is coupled with the provision of other services addressed to the broader community and the conduct of advocacy and lobbying activities. The services supplied range from home care, proximity, and green-space arrangements to the conservation and restoration of heritage sites. Insertion companies can be set up by third-sector organizations and may take various legal forms, including associations, cooperatives, foundations, or private institutions of social solidarity (Perista and Nogueira 2002). Interestingly, no participatory governance systems are envisaged by the law in force.

At the national level, between 1998 and 1999 the number of integration companies quadrupled from 67 to 284, and this growth continued until 2001, when it reached a peak of 611. The number of beneficiaries has increased steadily and in 2005 integration companies served 4,265 people. Women represent 75 per cent of all beneficiaries, which is probably because the main areas of activity of these enterprises are home care support, gardening, laundry, and restoration (Defourny and Nyssens 2008).

To conclude, insertion companies are a form of work integration social enterprise that appear to be relatively successful as a tool for promoting the social integration of disadvantaged groups (Perista and Nogueira 2006). However, the capacity of these companies to become self-sustainable enterprises is limited because they are mainly engaged in the supply of proximity services, which require regular state support (Defourny and Nyssens 2008).

Table 6.1 Main characteristics of work integration social enterprises in Italy, Portugal, Finland, and Poland

Country	Work integration social enterprise	Legal form	Goal	Products delivered	Threshold (disadvantaged workers over total labour force)	Typology of disadvantaged workers integrated	Relations with public policies	Participatory governance	Profit distribution	No. of work integration social enterprises
Italy	B-type social cooperative	Social cooperative	Work integration	Wide spectrum of services other than social services	30%	Wide category that includes people with physical or mental disabilities, drug addicts, alcoholics, minors with problem families, and prisoners on probation	More links with social policies than with labour policies	Participatory with multi-stakeholder structure	Direct and indirect distribution of profits prohibited	2,419 (2005)
	Social enterprise	Various legal forms (cooperative, investor-owned enterprise, and traditional non-profit organization)								
Portugal	Insertion company	Various legal forms (association, cooperative, foundation or private institution of social solidarity)	Both social services and work integration	Wide spectrum of services, including social services	No defined threshold	Wide category that includes long-term unemployed, unemployed who are at risk of social exclusion, and disabled	Direct links with public policies (run by the Ministry of Social Security and Labour)	Participatory governance not envisaged	Not allowed	521 (2005)
Finland	Social enterprise	All enterprises regardless of their legal form	Work integration	Wide spectrum of services, including social services	30%	People with disabilities and long-term unemployed	Marginal support by public agencies	Participatory governance not envisaged	Distribution of profits allowed with no constraints	69 (2006)

| Poland | Social cooperative | Social cooperative | Work integration | Wide spectrum of services other than social services | 80% | Wide category of disadvantaged workers (homeless people, former prisoners, mentally ill people, etc.) | Direct links with labour offices, which award seed money to social cooperatives | Participatory governance with single-stakeholder structure | Profits have to be reinvested as follows: 1/3 for the social integration of the members; 1/3 for community interest activities (education, culture); 1/3 in the enterprise | 169 (2008) |

Finland

Work integration is the only type of social enterprise that is provided for in Finnish law (Defourny and Nyssens 2008). The initial impetus for the development of non-profit initiatives in the field of work integration was the mass unemployment and deep economic crisis that hit Finland at the beginning of the 1990s. Against the background of structural unemployment, labour cooperatives established by unemployed people were set up. They managed to produce both new job opportunities and vocational training for thousands of the unemployed (Pättiniemi 2001).

A further incentive for the development of work integration initiatives was provided in 2004 by the Finnish Act on Social Enterprises. This legislation specifies that the purpose of social enterprises is to create employment opportunities for those who are disadvantaged or unemployed. Social enterprises must be market-oriented, and they can produce industrial goods as well as social services. According to the Act on Social Enterprises, all enterprises, regardless of their legal form and ownership structure, may apply to become social enterprises, provided they have been registered as an enterprise with the Trade Register of the Ministry of Trade and Commerce and at least 30 per cent of their employees are disabled or long-term unemployed.

Unlike laws in many other European countries, the Finnish Act on Social Enterprises does not impose a non-profit distribution constraint. Furthermore, it does not prescribe the adoption of participatory decision-making mechanisms designed to ensure the involvement of recipients (Pättiniemi 2006). By October 2006, 69 social enterprises had been registered according to the Act (Defourny and Nyssens 2008).

Poland

In Poland, initiatives in the field of work integration have grown considerably in recent years. This expansion was triggered by a mass increase of unemployment and poverty during the transition period and it has subsequently been supported by the European Union's policy recommendations and structural funds (Leś 2009).

The development of social cooperatives specifically designed to provide employment opportunities for disadvantaged people started after the introduction of two pieces of legislation in 2003: the Act on Social Employment and the Act on the Employment Promotion and Institutions of the Labour Market. Both acts contributed to the institutional and legal recognition of third-sector institutions and acknowledged social cooperatives as a special type of worker cooperative.

The Law on Social Cooperatives was introduced in 2006 to promote the social and work integration of people who are experiencing difficulties of various kinds, including social exclusion and unemployment. The law provides for the joint running of enterprises to empower stakeholders, including both founders and beneficiaries. With regards to the groups that are entitled to create social cooperatives, the law specifically refers to unemployed persons, as specified in the Law on the Promotion of Employment and Institutions of the Labour Market, and disadvantaged people, who are identified by the 2003 Law on Social Employment as the homeless, alcoholics, drug addicts or people addicted to other illicit substances, mentally ill people, former prisoners, and refugees. The spectrum of services delivered includes elderly home care, cleaning, building repair, maintenance of public green areas, and recycling.

At the end of 2006, over 60 social cooperatives were operating in Poland, and by the end of 2008 this number had grown to 169 (Gumkowska *et al.* 2008). The high legal threshold that 80 per cent of the workforce must consist of disadvantaged workers seems to be the cause of the relative isolation of these institutions from the surrounding environment and tends to qualify them more as sheltered workshops than as social enterprises (Galera 2008). Against this background, a new legal initiative that aims to change the Law on Social Cooperatives was launched in 2007 by a group of parliamentarians, politicians, and researchers. One of the crucial provisions of this initiative is to decrease the proportion of disadvantaged people to 50 per cent of the total workforce (Borzaga *et al.* 2008).

Conclusions

As emphasized in this chapter, mainstream labour policies have proved unable to ensure a balanced allocation of the available labour force. Against the background of both ethical valorization and efficient exploitation of labour resources, work integration social enterprises are an innovative institutional solution of supported employment favouring those workers who are discriminated against by conventional enterprises. Work integration social enterprises have demonstrated their ability to tackle crucial problems of labour exclusion that affect contemporary economies. Their competitive advantage over traditional labour policies, including sheltered workshops and traditional schemes of supported employment, can be ascribed to the full empowerment of workers that is promoted through the running of autonomous and self-sustainable economic activities. The specific features of these enterprises (e.g. their inclusive governance model and explicit social goals) contribute to strengthening their capacity as active labour market tools.

This chapter has highlighted how the development path followed by work integration social enterprises is strongly influenced by the interplay of a number of variables that shape the phenomenon at country level. Italy has emerged as a leader in this form of social enterprise, both from an institutional and quantitative point of view (Spear and Bidet 2005). By comparing Italy's pioneering development of work integration social enterprises with the growth of comparable enterprises in other European countries, specific enabling factors can be identified. These include the existence of a specific legal form—the type B social cooperative—since 1991; the clear specification in law of the work integration of beneficiaries as the exclusive goal to be pursued, the rules to be followed, and the public subsidies available; the existence of an appropriate threshold for the percentage of disadvantaged workers to be integrated; the focus on various typologies of disadvantages, including new pockets of marginalization; and the support of work integration in the open labour market.[6]

Comparative evidence from Portugal and Finland shows that the pursuit of a plurality of goals (i.e. work integration in conjunction with the supply of social services) hampers the capacity of social enterprises to integrate disadvantaged workers. Moreover, an excessively high compulsory threshold for the integration of disadvantaged workers appears to jeopardize the full integration of disadvantaged workers into local communities, leading instead to the creation of more traditional workshops.

Overall, the number of disadvantaged workers integrated remains far from being adequate if compared to the increasing demand for social inclusion. Furthermore, current global trends will increase the conditions for social exclusion and open the door to new solutions based on the active participation of local communities. There is a clear need for further theoretical and empirical research that can contribute to identifying successful institutional models and enabling policies that can jointly increase the number of disadvantaged workers integrated into work and society by means of social enterprises. Enabling policies underline the need for public schemes to exploit the competitive advantage of work integration social enterprises as active labour market tools that can both enhance social cohesion and reduce the public cost of social exclusion.

Notes

1 Commission Regulation No. 2204/2002 of 12 December 2002 on the application of Articles 87 and 88 of the Treaty of State Aid for Employment. Additional criteria are the following: 'any person recognized to be or to have been an addict in accordance with national law; any person who has not obtained his or her first regular paid employment since beginning a period of imprisonment or other penal measure; any woman in a NUTS II geographical area where average unemployment has exceeded 100 per cent of the Community average for at least two calendar years and where female unemployment has exceeded 150 per cent of the male unemployment rate in the area concerned for at least two of the past three calendar years.'
2 *Stigma* can be defined as the co-occurrence of various components, including labelling, stereotyping, separation, status loss, and discrimination (Link and Phelan 2001).
3 The acronym *WISE* has been used by some researchers to refer to both traditional and innovative initiatives (Davister *et al.* 2004).
4 See the Introduction of this volume for further information.
5 According to a study carried out in the Italian region of Lombardia, one way that for-profit enterprises assist social enterprises is by employing disadvantaged workers. According to this study, 7.8 per cent of all industrial enterprises operating in this region employ disadvantaged workers (Borzaga and Mori 2008).
6 The last trend is emerging in northern Italy as demonstrated by recent research carried out by Euricse (Borzaga *et al.* 2009).

7 The fair-trade debate and its underpinnings

Leonardo Becchetti

Ropi is a village situated in southern Ethiopia, about 320 km from the capital of Addis Ababa and 70 km from the town of Shashemane. The farmers of Ropi produce wheat during the wet season that they are forced to sell below the seasonal (low) market price to local intermediaries who bring the product to the Shashemane market. In the dry season, these farmers run out of wheat and have to buy it from the same traders at the seasonal market price, which is about double the wet season price.

This story of lack of bargaining power and dependence upon intermediaries is strikingly similar for Kenyan farmers on Mount Kenya's eastern slopes, for Peruvian handicraft producers in towns near Titicaca Lake, and for Thai organic rice producers in Yasothon Province. In many situations similar to these throughout the developing world, extreme poverty depends, among other factors, upon insufficient market access, weak organization and cooperation among producers, and lack of bargaining power with intermediaries. The goal of fair trade is to address these and related issues.

Fair trade is an original value chain created by alternative trade organizations to improve the welfare of marginalized producers in developing countries by selling goods in developed countries that have been produced according to social and environmental criteria. Fair-trade schemes have been devised to foster inclusion of poor and marginalized workers in global product markets via consumption and trade. The mechanism for achieving this goal is a package of benefits that include anti-cyclical markups on prices, long-term trade relationships, credit facilities, and 'business angel' consultancy that aims to strengthen the capacity of producers.

This meaning *of fair trade* is quite different from how the term is used in the field of industrial organization. This earlier meaning dates back to the 1930s and refers to schemes by industry trade associations to regulate competition among members, usually by requiring that prices be posted in advance and that no transactions take place except at the agreed prices. During the Great Depression of the 1930s, such schemes were part of the National Recovery Act in the US. More recently, *fair trade* has been used to specify the conditions under which trade should take place (Maseland and de Vaal 2002). In this framework, *fair trade* generally refers to the absence of duties, controls, and dumping practices in international trade. For a similar use of the term, see also Mendoza and Bahadur (2002), Bhagwati and Hudec (1996), Stiglitz (2002), and Suranovic (2002).

By contrast, the term *fair trade* as used in this book refers to food and artisan goods that have been produced according to strict criteria of social responsibility and environmental sustainability (Moore 2004; Hayes 2006). These goods are certified as *fair-trade products* and are promoted and distributed by networks of fair-trade importers and retailers.

A useful way to understand what is meant by fair trade is to examine the price breakdown of a typical fair-trade product. Table 7.1 presents in absolute value and as percentages the revenues going to the various actors involved in the production and distribution of a 250-gram packet of coffee produced by a cooperative in Mexico and distributed by world shops in Italy. Farmers get 22.6 per cent of the final consumer price, which is around twice the standard share for a non-fair-trade product. The impact of fair trade is not limited to the producer price. Three components of the final price—general expenses (6.4 per cent), social projects (5.5 per cent), and the organic premium (3.4 per cent)—are effectively transfers to the first-level producer organization that markets the coffee and provides technical and social services to the farmers. These transfers include contributions to the provision of local public goods (technical assistance and capacity building) to affiliated farmers. Note that two important components of the value chain—transportation and processing—are not under the control of fair-trade producers or importers. This feature is also common to other agricultural products and is an important issue since the high value-added activity of product transformation does not contribute to farmers' incomes. The reason is both technological and commercial: on

Table 7.1 Price breakdown of fair-trade coffee

	Euro	*%*
Farmer	0.55	22.6
UCIRI general expenses	0.16	6.4
UCIRI social projects	0.13	5.5
UCIRI organic premium	0.08	3.4
Transportation costs to the processor	0.06	2.4
Tariff and custom expenses	0.04	1.7
Toasting and packaging	0.46	18.8
Distribution costs and financial expenses	0.13	5.2
Importer margin	0.29	12.0
Retailer margin	0.54	22.0
Sale price	2.45	100.0
Value Added Tax (VAT)	0.49	
Total	2.94	

Source: Author's elaboration of CTM Altromercato data.

Note
Price of a 250-gram packet of Arabica coffee produced by Union Comunidad Indigenas de la Region de Istmo (UCIRI) in Mexico and distributed by Cooperazione Terzo Mondo (CTM Altromercato) in Italy in 2002.

the one hand, the skills and economies of scale required to operate these transformative activities are often not available to producers; on the other, escalating tariffs and non-tariff barriers create insurmountable obstacles to the start-up of transformation activities in countries where the products are produced.

A comparative examination of fair-trade and market prices helps to clarify the price difference between the standard and 'alternative' remuneration for farmers. Figure 7.1 refers to market prices of cocoa beans and Figure 7.2 to market prices of Robusta coffee; these figures illustrate that the fair-trade price is a sort of anti-cyclical markup on the commodity stock market price. The latter price is inherently volatile due, among other factors, to speculative trading, rigidities of supply in adapting to demand, and meteorological supply shocks.

In times of commodity market lows (generally due to overproduction or shocks caused by the entry of new producers), the markup goes above 100 per cent. In times of commodity market highs (typically caused by climatic shocks which destroy part of the crop), the markup is reduced to a much smaller margin. Figures 7.1 and 7.2 show that fair-trade importers fix a lower threshold for the price (which ideally coincides with the minimum earning needed by local producers not to fall below the poverty line), and maintain a slight markup on the market price in its upturns.

Fair trade and globalization

To understand why fair trade is becoming an increasingly important feature of the contemporary socio-economic environment, it is useful to consider how

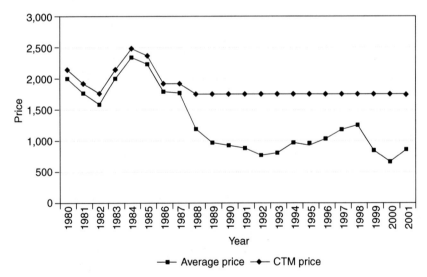

Figure 7.1 Average annual fair-trade and market prices for cocoa beans (source: Becchetti and Gianfreda 2007: 60).

Note

Cocoa prices in US dollars per 1,000 kg. The CTM price is that paid by CTM Altromercato, a leading Italian fair-trade importer, for cocoa beans produced according to Fairtrade standards.

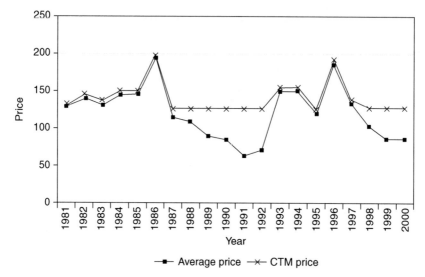

Figure 7.2 Average annual fair-trade and market prices for coffee (source: Becchetti and Gianfreda 2007: 60).

Note
Coffee prices in US cents per pound. The CTM price is that paid by CTM Altromercato, a leading Italian fair-trade importer, for coffee produced according to Fairtrade standards.

development of fair trade has depended upon the effects of global market integration. In short, globalization has provided a delocalization opportunity for firms and reduced the power of domestic welfare systems and trade unions to promote the well-being of workers in a given country. If welfare and trade union rules set social standards that are higher with respect to those enforced in other countries, firms may simply abandon that country to reduce their production costs, resulting in the paradox that higher social standards end up creating more unemployment. For this reason, bottom-up actions by socially responsible consumers may create the type of pressure that domestic governments find difficult to exert, thereby reducing the temptation by corporations to evade social and environmental responsibilities.

Consider how globalization processes have dramatically reduced transportation costs and deeply modified geographical patterns of trade around the world.[1] The driving forces of globalization include, on the real side, the rapid acceleration of worldwide economic integration under the principles of the market economy and, on the financial side, the increasing freedom and speed of capital movements. These phenomena have been facilitated by a worldwide technological revolution that originated in the convergence of software and telecommunications, and was further advanced by the introduction of digital technologies. By easing time–space constraints, this technological revolution has increased interdependence among individuals, which in turn has exacerbated problems involving global public goods or 'bads' and social costs from market failures generated by missing or insufficient global governance.

Many studies have shown that increasing skill wage differentials are associated with the globalization of labour and product markets (Deardorff 2000; Feenstra and Hanson 2003).[2] While 'superstars' and highly skilled workers in developed countries can take advantage of this extension of demand and are generally not harmed by increased competition, unskilled workers generally do not benefit from the enlargement of product markets, and they bear the costs of increased competition by unskilled workers from developing countries.[3] On the other hand, unskilled workers in developing countries should benefit from this process according to standard trade theory, though this may not hold when markets are uncompetitive. Unskilled workers in the primary product industry (above all in the agricultural and textile industries) may indeed find it difficult to step up the 'skill ladder' as distance from the coast, subsistence wage levels, and tariff and non-tariff barriers[4] imposed by developed countries prevent them from accumulating resources that could be invested in human capital to increase their productivity. A large proportion of those living below the poverty threshold according to world statistics—the 'bottom billion' (Collier 2007)—may fall into this category.[5]

Traditional welfare approaches are unable to solve these problems of trade and international labour markets since conflicts of interests among countries and the underrepresentation of the interests of the poorest countries at the international level prevent the emergence of a global benevolent planner (Rawls 1974). A poverty trap in which low skills lead to reduced bargaining power and monopsonistic labour market conditions is well known to economists. Several policy proposals to redistribute income to low-skilled workers have been advanced in the last two decades (Dixit and Norman 1986; Akerlof *et al.* 1991; Phelps 1997). The problem is that these schemes are conceived of as being administered by domestic governments and, consequently, will tend to provide only for domestic unskilled workers, while 'it makes sense to include the well-being of agents in other countries within any welfare criterion' (Feenstra 1998: 41). Therefore, it is highly likely that neither overly indebted local governments nor the domestically oriented governments of industrialized countries will provide for the welfare of unskilled workers in developing countries.

The experience of fair trade seems to suggest that a partial solution to this problem may be found by devising 'bottom-up' welfare mechanisms in which 'socially responsible consumers' in the North play a compensating role for weak or missing institutions.

To understand what is meant by 'bottom-up' welfare, consider economic development as the interaction among firms, institutions, and citizens (see Figure 7.3a). In this simple model, profit-maximizing firms make investment, production, and hiring decisions without considering the negative externalities that may potentially be generated by their productive activities. Individuals make their consumption and saving decisions based on a narrow definition of their preferences, which does not include social responsibility. The people who administer

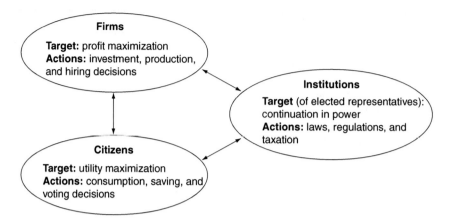

Limits of this system: A public-goods deficit is generated by insufficient internalization of social losses generated by selfish behaviour. Insufficient production of social capital reduces efficiency of market mechanisms.

Figure 7.3a The three-pillar economic system (source: Becchetti and Fucito 2000: 31).

the institutions are far from benevolent planners and maximize the duration of their stay in power. In domestic institutions, they try to satisfy the needs of domestic citizen-voters, while in international institutions they tend to satisfy the needs of voters living in countries that have dominant voting power within the institutions. The interaction among these three forces—firms, institutions, citizens—generates insufficient momentum for the solution of the existing market failures.

It is useful to compare this model with a more virtuous one in which bottom-up pressures are at work (see Figure 7.3b). The third pillar of the system now includes a small share of voters whose voting, consuming, and saving decisions are affected by social and environmental concerns. Even though they are a minority, they significantly influence the behaviour of profit-maximizing firms whose economic and financial success depends upon small changes in market shares, revenues, and profits. Institutions are nonetheless affected as politicians try to represent issues of these groups in order to avoid losing political support.

To sum up, this virtuous scenario is a 'bottom-up' welfare mechanism that includes those measures—such as ethical finance, ethical banking, and fair trade—that endogenize the active role played by socially responsible consumers and savers, who can crucially affect the behaviour of firms and institutions by their choices.[6]

Growth of fair trade

Fair trade has exceeded the rosiest expectations of experts in the field. Only a decade ago, socially responsible products were a very small niche of the market and few observers were prepared to predict that these products would conquer

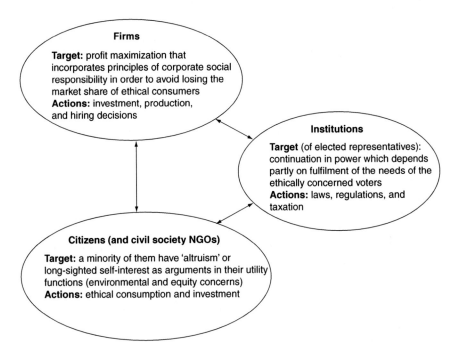

Figure 7.3b Virtuous circle for the globalized economy (source: Becchetti and Fucito 2000: 32).

significant market shares and create contagion among traditional market actors. A common mistake in commenting on fair-trade figures is to consider the ratio between fair-trade sales and the total volume of trade. This indicator is inappropriate, since it fails to take into account that fair-trade products do not exist for the entire range of products sold and traded in the market. Hence, a better approach is to calculate fair-trade market shares for those specific products for which a fair-trade alternative exists. In fact, while fair trade represents less than 0.01 per cent of world trade in physical merchandise (World Trade Organization 2008), fair-trade products generally account for sizeable market shares in their product categories in Europe and North America.

According to the Fairtrade Foundation, a UK-based licenser of products meeting international standards, consumer expenditure on Fairtrade-certified products amounted to £1.6 billion worldwide in 2007, a 47 per cent increase over the previous year. Among specific products, Fairtrade bananas rank first in terms of sales at £150 million, an increase of 130 per cent with respect to the previous year and a market share of 25 per cent in the UK. In the same year, Fairtrade coffee sales rose 24 per cent to over £117 million, and items made with Fairtrade cotton increased from over half a million to just under 9.5 million units. The annual rise in Fairtrade tea was 24 per cent, thereby achieving a 10 per cent market share in the UK by the end of 2008 (Fairtrade Foundation 2008).

This growth was mainly due to a process of fair-trade mainstreaming in which traditional corporations such as Nestlé and Starbucks started imitating 'pioneers' by creating their own fair-trade products (Becchetti and Solferino 2005). In 2008, Tesco and Sainsbury announced their decision to sell 100 per cent fair-trade bananas, boosting up the UK market share for this product to 25 per cent.[7] On 3 September 2008, EBay launched a dedicated platform (WorldOfGood.com) for fair-trade e-commerce, calculating that the US market for such goods was $209 billion in 2005 and forecasting a rise to $420 billion by 2010. The direct impact of fair trade does not fully take into account the indirect effects of contagion in the social responsibility of competitors. By the end of 2006, seven million producer households directly benefited from fair trade (Fairtrade Foundation 2008).

Institutional support for the fair-trade movement has grown in parallel with its diffusion. After previously timid support, in May 2009 the European Commission declared that 'Fair Trade has played a pioneering role in illuminating issues of responsibility and solidarity, which has impacted other operators and prompted the emergence of other sustainability regimes'. The Commisson defined fair trade succinctly as a 'private trade-related sustainability assurance scheme' that 'can influence mainstream business and government policy making'. The Commission also called for rigorous evaluation of the impact of fair trade on producers and stated its intention 'to explore the scope for further dialogue, co-operation and, where appropriate, convergence between different private labelling schemes to promote possible synergies and enhance clarity for the consumer'. Moreover, the Commission expressed its intention 'to continue funding for relevant Fair Trade and other sustainable trade related activities in accordance with its practice to date' (Commission of the European Communities 2009: 3–4, 11).

The debate over fair-trade criteria

The criteria used to include products in the fair-trade value chain have evolved over time and adapted to changing socio-economic conditions. One important promoter of fair-trade standards is the World Fair Trade Organization (WFTO), formerly the International Fair Trade Association, which was established in 1989 by fair-trade producer cooperatives and associations, export marketing companies, importers, retailers, national and regional fair-trade networks, and fair-trade support organizations; in February 2009, the WFTO had 350 members from 70 countries. Another influential group is the Fairtrade Labelling Organizations International (FLO), which was established in 1997 and is the umbrella organization promoting the Fairtrade Certification Mark; in June 2009, FLO (2009) promoted 19 labelling initiatives covering 23 countries.

The WFTO prescribes ten standards that fair-trade organizations must follow in their day-to-day operations and carries out continuous monitoring to ensure these standards are upheld:

- *Creating opportunities for economically disadvantaged producers.* Fair Trade is a strategy for poverty alleviation and sustainable development. Its purpose is to create opportunities for producers who have been economically disadvantaged or marginalized by the conventional trading system.

- *Transparency and accountability.* Fair Trade involves transparent management and commercial relations to deal fairly and respectfully with trading partners.
- *Capacity building.* Fair Trade is a means to develop producers' independence. Fair Trade relationships provide continuity, during which producers and their marketing organizations can improve their management skills and their access to new markets.
- *Promoting Fair Trade.* Fair Trade Organizations raise awareness of Fair Trade and the possibility of greater justice in world trade. They provide their customers with information about the organization, the products, and in what conditions they are made. They use honest advertising and marketing techniques and aim for the highest standards in product quality and packing.
- *Payment of a fair price.* A fair price in the regional or local context is one that has been agreed through dialogue and participation. It covers not only the costs of production but enables production that is socially just and environmentally sound. It provides fair pay to the producers and takes into account the principle of equal pay for equal work by women and men. Fair Traders ensure prompt payment to their partners and, whenever possible, help producers with access to pre-harvest or pre-production financing.
- *Gender equity.* Fair Trade means that women's work is properly valued and rewarded. Women are always paid for their contribution to the production process and are empowered in their organizations.
- *Working conditions.* Fair Trade means a safe and healthy working environment for producers. The participation of children (if any) does not adversely affect their well-being, security, educational requirements and need for play and conforms to the UN Convention on the Rights of the Child as well as the law and norms in the local context.
- *Child labour.* Fair Trade Organizations respect the UN Convention on the Rights of the Child, as well as local laws and social norms in order to ensure that the participation of children in production processes of fairly traded articles (if any) does not adversely affect their well-being, security, educational requirements and need for play. Organizations working directly with informally organized producers disclose the involvement of children in production.
- *The environment.* Fair Trade actively encourages better environmental practices and the application of responsible methods of production.
- *Trade relations.* Fair Trade Organizations trade with concern for the social, economic, and environmental well-being of marginalized small producers and do not maximize profit at their expense. They maintain long-term relationships based on solidarity, trust and mutual respect that contribute to the promotion and growth of Fair Trade. An interest free prepayment of at least 50 per cent is made if requested.

(WFTO 2009)

The most controversial and discussed criterion is undoubtedly that of the 'fair price', which means that the price paid to marginalized producers in low income countries must represent a higher share of the value of the product transferred to them than what is usually the case (for example, see Figures 7.1 and 7.2). Fair-trade organizations achieve this goal by shortening the value chain through the direct import and distribution of products through not-for-profit retailers ('world shops'). Thanks to this pricing mechanism, local producers' revenues are up to four times higher than those earned through traditional trade channels. Fair-trade organizations also fix a minimum price threshold that protects producers from the high volatility of market prices. This implies that fair-trade prices cannot fall below a minimum price (even when commodity market prices are lower), a mechanism designed to ensure a minimally decent standard of living.

The bilateral definition of a price different from that of the market has sound microeconomic grounds, since traditionally trade in primary products occurs when a monopolistic or oligopolistic transnational company buys from a large number of atomistic producers in developing countries at a price that is affected by the relative bargaining power of the two counterparts. The fair-trade price may therefore be ideally considered as the market price which would prevail if the two counterparts had equal bargaining power and may therefore be viewed as a non-governmental minimum wage measure taken by private citizens in developed countries (Adriani and Becchetti 2002; Becchetti and Solferino 2005).[8]

Using prices as a policy instrument to transfer resources to the South cannot be considered a market distortion because fair trade opens in the North a new market where 'contingent ethical' products are sold. In this sense, fair trade may be seen as a step towards market completeness, when consumers' preferences include social responsibility.

To sum up, a common criticism is that fair trade generates distortions in commodity market prices, providing incentives for producers to inefficiently invest resources in products for which there is scarce demand. Behind this kind of reasoning, there are two theoretical fallacies. First, as mentioned above, in many cases exchanges between producers and intermediaries do not occur in a competitive framework. Consequently, the market price is usually distorted because it does not reflect the productivity of producers but rather their lower market power. Second, the food industry produces highly differentiated products with a continuous wave of innovations that create new varieties. There is not a single (capital C) coffee but instead many different coffee products that are differentiated from one another in terms of quality, blends, packaging, and increasingly 'social responsibility' features. For each of these products, a specific and different market price is determined by consumer tastes for that kind of product. In this sense, fair trade is an innovation in the food industry that creates a new range of products. Moreover, it is important to take into account all the potential benefits of the fair-trade value chain in terms of the provision of local public goods, technical assistance that strengthens producers' market capabilities, and the democratization of markets through increasing consumer power.

Another important point about fair-trade principles is that products sold must be environmentally and socially sustainable. In this respect, care must be taken not to confuse fair trade with *ethical labelling*, which by banning child labour often disguises forms of strategic non-tariff barriers from the developed countries against the most impoverished developing countries. By pragmatically promoting workers' welfare through a transfer of resources to poorer households via the fair-price mechanism, fair trade tries to remove causes of marginalized producers' underinvestment in the human capital of their children without creating social non-tariff trade barriers.

A third feature of fair-trade products is the principle of transparency. Labels of fair-trade products must contain as much information as possible on production costs, wholesale prices, and nutritional characteristics. Transparency is fundamental for maintaining the ethical reputation of fair-trade importers and retailers and the conformity to fair-trade principles that is the crucial competitive factor of 'ethical' products.

Other important features of fair-trade projects are anticipated financing of investment for marginalized producers and the transfer of surplus provided to local producers through increased revenues to projects that reinforce the provision of public goods (such as health and education) to local communities. The development of a long-run partnership between fair traders and producers in the South leads to the construction of 'international social capital' and to the provision of export services and project consultancy, thereby creating positive 'learning through export' effects.

The anticipation of financing for production is important because it addresses the common problem of credit rationing that hinders many small non-collateralized producers. Fair trade provides alternatives to the traditional monopolistic intermediaries who buy products from local producers and bring them to the market; it thus serves as an antitrust instrument that reduces market power in trade and financial markets and increases the welfare of local producers.

By directing part of the surplus paid by consumers in the North to services for local communities in the South, fair trade entails private–private transfers that help offset the incapacity of highly indebted governments to provide public goods to their populations. The recent history of foreign aid suggests that it is more efficient to channel resources through civil society organizations when the strategic goals of the donors are appropriate and the corruption of domestic governments is high (Easterly 2003).

An argument that is sometimes raised against fair trade is that it would be more effective for consumers to buy standard (and usually cheaper) products and then combine this action with a charitable contribution. It should be clear from the above discussion, however, that this approach would fail to generate the same range of beneficial effects as fair trade. Charity does not create any contagion effects since it does not threaten the market shares of the profit-maximizing competitors of fair-trade organizations. Moreover, charity does not have the same effect as fair trade in countering the monopoly power of local transport and financial intermediaries. Finally, charity does not create a new variety of products that serves as a multi-purpose social innovation contributing to economic growth by 'creating economic value with values'.

Based on the arguments above, fair trade should be considered a potential solution to some important market failures. The model that follows explains an additional and little-examined contribution of fair-trade initiatives: the transformation of social responsibility into a competitive factor triggering imitative socially responsible actions by profit-maximizing competitors.

The contagion effects of fair trade

As examined in previous chapters of this volume, social enterprises have several unique characteristics. They compete in markets with for-profit competitors while pursuing alternative social goals. By achieving small but progressively increasing positive market shares with their innovative products (bundles of physical characteristics and values), social enterprises demonstrate that there is a significant minority of consumers with a positive willingness to pay for the social features of products. These consumers act as a contagion by pushing for-profit firms to compete for socially responsible consumers by behaving in ways that emulate social enterprises.

This section examines how this mechanism functions theoretically and illustrates it with anecdotal evidence. A striking illustration of contagion was provided by BBC news on 7 October 2005: 'Nestlé has launched a fair-trade instant coffee as it looks to tap into growing demand among consumers.' The BBC's comment on this report was 'ethical shopping is an increasing trend in the UK, as consumers pay more to ensure poor farmers get a better deal.' An interesting indication of motivations for Nestlé's initiative was provided by Fiona Kendrick, Nestlé's UK head of beverages, who argued that 'specifically in terms of coffee, fair trade is 3 per cent of the instant market and has been growing at good double-digit growth and continues to grow'.

Why have multinationals such as Kraft, Nestlé, or Starbucks decided to introduce new lines of socially responsible (fair-trade) products? Why have listed companies, which maximize shareholders' value voluntarily, compressed their profit margins on their newly created fair-trade products to increase their social and environmental sustainability?

The best framework to evaluate the contagion effects of fair trade is that of product differentiation models. In the conventional literature on horizontal product differentiation, geographical space is referred to as physical localization or as the space of product (d'Aspremont *et al.* 1979; Dasgupta and Maskin 1986; Economides 1986), even though it is clear from marketing textbooks that firms may compete on location in many other non-physical dimensions. The model proposed in the next section starts from these premises but assumes perfect information about the ethically responsible stance of players and asymmetric costs of ethical distance, and it interprets geographical distance as the 'space' of social and environmental responsibility (Becchetti and Solferino 2005).

A benchmark model

In the benchmark 'contagion model', a monopolist incumbent unconcerned about ethical issues sells a standard good to consumers uniformly distributed along a line segment [0, 1] that represents ethical and not geographical distance (see Figure 7.4). As in standard product differentiation models, consumers have inelastic unit demands. The monopolist transforms raw materials received from unskilled producers in the South, pays them a subsistence wage (w), and sells the final product to consumers in the North. The incumbent maximizes profits by fixing a price (P_A) for his product. The assumption of an absence of ethical concerns implies that the monopolist is set at the extreme of the ethical segment (or has a position $a=0$). A socially responsible entrant (the fair trader) starts to produce in this market by setting herself at the opposite extreme of the ethical segment ($a=1$) and selling her product at the zero profit price $P_B=w$.

With regard to consumers, it is typically assumed that their utility functions are decreasing in the product price and in the distance between a consumer's ethical stance and the ethical value incorporated in the purchased product. Furthermore, the psychological cost of buying a product that is below the consumer's ethical standards is t times the ethical distance, so that the consumer's welfare is

$$Wc = Rp - Pi - f(x-a) \text{ if } x-a \geq 0 \text{ or } Wc = Rp - Pi \text{ if } x-a < 0 \qquad (7.1)$$

where (Pi) is the price of the product sold by the i-th seller, (Rp) is the common consumer's 'conditional' reservation price—that is, the maximum price a

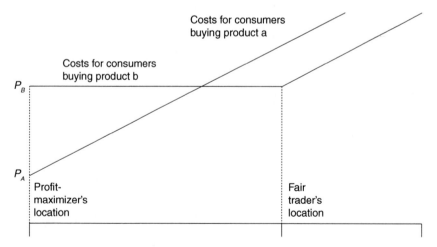

Figure 7.4 Hotelling game of ethical imitation and the asymmetric costs of ethical distance (source: Becchetti *et al.* 2003: 29).

Legend
Moving to the left implies choosing a product below the consumer's ethical standard (and therefore is costly), while moving to the right implies choosing a product above the consumer's ethical standards (and therefore does not provide any added psychological value).

common consumer is willing to pay in case of zero costs of ethical distance—and x denotes generic consumer location.[9]

The term 'f' measures the cost of ethical distance and has a clear monetary dimension. For the producer located to the right of the consumer, term 'f' represents the distance in monetary terms between the transfer which is considered fair by the consumer (indicated by consumer's location on the segment), and the transfer provided by the producer (indicated by producer's location on the segment). Hence, the coefficient (f) plays the role of mapping this objective measure into consumer preferences indicating whether its impact on consumer utility is proportional ($f=1$), more than proportional ($f>1$), or less than proportional ($f<1$) than its amount in monetary terms.

The difference between the benchmark in this approach and in horizontal differentiation models is clearly that a different position on the segment implies a different concern for the ethical features of the products and not a variation in physical distance from them.[10] This leads to a conception of the costs of distance that differs from the standard symmetric approach by assuming that the cost of moving along the line segment is positive only for those going from a more ethical to a less ethical point (see Figure 7.4). Taking the extreme right of the segment as the most ethical position, consumers move without costs to the right, while they incur costs proportional to the 'social responsibility' distance when they move to the left.[11]

This approach to modelling social responsibility is a departure from the vertical differentiation approach in which 'more is better' for all consumers. Descriptive evidence from the World Values Survey Association (2006)—in which 65,660 individuals were interviewed between 1980 and 1990 in representative samples of 30 different countries—provides empirical support for the hypothesis about the heterogeneity of individual attitudes towards social responsibility. In this survey, about 45 per cent of sample respondents expressed their unwillingness to pay in excess for the environmentally responsible features of a product. This percentage was 49 per cent when the same analysis was repeated on a sample of 15,443 individuals in seven countries between 1990 and 2000. These two surveys also show that the share of those arguing that the poor are to be blamed is around 29 per cent. This heterogeneity in the willingness to pay for social and environmental responsibility challenges the assumption that more social responsibility may be better for all individuals.

The above documented heterogeneity of opinions about the poor and the environment (to which must be added the perplexities of those who are socially responsible but do not believe in the effectiveness of fair trade) justifies the choice to introduce heterogeneity in preferences about fair-trade products into the theoretical model. In the debate over economic development, for example, a sizeable proportion both of the public and of experts believe that it is important not to send too much money to developing countries, since the absorption capacity of these areas is limited and the intervention may fall victim to corruption and/or reinforce rent-seeking lobbies in the recipient country. Another line of argument is that paying more for fair-trade products is a distortion of market incentives and leads to overproduction (LeClair 2002). The same reasoning may be applied more generally to corporate social responsibility (CSR) if it is assumed that some consumers accept Friedman's (1962) claim that CSR is a betrayal of managers' duties towards shareholders, or Jensen's (1986) argument that CSR is likely to lead to more opacity in managerial behaviour.

Variations on the benchmark model

One important improvement in the model that needs to be considered is the introduction of a law of motion for consumers' ethical tastes. It is reasonable to expect that consumer concern for social and environmental sustainability is not fixed and is affected by the duration of their fair-trade consumption habits, which are highly likely to be related to exposure to fair-trade promotion and educational campaigns (Becchetti and Rosati 2007). At the same time, it is reasonable to assume (and evidence in the field confirms) that profit-maximizing imitators will not put the same effort into investing in consumer awareness, since imitation is for them a cost in terms of their profit-maximizing goal.

Based on these premises, Becchetti et al. (2005b) propose a dynamic version of the model in which consumers' sensitivity to social responsibility varies according to the frequency they make ethical consumption purchases. In this version of the model, a standard profit-maximizing producer maximizes the following intertemporal profit function in continuous time:

$$\underset{(a,P_A)}{Max}\int_0^\infty e^{-\rho t}\left[P_A-w(1+as)\right]\left[\frac{P_B-P_A}{f}+a\right]dt \qquad (7.2)$$

subject to the law of motion of consumers' social responsibility

$$f''=-\theta f+1-\left(\frac{P_B-P_A}{f}+a\right)+a\left(\frac{P_B-P_A}{f}+a\right) \qquad (7.3)$$

under the non-negative location constraint $a\geq0$. All parameters in these equations are those of the benchmark model. Equation 7.2 describes the law of motion of consumers' social responsibility, which is affected, negatively, by depreciation from current levels of social responsibility (the parameter θ measures consumers' 'loss of ethical memory') and, positively, by the habit reinforcement generated by current consumption of socially responsible products.[12]

Finally, a crucial issue in modelling competition between the fair trader and profit-maximizing competitors is the problem of asymmetric information about the socially responsible features of the products. This problem is exacerbated by the fact that the ethical value of a product does not make the product an 'experience good'; in other words, it is not possible (as it is for other quality dimensions) to bridge the information gap after consumers purchase and have experience with the product. Becchetti and Gianfreda (2007) take this problem into account by introducing into the model the reasonable assumption that imitation in social responsibility needs to be advertised at some cost.

Links with the existing literature

The benchmark model combines features of horizontal product-differentiation models (for example, the assumption of the heterogeneity of consumer tastes for social responsibility corresponding to their location on the unit segment) with a feature of vertical product-differentiation models, since the model assumes that consumers have distance costs only when they move to the left. Hence, while the choice of symmetric costs of ethical distance links the model with the horizontal differentiation literature, the choice of asymmetric costs of ethical distance links it to the vertical differentiation literature.

The heterogeneity of competitors also links the model to the mixed duopoly literature (Cremer *et al.* 1991; Grilo 1994) in which competition between a public and a private enterprise is considered with the following qualifying differences: first, the not-for-profit producer is a private and not a public enterprise; second, the welfare problem is two-sided since it involves both consumers in the North and raw material producers in the South; and third, the not for profit pro ducer has the peculiar features of being mainly concerned with welfare in the South and not with product quality in the North. These differences between the model and the three main strands in the literature (horizontal and vertical product differentiation and mixed duopoly) are determined by the specificities of actual competition over social responsibility described in the sections above. From a strictly theoretical point of view, the model is a hybrid between the horizontal and vertical product-differentiation approaches. An analogy is models focusing on situations in which producers introduce 'quality' features about which consumers may have heterogeneous views.

Comments on the main theoretical findings

Based upon the benchmark model and the variations that have been examined, two broad observations about the contagion effects of fair trade can be proposed.

> *Proposition 1.* The entry of a socially responsible producer competing over price and ethical location in a horizontal differentiation model is Pareto improving for consumers in the North when consumers' costs of perceived ethical distance are sufficiently high.

Becchetti *et al.* (2005a) demonstrate the contagion effect by showing that, on the basis of the benchmark model described above, the entry of a fair-trade producer leads the profit-maximizing producer to reduce price and to emulate partially the entrant's social responsibility, when marginal benefits from imitation (gains of part of the concerned consumers' market share) are higher than marginal costs of imitation (the increase in costs and reduction of profit margins implied by the satisfaction of fair-trade criteria). This finding is robust for modelling variations since it holds both under linear and non-linear ethical distance costs, and it provides a theoretical rationale for the contagion effects described above.

Becchetti *et al.* (2003) demonstrate that the contagion effect generates important welfare consequences in terms of a Pareto superior equilibrium for consumers in the North. More specifically, they observe that the welfare change has four components. The first regards those still buying the incumbent product and are better off paying a lower price. The second and the third apply to those shifting their consumption from the incumbent to the entrant product (loss for the foregone consumption of the incumbent product and gain for the new consumption of the entrant product). These consumers are better off by revealed preferences: they prefer the entrant even though their welfare would be higher by simply remaining with the incumbent. The fourth component concerns those who were not buying before and now buy from the fair trader. Their welfare improvement is measured by the difference between their reservation price and the fair-trader price.

Starting from this basic finding, Becchetti *et al.* (2003) propose another proposition:

Proposition 2. If the location of the profit-maximizing producer is fixed, a policy of duty exemption only for the fair trader may be welfare improving for consumers in the North compared to a policy of collecting duties from both players and directing part of these revenues to the South. The relative preference for the first policy increases the fair-trade transfer to the South and decreases the ex ante duty–unit cost (d/w) ratio. Under reasonable conditions, the first policy will also increase the amount of resources transferred to the South.

In this proposition, the authors introduce a realistic feature in the model (tariffs) and speculate whether a social planner may find it optimal to support social responsibility with tax advantages. They then outline a 'subsidiarity principle' under which a policy of direct aid to the South is inferior to 'indirect intervention' through duty exemption for the fair trader or both players (see Figure 7.5). They also show that the conditions for the application of the subsidiarity principle (the relative convenience of an indirect rather than a direct aid policy) are less strict when the exemption is extended to both players. In essence, by exploiting consumers' willingness to pay to support marginalized producers and by stimulating such willingness with tax incentives, the government may spend less than it would with direct aid to the South. These results hold without considering the 'warm glow' effect: for two interventions with an equal impact on a social problem, individuals prefer to donate directly rather than indirectly through taxation and government action (Andreoni 1990).

The conclusion is that even when costs of domestic competitors under a reduction of duties are explicitly formalized with a reasonable representation of

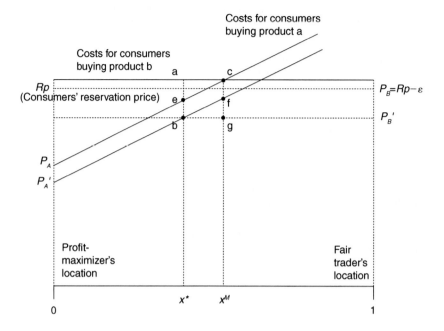

Figure 7.5 North consumer's welfare improvement under the fair trader's entry and the profit-maximizing producer's price reaction (source: Becchetti *et al.* 2003: 29).

Legend
Before fair trader entry, the profit-maximizing producer sells at P_A to consumers located on the segment from 0 to x^M and the North consumers' surplus is given by the triangle (P_A-Rp-c). Even though the fair trader sells products at the least convenient price for consumers $(Rp-\varepsilon)$, the consumers' surplus is enhanced since those who were not previously buying are now buying the fair trader's product and are better off (their welfare gain is given by the area ε $[1-c]$ since the consumers' segment has unit length). For a fair trader's price below $Rp-\varepsilon$, such as P_B' that maximizes the fair trader's transfers, the profit-maximizing producer's price reaction (P_A') generates a further aggregate increase in welfare—from the $(P_A-Rp-a-e)$ to the $(P_a'-Rp-a-b)$ area—for consumers who continue to buy from the profit-maximizing producer. For those consumers who have switched to purchasing from the fair trader, there is a welfare increase equal to $(e-c-g-b)$, while the rectangular area $[(1-c)(Rp-P_B')]$ represents the welfare for consumers unable to buy the product before the fair trader's entry. The new market share of the profit-maximizing producer is 0–x^* in response to the fair trader's entry.

consumers' utility functions, departures from a protectionist agricultural policy may be politically sustainable. If the subsidiarity principle is applied, consumers in the North may be better off due to their higher purchasing power when buying tariff-free products from the South. Consequently, some of their welfare gains may be transferred to North producers negatively affected by the removal of duties. Furthermore, an indirect development policy, together with the removal of duties, may be welfare improving for producers in the South.

The welfare paradox and the dynamic model

Other interesting insights may be obtained from the benchmark model by comparing the optimal locations of the fair trader and the profit-maximizing incumbent with those that would be chosen by a benevolent planner that maximizes the welfare of consumers in the North. The main finding is that under slightly different versions of the game all private equilibria with no government intervention (that is, left to the interplay of private players) in the game exhibit *too much social responsibility* from a domestic welfare perspective (Becchetti and Solferino 2005). This result is crucially determined by the assumption of a duopolistic product market and by the complementarity between prices and ethical location. The interesting point is that the result of excess social responsibility from the perspective of the domestic social planner might be reversed if an international social planner that incorporated and gave equal weight to the preferences of South producers aimed for a higher level of social responsibility than the domestic social planner. The rationale is that domestic governments do not care too much about world poverty since they need to serve the interests of their voters. If the decision is left to domestic governments, there would be an insufficient flow of resources from the North to the South in equilibrium. On the contrary, transfers to the South would be much higher in the dynamics of a duopoly of private producers in which a non-profit-maximizing producer concerned about the problem of the marginalized poor in the South (in other words, a fair trader) competes with the standard profit-maximizing firm.

In this version of the model, Becchetti and Solferino (2005) find that an oligopolistic market equilibrium creates an international socially optimal level of social responsibility. Therefore, an oligopolistic market mechanism exists based on the strategic complementarity between prices and social responsibility, and it compensates with entirely private and voluntary mechanisms the absence of an international social planner.

In this chapter it has been argued that the law of motion of consumer tastes for social responsibility make the proposed model closer to the reality of competition between fair traders and profit-maximizing firms. Results from the dynamic version of the model that incorporates this feature (see Equations 7.1 and 7.2) provide additional insight by showing that the present value of the profit-maximizing producer's shadow cost of changes in consumers' social responsibility determines differences in equilibria with respect to the static version. To sum up, the introduction of the law of motion of consumer tastes both enhances the profit-maximizing producer's price competition and lowers the threshold of the consumers' social responsibility that triggered the profit-maximizing producer's ethical imitation. These differences are justified by the fact that the cost of losing market share today is lower in an intertemporal than in a static perspective, since in the intertemporal perspective it enhances the formation of socially responsible consumer habits that are reinforced by current consumption of socially responsible products. The mechanism here seems to be that ethical consumption habits reinforce the ethical sensitivity of consumers and therefore create the ground for a progressive reduction of the market share of profit-maximizing producers; consequently, these producers will be more aggressive in lowering their prices. This move would in fact reduce the initial fair-trade market share and the conditions that lead to the reinforcement of consumers' sensitivities.

The dynamic model provides insights into the decision to partially (but not fully) adopt the fair-trade approach by profit-maximizing producers with and without the existence of fair traders. The issue is whether market entry by a fair trader is a necessary condition for a profit-maximizing producer to adopt socially responsible practices or whether an *awareness* of the tastes of socially respons-ible consumers is sufficient to elicit this behaviour. The dynamic model shows that mere awareness is not sufficient due to the law of motion of consumer tastes for social responsibility expressed by Equation 7.3. The profit-maximizing pro-ducer acting alone in the market has no interest in responding to the concerns of ethical consumers and therefore chooses a lower level of involvement in corpor-ate social responsibility. This finding further demonstrates the importance of pio-neering alternative trade organizations and their contagious effect on markets.

A final point worth considering is the impact of removing the assumption of perfect information and accepting that social responsibility must be promoted. An important finding is that the introduction of advertising costs generates an inverse U-shaped relationship between the profit-maximizing producer's imita-tion and the fair-trader's socially responsible engagement in relevant parametric regions of the benchmark model (Becchetti and Gianfreda 2007). The intuition behind this result is that if the social responsibility stance of a fair trader is above a given threshold, the profit-maximizing producer cannot afford the costs of imi-tation. By contrast, if the social responsibility transfer is below a minimum threshold, the fixed costs of advertising are too high relative to the potential benefit for the profit-maximizing producer operating under ethical imitation. By considering the stylized fact of competition between profit-maximizing imitators and the fair trader, the implication of these results are that imitation will be equally discouraged when commodity market prices are too high or too low.

A typical problem of informational asymmetries is that the profit-maximizing producer may be tempted to declare an intention to adopt social responsibility, but without actually doing so. A framework that explicitly takes into account information asymmetries and advertising also allows for the investigation of the incentives of the profit-maximizing producer to provide misleading advertising about the producer's ethical stance. In this respect, the model shows that if the information provided by the profit-maximizing producer is the only source of knowledge for consumers, there is a positive incentive for producing misleading advertising. The incentive to cheat depends positively upon the announced trans-fer to marginalized producers, consumers' sensitivity to ethical distance, and the marginal costs of additional advertising. The degree of the effect of social responsibility imitation on the incentive to cheat is mainly positive, but also has a negative component due to the complementarity between the profit-maximizing producer's price and ethical imitation.

Notes

1 Feenstra (1998) documents the phenomenon of disintegration in production by showing a significant rise in the ratio of imported to domestic intermediate inputs and in the ratio of merchandise trade to merchandise value-added in OECD countries.

2 Katz and Murphy (1992) show that the graduate–undergraduate wage ratio for workers with one to five years of working experience increased from 1.4 to 1.9 during the 1980s. Autor *et al.* (1998) find that college workers' wages rose by 25 per cent from 1970 to 1995, against an average yearly decline of 0.11 per cent between 1940 and 1970. The trade and wage debate highlights two main concurrent explanations for increasing skill wage differentials within industries: technological innovation and outsourcing within industries of the least skill-intensive processes to developing countries (Rodrik 1998).

3 The Stolper-Samuelson theorem suggests that trade integration should benefit the factor that is locally abundant and thus low-skilled workers in developing countries. This theorem holds only in cases of perfect competition and does not apply if purchasers of intermediate products from the North have excess market power.

4 Oxfam (2002) calculates that tariff and non-tariff barriers cost developing countries around $100 billion per year, twice as much as these countries receive in terms of international aid. The report also highlights that an increase by 1 per cent in the share of sub-Saharan countries in world trade could potentially bring 120 million people above the poverty line.

5 The empirical literature confirms that specialization in primary products is harmful to growth (Sachs and Warner 1997; Sala-i-Martin 1997) and is associated with relatively higher levels of child labour (Becchetti and Trovato 2005).

6 Bottom-up (grassroots) welfare may be viewed as a 'third generation welfare' mechanism that follows and complements the benevolent-planner and the reform-of-rules approaches. Bottom-up mechanisms, however, may be more realistic than some other approaches, since the benevolent planner seems to be a myth (Easterly 2003), while significant market shares for socially responsible consumption and saving suggests that this mechanism not only exists but also has an impact.

7 For a discussion of competition between dedicated fair-trade retailers and supermarkets distributing fair-trade products see Kohler (2007).

8 A minimum wage under perfect competition may have the perverse welfare effects of reducing labour demand and increasing unemployment (Basu 2000). This is obviously not the case when the wage rises from its equilibrium level to the perfect competition level in a monopsonistic labour market. Recent empirical studies confirm that when workers have low skills and are easily replaceable, labour markets tend to be monopsonistic or oligopsonistic. Card and Krueger (2000) found that the introduction of a minimum wage had a positive impact on output and employment in the fast-food industry in two US states. Shepherd (2000) explains this result as the typical effect of the introduction of a minimum wage measure in a monopsonistic labour market.

9 The design of consumer preferences is consistent with empirical evidence and consumer surveys in which values are shown to be a determinant of choices together with prices. From a theoretical point of view, this point has been analysed by Sen (1993), who shows that people also choose on the basis of their values and, for this reason, do not always choose what they would strictly prefer on the basis of prices.

10 This standard model abstracts from considerations of asymmetric information and divergences between consumers' and sellers' perceptions of the ethical value of the good by assuming that they coincide. Becchetti and Gianfreda (2007) analyse market equilibria under asymmetric information and with the presence of ethical labelling institutions in an extension of this model.

11 The rationale for these assumptions is that moving to the left implies choosing a product below the consumers' ethical standards (which is psychologically costly),

while moving to the right implies choosing a product above the consumers' ethical standards (which may be considered 'too much', and therefore it can be assumed that this choice does not entail a psychological cost for the buyer).

12 It is assumed that habit reinforcement is determined by the share of socially responsible consumption and, consequently, by the market share of fair-trade products. A rationale for this hypothesis is that fair-trade publicity may be positively related to revenues. Fair-trade retail shops provide a lot of information (such as leaflets and documentation) about social responsibility and therefore past consumption may foster future consumption due not only to a habit formation process, but also to the effect of additional information and motivation gained when buying fair-trade products.

8   An empirical test of fair trade

Leonardo Becchetti and Marco Costantino

Asymmetric information is an important problem in fair trade, as in many other areas of economics. Sellers have better information than consumers about products not only when second-hand cars are sold, but also when goods are marketed based on their ethical content. Specifically, fair traders have an information advantage over concerned consumers about the fundamental intangible incorporated in their products: the social and environmentally responsible content of the value chain. This immaterial element is not an 'experience good'—that is, a good for which repeated purchases and consumption can help consumers to bridge the information gap. For this reason, empirical analyses of fair-trade economics are useful to help consumers verify whether fair traders maintain their promises, so that the consumer's willingness to pay for the social content of the product actually promotes the interests of marginalized producers. On the other hand, fair-trade importers need to know whether fair-trade principles are effective and whether these principles and the procedures by which they are put into practice need to be adapted to changing socio-economic conditions. In addition, fair traders want to know more about consumers' preferences for their products. These needs can be satisfied by empirical research both on consumer demand for fair-trade products and on the impact of fair trade on producers. This chapter illustrates the main findings of both types of research.

The impact of fair trade on marginalized producers

Even though the beneficial impact on producers is the rationale for fair trade, the empirical literature on this topic is surprisingly scarce. One of the few studies that has tried to evaluate the statistical significance of the impact of fair trade was carried out by Bacon (2005) on a sample of Guatemalan coffee producers. Using a two-way ANOVA approach and controlling for other concurring factors, this study demonstrates a positive link between access to certified fair-trade markets and sale prices.

A similar approach was followed by Pariente (2000), who found that a minimum price level had a positive impact on producers' security in a coffee cooperative in Costa Rica. This research documents the narrower price variability (and a minimum price higher than the world price) when local producers sell to fair traders. Pariente identifies a virtuous circle in which lower price variability and higher sale prices positively affect investment.

Other impact analyses are based on non-systematic, though qualitatively rich, evidence collected from case studies. Castro's (2001a) impact analysis of fair trade on the Cooperativa de producciòn artesanal de vidrio Cantel (COPAVIC)[1] in Guatemala shows that handicraft producers belonging to this cooperative had significantly higher mean wages than those of traditional producers in the area and that fair traders had given significant support to the cooperative in terms of physical capital investment, technical and financial assistance, and employment benefits (including the introduction of life and medical insurance). An important impact, which is common to many fair-trade projects, was that imports from fair trade constituted only part of the sales by marginalized producers (around 42 per cent) and that technical assistance helped members to strengthen their position in the international market.

Castro (2001b) also studied the impact of fair trade on the cooperative Productores de Miel Flor de Campanilla in Oaxaca, Mexico. In this case, fair trade played the role of 'business angel' by providing financial and technical assistance and raising quality standards, but there were less measurable improvements in members' livelihoods than in the case of COPAVIC and the Productores de Miel Flor was struggling to survive in the international market.

Nelson and Galvez (2000) examined the impact of fair trade on cocoa producers that belong to MCCH, a cooperative in Ecuador.[2] This study found that cocoa farmers who belonged to the cooperative were paid a higher price than non-member neighbouring farmers, even though the price differential was small due to the generally positive effect of fair-trade prices in the area. The study identified the benefits of participating in the cooperative as capacity building, support for marketing skills, organizational development, and production and post-harvest technical assistance. MCCH had also contributed to breaking the monopolies of local intermediaries.

A study commissioned by the UK's Department for International Development (Oxford Policy Management 2000) highlighted the difficulty of discriminating between fair-trade and non-fair-trade aspects of producers' organizational activities. In two case studies of coffee markets in Africa, this study found that fair trade develops relationships with first-level producer organizations and not with individual producers themselves,[3] and also that the fair-trade premium is managed by the producer organizations in order to satisfy the welfare needs of their members. In such cases, the evaluation of the impact of fair trade hinges upon an assessment of the social and environmental responsibility of the specific producer organization. The study also found that the main contribution of fair trade is technical and business-skills capacity building, which is crucial for supporting members if they are going to participate successfully in international trade. Hence, fair trade is a 'way of empowering farmer groups to engage with non-FT [fair-trade] marketing channels on a more favourable basis' (Oxford Policy Management 2000: 33). Similar conclusions were drawn both by Hopkins (2000), who conducted 18 case studies of Oxfam's fair-trade partners and calculated an economic impact ratio—i.e. the ratio of earnings from fair-trade activities to the opportunity cost of labour—and by Ronchi (2002), who analysed a fair-trade coffee cooperative in Costa Rica and distinguished between the direct impact of fair trade on members and the cooperative, and the indirect impact of the cooperative on its members. Both of these studies note that capacity building is an important outcome of fair-trade commercial relationships.

These studies underline the importance of the rigorous evaluation of impact. Nelson and Galvez (2000: 25), for example, observe:

> As with many organizations involved in fair-trade, MCCH has not as yet been able to make an assessment themselves of the longer-term impact of its involvement in cocoa marketing for smallholders and their livelihoods. There is a growing recognition amongst organizations involved in fair trade that more attention needs to be paid to impact assessment.

Along similar lines, Oxford Policy Management (2000) argues that it is important to compare the level and changes in quality-of-living indicators for farmers affiliated to fair trade with non-affiliated farmers drawn from a randomly selected control sample.

Becchetti and Costantino (2008) address this concern in their impact analysis of the effects of fair trade on a specific group of Kenyan farmers. These farmers had the advantage of being a homogeneous community that benefits from the increased productivity generated by the irrigation infrastructure of the Ng'uuru Gakirwe Water Project. This study extracted a sample of producers affiliated with Meru Herbs (the local association which sells part of affiliated farmers' products to fair-trade importers) and compared this group to that of a control sample of farmers living in the same area but having no relationship with fair trade. This study utilized a series of well-being indicators and a variety of techniques ranging from descriptive statistics to multiple equation systems in which the effect of fair-trade affiliation is evaluated controlling for selection biases.

This study found that the most important impact of fair-trade affiliation is farmers' satisfaction. This satisfaction was traced to a combination of the in-kind benefits that affiliates received[4] and the reduction of risk that they enjoyed due to diversified product portfolios, the stability of prices and purchases provided by Meru Herbs, and the impact of fair trade in the export channel. These factors were the main drivers of the positive and significant effects of fair trade on price and income satisfaction, food consumption, dietary quality, and child mortality. Another interesting finding of this study was that product diversification, which is not included in fair-trade criteria, was one of the most important factors influencing producers' well-being. More specifically, fair-trade importers had introduced new products—such as mango, karkade, guava, and lemon—that were cultivated only by affiliated farmers.

In this study, evaluating the main fair-trade criterion—the price premium—was difficult due to a mismatch in the product portfolios of affiliated and control farmers: a first group of products (sorghum, maize, millet, and okra) was produced by both groups but sold only on the local market. For these products, there was no evidence of better price conditions for affiliated farmers. *Pili-pili*, a variety of red pepper, is the only product that was both sold to fair traders by affiliated farmers and produced and sold through traditional trade channels by control group farmers. For this product, the price premium was large and statistically significant.

The Becchetti and Costantino (2008) study shows that producers' relationships with fair-trade importers are not necessarily exclusive: farmers with longer affiliations with Meru Herbs sold 60 per cent of their production through fair-trade channels, while those with shorter affiliations sold less than 40 per cent. This is a widespread characteristic of relationships between fair traders and first-level producer organizations. In this respect, Hopkins (2000), Nelson and Galvez (2000), Oxford Policy Management (2000), Ronchi (2002), and Bacon (2005) all observe that fair-trade importers do not force affiliated farmers to sell exclusively through fair-trade channels, and these farmers often sell a small proportion of their produce in the local market and through traditional intermediaries. Production for self-consumption and for sale on local markets are also mentioned in Pariente (2000), Castro (2001a, 2001b), and in the previous studies cited.

An important methodological aspect of the Becchetti and Costantino (2008) study is that it discriminates between two possible explanations of the findings: the success of the affiliated producers is due to the direct effects of fair trade or, alternatively, to the superior ex ante characteristics of the affiliates. This issue arises since it is likely that farmers who are more skilled will choose to belong to producer associations. By using a treatment regression model,[5] the study shows that part of the beneficial effects of fair trade are due to an ex ante selection bias, but also that a larger part of the effects can be traced to the impact of fair trade.

Although this finding partially mitigates the impact of fair trade on producers' well-being and leads to the conclusion that effects of fair trade may be exaggerated, the existence of positive externalities and spillovers point in the opposite direction since the dampening of differences between fair-trade affiliated and control farmers would lead to an underestimation of the fair-trade effect. More precisely, externalities may arise if the knowledge assimilated by Meru-affiliated farmers is spread by verbal communication to farmers in the control group. Another transmission effect may occur if the existence of Meru Herbs also increases the bargaining power of non-affiliated farmers, since they may demand better price conditions from traditional intermediaries by threatening to affiliate with Meru Herbs.[6]

Using the data from the Meru Herbs study, the impact of fair-trade affiliation upon price conditions and received technical assistance can be tested econometrically. A standardized index of price conditions (SIPC) was constructed for the *i*-th farmer selling the *j*-th ($j=1,\ldots,n_i$)[7] product on the market:

$$SIPC_i = \frac{1}{n_i} \sum_{j=1}^{n_i} \frac{P_{ij} - \mu_{Pj}}{\sigma_{Pj}} \tag{8.1}$$

where μ_{P_j} and σ_{P_j} are, respectively, the mean and standard deviation of the product j price in the overall sample. The standardized index was regressed in a Tobit[8] specification on various potential determinants including fair-trade membership and producers' socio-demographic characteristics

The findings clearly show the positive and significant effect of affiliation to the Conversion group (Meru Herbs members of recent affiliation) on the index (Table 8.1, column 2). No other variables appear to be significant in the estimate.

As mentioned above, affiliated farmers receive goods and services (seeds and small fruit trees, organic fertilizers, and periodical training meetings about organic farming procedures) as benefits of their affiliation to Meru Herbs. In order to test this comparative advantage, a logit model was estimated in which the dependent variable takes the value of one if the farmer reported receiving technical assistance from the buyer and zero otherwise. The dependent variable was regressed on the usual set of controls, and two of these—the number of years of farmer's schooling and of the farmer's affiliation to Meru Herbs—have a positive and significant impact on it (Table 8.1, column 4). These findings show that technical assistance is an important difference between affiliated and non-affiliated farmers in the area.

The study of Meru Herbs proposes an approach to empirical impact studies of fair trade that should be further developed. The frontier of research in this field concerns the capacity of properly measuring externalities generated by fair trade. Does fair trade help affiliated farmers to increase their bargaining power and improve sales conditions in local markets? Does the introduction and development of fair-trade projects in a region affect wage and price conditions of non-affiliated as well as affiliated farmers? These two questions are important because in addition to easily measurable direct effects, fair trade influences demand and supply in local markets and has 'general equilibrium' effects on the local area involving prices, wages, and employment of affiliated and non-affiliated workers. Further refinements of estimation techniques and a better understanding of the affiliation criteria of first-level associations is also needed to disentangle the selection effect from the contribution of fair trade to farmers' well-being.

Another important issue for impact studies of fair trade is the choice of well-being indicators (purely economic ones such as consumption and income versus socio-economic or capability indicators). An interesting finding of the Meru Herbs study is that the superior life and income satisfaction of affiliated farmers depends upon their significantly lower wage aspirations with respect to the control sample. The apparent rationale for this finding is that the complimentary services offered to members reduce producers' dependence upon the market.

Effects of fair trade on social capital

Beyond the myth of the direct relationship between importers and individual producers, fair trade is a virtuous twinning between alternative trade organizations

Table 8.1 Impact of affiliation to Meru Herbs on the standardized index of price conditions (SIPC)

Dep. Var.	SIPC		TECHASS
Bio	0.033	Workyear	0.277**
	[0.235]		[0.073]
Conversion	0.648**	Male	−0.946
	[0.253]		[0.585]
Control	−0.020	Birth	−0.033
	[0.253]		[0.028]
Male	−0.152	Married	−1.221
	[0.176]		[1.054]
Birth	−0.012	Schoolyears	0.162**
	[0.008]		[0.062]
Married	0.032	Famsize	−0.026
	[0.150]		[0.124]
Schoolyears	−0.011	Catholic	−0.237
	[0.019]		[0.534]
Famsize	−0.028	Acres	−0.021
	[0.032]		[0.043]
Catholic	−0.053	Employees	−0.058
	[0.172]		[0.119]
Acres	−0.014	Othincome	0.826
	[0.008]		[0.693]
Employees	0.037	Peoplehome	0.206
	[0.055]		[0.135]
Othincome	0.062	Noothact	0.170
	[0.212]		[0.686]
Peoplehome	−0.020		
	[0.038]		
Noothact	0.069		
	[0.219]		
Constant	23.311	Constant	64.976
	[15.252]]		[55.999]
LR $\chi2(15)$	18.68	LR $\chi2(19)$	15.80
Prob $> \chi 2$	0.2857	Prob $> \chi 2$	36.83
Pseudo R^2	0.0845	Pseudo R^2	0.282
Observations	90	Observations	96

Notes
Variable legend
SIPC: standardized index of price condition (see Equation 8.1 in the text); TECHASS: dummy variable taking value of one if the farmer recieved technical assistance in the last two years and zero otherwise.
The two indexes are dependent variables (in columns 1 and 2) in Tobit specifications since both dependent variables have upper and lower bounds.
Legend of regressors
Control (Bio, conversion): dummy variable taking the value of one if the farmer belongs to the Control (Bio, conversion) group and zero otherwise; *Male*: dummy variable taking the value of one for male respondents and zero otherwise; *Birth*: year of birth; *Married*: dummy variable taking the value of one for married respondents and zero otherwise; *Schoolyears*: schooling years of the respondent; *Famsize*: number of respondent's children; *Catholic*: dummy variable taking the value of one if the farmer is Catholic and zero otherwise; *Acres*: extent in acres of the farmer's land; *Employees*: number of employees hired during the harvesting season; *Othincome*: dummy variable taking the value of one if the respondent has additional sources of income and zero otherwise; *Peoplehome*: number of people living in the respondent's home; *Noothact*: dummy variable taking the value of one if the respondent has another work activity and zero otherwise. Results on ethnic group affiliation dummies are omitted for reasons of space.
* 90 per cent significance, ** 95 per cent significance. Robust standard errors in square brackets.

and first- or second-level producer associations based in developing countries. Hence, an implicit and not duly emphasized effect of fair trade is its capacity to reinforce the social capital of local producers.

Social capital refers to trustworthiness in interpersonal relationships, civic sense, trust in institutions, and the willingness to pay for public goods. Economists have increasingly focused on the role of these factors since they crucially influence more easily measurable and traditionally studied factors such as input productivities and economic outputs. From this point of view, trust is a 'lubricant' (Arrow 1974) of the socio-economic system since most economic transactions occur in an asymmetric information framework in which mutual confidence is fundamental to ensure their functioning and success.

Becchetti and Michetti (2008) identify a channel through which economic activity and economic transactions reinforce rather than erode social capital. They demonstrate that fair trade may have positive effects on trust in institutions and on political participation by producers. Specifically, participation in elections by farmers affiliated to Meru Herbs was 25 per cent higher than by control-group farmers and the number of years of affiliation had a significant negative effect on the probability of mistrusting political parties, trade unions, and the government.

These findings are particularly relevant in light of the socio-political conflicts that exploded in Kenya after the 2008 elections. Due to a disagreement about the validity of elections between the two main parties, post-election violence escalated to the point that the country was on the brink of civil war.[9] The conflict eventually was contained thanks in part to the relatively high level of social capital that existed in Kenya in the form of trust in government, political parties, and trade unions. This development serves as a powerful reminder that civic associations, which are encouraged and supported by fair trade, are a form of social capital that is of foremost importance in developing countries.

The importance of reinforcing social capital is further confirmed by economists who identify this factor as one of the main determinants of success or failure of development policies in sub-Saharan Africa. Easterly *et al.* (2000) observe that efforts of pro-poor (growth plus equity) policies are often frustrated by insufficient leadership on the part of local rulers and, even more importantly, by these leaders' lack of manoeuvring room due to weak institutions and insufficient social cohesion. The relationship between social capital and the quality of institutions is therefore mutually reinforcing: greater trust and civil virtues strengthen and stabilize institutions, while the quality of institutions buttresses social capital. In this sense, it is argued that high-quality institutions—measured by factors such as rule of law, bureaucratic quality, freedom from government expropriation, and freedom from government repudiation of contracts—mitigate the adverse economic effects of ethnic fractionalization (Easterly and Levine 1997).

These considerations and the results of impact studies illustrate an important point. Trust, trustworthiness, and civic sense are the basis of the good functioning not only of markets but also of institutions. These values need to be constantly nourished by society in order to avoid their progressive deterioration. The fair-trade initiative contributes to this process by supporting capacity building and inclusion in global markets of those local productive organizations that are well equipped to reinforce social capital.

Externalities, human capital investment, and the role of tourism

Two recent impact analyses conducted in Peru highlight some unexamined aspects of fair trade.[10] Becchetti *et al.* (2007a) focus on the problem of externalities by evaluating whether fair-trade affiliation strengthens the bargaining power of marginalized producers and improves trading conditions in local markets vis-à-vis intermediaries. They also investigate whether the introduction of fair trade generates demand and supply changes that affect the well-being of non-affiliated producers in the area.

An important innovation in this study was the use of a retrospective panel approach to reconstruct the schooling decisions made by affiliated producers in order to evaluate the impact of years of fair-trade affiliation on human capital investment. To understand how this works, consider that a common problem with empirical field research in development economics is the costs and difficulties of repeating surveys on the same individuals at different moments in time. A partial solution is to reconstruct past information based on a single survey in which respondents are asked about memorable events that occurred in the past (McIntosh *et al.* 2008). The retrospective panel data approach to human capital reconstructs schooling decisions by asking simple information about the number of children, their ages, and years of schooling. The underlying assumption is that this information is easily remembered by respondents (and certainly easier than, for example, recalling past levels of income). A further innovation of this study was the comparative evaluation of fair-trade prices with sale prices not only to traditional local intermediaries but also to socially responsible travellers.[11]

Becchetti *et al.* (2007a) identify a positive and non-linear pattern in the impact of years of fair-trade affiliation on producers' income and food expenditure, along with a linear pattern determined by trade channel diversification. A plausible interpretation of this non-linearity is that year-to-year returns from capacity building and positive fair-trade externalities in the area are strong at the beginning but decline over time. In essence, there are two main effects. The first (non-linear effect) shows that each additional affiliation year promotes capacity building, helps producers to adapt their products to foreign markets, and increases productivity with effects that tend to be progressively smaller over time. The second (linear effect) shows that one of the main benefits of fair trade comes from its simple characteristic of providing marginalized producers with an additional market for sales that helps them to diversify risk and reduce their vulnerability. These findings, similar to those of many other impact studies, provide evidence against the myth that producers affiliated to fair-trade organizations are forced to sell only through fair-trade channels. On the contrary, this study shows that affiliated farmers diversify risk by continuing to sell part of their production on the local market and even to traditional transportation intermediaries, who are now forced to be competitive with fair-trade organizations.

Another finding of this study is that fair trade reinforces the bargaining power of marginalized producers vis-à-vis local intermediaries. This finding is based both on a comparison of prices with non-fair-trade intermediaries for the treatment and control samples and on producers' responses to a direct survey question on this issue. In contrast, evidence about the impact of externalities on other local producers is mixed since in only one of the two projects studied were the conditions of non-fair-trade producers in the area improved by the presence of fair-trade projects. This implies that LeClair's (2002) hypothesis that fair trade has negative effects on the demand of non-affiliated producers can only be rejected in one of the two cases.

A further point documented by this study for the first time is that the price premium paid by 'ethical travellers' is even larger than that paid by fair traders. This seems reasonable since the two groups are motivated by the same principles of social responsibility, but fair-trade importers must bear logistic costs for transporting products to responsible consumers in the North. In addition, sales to responsible travellers are shown to have greater positive effects on producers' self-esteem since they interact directly with the final consumers of their products.

Becchetti *et al.* (2007a) conclude with an observation that integrates the specific findings of many impact studies: the effects of fair trade depend upon the initial standard of living of the marginalized producers involved. In the study of the project in which the initial standard of living was much lower (the control sample of the Juliaca producers live on an average on 60 US cents per day) the effect on life satisfaction of the additional income arising from the price premium and other fair-trade benefits is markedly higher than in the project in which the initial standard of living was higher (the control sample of producers in the Chulucanas project live on about US\$4 per day).[12]

The other side of the coin, however, is that positive and significant effects on child schooling only occur when producers have sufficiently high initial standards of living. More specifically, the Juliaca producers used all their additional resources to increase their consumption and stabilize their incomes without significant effects on schooling decisions. The schooling effect was only clearly evident and significant for the Chulucanas producers, who initially had a far higher standard of living. Consistent with Basu's (2000) luxury axiom, the schooling decision was triggered when household incomes passed a given threshold that was between the standards of living of the project-affiliated producers in Juliaca and Chulucanas. The underlying assumption is that parents want to send their children to school but cannot when their incomes are below a subsistence level that makes schooling expenses and the opportunity cost of scholarization (the foregone income from child work) too high.

Important policy considerations follow from these results. First, descriptive evidence indicates that fair trade is an effective instrument for improving the economic well-being and life satisfaction of producers. Second, the findings documented above show that the most important mechanisms leading to these results are opportunities for export diversification and capacity building. Third, fair trade appears to be a finely tuned policy for addressing antitrust problems in transnational food and textile value chains. In the absence of proper antitrust measures against monopolies or conditions of unequal market power within the value chain, consumer purchases of fair-trade products serve as a bottom-up mechanism that strengthens the position of producers vis-à-vis transportation and credit intermediaries.

Finally, given the limits of fair trade, further progress needs to be made in infrastructural development by strengthening the link among fair trade, schooling decisions, and wealth accumulation. For this purpose, it may be useful in the future to link fair-trade intervention to complementary actions by international organizations and local governments involving infrastructure and schooling policies.

Consumers' willingness to pay for fair-trade products

In the static and dynamic versions of the contagion model presented above, several assumptions were made about consumers' tastes for social responsibility. Specifically, it was argued that these consumers have non-zero willingness to pay for the ethical features of fair-trade products and that their ethical tastes may evolve in different ways according to how long they have made purchases from fair traders or from profit-maximizing imitators. In this section, empirical evidence is provided to support these assumptions.

Several marketing surveys on consumers' tastes for social responsibility have been conducted over the last decade. A survey of a balanced sample of the Italian population documents that 40 per cent of the population claim to have purchased fair-trade products at least once in the previous year, while 20 per cent have done so more frequently (Demos & Pi 2004). The existence of a significant proportion of socially responsible consumers in the overall population is confirmed by similar studies in the UK (Bird and Hughes 1997), Belgium (De Pelsmacker *et al.* 2003), and Germany (Zick Varul 2009).

The limitation of these surveys is that they provide simple descriptive findings about the proportions of 'ethical' consumers that exist in various countries and uncritically assume that declarations about the willingness to pay reflect the actual extent to which consumers make fair-trade purchases. The contingent valuation literature, however, suggests that such declarations may be affected by many biases (Mitchell and Carson 1989), the most relevant in this case being that a self-declaration of ethical virtues is costless, so there will tend to be an upward bias in the estimates of the proportion of ethically concerned consumers.

Becchetti and Rosati (2007) examined demand and willingness-to-pay by performing descriptive and econometric analyses of a sample of about 1,000 Italian fair-trade consumers. Utilizing a simultaneous two-equation treatment effect model, they conclude that fair-trade products are a special kind of 'awareness goods'. The demand for these goods depends upon standard factors—such as

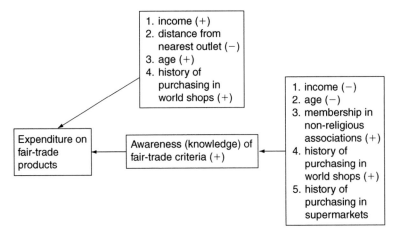

Figure 8.1 Model of 'awareness intensive' demand for fair-trade goods.

age, income, and geographical distance from the sales outlet—plus an additional factor of knowledge about fair-trade criteria, which is in turn affected by the same demographic variables that directly influence product demand (see Figure 8.1). This complex pattern of relationships provides the basis for interpreting econometric results that would otherwise be difficult to understand.

For instance, a simple standard regression of the demand for fair-trade products on various controls shows that demand is not significantly affected by income and age. The estimation of the two-equation model, however, indicates that this finding obscures a more complex pattern of relationships. Age and income have positive and significant effects on product demand similar to other consumption estimates of this kind, but older and richer individuals know significantly less about the fair-trade criteria that positively affect fair-trade purchases. This second effect dampens the combined impact of income and age on consumption.

Becchetti and Rosati's (2007) study has important policy implications. Age cohort effects exert a strong influence on fair trade, but fair-trade sales can greatly benefit by a higher investment in the diffusion of fair-trade knowledge in the older generation and in the highest income population. On the one hand, these findings imply that fair-trade sales can be boosted for consumers in their thirties, which is an age cohort that has stronger fair-trade consumption habits, and as they grow older these consumers increase their purchasing power. On the other hand, advertising campaigns targeting higher income groups and older age cohorts may have higher short-term returns given their relatively lower level of information and higher purchasing capacity.

Tables 8.2 to 8.6 provide further evidence about the characteristics of ethical consumers in Italy. These data were collected through interviews of a random sample of around 1,000 consumers purchasing products in world shops. The questionnaire included items about the socio-demographic characteristics and

Table 8.2 Daily expenditure (in €) by Italian consumers on fair-trade products

	Top third of income distribution	Middle third of income distribution	Bottom third of income distribution	Entire sample
Professional status				
Student	0.46	0.47	0.41	0.47
Teacher	1.07	0.73	0.78	0.73
Manual worker	0.89	1.17	0.72	1.17
Clerk	0.96	0.76	0.72	0.76
Retired worker	1.33	0.93	0.90	0.93
Membership				
Non-confessional associations	0.93	0.97	0.93	0.97
Confessional associations	0.61	0.71	0.91	0.71
Political party	0.81	0.61	0.66	0.61
NGOs	0.47	0.80	1.01	0.80
Distance from the nearest fair-trade outlet				
<10 minutes	0.65	0.72	0.80	0.72
10–20 minutes	0.82	0.86	0.78	0.85
20–40 minutes	0.66	0.67	0.64	0.65
>40 minutes	0.40	0.45	0.65	0.45
Gender				
Male	0.79	0.71	0.67	0.71
Female	0.62	0.74	0.77	0.74
Religious beliefs				
Believers	0.64	0.74	0.79	0.74
Consumers purchasing fair-trade products				
In world shops only	0.71	0.76	0.75	0.76
Also in supermarkets	0.51	0.56	0.70	0.56

Source: Becchetti and Rosati (2007: 821).

purchasing habits of fair-trade consumers, awareness of fair-trade criteria, qualities and/or disservices in the fair-trade product chain, and consumers' willingness to pay in excess for the social responsibility features of fair-trade products (Becchetti and Rosati 2007).

Table 8.2 shows daily expenditure on fair-trade products in relationship to income distribution. The average expenditure for fair-trade products is €0.75 per day, which is about €20 per month. The groups with the highest expenditure are volunteers in non-religious associations (€0.97) and retired workers (€0.93). Overall, these figures may seem low, but it should be noted that world shops do not sell fresh products that need to be acquired daily.[13]

Table 8.3 presents data on the declared willingness of Italian consumers to 'pay in excess' for the social characteristics of fair-trade products. The willingness to

Table 8.3 Declared willingness of Italian consumers to 'pay in excess' for the social characteristics of fair-trade products (€ per month for overall food expenditure)

	Top third of income distribution	Middle third of income distribution	Bottom third of income distribution	Entire sample
Professional status				
Student	51.54	51.86	51.49	51.86
Teacher	50.00	51.14	50.00	51.14
Manual worker	45.00	50.93	50.00	50.93
Clerk	52.89	55.58	52.74	55.58
Retired worker	50.00	53.13	42.86	53.13
Membership				
Non-confessional associations	52.94	58.25	52.43	58.25
Confessional associations	50.69	57.84	55.66	57.84
Political parties	50.00	55.09	67.50	55.09
NGOs	50.00	51.73	51.86	51.72
Distance from the nearest fair-trade outlet				
<10 minutes	46.64	54.19	51.58	54.19
10–20 minutes	52.27	54.54	54.28	54.54
20–40 minutes	52.14	53.23	50.54	53.23
>40 minutes	60.00	56.86	65.00	56.86
Gender				
Male	52.36	55.06	51.58	55.06
Female	49.72	54.23	54.58	54.23
Religious beliefs				
Believers	50.00	55.14	54.47	55.14
Consumers purchasing fair-trade products				
In world shops only	50.20	55.02	53.80	55.02
Also in supermarkets	54.41	52.01	52.54	52.01

Source: Becchetti and Rosati (2007: 828).

pay in excess for fair-trade food products (against non-fair-trade products of the same quality sold at the same geographical distance) is about €50 per month and goes up to €58 for volunteers in non-religious associations. This is clearly not in line with actual expenditure, since Italian consumers do not spend on average more than €35 per month for these products. If the declared willingness to pay in excess was truthful, it would incur an actual expenditure of at least €50.

In order to interpret this data, it must be kept in mind that the willingness to pay in excess with respect to equivalent non-fair-trade products is a far different concept than effective expenditure. It is an ideal situation that implies an exactly equivalent non-socially responsible product can be found with no distance differential and that full information on the socially responsible features of fair-trade products is available.

This may not be the case if consumers do not find enough products (equivalent to the non-fair-trade product that they would have bought) in a world shop. Furthermore, asymmetric information may be such that consumers maintain some doubts about the fair-trade features of the products. These doubts are likely to affect the gap between actual expenditure and willingness to pay in excess. Other reasons that may explain this inconsistency are difficulties in understanding the question or a form of interview bias in which consumers aim to convey their sensitiveness to the issue by exaggerating social preferences.

Table 8.4 examines the determinants of fair-trade expenditure in single-equation estimates under different model specifications. The most significant regressor is the knowledge of at least five of the fair-trade criteria. Other significant factors are a purchasing history of fair-trade products in world shops and supermarkets.

Table 8.5 identifies those factors correlated with Italian consumers' perceived limitations of fair-trade products. These results indicate that distance from the nearest fair-trade outlet positively affects the probability of complaining about distance. This may seem obvious, but it is a useful check since it indicates that the two reported variables are reliable. Family income is positively and significantly related with complaints about distance and about the limited range of products. This illustrates another potential difficulty for fair-trade marketing: high-income individuals have a high opportunity cost of time and are accustomed to choosing among a wide range of products. The evidence suggests that when fair-trade products are distributed on a large scale, there is an increased probability of complaints about the limited range of products (the effect is around 10 per cent).

As has been shown, knowledge of fair-trade criteria is the most important determinant of expenditure on fair-trade products. Table 8.6 identifies the effects of different control variables on the knowledge of specific fair-trade criteria. A first important finding is the positive role of a history of purchasing in world shops. This variable raises by about 10 per cent the probability of a respondent's awareness of each criterion. By comparison, a history of purchasing in supermarkets significantly raises awareness of only one criterion—the environmental sustainability of fair-trade production processes.

Table 8.4 Determinants of fair-trade expenditures by Italian consumers

Log(Distance)	−0.220	−0.223	−0.212	−0.208	−0.188	−0.150
	(−3.86)	(−3.86)	(−3.63)	(−3.63)	(−3.46)	(−2.87)
Log(Income)	−0.009	−0.004	0.010	0.066	0.141	0.154
	(−0.11)	(−0.06)	(0.12)	(0.76)	(1.69)	(1.88)
Male		0.013	0.010	−0.019	−0.071	−0.081
		(0.14)	(0.11)	(−0.21)	(−0.85)	(−0.98)
Log(Age)		0.738	0.735	0.371	0.400	0.437
		(5.36)	(5.27)	(2.14)	(2.42)	(2.58)
Log(School)		0.223	0.243	0.065	−0.061	−0.108
		(0.94)	(1.02)	(0.29)	(−0.28)	(−0.51)
North-East			−0.071	−0.018	0.100	0.094
			(−0.36)	(−0.09)	(0.53)	(0.49)
North-West			0.284	0.289	0.324	0.270
			(1.99)	(2.00)	(2.36)	(2.01)
South			0.166	0.191	0.211	0.176
			(1.42)	(1.61)	(1.92)	(1.66)
Faith				−0.103	−0.156	−0.128
				(−1.15)	(−1.77)	(−1.47)
Student				−0.519	−0.360	−0.347
				(−3.48)	(−2.52)	(−2.45)
Teacher				−0.048	0.111	0.127
				(−0.19)	(0.52)	(0.60)
Manualworker				−0.023	0.124	0.138
				(−0.06)	(0.31)	(0.35)
Clerk				−0.219	−0.191	−0.171
				(−2.01)	(−1.91)	(−1.74)
Ncvol					0.572	0.461
					(6.57)	(5.19)
Cvol					0.081	0.038
					(0.77)	(0.37)
NGO					0.232	0.173
					(2.06)	(1.53)
Log(FidelWS)					0.252	0.188
					(3.43)	(2.56)
WSonly					0.353	0.350
					(2.92)	(2.91)
Log(FidelS)					0.273	0.245
					(3.37)	(3.13)
Knowmostcriteria						0.466
						(5.44)
Nocomplaints						0.127
						(1.38)
Constant	−0.274	−3.473	−3.709	−2.12	−3.438	−3.700
	(−0.42)	(−3.76)	(−3.96)	(−1.93)	(−3.20)	(−3.41)
No. of Obs.	725	701	701	701	701	701
F-test on overall	(2, 722)	(5, 695)	(8, 692)	(13, 687)	(19, 681)	(21, 679)
significance	7.59	9.79	7.28	5.85	12.15	13.14
Adj. R^2	0.021	0.063	0.069	0.088	0.212	0.241

Source: Becchetti and Rosati (2007: 826).

Notes
Legend
Dependent variable: daily expenditure on fair-trade products.
Explanatory variables
Numdistance: declared distance from the nearest fair-trade world shop in minutes; *Income*: average net family income calculated as monthly after-tax family income minus or plus all other income flows (i.e. mortgages, housing rents, etc.); *School*: average schooling years; *North-East*: dummy for consumer location in the north-east of the country (Trentino-Alto Adige, Veneto, Friuli-Venezia Giulia, Emilia Romagna); *North-West*: dummy for consumer location in the north-west of the country (Piemonte, Valle D'Aosta, Lombardia, Liguria); *South*: dummy for consumer location in the south of the country (Calabria, Campania, Puglia, Sardegna, Sicilia); *Faith*: dummy taking value of one if the respondent is believer and zero otherwise; *Ncvol*: volunteer in non-confessional associations; *Cvol*: volunteeer in confessional associations; *NGO*: members of a non-governmental organization; *FidelWS*: duration of fair-trade purchasing habits (number of years); *WSonly*: dummy for those purchasing from world shops only; *FidelS*: duration of purchasing habits of fair-trade products in supermarkets (number of years); *Knowmostcriteria*: knowledge of at least five out of eight fair-trade criteria; *Nocomplaints*: absence of complaints about fair-trade sale organization.

Table 8.5 Limitations of fair-trade products as perceived by Italian consumers

	Limitfood	Limitidress	Limitiobject	Badtime	Badpers	Badplace	Noprod	Noonline
Male	-0.043 (-1.55)	-0.054 (-1.42)	-0.027 (-0.73)	-0.015 (-0.58)	0.037 (1.78)	0.005 (0.16)	-0.059 (-1.68)	0.006 (0.25)
Log(Distance)	0.0001 (0.19)	-0.0008 (-0.57)	0.001 (0.87)	-0.001 (-1.31)	0.0006 (0.86)	0.007 (6.02)	-0.002 (-1.52)	-0.0008 (-0.86)
Log(Income)	-0.00001 (-0.47)	-0.00004 (-1.52)	0.0001 (1.93)	-0.0001 (-0.22)	-0.00002 (-1.29)	0.00005 (2.54)	-0.00003 (-1.32)	0.00001 (0.71)
Log(Age)	0.040 (0.72)	-0.123 (-1.65)	0.184 (2.48)	-0.015 (-0.31)	-0.046 (-1.17)	-0.076 (-1.12)	0.024 (0.34)	-0.060 (-1.25)
Log(School)	0.034 (0.46)	0.070 (0.70)	-0.111 (-1.16)	0.115 (1.57)	0.0228 (0.43)	0.012 (0.13)	0.030 (0.32)	0.207 (2.77)
Faith	0.023 (0.80)	0.008 (0.21)	0.075 (1.98)	-0.00003 (-0.00)	0.011 (0.52)	0.030 (0.86)	0.030 (0.82)	0.041 (1.68)
Student	0.032 (0.69)	-0.021 (-0.35)	0.089 (1.46)	-0.028 (-0.70)	-0.041 (-1.39)	0.025 (0.45)	0.010 (0.18)	0.068 (1.68)
Teacher	-0.016 (-0.20)	0.187 (1.75)	-0.024 (-0.22)	-0.090 (-1.34)	0.012 (0.21)	-0.067 (-0.71)	0.013 (0.12)	-0.045 (-0.70)
Manualworker	-0.023 (-0.26)	0.133 (1.17)	-0.210 (-2.01)	-0.006 (-0.22)	0.076 (1.13)	-0.123 (-1.30)	0.138 (1.24)	-0.029 (-0.34)
Clerk	0.010 (0.30)	0.067 (1.49)	0.015 (0.35)	-0.006 (-0.22)	0.003 (0.13)	-0.002 (-0.05)	0.011 (0.25)	-0.023 (-0.80)
Ncvol	0.023 (0.78)	-0.006 (-0.15)	0.049 (1.26)	0.002 (0.08)	0.008 (0.40)	-0.037 (-1.05)	0.068 (1.83)	0.031 (1.23)
Cvol	0.012 (0.34)	0.052 (1.11)	0.033 (0.75)	0.051 (1.60)	-0.032 (-1.35)	-0.082 (-2.01)	0.008 (0.19)	-0.014 (-0.47)
NGO	0.077 (1.84)	0.062 (1.13)	0.024 (0.46)	0.001 (0.03)	0.004 (0.13)	-0.065 (-1.36)	0.047 (0.92)	0.008 (0.22)
Log(FidelS)	0.114 (4.51)	0.122 (3.13)	0.091 (2.45)	-0.009 (-0.34)	-0.002 (-0.13)	0.052 (1.53)	-0.002 (-0.06)	-0.046 (-1.71)
Log(FidelWS)	0.016 (0.74)	0.049 (1.70)	-0.060 (-2.14)	0.013 (0.68)	-0.013 (-0.90)	-0.056 (-2.16)	0.047 (1.75)	0.002 (0.12)
North-East	-0.099 (-1.70)	-0.114 (-1.41)	-0.078 (-1.00)	0.029 (0.53)	0.015 (0.35)	-0.0128 (-1.89)	-0.018 (-0.24)	-0.080 (-1.85)
North-West	-0.004 (-0.08)	-0.020 (-0.31)	-0.104 (-1.69)	0.038 (0.87)	0.042 (1.19)	-0.155 (-2.67)	-0.100 (-1.72)	-0.045 (-1.12)
South	0.071 (1.89)	0.147 (2.96)	0.018 (0.37)	0.035 (1.01)	-0.064 (-2.50)	-0.083 (-1.97)	-0.015 (-0.32)	-0.010 (-0.34)
Num.Obs	793	793	793	769	793	793	793	793
$LR\chi^2$	(18) 40.87	(18) 44.22	(18) 36.70	(17) 14.71	(18) 21.85	(18) 81.55	(18) 21.16	(18) 32.01
PseudoR^2	0.0016	0.0403	0.0348	0.0246	0.0457	0.0862	0.0211	0.0526

Source: Becchetti and Rosati (2007: 825).

Notes

Variable legend
Disservices
Limitfood: limitations in the fair-trade food product range; Limitidress: limits in the fair-trade clothing product range; Limitiobject: limitations in the fair-trade product range; Badtime: reduced opening times of fair-trade shops; Badpers: lack of courtesy by world-shop personnel; Badplace: unsatisfactory location of the fair-trade outlet; Noprod: limitations in the fair-trade product range; Noonline: absence of online sales.

Regressors
Distance: declared distance from the nearest fair-trade world shop in minutes; Income: average net family income is calculated as monthly after-tax family income minus or plus all other income flows (i.e. mortgages, housing costs, etc.); Faith: dummy taking value of one if the respondent is believer and zero otherwise; Ncvol: volunteer in non-confessional associations; Cvol: volunteer in confessional associations; NGO: member of a non-governmental organization; FidelWS: history of purchasing in world shops (number of years); FidelS: history of purchasing in supermarkets (number of years); North-East: dummy for consumer location in the north-east of the country (Trentino-Alto Adige, Veneto, Friuli-Venezia Giulia, Emilia Romagna); North-West: dummy for consumer location in the north-west of the country (Piemonte, Valle D'Aosta, Lombardia, Liguria); South: dummy for consumer location in the south of the country (Calabria, Campania, Puglia, Sardegna, Sicilia).

Table 8.6 Determinants of Italian consumers' awareness of fair-trade criteria

	Fairprice	Prefin	Pricestab	Labour	Environ	Longrun	Transpar	Pgood
v	0.00065 (0.02)	-0.013 (-0.35)	0.030 (0.85)	-0.059 (-1.67)	-0.023 (-0.60)	0.014 (0.42)	-0.048 (-1.26)	-0.034 (-0.90)
Log(Income)	0.000015 (0.70)	-0.00001 (-0.39)	-0.00006 (-2.03)	-0.00001 (-0.14)	-0.00003 (-1.03)	-0.00002 (-0.76)	-0.00003 (-1.24)	-0.00001 (-0.039)
Age	-0.108 (-1.82)	0.067 (0.91)	-0.032 (-0.47)	-0.185 (-2.61)	-0.175 (-2.26)	-0.152 (-2.23)	-0.328 (-4.32)	-0.086 (-1.15)
School	0.183 (2.33)	0.153 (1.52)	0.135 (1.41)	0.199 (2.28)	0.108 (0.08)	0.103 (1.11)	-0.040 (-0.40)	0.036 (0.36)
Faith	-0.009 (-0.27)	0.027 (0.70)	-0.039 (-1.05)	-0.040 (-1.13)	-0.101 (-2.54)	-0.063 (-1.73)	-0.093 (-2.31)	-0.007 (-0.18)
Student	-0.095 (-1.83)	0.038 (0.63)	-0.038 (-0.68)	-0.132 (-2.25)	-0.131 (-2.10)	-0.074 (-1.39)	-0.054 (-0.89)	-0.084 (-1.41)
Teacher	-0.111 (-1.17)	0.127 (1.12)	-0.119 (-1.22)	0.083 (0.84)	-0.066 (-0.58)	0.083 (0.81)	-0.035 (-0.31)	0.098 (0.90)
Manualworker	-0.044 (-0.47)	-0.016 (-0.14)	-0.022 (-0.20)	-0.073 (-0.69)	-0.136 (-1.14)	0.026 (0.24)	-0.071 (-0.61)	-0.143 (-1.27)
Clerk	-0.006 (-0.17)	-0.108 (-2.47)	-0.034 (-0.83)	-0.058 (-1.35)	-0.015 (-0.33)	-0.039 (-0.98)	-0.032 (-0.70)	-0.071 (-1.62)
Ncvol	0.090 (2.72)	0.290 (7.43)	0.111 (2.96)	0.132 (3.61)	0.110 (2.73)	0.162 (4.45)	0.180 (4.51)	0.144 (3.65)
Cvol	0.079 (2.08)	0.065 (1.39)	0.083 (1.87)	0.077 (1.81)	0.112 (2.38)	0.078 (1.79)	0.111 (2.33)	0.058 (1.25)
NGO	-0.041 (-0.89)	0.105 (1.90)	0.129 (2.47)	0.026 (0.53)	0.080 (1.45)	0.089 (1.75)	0.036 (0.66)	0.149 (2.70)
Log(FidelS)	0.039 (1.14)	0.040 (1.06)	0.050 (1.43)	0.045 (1.19)	0.103 (2.57)	0.012 (0.35)	0.047 (1.22)	0.027 (0.71)
WSonly	0.044 (1.10)	0.057 (1.19)	-0.084 (-1.82)	-0.006 (-0.13)	0.083 (1.70)	-0.006 (-0.13)	0.063 (1.30)	0.041 (0.86)
Log(FidelWS)	0.050 (2.10)	0.129 (4.60)	0.139 (5.18)	0.104 (3.92)	0.098 (3.36)	0.111 (4.27)	0.127 (4.33)	0.117 (4.11)
North-East	0.043 (0.66)	-0.054 (-0.68)	-0.043 (-0.57)	0.019 (0.26)	0.085 (1.05)	0.009 (0.12)	0.018 (0.22)	0.022 (0.27)
North-West	0.089 (1.71)	-0.057 (-0.89)	-0.005 (-0.08)	0.119 (2.06)	0.020 (0.30)	0.098 (1.63)	-0.040 (-0.61)	0.079 (1.23)
South	0.016 (0.40)	-0.014 (-0.29)	-0.007 (-0.15)	0.037 (0.84)	0.024 (0.49)	-0.020 (-0.45)	-0.028 (-0.57)	-0.017 (-0.35)
Num. obs	793	793	793	793	793	793	793	793
$LR\chi^2(18)$	51.14	130.03	80.12	77.44	70.65	75.60	91.52	65.70
PseudoR²	0.0595	0.1251	0.0807	0.0794	0.0646	0.0792	0.0846	0.0614

Source: Becchetti and Rosati (2007: 826).

Notes
Variable legend
Awareness of fair-trade criteria
Fairprice: premium on the price paid on primary products by local intermediaries or food transnationals; *Prefin*: anticipated financing which reduces the impact of credit rationing of small uncollateralized producers; *Pricestab*: price stabilization mechanisms which insulate risk-averse primary product producers from the volatility of commodity prices; *Labour*: the intervention to improve working conditions and to remove factors leading to child labour through monetary integration of poor household income; *Environ*: attention to the environmental sustainability of production processes; *Longrun*: creation of long-run relationships between importers and producers and provision through them of export services; *Transpar*: transparency with customers about the characteristics of the product value chain; *Pgood*: preferential inclusion in the fair-trade chain of projects reinvesting part of the surplus arising from the fair price in the provision of local public goods (health, education, job training). For further details on these criteria, see the section 'The impact of fair trade on marginalized producers'.

Regressors
Income: average net family income is calculated as monthly after-tax family income minus or plus all other income flows (i.e. mortgages, housing rents, etc.); *School*: average schooling years; *Faith*: dummy taking value of one if the respondent is believer and zero otherwise; *Ncvol*: volunteer in non-confessional associations; *Cvol*: volunteer in confessional associations; *NGO*: membership in an NGO; *FidelS*: history of purchasing in world shops (number of years); *WSonly*: dummy for those purchasing from world shops only; *FidelS*: history of purchasing in supermarkets (number of years); *North-East*: dummy for consumer location in the North-East of the country (Trentino-Alto Adige, Veneto, Friuli-Venezia Giulia, Emilia Romagna); *North-West*: dummy for consumer location in the North-West of the country (Piemonte, Valle D'Aosta, Lombardia, Liguria); *South*: dummy for consumer location in the South of the country (Calabria, Campania, Puglia, Sardegna, Sicilia).

A second important finding is that higher education increases the likelihood that consumers are aware of the fair price, pre-financing, price stabilization, and labour standard criteria.[14] This may also be a limitation since full understanding of the fair-trade criteria seems to correspond to a minimum level of educational background. Other findings include that membership of non-religious volunteer associations increases the likelihood of respondents being aware of fair-trade criteria by about 30 per cent. This effect is greater than the positive and significant impact on awareness by membership in a religious organization of volunteers, which is only around 10 per cent.

Finally, it is interesting to note that a history of purchasing in supermarkets also contributes to the knowledge of several criteria including price stabilization, the environmental sustainability of fair-trade products, and purchases in world shops. This implies that product sales in supermarkets may not fully substitute for purchases from world shops, but rather produce positive externalities for such purchases.

A clear conclusion based on these findings is that education and membership of religious and non-religious organizations are the main drivers of fair-trade awareness, which in turn has a strong positive effect on purchases of fair-trade products.

The evolution of fair trade: hopes and reality

The increasing success of fair trade has paradoxically been accompanied by a series of conflicts of interest among the actors in this value chain. Most such conflicts directly stem from the success of fair trade and from its main beneficial effect: the capacity to trigger partial imitation in social responsibility by profit-maximizing competitors. The entry of large transnational competitors into the production and distribution of fair-trade products generates a range of reactions by original fair-trade promoters, since the new entrants are simultaneously both a sign of success and a threat. The decision of labelling organizations to certify fair-trade products of partial imitators (such as those of Nestlé or of supermarket chains) was not appreciated by many fair-trade importers and world shops, who reacted by creating an alternative label, the WFTO (World Fair Trade Organization) Mark, that certifies that not only a specific product but also the entire organization follows fair-trade rules. These are criteria that are difficult, if not impossible, for profit-maximizing transnationals to follow.

This development may have been the predictable outcome of competition in social responsibility among actors with different interests and objective functions. Some labelling organizations, such as members of the Fairtrade Labelling Organizations International (FLO), have benefited by certifying products of partial imitators who are not part of the fair-trade movement, while fair-trade importers and world shops have been averse to this development since it has created new competitors for them. The reaction of the fair-trade movement has been to communicate to consumers its ethical 'difference' of being fully dedic-ated to fair trade in its entire product line and investing significantly in increasing consumer awareness and promoting advocacy campaigns for fairness in international trade rules.

These developments confirm that fair trade has introduced significant changes in the way markets are conceived. First, fair trade has generated a new wave of products that are bundles of physical and ethical characteristics. Second, fair trade has improved the reputation of the market, which is no longer the place in which efficiency cannot be reconciled with redistribution and social inclusion. With fair trade, the market becomes a place where people vote for values promoting social inclusion and redistribution through their purchasing decisions. Finally, fair trade has promoted pioneering social entrepreneurs (fair-trade importers), partial imitation by profit-maximizing corporations, and competition in labelling processes; these developments have all contributed to transforming social responsibility from a residual value that inspired philanthropic activities into a competitive force.

These final considerations demonstrate that the overall goal of fair trade is hugely ambitious and considerably exceeds the effects it may have on marginalized producers. The real issue at stake is overcoming the dichotomy between the creation of economic value, which generates adverse social and environmental externalities, and the successive phase of social actions by philanthropic organizations that aim to ameliorate the negative by-products of economic activities. Social entrepreneurs demonstrate that it is possible to 'create value with values' by generating economic value in socially and environmentally responsible ways and by internalizing the negative externalities of many standard productive processes. This ambitious goal has implications not only for the future material well-being of marginalized producers, who are the intended beneficiaries of fair trade, but also for the quality of life and job satisfaction of the entire population of the planet.

Notes

1 This cooperative was formed in 1976 by the former employees of a glass factory in the village of Cantel, near Quetzaltenango.
2 The acronym MCCH stands for Maquita Cushunchic Comercializando como Hermanos, which in a mix of Quechua and Spanish means 'let's join hands and market as brothers'. This cooperative represents 400 Ecuadorian groups that produce handicrafts and agricultural products.
3 One of the goals of fair trade is to strengthen producers' capacities to organize themselves in associations or cooperatives in order to increase their bargaining power with credit and transportation intermediaries. This is why fair-trade importers prioritize the establishment of links with producers' organizations. Among these organizations, it is useful to distinguish 'first-level' associations or cooperatives whose members are individual producers from 'second-level' marketing or export consortia whose members are first-level cooperatives or associations.
4 Meru Herbs provides complimentary seeds and organic fertilizers to farmers, sells fruit trees for production at subsidized prices, organizes training courses in the implementation of organic farming techniques, and offers the services of two technicians to supervise and assist the affiliated farmers.
5 According to this approach, the standard performance equation in which the performance indicator is regressed on individual characteristics and fair-trade membership is

re-estimated jointly with a selection equation in which affiliation/non-affiliation to fair trade is regressed on a set of individual controls. This estimate allows for the disentangling of the presumed positive impact generated by the project (affiliated farmers perform better in a given indicator for the effects of fair trade) from the selection effect (affiliated farmers outperform the control sample simply because affiliation to fair trade is somewhat related to their ex ante characteristics correlated to high outcome). Disturbances of the two equations in the system are assumed to be correlated with each other and the likelihood function for its estimation is the standard one provided by Maddala (1983) and Greene (2000).

6 See Armendáriz and Morduch (2005) for the problem of externalities from treatments of control samples in impact studies.

7 The number of products sold (n) is indexed by i in order to take into account that it is different for any i-th farmer.

8 A Tobit model is used because the dependent variable has, by design, the value of one as its upper limit and zero as its lower limit.

9 It has been estimated that up to 1,000 people died during the eruption of post-election violence. Two notable economic consequences of this crisis were a sharp drop in tourist revenues with an estimated loss of 150,000 jobs and a health crisis due to a slowdown and interruption of treatments for HIV and other illnesses.

10 Becchetti *et al.* (2007a) examined associations of handicraft producers in Chulucanas and of wool-clothing producers in Juliaca. Both associations sell part of their production through fair-trade channels.

11 Ethical tourism is an initiative that aims to organize tourist activities while promoting environmental and social sustainability and fostering social–cultural exchange with the people that visitors meet. The socially responsible element generally implies that a higher share of the value generated by this kind of tourism goes to the local population.

12 Average living standards are always downward biased if self-consumption and self-production are taken into account. Therefore, these figures need to be revised upward by adding the market value of consumed goods that are directly produced and not purchased on the market.

13 In 2004, the average monthly expenditure of Italian consumers for the range of food products that can be bought in world shops was estimated to be around €32.80. Given that non-food products account for approximately one-third of fair-trade expenditure (€20 on average), it can be roughly determined that fair-trade consumers in the sample shifted, on average, around 45 per cent of their food consumption from non-fair-trade to fair-trade products.

14 Recall that pre-financing and price stabilization are among the less-known fair-trade criteria, with less than 40 per cent of consumers expressing awareness of them.

9   Microfinance

A frontier social enterprise

Leonardo Becchetti

> The rich can evade the consequences of non-payment; the poor cannot. They
> value access to credit so highly, and dislike the loan sharks so much, that they
> are only too grateful for a once-in-a-lifetime opportunity to improve
> themselves.
>
> Muhammad Yunus, founder of Grameen Bank

Over the last two decades, there has been an explosive growth of interest in
microfinance as a tool for alleviating poverty. One important reason for this is
that microfinance satisfies the twin goals of economic development and the
inclusion of marginalized people, reducing the mismatch between individuals
with talent but no wealth and those with wealth and no talent. Even though it is
obvious that not all loans end up in the hands of talented individuals, microfinance has this potential. Another reason is that in the field of banking, microfinance represents a breakthrough innovation that extends access to credit to the
'unbankable'—that is, to individuals lacking financial resources that can be used
as collateral for the sums borrowed.

Microfinance is an innovation that can make an important contribution to sustainable development and the conditional convergence of developing countries
to the level of economic well-being in developed countries. As shown in Chapter
4 of this volume, *conditional convergence* is a conceptual framework that has
been influential in empirical studies of growth and establishes that less-
developed countries can begin to catch up to developed ones by bridging the
gaps through convergence factors such as human capital, physical capital, physical and digital infrastructure, and quality of institutions. A microeconomic analysis of the laws governing economic growth shows that a crucial convergence
factor is the pursuit of equal opportunities (Aghion *et al.* 1999).

At the beginning of the industrial revolution, capital accumulation was the
priority and a degree of inequality was necessary in order to allow higher savings
by the rich to fuel economic growth. Today, however, financial resources are
abundant at the world level, and the growth potential of a given country is
achieved when all its inhabitants have access to credit and education and can
fully exploit their talents. By providing access to credit for the 'unbankable',

microfinance marks an important step forward in assuring such access and reconciling equal opportunities and economic development.

In terms of the specific contributions made by microfinance institutions (MFIs), the microfinance revolution marks the passage from the second to the third stage of development in the financial system. The first stage is characterized by individual moneylenders who were the only source of finance in pre-industrial societies and still perform this role in villages of less developed countries.

The second stage began with the rise of the modern banking system during the industrial revolution. The advent of this financial institution marked a significant improvement in social well-being, since banks provide several immaterial services and perform the crucial role of financial intermediaries between entrepreneurs and investors. By having illiquid assets and liabilities on their balance sheets, banks accept an element of vulnerability in order to provide those liquidity services that are essential for the continuity of productive investment. The other 'social virtues' of the banking system are its capacity to aggregate the savings of individual investors, allocate financial resources to the most productive activities, and restructure the duration and maturity of financial assets.

A general limitation of this second stage of finance is that access to credit is restricted to individuals who have sufficient financial resources to provide collateral, the value of which must generally be at least equal to that of the amount borrowed. This restriction occurs because asymmetric information between lenders and borrowers prevents banks from efficiently performing their role of allocating financial resources to the most productive destinations. Asymmetric information is influential in three specific phases of the financing process: *ex ante*, when lenders cannot assess precisely the quality of the projects and entrepreneurs; *in the interim*, when lenders cannot constantly monitor the behaviour and effort of borrowers; and *ex post*, when borrowers may be tempted to default strategically in order to avoid paying back their loans. For all these reasons, the requirement of collateral as a guarantee for a loan is the shortcut that overcomes (Wydick 1999; Karlan 2005) the problems of informational asymmetries by reducing or eliminating bank losses in cases of non-performing loans. This solution, however, is a problem for those borrowers who remain without credit due to their lack of financial assets.

The third stage of the financial system is the rise of MFIs, which were created precisely to address this problem. Empirical evidence demonstrates that these institutions are surprisingly successful in lending to uncollateralized borrowers without endangering their financial performance and actually have a proportion of non-performing loans that is lower than the average for the standard banking system (Armendáriz de Aghion and Morduch 2005).

The reasons for this success are open to debate. Some scholars emphasize technical features of MFIs such as group lending with joint liability (Banerjee *et al.* 1994; Gangopadhyay *et al.* 2005), individual progressive loans (Wydick 1999; Karlan 2005), and individual loans with notional collateral. Other scholars point to organizational and immaterial elements, including systematic monitoring and training activity by loan officers, social sanctions that discourage delinquent behaviour by borrowers, and the capacity to trigger borrowers' hidden resources such as promotion of their dignity and self-esteem.

The forerunners of microfinance

Even though microfinance is considered a recent development, it is not entirely new and has historical precedents. *Raiffeisen* (agricultural) banks were initially established in Austria and Germany at the end of the nineteenth century for the purpose of extending credit to poor farmers. These banks operated in an environment devoid of liquidity, where the only illiquid assets were land, houses, and livestock. In order to get access to credit, local farmers decided to consolidate their holdings as a guarantee for the loans their bank was giving to each of them. Raiffeisen banking was an extremely risky activity for bank members since it was based on unlimited liability. The high penalty implied by insolvent behaviour created a strong incentive for the borrowers and other bank members to restrain from monitoring moral hazard and strategic default behaviour, but did not protect them entirely from financial shocks and losses. Other institutions that belong to the same family of financial intermediaries are tontines, which were popular in Europe and the US in the eighteenth and nineteenth centuries, and rotating savings and credit associations (ROSCAs), which operate mainly in Africa and Asia to promote financial services for low-income individuals.

Tontines are informal financial organizations that provide life insurance services in informal credit markets. Tontines gather contributions from members, who receive interest payments during their lives; following a death, the capital of the tontine is redistributed among the remaining members. ROSCAs, on the other hand collect equal contributions from a set number of members into a common pool; on a rotating basis, members can withdraw part of the group's funds to finance the purchase of a durable good. This system has the advantage of fostering collective savings and easing access to financial services to uncollateralized poor individuals. The use of financial resources, however, is constrained to a proportion of the contribution to the pot and is not liquid (not immediately available) given the rotation principle. While sharing with these informal methods of collective savings the goal of easing access to 'unbankables', microfinance has the advantage of providing poor borrowers conventional bank debt with all the advantages of the standard banking system.

Microfinance is also clearly different from the traditional activity of local moneylenders, who are pervasive in financial markets in developing countries. Moneylenders usually have the advantage of bridging informational asymmetries with local borrowers and exploiting the opportunity of having more than one relationship (interlinkage) with them. Moneylenders are frequently not just lenders but also the borrowers' landlords, employers, or suppliers of essential goods and services. The existence of these multiple linkages allows moneylenders to reduce their risk even in the absence of collateral, since in cases of default they can compensate by exploiting the other economic relationships they have with borrowers (e.g. by reducing wages or increasing rents (Ray 1998)). These interlinkages are also such that it is not necessary for lenders to increase rates when loans are riskier. This explains why the empirically observed distribution of real rates of local moneylenders is highly heterogeneous, ranging from values close to zero to upper double digits. Paradoxical situations may exist in which the value of the collateral for the lender is higher than the value of the outstanding loan, such as when the collateral is a piece of land adjoining that of the moneylender. In such cases, moneylenders may actually prefer borrowers to default on their loans. In sum, even though moneylenders, in a sense, allow poor borrowers access to credit, the well-being of borrowers and their social and economic inclusion are not the moneylenders' goal.

The joint liability debate

The most important and widely debated technical feature of microfinance is that of group lending with joint liability, which entails making individual loans to a self-selected group of borrowers who are financially responsible if one of the members becomes insolvent. Since borrowers in small villages are generally more informed about their neighbours than a bank can be, MFIs exploit their informational advantage by utilizing joint liability to create a penalty in cases when there is the non-virtuous selection of groupmates (Morduch 1999; Ghatak and Guinnane 1999). It is in the interest of borrowers to create groups with the most productive villagers in order to reduce the probability of having to pay the joint liability penalty.

Joint liability is not a magic solution for all problems. First, even though the reduction of risk reduces the cost of loans when MFIs are not-for-profit, joint liability poses a heavy burden on groupmates' shoulders and requires them to perform a monitoring activity that is usually done by the bank. Furthermore, the incentive to virtuous selection does not prevent low-quality borrowers from creating groups among themselves when the alternative of joining productive borrowers is not available.

In addition, size is important since groups that are too small may increase borrowers' burdens in terms of monitoring costs and the joint liability penalty, while groups that are too large create free-rider effects and reduce the responsibility and incentive that individuals have for monitoring groupmates.

Last but not least, the dynamics of the interim phase in the lending process may create the phenomenon of 'borrowers run' (Bond and Rai 2009), which may happen if a borrower comes to know in advance that a groupmate is unable to repay. In such cases, the incentive to stop productive effort and refuse to repay is greatly enhanced, given that in situations of personal success but a groupmate's failure, joint liability will impose repayment costs significantly higher than individual borrowing.

The decision by Muhammad Yunus to move from Grameen I to Grameen II by abandoning joint liability was due to this concern and signalled a crucial passage to a microfinance model that tries to improve the welfare of borrowers without increasing the risk of uncollateralized loans for the bank. The main idea of this new approach is that incentives to repay the loan may be maintained by shifting the penalty from groupmates to the insolvent borrower in the future by dividing each individual loan into small tranches distributed at close intervals. The penalty is now on the individual insolvent borrower because his or her inability to repay a previous tranche halts the lending process. The Grameen II system thus seeks to discriminate between problems of insolvency (structural inability to repay) and liquidity (momentary inability to repay due to a mismatch between revenues and expenses). When liquidity is the issue, the system creates a special track that tries to restore the repayment capacity of the borrower.

Another alternative to group lending and joint liability is the principle of *notional collateral* (Armendáriz de Aghion and Morduch 2005), in which banks make individual loans based on collateral that has a high 'notional' value for the borrower, but lower or negligible market value. Examples of notional collateral are a taxi driver's car, a farmer's livestock, or a family's valuables. Notional collateral has the advantage of stimulating borrowers' effort, thereby protecting lenders from strategic default, though it provides no protection against bank losses when the default is not the borrower's responsibility.

To conclude the discussion on joint liability, there are advantages and disadvantages that justify the heterogeneity in its adoption and utilization by MFIs around the world. Some pioneers such as Grameen Bank and BancoSol have shifted to individual-based contracts, while developing alternative mechanisms to solve the problem of the lack of individual collateral, such as progressive loans, notional collateral, and forced savings. Nevertheless, group lending with joint liability remains one of the most important and successful approaches to microfinance. The degree to which it is successful depends upon several factors, including efficient self-selection, the capacity to replace a lack of individual collateral, peer pressure, a cultural tradition of lending money to members of savers' groups, and group performance of administrative duties in managing loans.

The role of intangibles

There is far more involved in making microfinance successful than the simple technical device of joint liability. Social norms, for example, play a fundamental role since MFIs often operate in village communities in which social sanctions on members who break rules are strong and insolvent borrowers risk being isolated by the community. On the positive side, social norms crucially explain why the motivation by borrowers to repay is not simply fear of economic sanctions. Microfinance loans are often directed to the marginalized poor and represent for them a unique opportunity for inclusion and growth of social recognition.

In this sense, the 'dignification' of loan beneficiaries is a hidden source of productivity and compliance. Reflecting upon the characteristics of standard effort and motivation mechanisms in professional life, it seems evident that a lack of trust and social recognition may dramatically undermine an individual's confidence and capacity to perform a task. By the same token, a powerful process that strengthens motivation and effort is enacted when dignity is restored by providing an individual the opportunity to improve her or his situation with a microfinance loan.

The principal–agent framework seems inadequate for characterizing the microfinance relationship between lender and borrower given the pathologies of adverse selection, moral hazard, and strategic default.[1] The assumption that the first instinct of a borrower is to be financially delinquent and that delinquency is only preventable by the threat of financial penalty seems applicable to the cold and anonymous relationships between large banks and limited liability corporations. This assumption seems much less plausible in the context of the personal relationship between a village loan officer and an individual borrower. To put it more bluntly, corporate screens and complex group structures may reduce incentives to virtuous behaviour for a defaulting manager since they relax the direct individual responsibility from an economic failure, while the individual borrower in a village in which social control is high has no golden parachutes and no alternatives to debt repayment.

These considerations help explain the puzzle of the unexpected success of these unorthodox lenders that ease access to credit to uncollateralized and marginalized individuals. Nevertheless, this puzzle cannot be completely solved by focusing on the advantages and limitations of lending techniques.

The issue of subsidies

While not all MFIs fit the definition of social enterprises used in this book, Yunus uses this concept to characterize the Grameen Bank. The activities and organization of this bank clearly fit what we mean by a social enterprise: Grameen's primary goal is to promote the interests of the poor, and this goal is pursued by competing with other financial intermediaries in the market. Thus, this bank creates value added, contributes to domestic growth, and resolves the dilemma between growth and distribution by generating economic value that yields substantial social benefits and avoids negative social externalities.

Other MFIs ease access to credit for the 'unbankable', but they have an explicit profit-maximization goal, such as the BancoSol which is an MFI that aims to attract equity capital (and resources from investors choosing microfinance investment funds for diversification purposes) by offering high returns. This difference between BancoSol and Grameen entails a gap in terms of real lending rates. Assuming that the productivity of loan officers and screening techniques are about equivalent and that the two types of MFIs bear the same types of risk, the profit-maximizing goal of commercial banks will result in much higher rates for borrowers.

An important consequence is that subsidies are justifiable mainly for the first type of not-for-profit MFIs, where their benefits are immediately transferred to borrowers. From a historical point of view, subsidies were fundamental for the start-up and initial operation of Grameen, and they played an important role in achieving financial equilibrium.

The debate over the role of subsidies in microfinance is highly polarized. On the one hand, opponents argue that subsidies weaken the incentives of MFIs to increase their productivity and develop refined scoring techniques. Subsidies thus create the typical situation of an 'infant industry', where the move towards self-sufficiency is delayed by the desire not to lose access to the subsidy. On the other hand, supporters of subsidies argue that the more microfinance is directed to 'low-end' beneficiaries, the more it requires financial support. In this respect, consider that the Microfinance Information Exchange (2008) found that only 40 per cent of microfinance lenders working with low-end borrowers achieve financial sustainability.[2] The reason for this lies in the social role performed by MFIs in cases where they act as substitutes for more costly welfare provisions in accordance with the subsidiarity principle.[3]

The effects of subsidies in microfinance also depend upon a series of conditions. Armendáriz de Aghion and Morduch (2005) emphasize that subsidies are justifiable and have important positive effects when credit demand is elastic to lending rates, adverse selection effects and positive spillovers on other lenders arise, and higher weight is given by policymakers to the well-being of the poor than to those who are better off. The application of Rawls's 'veil of ignorance' assumption provides the basis for a pro-subsidy argument: if people are uncertain of knowing whether they will be born rich and collateralized or poor and devoid of financial resources, they would rationally choose to subsidize microfinance, even if it would sacrifice some efficiency gains in the economic system as a whole.

Socially responsible investing as a form of private subsidization

What must be taken into account in the discussion about subsidies is that in most cases subsidized funds channelled to MFIs come from private and not from public sources. The existence of private subsidies alters the terms of discussion. When a group of financial investors who are socially responsible decide to sacrifice some of their gains in exchange for the satisfaction they receive by serving an ideal, there is no 'arbitrary' use of public resources or diversion of contributions by non-socially responsible taxpayers. Socially responsible savers are also rational and maximizing individuals but their preferences are different from those usually depicted in textbook models. These savers are characterized by inequity aversion, fairness, or altruism, and therefore their decisions to provide subsidized finance to MFIs are not suboptimal, but rather fully satisfy their goals. Nevertheless, the issues of whether their generosity is appropriate and their financial resources are used efficiently remains. In the simple benchmark model of microfinance proposed below, the intervention of socially responsible savers will be shown to be beneficial since socially responsible depositors assume part of the asymmetric information costs incurred by MFIs. These interventions both narrow the gap between the private and social optimum volume of financed projects and reduce the effect of shocks that are not diversifiable among borrowers (Becchetti *et al.* 2006).

Representative evidence on microfinance

An initial picture of the microfinance industry can be provided by examining the size distribution of MFIs. Table 9.1 shows that there is a high degree of concentration, with a few big players and a large number of very small ones. Eight MFIs with more than one million borrowers serve 34.7 per cent of the total customers, while at the bottom of the size distribution 2,190 small intermediaries have fewer than 2,500 customers and serve less than 2.2 per cent of the market. For this reason, figures from a small group of large players are highly representative of the microfinance industry.

Table 9.2 provides data on four MFIs: two top players (Grameen and BancoSol), one large (Finca International), and one small (Accion USA). These data show that the gender effect is very strong for Grameen (97 per cent of the bank's microloans are given to women) but the share of women borrowers is far below average for the other banks (with Accion USA at 40 per cent). Average loan size per borrower is confirmed to be small (only $104 for Grameen), even though to make comparisons across different countries these raw figures would have to be converted into purchasing power parity values (the average $6,980 per loan in the US is also small given the context). In terms of lending techniques, group sizes are extremely heterogeneous (ranging from five in Grameen and between ten and 50 in Finca International). Another interesting feature is the heterogeneity in the requirement of compulsory savings for microfinance clients. Since most MFIs are small and scattered around the world, it is very difficult to move from MFI-level data to aggregate statistics.

One useful source of information is the Microfinance Information Exchange (2008), which has created a representative sample of 231 MFIs that have been consistently monitored over a period of years. A large proportion of these MFIs (134) are NGOs and a majority (174) are not financial intermediaries (see Table 9.3). These findings confirm that a typical scheme in microfinance entails coordination between an MFI that assumes all of the operating tasks (such as monitoring and training) and expenses, and a bank that formally lends the money. About two-thirds of the monitored MFIs are non-profits operations,

Table 9.1 Concentration of the microfinance industry in 2004

Size (number of poor borrowers)	Number of MFIs	Total number of borrowers	Per cent of total borrowers
1 million or more	8	19,027,342	34.7
100,000–999,999	34	8,302,482	15.2
10,000–99,999	253	6,952,768	12.7
2,500–9,999	464	2,240,032	4.0
Less than 2,500	2,169	1,184,729	2.2
Networks	3	17,078,080	31.2

Sources: National Bank for Agriculture and Rural Development (NABARD) in India; Association of Asian Confederation of Credit Unions (ACCU), and Bangladesh Rural Development Board (BRDB).

Table 9.2 Summary features of some representative MFIs in 2008

	Grameen Bank	BancoSol	Finca International	Accion USA*
Date established	1976	1986	1984	1991
Number of clients	7,670,203	82,051	744,756	1,458
Proportion of women	97%	46%	70%	40%
Average loan per borrower	$104	$2,547	Varies by country	$6,980
Target clientele	Small rural entrepreneurs	Small rural and urban entrepreneurs	Small rural entrepreneurs	Small urban entrepreneurs
Lending modality	Group lending	Individual and group lending	Group lending	Individual lending
Group size	5	4–6	10–50	–
Forced savings	Compulsory	Optional	Compulsory	Optional

Sources: Accion USA (2009), BancoSol (2009), Finca International (2009), and Grameen Bank (2009).

Note
* Data for 2007.

while one-third are for-profit firms. This information is important since it indicates the ratio between two alternative models: the Grameen-type model of the 'social entrepreneur', the goal of which is the inclusion of the marginalized, and the BancoSol-type MFI, which performs the task of extending credit to uncollateralized individuals with the aim of making profits. A typical difference between these two alternative models is their lending rates. For Grameen, the rate is about equal to a zero-profit condition and is therefore quite moderate in real terms. For BancoSol, its profit-maximizing goal and the interest-increasing factors of higher borrower risk and lack of collateral push its interest rates to very high levels in real terms. Empirical evidence from the Microfinance Information Exchange suggests that Grameen-type MFIs represent about two-thirds of the total.

Data from the Microfinance Information Exchange confirm that the gender effect is widespread since 62 per cent of borrowers in its sample MFIs are women, with the notable peaks of 94 and 92 per cent for the village and all-Asian MFI subsamples. The average loan per borrower is $423, which represents around 41 per cent of the gross national income per capita.

MFIs that do not have an explicit profit goal may still make profits; in fact, the average profit margin of their loan portfolios is around 4.9 per cent. The data confirm that providing loans to low-end beneficiaries is costly since this subgroup of MFIs has a 2.1 per cent rate of profit, while MFIs that serve small businesses have an average 9.8 per cent rate. In the model proposed below, the decision to assume that the MFI is a zero-profit financial intermediary is justified by the fact that MFIs providing loans to low-end beneficiaries are close to this threshold and even below it. This is the case with solidarity MFIs, which have a negative 2.3 per cent rate, and of African MFIs, which have a negative 5 per cent rate; small African MFIs plunge to a negative 20.5 per cent rate. This evidence confirms that MFIs are not insulated from the broader macroeconomic and institutional contexts in which they operate, and that in countries in which factors of conditional convergence are weaker, microfinance performance is less sustainable.

From another perspective, the Microfinance Information Exchange data illustrate the success with which MFIs generally select solvent borrowers. The loan loss rate is about 1.4 per cent, with a maximum of 2.0 per cent for African banks and a minimum of 0.6 per cent for Middle Eastern and North African banks.

Productivity indicators confirm that one of the advantages of village over individual lending is its capacity to transfer some monitoring costs from bank officers to village peers. This tendency is reflected in the differences in the average number of loans per staff member from 82 for individual lending to 161 for village banking. This difference reduces the average cost per loan from $190 to $57 (see Table 9.3).

Another interesting point is that there does not seem to be relevant differences in efficiency between profit and non-profit institutions. The ratio between personnel expenses and the loan portfolio is quite similar ($10 for for-profits versus $10.20 for non-profits) and the same is true for the ratio between operating expenses and the loan portfolio (19.3 versus 19.1 per cent). As to be expected, the gap in the ratio between financially sustainable and non-financially

Table 9.3 Selected MFI characteristics according to peer groups

Units	Number of MFIs	Age	Return on equity	Profit margin	Yield on gross portfolio (nominal)	Provision for loan impairment assets	Operating expense loan portfolio	Personnel expense loan portfolio	Cost per borrower	Loans per staff member
			%	%	%	%	%	%	US$	
Year	2007	2007	2007	2007	2007	2007	2007	2007	2007	2007
Age										
New	144	3	(0.9)	(1.6)	37.6	1.5	34.8	17.0	119	83
Young	203	7	2.5	5.5	31.0	1.2	21.0	10.9	114	113
Mature	543	14	4.5	5.7	28.7	1.5	17.2	9.3	117	123
Methodology										
Individual	277	11	5.8	7.2	27.6	1.5	14.6	7.4	211	82
Individual/Solidarity	440	10	2.8	3.8	31.4	1.4	21.2	12.0	101	115
Solidarity	79	7	(0.1)	(2.3)	28.3	1.3	24.0	14.5	32	163
Village Banking	94	9	2.2	4.6	32.9	1.4	25.4	14.0	57	161
Profit status										
For-profit	309	9	5.1	6.9	31.2	1.3	19.3	10.0	149	95
Not-for-profit	581	10	2.5	3.6	29.4	1.5	19.1	10.2	101	125
Region										
Sub-Saharan Africa	159	10	(3.2)	(5.0)	33.4	2.0	31.7	14.0	114	127
East & Central Asia	244	11	2.3	2.6	26.8	1.3	16.0	9.4	37	131
E. Europe & Cen. Asia	158	8	4.3	7.2	29.5	1.1	15.4	8.2	278	66
Latin Am. & Caribbean	283	12	7.2	8.1	31.7	1.6	19.5	10.5	152	123
Mid. East & N. Africa	46	8	0.9	2.1	30.8	0.6	19.5	13.2	67	119
Target beneficiaries										
Low end	335	9	1.3	2.1	34.8	1.5	28.6	15.6	53	157
Broad	454	10	5.1	5.7	28.9	1.5	16.7	8.7	144	101
High end	57	10	8.1	9.3	22.6	1.2	15.1	6.9	252	62
Small Business*	44	11	3.8	9.8	23.2	1.4	16.8	7.0	441	44

Source: Microfinance Information Exchange (2008).

Note
* Gross Loan Portfolio < $2,000,000.

sustainable organizations is large (37.1 versus 19.5 per cent), but it is impossible to know whether this low efficiency is due to the decision to serve the poorest clients or to a true internal organizational inefficiency.

Impact studies

While there is lot of anecdotal and descriptive evidence that MFIs are effective in improving the well-being of the poor in a variety of contexts, impact studies provide rigorous scientific evidence and have a fundamental role to play in improving the efficiency of MFIs and demonstrating the impact of microfinance for external donors.

In general, the main indicators assessed in impact studies are economic conditions—measured in terms of household income, household consumption, income diversification, and changes in household assets—and social indicators—measured by improvements in child schooling, health outcomes for women and children, the empowerment of women, social capital, and self-esteem and dignity. There are few serious impact studies of microfinance, however, since almost insurmountable methodological problems exist (Hulme and Mosley 1996; Pitt and Khandker 1998; Coleman 1999).

First, the optimal impact study in principle should compare borrowers' performance with the counterfactual. The counterfactual is the performance of treated individuals if they were not subject to the treatment. The ideal comparison of the performance of treated individuals with the counterfactual is actually a first-best impossible scenario that impact studies attempt to approximate with their methodologies.

In the absence of a counterfactual, a good impact study must have a homogeneous control sample of individuals not financed by the MFI as a benchmark to compare variations in socio-economic indicators. Although difficulties exist in finding homogeneous control samples for all impact studies, this problem is exacerbated in the case of microfinance since any correlation between the factors associated with the selection of the samples will mean that the impact of microfinance cannot be disentangled from a selection effect. To put it more simply, if the most productive individuals tend to self-select themselves into the treatment sample, it is impossible to determine whether any observed differences in socio-economic indicators between the treatment and control samples are due to the effects of the microfinance programme or the selection process.

The selection problem is particularly strong in banking studies, since the ex ante activity of financial intermediaries is precisely to screen and select good projects. If this screening activity is efficient and successful, it becomes very difficult to ascertain whether the out-performance of treated individuals is due to the impact of the loan or stems from the screening process.

For impact studies of microfinance, a possible solution to this problem is to identify a neighbouring village where an MFI does not operate and there exists a group of potentially eligible individuals who are homogeneous with the MFI borrowers. The alternative 'internal' solution is to compare borrowers with younger and older credit records within the MFI to evaluate how benefits grow over time. This approach has limitations, since if survivorship in the programme is an issue, then the sample of older borrowers is biased since it includes only the fittest who survived. This problem would lead to an overestimation of the benefits of microfinance.

A second issue is specifying the time interval in which the benefits of microfinance loans should materialize. With regards to a single loan, this period should generally not be too long (i.e. more than three years) given the potential uses of such loans (for working capital, start-up of small entrepreneurial activities, and, in some cases, consumption), but the effects may not be immediate. Consequently, this type of research requires comparisons to be made of values over time, thus necessitating repeated surveys at considerable cost.

A third problem in microfinance impact analyses is that the research can clash with the social goal of the borrowing activity itself. In order to create conditions for the 'experiment' which limits as much as possible the risk of selection bias, it is necessary to identify a group of potential beneficiaries with good projects and then to lend money only to a subgroup of them (the treatment sample), while refusing it to the rest of the potential beneficiaries (the control sample). If the latter are poor and in need, the quality of the experiment conflicts with the objective of microfinance activities and poses ethical issues.

For all these reasons, rigorous empirical studies of the effects of microfinance are scarce with respect to both theoretical and descriptive analyses.

A benchmark model

The most convenient way to analyse the characteristics and role of microfinance from a more formalized theoretical perspective is to start from a simple scheme that initially follows Prescott (1997) and Ghatak and Guinnane (1999) and then to progressively enrich it. In Prescott's (1997) framework, the world is populated by two different kinds of people—lenders and borrowers. Lenders are risk neutral and endowed with $1/m$, $m>1$ units of the investment good. They therefore have fewer resources than those needed to finance an investment project, so one of the main roles of the financial system—the aggregation of savings—is taken into account. The investment good can be used for two different purposes: the creation of consumption goods with either a risky investment project or a low-return investment technology. This technology takes x units of the investment good and turns it into Rx units of the good, with a return rate of $R-1$ per cent. The second group of individuals is composed of risk-neutral borrowers who possess specific skills to produce the consumption good, but have no units of the investment good.

This model reproduces the typical mismatch between those who have productive skills and those who have the resources needed to finance them. This mismatch is one of the main reasons why a financial system and a banking intermediary are necessary. The risky investment is indivisible so that each borrower's investment technology requires an input I of exactly one unit of the investment good. Indivisibility also implies that an investment of less than one produces an output of zero and any investment above one unit is wasted.

The investment needed to produce the consumption good is risky because its output is X with probability p and f with probability $1-p$. The expected value of the investment is $pX+(1-p)f>R$. In this way, the typical situation in which the project fails due to a poor business climate is reproduced. Project return goes below the opportunity cost of money, but its expected value is higher.

In the model, lenders can opt for the low return technology or choose among four lending options: (i) lend directly to borrowers and use a liquidation contract; (ii) lend directly to borrowers and monitor them; (iii) lend directly to the group and use a liquidation contract; (iv) lend to the large financial intermediary. The choice of lending to the large financial intermediary is optimal due to its capacity to economize the costs of screening and monitoring that would otherwise be borne by individual lenders.

The financial intermediary has three options for lending funds: (i) lend to borrowers, not monitor them, and use the threat of liquidation; (ii) lend to borrowers and monitor them; or (iii) lend to borrowers through groups. Consistent with the choice of modelling the Grameen-type MFI that does not maximize profits, the financial intermediary has no profits and receives just R, the opportunity cost of the lenders' funds. Thus, any excess goes to the borrower.

Under these assumptions, Prescott (1997) shows that it is possible and convenient to divide the expected returns to a project into five components: the expected payment to the financial intermediary R, the expected utility (return) of the borrower U, the liquidation costs L, the monitoring costs M, and the screening costs Ks. The sum of the five components is equal to $pX+(1-p)f$, that is the project's expected output.

Individual lending with no monitoring but liquidation

In this first case, the borrower must pay F or the borrower's project is liquidated where $f<F<X$. The cost of liquidation for the borrower is the value of destroyed output. When the project's return is f, both the borrower and financial intermediary take zero. The zero-profit condition for the financial intermediary is $R=pF+(1-p)0-K_S$, where Ks are the intermediary screening costs. As a consequence, $F_{NM} = \dfrac{R+K_S}{p}$. Consider that the required rate of return of the financial intermediary does not depend upon the project's value in the good state of nature, but rather depends upon the probability of the occurrence of this state (p). The decomposition of project output into its five components is the following:

$$\begin{cases} U_{NM} = pX - R - K_S \\ R = R \\ L = (1-p)f \\ M = 0 \\ S = K_S \end{cases}$$

Note that under the assumption of no monitoring with liquidation in case of failure, the output is destroyed (liquidated) but has no value for the lender. The lender therefore imposes liquidation but cannot recover the bad-state value.

Individual lending with monitoring

The difference with respect to the previous case is that the financial intermediary monitors the borrowers and obtains f if the low return occurs and F if the high return X occurs. The zero-profit condition becomes $R=pF+(1-p)f-K-K_S$, where K (costs of monitoring) are added to screening costs. The equilibrium payment to the financial intermediary required to satisfy its zero-profit condition is

$$F_M = \frac{R+K+K_S-(1-p)f}{p}$$. By comparing this with the previous solution, it is

clear that $U_M \geq U_{NM}$ and $F_{NM} \geq F_M$ if $K \leq (1-p)f$. This implies that individual lending with monitoring is preferred if monitoring costs of the financial intermediary are lower than the liquidation costs. The rationale is that with monitoring costs, the intermediary recovers f and the loss of f is not charged to the loan.

Under individual lending with monitoring, the decomposition of project output into its five components is the following:

$$\begin{cases} U_M = pX +(1-p)f - R - K - K_S \\ R = R \\ L = 0 \\ M = K \\ S = K_S \end{cases}$$

Group lending

The analysis of the two cases of individual monitoring examined above provide the basis for comparing standard with group lending to see when and under what circumstances the latter is preferable.

As will be shown below, the Prescott (1997) model focuses on one specific aspect of group lending—the joint liability effect. In the current microfinance debate, there is no consensus on the effectiveness of joint liability since the Grameen Bank initially used it, but later determined that it was too burdensome for the borrowers and eliminated it. Currently, some MFIs follow the older approach while others the newer one. It is therefore important to analyse why the application of joint liability remains controversial.

The model considers a group consisting solely of two individuals. Both members receive an individual loan and monitor each other, but since the large financial intermediary does not know the results of their monitoring, it needs to include a liquidation provision in the contract. The face value of the group's debt is $2F$. The expected value of the joint project is $p^2 2X+2p(1-p)(X+f)+(1-p)^2 2f$.

It assumed that joint liability takes its extreme form—i.e. that borrowers are committed to repay in full the debt of the insolvent group member.

The advantage of group lending for the bank is clear. Considering the four possible combinations of success and failure of the two members, the bank will get back all its money in three out of four cases (success–success, success–failure, and failure–success), while with individual lending in two of these cases it would have lost the money from one of the two loans. A crucial assumption for the effectiveness of group lending is therefore that the sum of the good-state and the bad-state output is higher than what the group has to pay back, or $X+f>2F$. With liquidation and screening costs, the zero-profit condition for the financial intermediary becomes $2R=p^2 2F+2p(1-p)2F+(1-p)^2 0-2K_S$.[4] This condition is satisfied by the equilibrium payment $F_{GL} = \dfrac{R+K_S}{p^2+2p(1-p)}$. If the MFI has zero profit, as this model assumes, then the advantage of the reduced risk is transferred to borrowers in terms of a lower cost of debt. This is evident from the observation that $F_{GL}<F_{NM}$ since $p^2+2p(1-p)>p$. Hence, the lower the probability of the good-state output, the more helpful is group monitoring in reducing the equilibrium payment to the financial intermediary, under the condition that $X+f>2F$ remains satisfied. Under group lending the decomposition of project output into its five components is the following:

$$\begin{cases} U_{GL} = pX +(1-p)f - R - K_S - K_G -(1-p^2)f \\ R = R \\ L = (1-p)^2 f \\ M = K_G \\ S = K_S \end{cases}$$

Why did the Grameen Bank abandon this scheme? The reason is that even though group lending may be the only credit opportunity available, borrowers are not necessarily better off with group lending than with individual lending: $U_{GL}>U_M$ if $K>(1-p)^2f+K_G$.[5]

Therefore, borrowers' welfare is higher under group lending than under individual lending with monitoring only if the financial intermediary's monitoring costs are higher than the liquidation cost plus borrowers' monitoring costs.

If the borrowers' utilities under group lending and the no monitoring (liquidation) scheme are compared, then $U_{GL}>U_{NM}$ if $K_G+(1-p)^2f<(1-p)f$. Hence, group lending is preferred to individual lending without monitoring if its monitoring and liquidation costs are lower than the liquidation costs of individual lending without monitoring.

To provide a simple intuition for these results, joint liability in group lending definitely reduces bank risk and the cost of debt for borrowers if the bank has zero profit. In spite of this, the relative advantage of the first or second choice is more uncertain from the perspective of the borrowers' welfare. On the one hand, the bank saves on monitoring costs and its reduced risk implies lower lending rates for borrowers; on the other hand, borrowers have monitoring costs and must pay the joint liability in case of insolvent groupmates. Group lending in joint liability may therefore represent just a 'second best' with respect to a first-best of individual lending, which is often not viable when borrowers lack collateral.

Extensions of the benchmark model

The model described above may sacrifice too many aspects of the reality of microfinance, where groups often consist of variable numbers of individuals, project outcomes are rarely independent, and informational asymmetries on their qualities are common. This section examines how the benchmark model varies when some restrictive assumptions are removed, including no correlation among projects of group borrowers, a fixed level of borrower's effort, and homogeneity in borrower's quality.

The role of group size

Table 9.2 shows that some well-known MFIs that follow the group-lending approach choose different group sizes. To understand in a simple way what are the costs and benefits of group enlargement, the effects on the previous findings were examined when the number of lenders was increased from two to three (see Becchetti *et al.* 2006). There are two completely different scenarios depending upon whether or not a borrower's default can be avoided if only one out of three borrowers is successful.

From a general point of view, it can be concluded that a marginal increase in group size may reduce or increase the odds depending upon whether the failure of the additional member can be accommodated by the members whose success was sufficient to avoid group default. To simplify, consider a group of three borrowers and assume at first that one successful borrower is enough to repay for the group of three: $X+2f \geq 3F$. In this case, it is easy to verify that the risk of default will be lower for the MFI that transfers the benefits of risk reduction in terms of lower cost of debt for the borrower when it acts as a zero-profit lender. If, however, two successful borrowers are needed to repay a group of three, then the alternative condition $(2X+F \geq 3F)$ will hold. In this case, the bank's risk will be higher as will the cost of debt for the borrower. Becchetti *et al.* (2006) generalize this problem and demonstrate the following propositions.

Proposition 1 (comparison within groups): For a group of given size s, F increases and borrowers' welfare decreases as long as the number of successful groupmates that are necessary to make the group solvent grows.

Proposition 2 (comparison between groups): F decreases and borrowers' welfare increases as the size of the borrowers' group grows if the number of groupmates necessary to make the project solvent is constant. This is so because as the group grows, the value of F increases due to the reduction of the joint probability of failure.

Proposition 3 (comparison between different schemes): The inequalities $F_{GL+1} > F_{DR} > F_{GF}$ and $U_{GL+1} < U_{DR} < U_{GF}$ hold for any group size and hypothesis.

These three propositions are represented graphically in Figure 9.1.

In this figure, the number in the circles represents the number of borrowers who must be successful in order to repay the debt of their unsuccessful group-mates (depending upon the ratio between costs of group debt and profits of the individual borrower in the good state of nature). The arrows indicate the prefer-ence of one hypothesis over the adjoining ones in terms of both reduced cost of debt and increased borrowers' welfare. The dashed arrows indicate relative dom-inance based on the value of the overall probability of success.

Clearly, the proposed framework neglects several other important effects of changes in group size since it considers borrowers' effort exogenous and does not analyse the feedback of changes in size on monitoring the costs and effort of group borrowers. The problem with larger groups is that they may generate free-rider problems in monitoring within the group. Furthermore, if it is assumed, as happens in reality, that there is unequal timing of project realiza-tion by borrowers, verification of anticipated failure by some of them could have negative effects on effort and repayment decisions by others, thereby

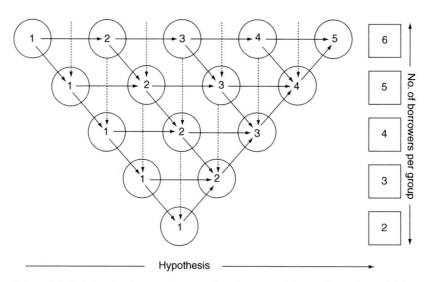

Figure 9.1 Relative dominance of group sizes (in terms of lower face values of debt and higher borrowers' welfare) under different group solvency hypotheses (source: Becchetti *et al.* 2006: 15).

generating the phenomenon of 'borrowers' run' (Bond and Rai 2009). Again, invisible factors such as social norms and sanctions, dignity, and trust can play an important role in avoiding these adverse effects in larger groups. In this sense, the assumption of exogenous borrowers' effort is a limiting case in which social sanctions are effective in eliciting the maximum level of effort from borrowers and eliminating any problem of moral hazard.

Correlated risk

As has been shown, the essential advantage of group lending with joint liability over individual lending is that it allows full repayment from a group of borrowers when their projects generate opposite outcomes (one success, one failure). Consequently, the benefits from joint liability are higher when projects of groupmates are inversely correlated. Unfortunately, the typical environment in which MFIs operate presents exactly the opposite situation: geographically delimited areas where there is a high probability that common (i.e. meteorological, industry-specific, or business-cycle-related) shocks increase the probability of positive correlation of loans in bank portfolios.

To illustrate this point from an analytical point of view, Becchetti *et al.* (2006) follow an approach developed by Armendáriz de Aghion (1999), who defines the following conditional probabilities:

$$\alpha = pr(Y_i = XY_j = X), (1-\alpha) = pr(Y_i = fY_j = X), \beta = pr(Y_i = XY_j = f), 1-\beta = pr(Y_i = fY_j = f)$$

where i, j denote the two borrowers being part of the same loan group. These conditional probabilities imply that $p^2 = \alpha p, (1-p)^2 = (1-p)(1-\beta), p(1-p) = (1-p)$ β or $p(1-\alpha)$. To put it simply, project returns are uncorrelated if $\alpha = p = \beta$, positively correlated if $\alpha > p > \beta$, and negatively correlated if $\alpha < p < \beta$. When project correlation exists, the new MFI zero profit condition therefore becomes

$$2R = p\alpha 2F + 2(1-p)\beta 2F - 2K_s \tag{9.1}$$

And the total amount due by a group borrower to the bank for a single project is

$$F = \frac{R + K_s}{p\alpha + 2(1-p)\beta} \text{ or } F = \frac{R + K_s}{p(2-\alpha)}$$

This implies that with a positive correlation ($\alpha > p$), F will be higher and, with a negative correlation ($\alpha < p$) it will be lower than the benchmark in which there is no correlation between group projects.

The intuition for this result is that project correlation limits the risk diversification opportunities created by group lending plus joint liability. As a consequence, this correlation reduces the capacity of group lending plus joint liability to lower the cost of loans when MFIs have zero profits and transfer their reduction of risks to the borrowers.

Assortative matching[6]

A restriction in the benchmark model is the assumption of homogeneity of borrower types. This restriction prevents an exemption of the problem of asymmetric information between borrowers and the MFI before the project is financed. The typical story of ex ante asymmetric information is that of adverse selection. Borrower types are heterogeneous either because of the intrinsic characteristics of their projects or due to their ability to operate them. The problem with standard individual debt is that if project types follow a probability distribution in which there is a mean preserving spread in revenues,[7] an increase in interest rates may make the pool of financed projects riskier since it is no longer convenient for borrowers to finance safer projects (Stiglitz and Weiss 1981).

The microfinance literature suggests that group lending with joint liability may create an important deterrent to adverse selection. Consider a situation in which borrowers are of two types, safe (S) and risky (R). Following previous assumptions about project distribution, a project of type I ($i=S,R$) output takes two values, X_i and f_i, and the probability of high output is p_i, $i=S,R$, with $p_S>p_R$. Since the bank does not know the borrower types (and standard screening instruments such as collateral are not available), it has to offer loans to all borrowers at the same nominal interest rate. It is clear that in this case safe borrowers end up cross-subsidizing risky borrowers given that both types of borrowers repay the same amount when they succeed, but safe borrowers succeed more often.

The final issue illustrated by this model is that the existence of a large number of risky borrowers drives the equilibrium interest rate high enough to discourage access to the bank by safe borrowers. If this is not the case, safe borrowers subsidize some undeserving risky projects. The microfinance literature suggests that in this situation a joint-liability contract can ensure assortative matching and restore full efficiency. Assume that the joint liability provision is such that a borrower must repay her loan F, whenever her project yields high returns, while she must pay an extra amount $c=F-f>0$ if her partner's project yields low returns. The expected payoff from a joint-liability contract for a borrower of type i when her partner is type j is:

$$U_{ij}=p_i p_j(X_i-F)+p_i(1-p_j)(X_i-F-c) \tag{9.2}$$

The net expected *gain* for a risky borrower from having a safe partner is

$$U_{RS}(F,c)-U_{RR}(F,c)=p_R p_S(X_R-F)+p_R(1-p_S)$$
$$(X_R-F-c)-[p^2{}_R(X_R-F)+p_R(1-p_R)(X_R-F-c)=p_R(p_S-p_R)c>0 \tag{9.3}$$

Similarly, the net expected *loss* for a safe borrower of having a risky partner is

$$U_{SS}(F,c)-U_{SR}(F,c)=p^2{}_S(X_S-F)+p_S(1-p_S)$$
$$(X_S-F-c)-[p_S p_R(X_S-F)+p_S(1-p_R)(X_S-F-c)=p_S(p_S-p_R)c>0 \tag{9.4}$$

It is easy to verify that (9.4) is larger than (9.3) since $p_S > p_R$.[8] Given that the expression depends on $c = F - f$ it is clear that socially responsible savings under both options, by reducing the lending rate, weaken conditions for assortative matching. The implication of this finding is that choosing a risky partner is a cost since it raises the probability of paying for the insolvent groupmate.

It is interesting to note that the joint-liability condition is not sufficient to avoid adverse selection. The assortative matching result indicates that both safe and risky borrowers will try to form groups with safe borrowers. However, this is not sufficient to ensure that the bank will be able to select only groups of safe borrowers. The reason for this is that after all existing safe borrowers have formed their homogeneous groups, risky borrowers will have an incentive to create groups among their peers and try to present themselves to the lender as safe borrowers. Becchetti and Pisani (2007) show that only when project size varies is a bank able to offer contracts that will be efficient in screening among groups of safe and risky borrowers in order to avoid adverse selection.

Moral hazard in cooperative and non-cooperative games

To analyse the effect of group lending on borrowers' productive effort, the restrictive assumption of exogeneity for this variable must be relaxed. Following Ghatak and Guinnane (1999) and Becchetti *et al.* (2006), it is assumed that effort is endogenously chosen by the utility-maximizing borrower. Project output is equal to X with probability $p[0,1]$, where this probability also represents the level of effort selected by the loan beneficiary. The corresponding cost function is equal to $(1/2)\gamma p^2$, with $\gamma > 0$. The bank cannot observe the borrower's choice and $X < \gamma$ is a parametric condition needed to ensure an interior solution.

Abstracting from the lending activity, social welfare can be defined as the difference between project revenues and borrower costs. The socially optimal level of effort is that which maximizes this function or $p^* = X/\gamma$. Since the bank cannot observe the borrower and force the borrower to choose $p = p^*$, the problem of moral hazard exists. This problem can be formulated by considering that the optimal effort chosen by the borrower is the p that maximizes the utility function

$$\hat{p}(F) = arg\ max \left[p(X - F) - \frac{1}{2}\gamma p^2 \right] = \frac{X - F}{\gamma} \tag{9.5}$$

by substituting in the first order condition the value of F for which the MFI breaks even ($F = R/p$), then $\gamma p^2 - Xp + R = 0$. Assuming that the higher effort value is chosen in equilibrium,[9]

$$p^{eq} = \frac{X + \sqrt{X^2 - 4R\gamma}}{2\gamma} \tag{9.6}$$

Starting from the finding in (9.6) that illustrates equilibrium effort with individual lending, the issue is whether the introduction of group lending with joint liability generates higher or lower effort.

In order to move to group lending, it is assumed for simplicity that the joint-liability penalty is equal to $c < \gamma$ and that borrowers can act cooperatively by contracting among themselves the level of p, observing each other perfectly and without costs and enforcing each other to exert their maximum effort level. The introduction of group lending with joint liability turns the utility function of the borrower into

$$U_{GL} = p^2(X - F) + p(1 - p)(X - F - c) - \frac{1}{2}\gamma p^2 =$$

$$p(X - F) - p(1 - p)c - \frac{1}{2}\gamma p^2 \tag{9.7}$$

By solving the problem with the standard procedure described above, Becchetti *et al.* (2006) obtain[10]

$$p_{GL}^{eq} = \frac{X + \sqrt{X^2 - 4R(\gamma - c)}}{2(\gamma - c)} \tag{9.8}$$

By comparing this and the individual lending solution, the equilibrium value of p and, hence, the optimal borrowers' effort (as well as the repayment rate) is higher under joint liability. The rationale for this result is that when acting cooperatively, borrowers internalize the negative joint-liability externality and understand that by increasing their effort they can reduce the groupmate probability of paying the joint-liability penalty c.

This result shows that the capacity of the joint-liability mechanism to reduce the moral hazard problem under group lending is valid only if borrowers act cooperatively. This condition is realistic in environments in which social control or social ties are high and impose cooperation among borrowers. In order to determine whether it may also hold in non-cooperative games, consider the following alternative framework proposed by Becchetti *et al.* (2006) in which there are two borrowers—A and B—and two exogenous alternative strategies—no effort or shirking (SH) and maximum effort with $p = \bar{p}$. With group lending the individual borrower has the following utility function

$$U_i = p_i(X - F) - p_i(1 - p_j)c - (1/2)\gamma p_i^2 \text{ with } i,j = A,B \tag{9.9}$$

where c is the fixed penalty for the solvent borrower when a groupmate is not solvent. Under the assumption that $p = \bar{p} = 1$, the structure of the game is described by the payoff matrix in Figure 9.2.

As illustrated in Figure 9.3, the game has different solutions according to the assumptions made about the disutility of effort parameter γ. When the disutility is low ($\gamma < 2(X - F - c)$), region 1 applies in which both groupmates select the

		Borrower B	
		SH ($p=0$)	HF($p=\bar{p}$)
Borrower A	SH ($p=0$)	0,0	0, $X-F-c-(1/2)\gamma$
	HF($p=\bar{p}$)	$X-F-c-(1/2)\gamma$, 0	$X-F-(1/2)\gamma$, $X-F-(1/2)\gamma$

Figure 9.2 The non-cooperative microfinance game (source: Becchetti *et al.* 2006: 21).

maximum level of effort (the Nash Equilibrium is EF, EF). When the value of the disutility is intermediate $(2(X-F-c)<\gamma<2(X-F)$, region 2), there are two alternative Nash Equilibria where both borrowers exert maximum effort (EF, EF) or no effort at all (SH, SH). Finally when disutility of effort is high $(\gamma>2(X-F)$, region 3), the unique equilibrium of the game is that in which the no effort strategy is selected by both players (the Nash Equilibrium is SH, SH).

The interesting point here is that the joint liability in this case has a negative effect on borrowers' effort since it reduces region (1) in which both players unequivocally choose the maximum effort strategy.

The role of government subsidies in the benchmark model

One of the main issues in the microfinance debate is whether it is justifiable from an economic and social point of view that MFIs be supported by government or private subsidies. To evaluate the effect of subsidy in the benchmark model, consider that a subsidy has the role of reducing the cost of financial resources for the MFI from R to R', where $R'<R$. MFIs can use subsidies in two ways. First, the MFI may directly transfer into its zero-profit condition the reduced cost of money on the total amount required from borrowers, thereby reducing the level of F. Second, the MFI can use the subsidy to create a guarantee fund that intervenes in cases of non-performing loans.[11]

The obvious result in the case of exogenous effort in the first version of the benchmark model is that non-profit MFIs will transfer the benefit of the reduced costs directly to the borrowers. To test this proposition, Becchetti *et al.* (2006) propose a comparison of the different lending schemes analysed in terms of social welfare under given parametric conditions. Taking as a benchmark an

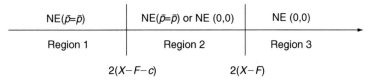

Figure 9.3 Effort regions in the non-cooperative microfinance game (source: Becchetti *et al.* 2006: 21).

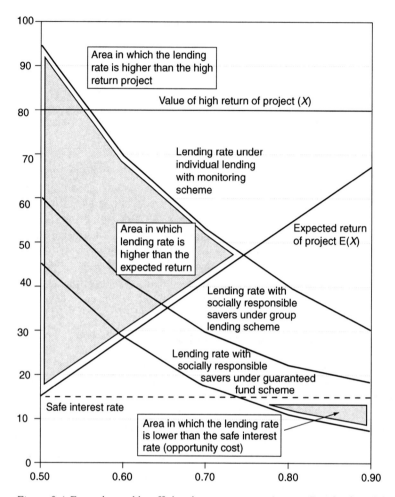

Figure 9.4 Excessive and insufficient investment areas (source: Becchetti *et al.* 2006: 25).

Legend

Horizontal axis: p Vertical axis= *X/I*.

Parametric values in this example (*X*=1.8, *F*=0.5, *R*=1.15, K_S=0.02, *K*=0.05, π=0.1) are scaled on the unit value of the investment (*I*=1). This implies that the project return (*X*) is 80 per cent, the cost of funds for the MFI is 15 per cent of the investment value (*R*=1.15), screening and monitoring costs are respectively 2 and 5 per cent (K_S=0.02, *K*=0.05), the total financing cost for the borrower is 50 per cent (*F*=0.5), and the MFI contribution to a guarantee fund is 10 per cent in a guaranteed fund scheme.

The guaranteed fund scheme introduced by the MFI enlarges the volume of profitable loans financed. Since the social welfare feasibility area is the area where *E(Y)>R* and the private feasibility is the area where *E(Y)* is higher than the cost of lending conditional to a given scheme, under the assumption that the only alternative to financing investment is the riskless rate *R*, the passage from individual to group lending—and from group lending to socially responsible group lending—reduces the gap between socially and individually optimal feasibility areas.

investment cost of unit value, in the numeric example they assume a lending rate of 15 per cent, a deposit rate of 5 per cent, a project return of 80 per cent and of minus 50 per cent in cases of default, plus a reserve requirement of 10 per cent. With these data it is possible to map (see Figure 9.4) the dynamics of the expected value of the project and of the cost of lending under different options (individual lending with and without monitoring, group lending, and group lending with socially responsible savers) against changes in the probability of project success (or the probability of occurrence of the good state output). It is possible to define the social welfare feasibility area as $E(Y) > R$, since under this condition financing the project implies that resources yield on average more than the opportunity cost. On the other hand, the private feasibility areas are those where $E(Y)$ is higher than the cost of lending for that scheme. The numeric example proposed in the figure clearly shows that the passages from individual to group lending and from group lending to socially responsible group lending reduce the gap between the socially and individually optimal feasibility areas, under the assumption that the only alternative to financing investment is the risk-less rate R.

The role of subsidies in the extension of the benchmark model

The impact of subsidies on the cost of debt and on borrowers' utility immediately changes with different extensions of the base model and when the problems of group size, project correlation, assortative matching, and moral hazard in cooperative and non-cooperative frameworks are taken into account.

Based on the findings about optimal group size and exogenous borrowers' effort developed above, it is clear that a subsidy which reduces the average remuneration on savings for non-profit MFIs is transferred to the cost of the loan for the borrower and may be crucial in triggering a change in the required ratio between successful and unsuccessful borrowers to avoid group default.

When project correlation is taken into account in the benchmark, the positive effect of the subsidized cost of money for the MFI increases as the level of positive correlation among projects increases. This implies that subsidies are effective in alleviating the negative impact of correlation on bank risk and on the cost of loans.

Subsidies also weaken, though they do not eliminate, the problem of assortative matching. The reason for this is that the penalty for the selection of a lower-quality and riskier borrower into a group is represented by the expected cost of the joint liability, which is inevitably correlated with the cost of money for the MFI. The lower the cost of money due to the subsidy, the lower the cost for selecting a low-quality borrower into one's group.

The situation changes in the moral-hazard cooperative framework, where the cost of debt for the borrower acts like a tax on success and therefore has a negative effect on the borrower's effort. From this perspective, the impact of the subsidy on the borrower's productivity is positive since it generates a reduction of the cost of debt and of the implicit tax on success. In essence, a subsidy reduces the amount of project revenues that the successful borrower has to give back to the bank to repay the borrower's debt (the tax on success) and therefore strengthens the incentive to exert more effort in order to increase project revenues.

If the problem of moral hazard is re-proposed in a non-cooperative context, the subsidy is again beneficial. Figure 9.3 shows that the threshold delimitating the full-effort from no-effort regions depends on the cost of debt. Again, a reduction of the cost of debt increases the likelihood of falling into a full effort region for a given disutility of the productive effort.

To sum up, the effect of subsidies seems to be beneficial in the benchmark model and in most of its variations. Obviously, this conclusion is seriously undermined if it is assumed that there is a negative impact on the dynamics of incentives for MFIs to improve their productivity and efficiency. What should be emphasized here, however, is that subsidies may reduce the wedge that risk and asymmetric information costs create between the private and socially optimal loan rate. In addition, subsidies can reduce moral hazard in cooperative and non-cooperative contexts and weaken but not eliminate incentives for assortative matching.

Consider, however, that a crucial characteristic of the microfinance framework is that the subsidies do not come from governments but from private foundations or directly from 'socially responsible savers'. In both cases, the sponsors of the subsidies are willing to accept lower remuneration in exchange for the social benefit that is obtained by promoting inclusion of the poor. This is an added positive element of subsidies.

It is therefore evident that socially responsible finance is crucial for the success of MFIs that start operations in difficult contexts involving low-end beneficiaries. The effect on borrowers' incentives to repay is generally positive but the potential negative effects on MFIs' effort to increase efficiency (subsidized financing may reduce the incentive to stand on one's own feet) need to be taken into account.

Conclusions

The impressive success of microfinance in the last two decades is good news since it provides an effective tool for promoting social and economic inclusion of the poor; this success has also posed a challenge to orthodox economics. Traditional banking theory depicts lending activity as a confrontation between two self-interested actors—the bank and the borrower—who have conflicting goals in a framework of informational asymmetry. In order to avoid various forms of opportunism by the borrower (such as moral hazard, asymmetric information, and strategic default) the lender devises contractual instruments that provide the optimal set of incentives and punishments in order to align the interests of the borrower with those of the lender.

A generally undisputed principle of this theory is that collateral is a crucial instrument that shields the bank from loan non-performance; the amount of the collateral required can also be used to screen good from bad borrowers. The problem is that the collateral requirement significantly limits the potential set of borrowers and prevents banks from lending to those who do not have adequate resources to use as collateral. Since one of the goals of financial intermediation is to match individuals who have productive ideas with those who are endowed with money, 'slavery to collateral' prevents standard financial intermediaries from fulfilling their role.

From this perspective, microfinance constitutes a revolution. After an initial moment of disbelief about the success of microfinance, the reaction by theorists has been to try to understand how it works. The explanation provided in the analytical framework of the standard debt contract is based on the role of group lending and joint liability. This specific form of microfinancing enhances peer monitoring and can reinforce the borrowers' incentive to repay even in the absence of the threat of losing their collateral.

The big puzzle, however, is why microfinance also works without group lending, as the success of Grameen II and of many other MFIs following this approach demonstrate. It seems implausible that microfinance can be explained without challenging the conventional paradigm of *homo economicus* uniquely animated by self-interest.

The epigraph of this chapter provides some hints. The standard cliché that a borrower's main goal is to avoid repaying the lender is probably not the univocal perspective from which to examine the microfinance lending relationship. Microfinance borrowers are certainly self-interested but operate in a framework in which the microfinance loan is an opportunity to promote individual dignity and social inclusion. This chapter has presented promising avenues of research by arguing that microfinance success provides insights into the immaterial resources that are usually neglected but are important drivers of individual productivity and performance. In the case of microfinancing, the opportunities offered for inclusion restore the dignity of disadvantaged individuals and seem to be a powerful incentive that pushes them to succeed and to repay their loans.

Another issue addressed in this chapter has been the role of subsidies in microfinance. The trade-off between outreach (capacity of financing the poorest) and profitability suggests that subsidies are unavoidable at least in the start-up phase if an MFI aims to serve the lowest income borrowers. Most of these subsidies come from private sources and express the willingness of socially concerned investors to pay for the inclusion of the 'unbankable' in financial markets. In this respect, the challenge is to prevent subsidies from weakening the incentive of MFIs to become more efficient and financially self-sufficient.

A final issue addressed in this chapter is differences between for-profit and not-for-profit MFIs. Far from the philanthropic description often provided by the press, many MFIs operate with a straightforward profit-maximization approach and therefore represent a different model from that proposed by the Grameen Bank, which is a not-for-profit organization whose main goal is social inclusion.

It is useful to examine differences in structure and performance between the two different startegies. The simplification of the proposed model probably captures the most important difference: while non-profit organizations transfer organizational efficiency and reduced risk from group lending into lower costs for borrowers, this is not the case for profit-maximizing MFIs. The large difference in lending rates between the two demonstrates that non-profit MFIs are better able to target low-end borrowers and that their actions have more favourable effects on the welfare of these borrowers.

Future research in microfinance needs to deepen the interaction between the 'emerged side' of borrowers' productivity and the invisible side of those factors (such as dignity, self-esteem, and social status) that contribute to the successful performance of microfinance loans. Microfinance studies can also contribute to developing a new anthropological paradigm that integrates the interplay of extrinsic and intrinsic motivations by combining insights from principal–agent theory with those arising from the unexpected and paradoxical success of lending to the uncollateralized poor.

Notes

1 These are the typical problems caused by informational asymmetries between borrowers and lenders. Adverse selection is a perverse mechanism through which the lender who sets higher lending rates ends up selecting riskier projects. Moral hazard occurs when borrrowers reduce their effort to pursue their projects, while strategic defaults occur when the borrowers interrupt payments for strategic purposes.

2 The Microfinance Information Exchange considers poorer ('low end') borrowers to be those who have an average balance per borrower that is both less than 20 per cent of the gross national income per capita and lower than $150.

3 The subsidiarity principle states that if an economic or social activity may be performed by smaller local organizations that are closer to the problem, it should be delegated to them by larger entities that operate at a broader geographical level.

4 The financial intermediary has no monitoring costs in this case since borrowers monitor each other in the group-lending scheme.

5 Consider that under group lending $L = (1 - p)^2 f$, which is dramatically lower than the case in which the intermediary lends but does not monitor (recall that the liquidation cost in that case was $[1 - p]f$). The reason for the dramatic reduction is that the distribution of group output has less variance than the distribution of individual output.

6 This tecnical term refers to a condition in which safe borrowers have no interest in mixing with risky borrowers.

7 The term *mean preserving spread* refers to two symmetric distributions that have the same mean but differ in the 'tails' and therefore have different variance.

8 Equation (9.4) is the assortative matching condition, from which it can be inferred that a safe borrower will not find it profitable to have a risky partner. A borrower of any type prefers a safer partner, but the safer the borrower herself is, the more she values a safe partner. A risky borrower in theory could pay the safe borrower to accept her as a partner, but the equation above implies that such payments would have to be so large that the risky borrower would not want to make them. As a result, group formation will display positive assortative matching under a joint-liability contract.

9 The existence and admissibility conditions are discussed in Becchetti *et al.* (2006).

10 The existence and admissibility conditions are available in Becchetti *et al.* (2006).

11 MFIs finance risky borrowers and often operate in risky areas. To protect themselves

from the risk of depleting their financial resources, MFIs are often supported by guarantee funds that are financed by donors or international institutions. If socially responsible funds are not available, MFIs usually must fulfil some regulator-imposed or prudentially self-imposed reserve requirement. To include this case in the benchmark, it must be assumed that for any successful project the MFI saves an amount PR when the loan is repaid and withdraws money from the accumulated reserve fund when the project fails. By starting from a base case in which socially responsible finance is not available, it is possible to calculate the impact of socially responsible finance when it is used to create a guarantee fund that satisfies the reserve requirement, and then compare such impact against the alternative strategy of a direct transfer of the reduced cost of financial resources ($R' < R$) on lending rates.

10 Only the fittest survive?

A test of the sustainability of corporate social responsibility[1]

Leonardo Becchetti and Rocco Ciciretti

Corporate social responsibility (CSR) involves a set of practices that aim to improve the social and environmental regulatory standards of the markets in which the subscribing corporations operate (Paul and Siegel 2006). According to this definition, a socially responsible firm should be interested not simply in maximizing shareholders' wealth, but also in the social and environmental consequences of its actions.

When CSR is actually practised—and not merely proclaimed—it should shift corporate goals from the maximization of shareholders' value to the satisfaction of the broader needs of such stakeholders as workers, customers, subcontractors, and local communities. This expanded focus has potential practical consequences since the goals of firms that aim solely to maximize profits can conflict with the subordinated interests of stakeholders. One relevant example of this is the conflict between shareholders and consumers. In many industries in which sellers have superior information about the characteristics of products and consumers cannot verify this quality in the short run, profit-maximizing firms may be tempted to reduce quality at the expense of consumers.

Strangely enough, the topic of CSR was generally ignored by economists until the late 1990s. The reason for this neglect probably lies in the 'tombstone' argument that many economists uncritically share: in an ideal world, benevolent institutions devise proper regulation and fiscal instruments to correct for the divergence between the individual and social welfare generated by negative externalities and the insufficient provision of public goods. In such a world, any departure by corporate managers from their task of maximizing shareholders' wealth is considered a betrayal of their mandate (Friedman 1962).

This recurring argument has been clearly expressed by the *Economist* (2005: 11): 'The goal of a well-run company may be to make profits for its shareholders, but merely in doing that—provided it faces competition in its markets, behaves honestly and obeys the law—the company, without even trying, is doing good works.' An additional argument against CSR is that managers may generate cash flow waste in a context of asymmetric information, given the undeniably greater difficulty in measuring the outcome of a complex multi-stakeholder target such as CSR in comparison to the simpler mono-dimensional goal of profit maximization (Jensen 1986).

These critiques of corporate social responsibility (and especially Friedman's argument) may be partly valid in a closed economy of industrialized countries, where strong trade unions and institutions with their redistributive claims act as checks and balances to corporate pressures in order to reconcile economic development with social cohesion. In the globalized world in which we live, however, benevolent planners do not exist and institutions are riddled by conflicts between their statutory objective functions and the personal goals of those who manage them. As a consequence, governance and rules are far from optimal, inevitably imperfect and incomplete, and sometimes altogether lacking. This is particularly true as the increasing integration of financial and real markets generates higher interdependence among countries and makes the problem of global public goods more urgent and compelling in a vacuum of global rules and institutions.

To sum up, it is one thing to assert that managers should not care about social responsibility in the US of the 1960s, as Friedman does, but it is quite another to argue that managers should have this attitude when they delocalize part of their productive activities to some of the 'ruleless lands' of the globalized economy or they fail to adopt an environmentally sustainable policy of reducing emissions in a world that has become conscious of the risk of global warming.

In a sense, recent history suggests that CSR is not an autonomous corporate initiative but rather should be seen as a response to grassroots protest over the failure of the old system of checks and balances. With the context of delocalizing production, the bargaining power of domestic trade unions and domestic institutions is greatly reduced and corporate power is immensely increased. This is why concerned consumers and investors have started to use their 'portfolio votes' to demand that firms take responsibility for the social and environmental sustainability of their actions.[2] As will be shown in this chapter, bottom-up pressures have been crucial in this process since when they are strong they can reduce the costs of social responsibility for firms and minimize conflicts with stakeholders (Freeman 1984).

Once it is recognized that CSR behaviour exists and is an important part of the contemporary corporate practices, a crucial question is whether it is sustainable. This issue can be posed in the following terms: if CSR is not a 'free lunch' and implies higher costs, how can 'socially responsible' firms not end up being less profitable than their traditional counterparts and survive in competitive environments?

This issue is of foremost importance, since evidence of a positive relationship between CSR and corporate performance may create the suspicion that firms practise CSR simply to increase profits; evidence of a negative relationship, on the other hand, may have the worse consequence of suggesting that the CSR choice is unfeasible in the current competitive climate.

In order to examine this issue empirically, three main types of CSR choice effects can be identified: first, a cost increase generated by improved conditions for non-investor stakeholders (workers, subcontractors, local communities) or by the adoption of more costly and environmentally responsible production processes; second, a potentially positive productivity effect generated by better working conditions and improved worker motivation; and third, increased demand from consumers who are sensitive to social responsibility issues.

Based on these considerations, this chapter tests a *strong* and a *weak sustainability condition* of the CSR choice. According to the strong sustainability condition, the productivity effect generated by the superior motivation of employees is sufficient to offset the costs of social responsibility. Paradoxically, the consequence of this condition is that the CSR choice would in principle be sustainable even if it were not communicated to consumers. According to the weak sustainability condition, the employees' motivation effect is not sufficient to offset additional costs. Hence, an additional positive demand effect from socially responsible consumers is necessary to make the CSR choice sustainable.

These weak and strong sustainability conditions are tested by comparing the impact of social responsibility separately for firms selling intermediate goods and for those selling final consumer goods for which consumer demand is sufficiently elastic. The assumption is that the first group of firms, unlike the second, cannot benefit (except indirectly) from the positive demand effect of socially responsible consumers who 'vote with their wallet' by purchasing final products. The relative weight of the weak and strong sustainability conditions may be tested by looking separately at the impact of CSR on these two groups of firms. If a positive and significant difference in profitability of the CSR choice exists between firms selling final and intermediate products, this would confirm the importance of the demand effect.

The chapter is developed as follows. The first section outlines the theoretical framework and illustrates the three effects of the CSR choice that define the weak and strong sustainability conditions. The subsequent sections examine the rationales provided in the literature for the three effects, describe the criteria chosen for discriminating between socially responsible and non-socially responsible firms, and survey the empirical research on social responsibility and corporate performance. The empirical test of the weak and strong sustainability conditions is then described and the econometric checks are explained.

Theoretical framework

To evaluate the impact of social responsibility on corporate performance, consider a firm with the following standard profit function

$$\pi(rs) = p(sr)F[x(sr)e(sr)] - w(sr)x(sr) \qquad (10.1)$$

where p is the product market price, $F[.]$ is the firm production frontier, with output being a function of labour input (x) in efficiency units (e) whose unit cost is w. It is assumed that social responsibility (sr) influences corporate performance in three ways: a demand-side effect, a productivity effect, and a cost effect.

Demand-side effect

$$\frac{\partial p(sr)}{\partial sr} F[.] + \left[p(sr) \frac{\partial F[.]}{\partial x(sr)} - \frac{\partial w(sr)}{\partial x(sr)} \right] \frac{\partial x(sr)}{\partial sr} \qquad (10.2)$$

On the demand side, the existence of a non-zero share of socially responsible consumers (i.e. consumers with social preferences) is assumed. The influence of such consumers is modelled by assuming that the social responsibility choice of a firm selling (demand elastic) consumer goods may generate a positive shift in the aggregate inverse demand function (*sr*) and therefore, *ceteris paribus*, on prices, the quantity sold, and the number of employed workers.[3]

Productivity effect

$$p(sr) \frac{\partial F[.]}{\partial e(sr)} \frac{\partial e(sr)}{\partial sr} \qquad (10.3)[4]$$

On the supply side, it is argued that workers' motivation and effort may be positively affected by a firm's CSR choice.

Cost effect

$$\frac{\partial w(sr)}{\partial sr} x(sr) \qquad (10.4)[5]$$

As can be shown, in most standard criteria used for identifying socially responsible firms, social responsibility choices imply a set of costly measures whose goal is to improve firm relationships with various stakeholders (subcontractors, employees, and local communities). It can thus be expected that the CSR choice will imply an increase in input costs (under the simplification here, wage costs).

The three effects (Equations 10.2, 10.3, and 10.4) can be combined to evaluate the impact of the CSR choice on corporate performance:

$$\frac{\partial \pi(sr)}{\partial sr} = \frac{\partial p(sr)}{\partial sr} F[.] + \left[p(sr) \frac{\partial F[.]}{\partial x(sr)} - \frac{\partial w(sr)}{\partial x(sr)} \right] \frac{\partial x(sr)}{\partial sr} +$$

$$p(sr) \frac{\partial F[.]}{\partial e(sr)} \frac{\partial e(sr)}{\partial sr} - \frac{\partial w(sr)}{\partial sr} x(sr) \qquad (10.5)[6]$$

Based on the three effects, strong and weak sustainability conditions can be defined.

Weak sustainability condition

$$\frac{\partial \pi(sr)}{\partial sr} = \frac{\partial p(sr)}{\partial sr} F[.] + p(sr) \left[\frac{\partial x(sr)}{\partial sr} e(sr) + \frac{\partial e(sr)}{\partial sr} x(sr) \right] - \frac{\partial w(sr)}{\partial sr} x(sr)$$

$$- \frac{\partial x(sr)}{\partial sr} w(sr) \geq 0 \tag{10.6}$$

By conjecturing that $\dfrac{\partial p(sr)}{\partial sr} F[.] + \left[p(sr) \dfrac{\partial F[.]}{\partial x(sr)} - \dfrac{\partial w(sr)}{\partial x(sr)} \right] \dfrac{\partial x(sr)}{\partial sr} > 0,$

$$p(sr) \frac{\partial F[.]}{\partial e(sr)} \frac{\partial e(sr)}{\partial sr} > 0, \text{ and } \frac{\partial w(sr)}{\partial sr} x(sr) > 0.$$

This condition holds when the (positive) productivity and demand-side effects compensate the (negative) cost effect and therefore the social responsibility choice generates a non-negative impact on profits.

Strong sustainability condition

$$\frac{\partial \pi(sr)}{\partial sr} = \frac{\partial p(sr)}{\partial sr} F[.] + p(sr) \left[\frac{\partial F(sr)}{\partial sr} e(sr) + \frac{\partial e(sr)}{\partial sr} x(sr) \right] - \frac{\partial w(sr)}{\partial sr} x(sr)$$

$$- \frac{\partial x(sr)}{\partial sr} w(sr) \geq 0 \tag{10.7}$$

By conjecturing that $p(sr) \dfrac{\partial F[.]}{\partial e(sr)} \dfrac{\partial e(sr)}{\partial sr} > 0, \ \dfrac{\partial x(sr)}{\partial sr} x(sr) > 0,$ and

$$\frac{\partial p(sr)}{\partial sr} F[.] + \left[p(sr) \frac{\partial F[.]}{\partial x(sr)} - \frac{\partial w(sr)}{\partial x(sr)} \right] \frac{\partial x(sr)}{\partial sr} = 0.$$

This condition is stronger as it implies that CSR may have a non-negative impact on corporate performance even without consumers' participation, since the positive productivity effect is strong enough to offset the negative cost effect. It is important to test this condition since its existence would imply that the social responsibility choice would be feasible and have a positive impact on profits, even if not advertised to consumers.

Rationales for the three effects

This section provides an economic description of the three effects formally derived from the analytical framework.

Demand-side effect

The assumption of a significant positive effect of social responsibility on consumer demand is supported by numerous theoretical studies and extensive empirical findings. These theoretical studies depart from the standard microfoundation of consumer preferences, which generally considers purely self-interested utility-maximizing individuals taken in isolation. Recent contributions provide broader motivations for individual preferences by focusing on issues such as intrinsic motivation, non-pecuniary incentives, inequity aversion, and social preferences (Fehr and Falk 2002).

An interesting branch of this literature analyses how worker and consumer choices that cannot be explained according to standard formulations of consumer preferences are indeed consistent with approaches that focus on 'social preferences'.[7] Another parallel strand of this literature builds on the idea of reciprocity and tries to capture elements of inequity aversion (Fehr and Schmidt 1999, 2002; Sobel 2005).

Inequity aversion models generally consider interaction and externalities among co-workers (Campbell and Kamlani 1997; Bewley 1999; Agell and Lundborg 2003). Becchetti and Rosati (2007) argue that the compression of distance caused by globalization allows for the extension of models of inequity aversion to account for North–South world inequality.

Based on these approaches, it is reasonable to assume the existence of a given share of socially responsible consumers whose demand is positively affected by the socially responsible features of goods and services sold on the market. Empirical evidence supporting this assumption is extensive. Based on the findings of the World Values Survey, Israel and Levinson (2004) and Torgler and Garcia-Valinas (2005) show that on average 40 per cent of respondents from 65 countries are willing to pay more taxes, accept reductions in income, or pay higher prices on products in order to help fight environmental degradation. Additional evidence is provided by Becchetti and Rosati (2007), who show that Italian consumers are willing to pay in excess for the socially responsible features of fair-trade products (see also Chapter 7 of this volume).

A series of studies have evaluated the share of socially responsible consumers in representative population surveys. In Italy, a 2004 study found that 40 per cent of respondents purchased fair-trade products at least once a year and 20 per cent of them purchased these products more frequently (Demos & Pi 2004). An earlier study classified consumers in the UK as ethical (23 per cent), semi-ethical (56 per cent), and selfish (17 per cent) and reported that 18 per cent of the surveyed consumers declared their willingness to pay a premium for socially responsible products (Bird and Hughes 1997). In Belgium, about 10 per cent of the population expressed a willingness to buy fair-trade coffee at a premium (De Pelsmacker *et al.* 2003), while in Germany 2.9 per cent of the population report buying fair-trade products regularly, 19 per cent rarely, 6 per cent almost never, and 35 per cent said they support the idea but do not buy them (Vantomme *et al.* 2006).

Cost effect

It is intuitively evident that social responsibility criteria are generally cost increasing given that they usually involve improved conditions for a firm's stakeholders (workers, subcontractors, and local communities). The main cost-increasing components of CSR are examined below.

Employee motivation effect

The same CSR criteria that improve workers' conditions (retirement benefits, implementation of job safety measures, participation in profits and corporate decision making) may provide important incentives for workers. The efficiency wage literature identifies four rationales for a positive relationship between wages (and more generally monetary and non-monetary working benefits) and employee effort (Yellen 1984). In a group of shirking models, higher wage (and non-wage) benefits increase the penalty of workers being fired when they are caught shirking and therefore increase workers' effort in equilibrium. In these models, the optimal wage is above the market clearing level and unemployment in equilibrium acts as a disciplining device since it increases the penalty for being caught shirking (Shapiro and Stiglitz 1984). Higher wage and non-wage benefits may also serve to reduce the probability of employees looking for another job and therefore reduce turnover costs (Salop 1979). Moreover, 'adverse selection efficiency wage' models show that if ability and workers' reservation wages are positively correlated, better wage and non-wage benefits attract more productive workers and reduce the risk of adverse selection (Malcomson 1981). Finally, Akerlof's (1982) gift exchange model shows that the decision to provide workers a 'gift' in the form of wage and non-wage working conditions positively affects implicit working norms and productivity.

Comparison with a benchmark

The best-known benchmarks of social responsibility are the selection criteria used for the FTSE KLD 400 Social Index (KLD400) by the firm KLD Research and Analytics (2009b). The KLD400 Index is a market-capitalization-weighted stock index of 400 publicly traded US companies that have met high standards of social and environmental excellence. These companies have been selected based on KLD's CSR criteria, which constitute a widely accepted international standard for selecting stocks to include in ethical fund portfolios. The application of these criteria for the period from 1990 to 2001 on a wide and representative sample of corporations provides a large number of observations for testing the impact of social responsibility on corporate performance.

The KLD400 criteria are divided into eight broad categories: community, corporate governance, diversity, employee relations, environment, human rights, product quality, and controversial business issues. For each category, the KLD400 Index identifies strengths and weaknesses of corporate actions with respect to CSR (see Appendix).

KLD400 criteria with cost-increasing potential

Since CSR mainly involves the (costly) improvement of relationships with various stakeholders, it is not surprising that several KLD400 criteria are potentially cost increasing, including the following specific items:

*   charitable giving, support for education, and support for housing (Community section);
*   work benefits ('employee benefits or programs addressing work/life concerns, e.g. childcare, elder care or flextime') (Diversity section);
*   profit-sharing, health and safety, and retirement benefit programmes (Employee Relations section);
*   climate protection ('significant measures to reduce corporate impact on climate change and air pollution through use of renewable energy and clean fuels or through energy efficiency or a commitment to promoting climate-friendly policies and practices outside its own operations') (Environment section);
*   support for indigenous peoples and labour rights ('the company has established relations with indigenous peoples near its proposed or current operations—either in or outside the U.S.—that respect the sovereignty, land, culture, human rights and intellectual property of the indigenous peoples' and 'the company has outstanding transparency on overseas sourcing disclosure and monitoring or has particularly good union relations outside the U.S.') (Human Rights section).

While CSR criteria that entail benefits to stakeholders imply additional costs, some CSR criteria may have the opposite effect.

KLD400 criteria with cost-reducing or productivity-enhancing potential

An inspection of the KLD400 criteria reveals that one domain (product quality) is profit enhancing and another (corporate governance) is cost decreasing (since it limits compensation for managers), with additional productivity-enhancing effects if workers have inequity aversion in their preferences. On the other hand, several of the criteria identified above as cost increasing may also have cost-decreasing effects if they have a positive impact on workers' motivations and productivity. These include programmes of work/life benefits ('the company has outstanding employee benefits or other programmes addressing work/life concerns, e.g. childcare, eldercare, or flextime') in the Diversity section and several factors in the Employee Relations section, such as:

*   profit-sharing ('the company has a cash profit-sharing program through which it has recently made distributions to a majority of its workforce');

- employee involvement ('the company strongly encourages worker involvement and/or ownership through stock options available to a majority of its employees, gain sharing, stock ownership, sharing of financial information, or participation in management decision-making');
- health and safety ('the company is noted by the US Occupational Health and Safety Administration for its safety programs');
- retirement benefits ('the company has a notably strong retirement benefits program');.
- union relations ('the company has a history of notably strong union relations');
- employee relations ('the company has strong employee relations initiatives not covered by other KLD ratings').

(KLD Research and Analytics 2009a; see Appendix)

The aim of this study is to evaluate the net aggregate impact of cost-increasing and potentially productivity-enhancing effects on sales per worker and then to investigate whether this impact differs between companies that sell intermediate and final goods. The assumption is that the effect of the CSR choice is less positive for firms selling intermediate goods since they do not benefit directly from the impact of socially responsible consumers.

Empirical literature on the impact of CSR

Empirical studies on the relationship between the CSR choice and corporate performance can be divided into three groups. The first group finds that there is a positive relationship between CSR and corporate performance and that the costs of having a high level of CSR are more than compensated by benefits in employee morale and productivity (Solomon and Hanson 1985). Moreover, CSR is positively associated with financial performance (Pava and Krausz 1996; Preston and O'Bannon 1997), positive synergies exist between corporate performance and good relations with stakeholders (Stanwick and Stanwick 1998; Verschoor 1998), and the adoption of CSR is positively associated with growth in sales and returns on sales (Ruf *et al.* 2001) or with higher value added even when there is a non-positive effect on the return on equity (Becchetti *et al.* 2007b).

The second group of studies does not identify any significant direction in the link between CSR and corporate performance. For example, McWilliams and Siegel (2000) observe that when per capita R&D expenditure is added to the regressors, the positive correlation between financial performance and KLD400 affiliation disappears. Equally inconclusive results are reported by Anderson and Frankle (1980), Freedman and Jaggi (1986), and Aupperle *et al.* (1985).

The third group highlights the existence of an inverse relationship between CSR and performance and seems to support the managerial opportunism hypothesis, which maintains that CSR reduces the loyalty of management to shareholders and increase management's room for arbitrary action and the possibility of cash flow waste with negative consequences for a firm's performance (Preston and O'Bannon 1997; Freedman and Jaggi 1986; Ingram and Frazier 1980; Waddock and Graves 1997).

The lack of clear unidirectional findings in this literature is highlighted by Margolis and Walsh (2001: 15): 'When treated as an independent variable, corporate social performance is found to have a positive relationship to financial performance in 42 studies (53 per cent), no relationship in 19 studies (24 per cent), a negative relationship in 4 studies (5 per cent), and a mixed relationship in 15 studies (19 per cent).' This lack of a consensus about the direction of the relationship between corporate performance and CSR is partially justified by the different frames (observation periods, companies included, measures of corporate performance, and methodological approaches adopted) in the various studies.

What is needed to shed light on this puzzle is a deeper understanding of the expected effects from the CSR choice in order to specify more clearly testable hypotheses and an improvement in the estimation techniques in order to disentangle the CSR effect from the larger set of concurring factors. Our study builds upon the existing research from several points of view. First, it uses panel data and panel cointegration techniques and takes into account a significantly long period, accounting specifically for business cycle effects with year dummies. Second, it introduces firm-specific intercepts (fixed effects), thereby separating the impact of CSR from time-invariant and firm-idiosyncratic characteristics. Third, it checks the robustness of panel fixed-effect findings with autoregressive generalized method of moments (GMM) estimates to control properly for endogeneity in the relationship between CSR and corporate performance. Fourth, on the basis of the decomposition of the CSR impact on corporate performance, it tests the significance of the socially responsible consumer demand effect by distinguishing between firms for which this effect may or may not apply. Finally, it explores whether the CSR demand effect is stable or has grown in recent years.

The econometric model

Based upon the definitions of weak and strong sustainability discussed above, the following hypothesis was formulated for empirical testing:

$H_0(1)$: If the weak sustainability condition holds, but the strong sustainability condition does not, the consumer effect of social responsibility is relevant and

$$\frac{\partial p(sr)}{\partial sr} F[.] + \left[p(sr) \frac{\partial F[.]}{\partial x(sr)} - \frac{\partial w(sr)}{\partial x(sr)} \right] \frac{\partial x(sr)}{\partial sr} > 0$$

In order to test this hypothesis, firms were divided between those selling intermediate goods and those selling to final consumers. The argument is that $H_0(1)$ is not rejected if the effect of inclusion in the KLD400 Index generates nonnegative changes in cash flow per employee in firms selling to final consumers and negative changes in cash flow per employee for firms selling intermediate products.[8]

An alternative approach to check for the relevance of the socially responsible consumer effect is to consider net sales per worker as the dependent variable and test whether the latter is significantly higher for firms selling final consumer goods. This variable should incorporate productivity-enhancing and socially responsible consumer effects and, to a lesser extent, cost-increasing effects since they may affect competitiveness and therefore net sales. This approach is the basis for the second hypothesis:

$H_0(2)$: the social responsible consumer effect is relevant if the impact of CSR on net sales per worker is significantly higher in firms selling final consumer goods with elastic demand than in firms selling intermediate goods.

This hypothesis may be considered controversial as some counterexamples exist. For instance, consider that in some cases intermediate good producers may signal (with advertising or with a certification of upstream productive processes) their CSR actions and thereby capture the willingness to pay of socially responsible consumers. An illustration would be timber companies using sustainable yield harvesting and then encouraging retailers who buy the lumber for resale to homebuilders and consumers to label the products as socially responsible at the store level. Nonetheless, this is probably not the usual pattern, and the purpose is to test whether firms selling final consumer goods may have a stronger interest and advantage in being socially responsible. A second rationale for the hypothesis is that CSR may be an important signal of product quality (and indeed is a criteria in KLD400 screening) that helps to overcome informational asymmetries with consumers in contexts where low product quality may have high pecuniary and non-pecuniary costs for consumers. This would explain why food and banking are leading industries in the CSR movement.

In order to test the impact of KLD400 screening on corporate performance, the following specification was made:

$$Y_{it} = \alpha_0 + \alpha_i + \alpha_1 KLD400 + \alpha_2 KLD400consumer(KLM\,400intermediate)$$

$$+\alpha_3 Entry + \alpha_4 Log(postexit_{it}) + \sum_{k=1}^{n-1} \beta_k ReasExit_k + \sum_{t=1}^{m-1} \gamma_t Year_t$$

$$+\alpha_5 Log(Size_{it}) + \varepsilon_{it}$$

$$(10.8)$$

where Y_{it} is a chosen performance variable (e.g. cash flow per employee or total sales per employee), α_i is the time-invariant firm idiosyncratic (fixed) effect, *Size* is the number of firm employees, *KLD400* is a (zero/one) dummy measuring affiliation to the KLD400 Index, *KLD400consumer* and *KLD400intermediate* are two additional dummies measuring affiliation to the KLD400 Index when the firm sells final consumer demand elastic (intermediate or consumer demand inelastic) goods, *Entry* is a dummy which takes the value of one in the year of entry into the KLD400 Index and zero otherwise, *Postexit* is a variable measuring the number of years following exit from the KLD400 Index, $Reasexit_k$ is the kth dummy taking the value of one in the year of exit when the specific exit rationale (*Military, Environment, Productquality, Badgovnce* and *Badlabour*) applies, and $Year_t$ is the year dummy picking up business cycle effects.

This specification helps to disentangle the effects of CSR (proxied by KLD400 affiliation) from business cycle effects (year dummies) and idiosyncratic characteristics (e.g. management quality) of each firm (proxied by the fixed effect measured through the firm specific intercept component u_i).

In selecting firms to be included in the estimate, several specific characteristics of the index were considered. Fictitious exits or exits not caused by a decline in CSR were ruled out; these included changes of ticker symbols, mergers or acquisitions, and bankruptcy. Given the characteristics of the KLD400 Index, two types of bias partially compensate for each other: on the one hand, firms selected tend to be those that not only are good in CSR but are also able to market it, thereby enhancing positive CSR effects on performance in the estimates; on the other hand, entry into the index is possible only when there is a dropout in order to maintain a constant number of index constituents. This implies that some of the firms in the control sample may be CSR firms on the waiting list, thereby reducing the CSR differences between the two subgroups. In spite of these limitations, the KLD database is at present the most reliable source of information on CSR and remains a good benchmark for testing the impact of CSR on corporate performance.

Results

Table 10.1 provides descriptive statistics on the distribution of the dependent variables (net cash flow per employee and net sales per employee) for the three subgroups in the analysis: *KLD400consumer, KLD400intermediate*, and *NonKLD400* firms. These values were calculated for the overall sample and for the subsamples of large, small, R&D investing, and non-R&D investing firms in order to test whether findings were robust in size and R&D investing splits.

In the distribution of cash flow per employee in the overall sample, this variable is always larger for *KLD400consumer* than for *KLD400intermediate* firm years in the highest percentiles (Table 10.1, columns 2 and 3). This finding is quite stable in size and R&D investment breakdowns. The dominance of the *KLD400consumer* on the *KLD400intermediate* subsample distribution is more clear-cut for net sales per worker (Table 10.1, columns 5 and 6).

Standard techniques applied to time series require that before estimating a model the series are $I(0)$ or, if not, that they have at least one cointegrating vector. This is to avoid spurious relationships due to significant relationships between the dependent variable and the regressors. These techniques can also be

Table 10.1 Net sales and net cash flow per employee

Total

Centiles	Net cash flow			Net sales		
	KLD400-consumer	KLD400-intermediate	Non-KLD400	KLD400-consumer	KLD400-intermediate	Non-KLD400
1	−465.17	−286.91	−407.81	7.21	6.33	0.81
10	−17.05	−13.68	−19.13	57.43	25.73	12.78
20	−4.02	−3.52	−4.10	115.84	63.47	37.06
30	−0.95	−0.69	−0.74	167.76	120.51	92.12
40	−0.08	0.01	0.00	224.36	159.27	149.81
50	0.37	0.48	0.56	336.11	220.97	212.60
60	1.62	1.65	1.86	511.24	314.24	320.65
70	4.83	4.65	5.33	858.91	428.58	506.52
80	12.24	10.33	14.07	1,977.71	681.45	886.18
90	44.52	29.58	52.98	5,856.46	1,770.72	2,090.92
99	1,073.96	413.98	1,095.18	66,154.65	20,636.73	48,830.65
No. of firm years	2,388	1,252	3,193	2,474	1,300	3,288

Large

Centiles	Net cash flow			Net sales		
	KLD400-consumer	KLD400-intermediate	Non-KLD400	KLD400-consumer	KLD400-intermediate	Non-KLD400
1	−1,382.19	−515.46	−486.95	8.46	27.91	2.11
10	−38.04	−19.85	−19.19	115.13	73.04	38.50
20	−6.51	−4.33	−5.62	192.77	123.67	159.78
30	−1.41	−0.92	−1.34	255.05	158.71	235.03
40	−0.02	0.02	0.03	371.18	199.88	342.35
50	1.09	1.05	1.16	595.38	290.58	482.40
60	4.20	3.88	2.94	1,339.12	382.50	718.72
70	10.74	8.76	7.39	2,462.53	485.44	1,171.27
80	27.59	17.16	16.34	5,045.65	790.32	1,899.38
90	136.22	49.72	49.88	11,582.26	2,310.58	3,940.17
99	1,545.95	1,129.66	1,188.15	100,945.30	19,439.40	169,408.20

Small

No. of firm years	960	359	620	989	373	655
	Net cash flow			Net sales		
Centiles	KLD400-consumer	KLD400-intermediate	Non-KLD400	KLD400-consumer	KLD400-intermediate	Non-KLD400
1	−190.31	−79.76	−246.04	7.65	1.37	0.91
10	−7.20	−5.88	−13.86	60.26	14.15	5.14
20	−2.31	−0.88	−1.99	90.93	26.03	12.23
30	−0.51	−0.24	−0.36	117.05	38.67	34.36
40	−0.08	0.01	−0.01	152.48	54.46	60.06
50	0.22	0.17	0.22	215.90	82.94	102.11
60	0.78	0.58	0.93	361.30	133.61	172.20
70	2.20	1.60	2.71	504.51	230.67	291.70
80	4.72	4.36	6.51	815.56	406.93	543.39
90	12.80	17.97	26.48	1,595.26	537.74	1,381.78
99	288.19	169.67	2,956.00	64,611.91	1,118.60	44,759.86
No. of firm years	559	237	691	577	252	717

R&D investing firms

	Net cash flow			Net sales		
Centiles	KLD400-consumer	KLD400-intermediate	Non-KLD400	KLD400-consumer	KLD400-intermediate	Non-KLD400
1	−397.01	−1,034.67	−261.92	2.93	10.95	1.21
10	−20.50	−18.84	−22.08	43.77	45.46	23.27
20	−4.76	−5.12	−5.90	123.62	110.19	87.61
30	−0.80	−0.88	−1.28	170.80	152.61	137.18
40	−0.02	0.04	−0.01	215.83	194.17	176.76
50	0.55	0.83	0.63	271.21	255.47	239.92
60	2.16	2.36	2.65	383.51	339.58	317.02
70	6.58	6.69	7.44	532.59	424.81	450.20
80	16.48	14.53	16.71	1,264.74	816.74	748.63
90	53.26	37.59	61.23	5,690.47	2,423.01	1,853.25
99	782.01	1,159.29	1,030.18	65,271.88	43,132.80	88,147.78

Table 10.1 Continued

No. of firms years	608	309	924	629	319	936

Non-R&D investing firms

	Net cash flow			Net sales		
Centiles	KLD400-consumer	KLD400-intermediate	Non-KLD400	KLD400-consumer	KLD400-intermediate	Non-KLD400
1	-550.88	-209.96	-545.36	8.47	5.39	0.76
10	-16.36	-12.20	-17.51	60.99	21.22	10.96
20	-3.85	-3.13	-3.45	112.38	56.34	30.35
30	-1.05	-0.67	-0.65	166.17	105.46	70.60
40	-0.11	0.00	0.01	230.49	147.38	133.78
50	0.29	0.38	0.56	379.84	208.15	202.75
60	1.45	1.53	1.74	583.99	304.94	322.85
70	4.36	4.24	4.64	990.88	429.12	547.64
80	11.74	9.28	12.77	2,084.06	630.97	914.47
90	41.97	26.47	47.92	5,887.76	1,635.18	2,197.75
99	1,173.65	342.78	1,240.26	73,770.91	19,019.40	43,850.36
No. of firms years	1,780	943	2,269	1,845	981	2,352

Notes
Legend
The social responsibility criteria of the KLD400 Index are reported in the Appendix. The database includes 1,077 firms for 12,001 valid firm-year observations. Firm KLD400 years are divided into two subgroups (*KLD400consumers* and *KLD400intermediate*). *KLD400consumers* are firms having at least one important final product with elastic consumers' demand. Firms selling intermediate products only or consumer products with inelastic consumer demand are included in the *KLD400intermediate* subgroup.

applied to the time dimension of individuals in panels. The application of these techniques to panel data is complex and requires the formulation of joint hypotheses on the stationarity of the time series of each of the individuals (in this case firms) being part of the panel.

The first test for the stationarity of non-discrete series in the estimates (firm size, net cash flow per worker, net sales per worker) was done using Fisher's test, developed by Maddala and Wu (1999), based on the *p*-values from *N* independent unit root tests. The null hypothesis assumes that all series are nonstationary. The test has two alternatives: the homogeneous (all series are stationary) and the heterogeneous (some series are stationary and others are not). The null hypothesis is rejected for the dependent variables (see Table 10.2a).

The problem with the Fisher test is that it cannot discriminate between the homogeneous and the heterogeneous alternatives. For this reason, Im *et al.* (2003) added a diagnostic that tests the null hypothesis that all series are nonstationary against the heterogeneous alternative. This test does not lead to the rejection of the null hypothesis for the net sales and net cash flow per employee series. This finding is consistent with the result of the Fisher test performed on individual (firm) series of the additional continuous variables (such as firm size), which shows in some cases stationarity and in some others nonstationarity.[9]

Once the existence of nonstationarity in at least some of the time dimensions of the individual firm series is verified, regression in levels with these variables can still be done if the presence of common stochastic trends (i.e. of cointegration) is found. To check this, the Nyblom and Harvey (2000) test was used, since it has the advantages of allowing for serial correlation in residuals and of not requiring a model to be estimated.[10] This test rejects the null hypothesis of

Table 10.2a Panel unit root test on two performance variables

		Size	Net sales per worker	Net cash flow per worker
Fisher *t*-test	*p*-value	0.001	0.001	0.001
	T*	−0.774	−1.631	−3.312
	Critical value 10%	−1.64	−1.69	−1.64
	Critical value 5%	−1.67	−1.67	−1.67
	Critical value 1%	−1.73	−1.73	−1.73
	N	568	414	192
IPS test	*W**	17.286	−2.584	−24.924
	p-value	1.000	0.005	0.000

Notes
Legend
Fisher t-test: The null hypothesis is that all series are non-stationary against the homogeneous alternative (all series are stationary) and the heterogeneous alternative (some series are stationary and some others are not).
IPS test: The null hypothesis of the test is that all series are non-stationary (H_0: $\rho_i=1$) under the assumption of serially uncorrelated (T*) or serially correlated (W*) errors against the alternative heterogeneous hypothesis (H_1: $\rho_i<1$ for each $i=1,\ldots,N_1$ and $\rho_i=1$ for each $i=N_1+1,\ldots,N$ for some N_1).

Table 10.2b Test for panel cointegration

		Size	Net sales per worker	Net cash flow per worker
	NH-t	74.667	8.412	7.153
	NH adj-t	44.800	41.230	38.450
Fixed effects	Critical value 10%	18.36	18.36	18.36
	Critical value 5%	19.01	19.01	19.01
	Critical value 1%	20.25	20.25	20.25
	N	N > 100	N > 100	N > 100

Notes
Legend
The null hypothesis of the Nyblom and Harvey (2000) test for panel cointegration is absence of cointegration (H_0: rank(var-cov)=K=0) against the alternative hypothesis of cointegration (H_1: rank (var-cov)=$K \neq 0$). *NH-t*: The test is performed under the hypothesis of independent and identically distributed errors. *NH adj-t*: Errors are allowed to be serially correlated, and the test is performed using an estimate of the long-run variance derived from the spectral density matrix at frequency zero.

absence of common stochastic trends under the assumption of non-independent and identically distributed (non-IID) standard errors (*NH adj-t* in Table 10.2b), thereby identifying the presence of cointegrating vectors which allow the model to be estimated in levels.

Table 10.3a illustrates the econometric findings on the test of the null hypotheses $H_0(1)$ (strong and weak sustainability conditions) and $H_0(2)$ on the overall sample. The dependent variable is the net cash flow per worker in columns 1 and 2 and net sales per worker in columns 3 and 4.

Cash flow per worker estimates show that KLD400 affiliation does not affect the dependent variable either positively or negatively (Table 10.3a, columns 1 and 2). These estimates also show that the same result applies to the marginal effect of being part of the specific *KLD400consumer* subgroup (Table 10.3a, column 3) while the marginal effect of *KLD400 affiliation* for the *KLD400intermediate* subgroup is significantly related to a downward shift in the net cash flow per worker. These findings do not contradict the weak sustainability hypothesis (Table 10.3a, column 2). If it is assumed that *KLD400intermediate* firms do not have the benefit of the socially responsible consumer effect, then KLD400 affiliation is sustainable only when this effect is added to the other two expected ones of higher costs and higher employee motivation.

All other variables with estimates shown in Table 10.3a are not significant, with the exception of the strong relevance of size (documenting that cash flow per worker does not grow proportionally to the number of employees) and of the joint significance of fixed effects, which confirms the importance of time-invariant firm-idiosyncratic characteristics.

Further indirect confirmation of the relevance of the consumer effect is provided by an analysis of the impact of the CSR choice on performance by estimating the same model with net sales per worker as the dependent variable

(Table 10.3a, columns 3 and 4). Unlike the previous case, there are no subtracting costs (and therefore controlling for costs) in the dependent variable. It is therefore to be expected that the impact of CSR on the dependent variable depends mainly on the remaining two effects (employee motivation and the socially responsible consumer effect), even though net sales indirectly depend also on cost variations that may significantly reduce competitiveness and market demand for firm products. To sum up, the expected impact of the cost effect should be much smaller when using net sales instead of cash flow.

Consistently with these expectations on the reduced impact of the cost effect on the dependent variable, affiliation to the KLD400 Index has a significant positive effect on net sales per worker (compared to the insignificant effect on net cash flow per worker), net of the impact of fixed effects, firm size, and length of exit from the KLD400 Index calculated in years, and motivation for exit. Not surprisingly, the positive effect of CSR on the dependent variable almost disappears for the *KLD400intermediate* subgroup (Table 10.3a, column 3). This finding does not contradict the hypothesis that most of the positive impact on net sales depends on the socially responsible consumer demand effect.

Net sales per worker estimates also reveal the interesting finding of a positive impact of exit from the KLD400 for violating the Military section of the KLD400 criteria and of a negative impact for the number of years after exiting the KLD400. This last result does not contradict Freeman's (1984) hypothesis that CSR minimizes transaction costs with stakeholders, if it is assumed that an increase in the number of years of exit from the KLD400 raises the possibility that such conflicts generate negative effects on firm net sales.

It is important to note that the significance of exit compared to the lack of significance for entry (both in net sales and cash flow per worker estimates) is consistent with one of the features of the KLD400 Index criteria discussed above: since the number of index constituents is fixed, newly qualified entrants can only become part of the index when one of the existing constituents is excluded.

To check whether the CSR choice corresponds to firm time-invariant characteristics, an examination was conducted to determine whether there existed a systematic difference in mean between fixed effect of the *AlwaysKLD400* (firms always included the KLD400 Index throughout the sample period) and of the *NeverKLD400* subgroups (firms never in the KLD400 Index throughout the sample period). These fixed effects were then regressed on industry and size dummies to extract firms' idiosyncratic characteristics that do not depend on size or industry affiliation. The findings show that, before and after correcting for these two groups of variables, *AlwaysKLD400* firms have significantly higher net sales per worker than *NeverKLD400* firms.

The interpretation is that differences in net sales and cash flow per worker between KLD400 and non-KLD400 firms may in part depend on idiosyncratic characteristics, even though it is not possible to exclude that the difference depends on factors related to the entry of the *AlwaysKLD400* firms into the KLD400 Index before the beginning of the sample period. A robustness check

Table 10.3a The effect of CSR choice on net cash flow and net sales per employee (fixed effect estimates)

	Log (1 + Net cash flow per employee)		Log (Net sales per employee)	Log (Net sales per employee)
KLD400	−0.10 (−0.72)	0.15 (1.31)	0.07 (1.92)	0.17 (5.72)
KLD400consumer	0.22 (1.28)		0.08 (1.89)	
KLD400intermedi		−0.35 (−2.01)		−0.14 (−3.00)
Entry	0.13 (0.79)	0.13 (0.80)	0.02 (0.43)	0.02 (0.40)
Log (Postexit)	−0.20 (−1.12)	−0.20 (−1.09)	−0.20 (−4.09)	−0.20 (−4.07)
Military	0.58 (0.84)	0.55 (0.80)	0.46 (2.71)	0.45 (2.63)
Environment	−0.03 (−0.06)	−0.06 (−0.12)	0.14 (0.96)	0.13 (0.90)
Productquality	0.18 (0.35)	0.16 (0.31)	0.26 (1.96)	0.25 (1.86)
Badgovernance	−0.48 (−0.92)	−0.44 (−0.84)	0.001 (−0.03)	0.01 (0.06)
Badlabour	0.43 (0.94)	0.44 (0.95)	0.16 (1.31)	0.16 (1.33)
Log (Size)	−0.81 (−23.56)	−0.81 (−23.52)	−0.70 (−78.74)	−0.70 (−78.69)
Constant	9.45 (29.28)	9.43 (29.24)	12.14 (144.21)	12.13 (144.16)
R-sq: Within	0.12	0.12	0.43	0.43
R-sq: Between	0.48	0.48	0.40	0.41
R-sq: Overall	0.38	0.37	0.39	0.39
Observations	6,929	6,929	12,001	12,001
Groups	1,076	1,076	1,077	1,077
Overall regression significance (F-test)	34.27**	34.38**	339.35**	339.75**
Significance of fixed effects (F test)	6.61**	6.63**	94.14 **	94.79**
Fixed Effects ±				
AlwaysKLD400	0.06956*	0.06953*	−0.00462	−0.00489
NeverKLD400	−0.18434*	−0.18426*	0.01203	0.01275
Fixed Effect net of industry and size ± ±				
AlwaysKLD400	0.03523*	0.03532*	0.01641	0.01648
NeverKLD400	−0.09335*	−0.09361*	−0.04277	−0.04294

Notes

Legend

The table reports results of panel fixed effect estimates for the impact of social responsibility (affiliation to the KLD400 Index) on net sales per employee and net cash flow per employee. The social responsibility criteria of the KLD400 Index are reported in the Appendix. The database includes 1,077 firms for 12,001 valid firm-year observations. Firm KLD400 years are divided into two subgroups (*KLD400consumers* and *KLD400intermediate*). *KLD400consumers* are firms having at least one important final product with elastic consumers' demand. Firms selling intermediate products only or consumer products with inelastic consumer demand are included in the *KLD400intermediate* subgroup.

Regressors

Size is the number of firm employees; *KLD400* is a (zero/one) dummy measuring affiliation to the KLD400 Index; *KLD400consumer* (*KLD400intermediate*) are two additional dummies defined as described above; *Entry* is a dummy which takes the value of one in the year of entry into the KLD400 Index and zero otherwise; *Postexit* is a variable measuring the number of years following exit from the KLD400 Index; *Reasexit* is the *k*th dummy taking the value of one in the year of exit when the specific exit rationale (*Military, Environment, Productquality, Badgovernance,* and *Badlabour*) applies; *Year* is a year dummy picking up year effects. Industry and Year dummies are included but their results are omitted for reasons of space.

± subgroup means ± subgroup mean residuals after regressing fixed effects on size and industry dummies.

T-stats in parentheses. *significant at 5 per cent level **significant at 1 per cent level.

was thus performed to shed additional light on the causality direction of the CSR–corporate-performance nexus.

Robustness check

Firm-specific time-invariant dummies in fixed-effect models allow for the interpretation of the dependent variable values as deviations from a time-invariant firm sample average, with industry and year dummies adding other important controls to the analysis. In a robustness check of the previous estimates, it was tested whether the findings persist in autoregressive models in which the lagged dependent variable is added as a regressor to the previous specification. Tests were also conducted to determine whether findings were robust to endogeneity issues since a reverse causation hypothesis on the CSR corporate-performance nexus might apply if KLD400 affiliation was preferentially chosen by better performing firms. The use of instrumental variables in the generalized method of moments (GMM) estimates helped control for endogeneity. The use of GMM was also necessary because correlation between the lagged dependent variable and the error term makes in this case Ordinary Least Squares (OLS) estimates biased and inconsistent, even when error terms are not serially correlated (Arellano and Bover 1995; Blundell and Bond 1998).

A widely used alternative is that of the 'first generation', first-differenced GMM approach. The problem with this approach is that the use of lagged levels are often poor instruments for first differences (Blundell and Bond 1998). Another limit is that if the autoregressive parameter is close to unity or the variance of the individual effects is large with respect to time varying and transient shocks, this estimator has poor finite sample properties (Bond *et al.* 2001). In this case, Arellano and Bover (1995) and Blundell and Bond (1998) suggest the use of 'second generation', system GMM in which the standard set of equations in first differences is combined with a second set of equations in levels with suitably lagged first-differences as instruments.

The two specifications were estimated on the determinants of net cash flow and net sales per employee with a system GMM approach (Table 10.3b). These findings show that the difference in the impact of KLD400 affiliation on net cash flow per employee between the *KLD400consumer* and the *KLD400intermediate* subgroup persists (even if it is weaker) after controlling for the autoregressive component of the dependent variable and for endogeneity in the relationship between CSR and corporate performance. Table 10.3b (columns 1 and 2) shows that *KLD400consumer* firms deviate positively and *KLD400intermediate* (weakly) negatively from a non-significant impact of KLD400 affiliation on the dependent variable. The difference between the impact on the two subgroups is even more clear-cut when the CSR effect on net sales is considered: the results (columns 3 and 4) clearly show that the *KLD400consumer* subgroup significantly overperforms and the *KLD400intermediate* significantly underperforms the control sample. Overall, findings from Table 10.3b confirm the hypothesis of the weak sustainability of the CSR choice.

Table 10.3b The effect of CSR choice on net cash flow and net sales per employee (GMM autoregressive estimates)

	Dependent variable (Y)			
	Log (1 + Net cash flow per employee)		Log (Net sales per employee)	
$Y_{(t-1)}$	0.001 (−0.36)	0.001 (−0.36)	0.58 (25.65)	0.59 (26.61)
KLD400	−1.48 (−1.05)	1.11 (1.33)	−0.61 (−4.09)	0.34 (3.94)
KLD400consumer	2.86 (1.87)	—	1.09 (5.02)	—
KLD400intermedi	—	−2.38 (−1.48)	—	−0.79 (−3.78)
Entry	0.43 (0.93)	0.48 (1.05)	−0.05 (−0.68)	−0.06 (−0.84)
Log(Postexit)	0.88 (1.30)	0.92 (1.37)	0.14 (1.46)	0.13 (1.36)
Military	1.64 (0.49)	1.28 (0.39)	0.37 (0.84)	0.48 (1.11)
Environment	−0.82 (−0.18)	−0.64 (−0.14)	0.59 (1.70)	0.69 (2.04)
Productquality	−0.84 (−0.32)	−0.45 (−0.17)	0.02 (0.08)	0.02 (0.08)
Badgovernance	−0.08 (−0.02)	−0.48 (−0.12)	0.26 (0.82)	0.35 (1.15)
Badlabour	1.20 (0.71)	1.07 (0.64)	0.38 (1.69)	0.39 (1.77)
Log(size)	−1.17 (−7.48)	−1.18 (−7.64)	−0.23 (−6.86)	−0.22 (−6.64)
Constant	11.55 (5.71)	11.39 (5.72)	4.29 (9.36)	4.17 (9.29)
Obs	6,182	6,182	10,832	10,832
Groups	1,064	1,064	1,073	1,073
Sargan test	481.17	446.71	101.17	96.90
AR(1)	−5.92	−6.05	−9.28	−9.72
AR(2)	0.48	0.49	−0.44	−0.48

Notes
Legend
The table reports results of Generalized Method of Moments (GMM) estimates in which the effect of social responsibility (affiliation to the KLD400 Index) is tested on net sales per employee and net cash flow per employee. The social responsibility criteria of the KLD400 Index are reported in the Appendix. The database includes 1,077 firms for 12,001 valid firm-year observations. Firm KLD400 years are divided into two subgroups (*KLD400consumers* and *KLD400intermediate*). *KLD400consumers* are firms having at least one important final product with elastic consumers' demand. Firms selling intermediate products only or consumer products with inelastic consumer demand are included in the *KLD400intermediate* subgroup.
Regressors
$Y_{(t-1)}$ is the one-period-lagged dependent variable. For additional regressors see Table 10.3a. Industry and year dummies are included but their results are omitted for reasons of space.
T-stats in parentheses. *significant at 5 per cent level **significant at 1 per cent level.

Finally, the sample was split into two time periods to test whether the relevance of the socially responsible consumer demand effect, which seemed to emerge from previous findings, is stable across sample subperiods. The results in Table 10.3c clearly show that it is not, indicating that the bulk of the socially responsible consumer demand effect arises in the second subperiod. This finding—along with the negative impact of the *Postexit* variable only during the second subperiod—demonstrates that the role of socially responsible bottom-up pressure has significantly increased in recent years as suggested by the Social Investment Forum (2007).

Conclusions

Establishing the relationship between CSR and corporate performance is analogous to a biological experiment. Social scientists are interested in evaluating what happens when a 'new species' of socially responsible firms is introduced into a competitive 'ecosystem'. One important issue is whether this new species is too weak to survive or is successful due to the competitive advantages linked to the CSR choice.

In this chapter, the impact of the CSR choice on corporate performance has been examined by focusing on the *cost effect*, the *employee motivation effect*, and the *socially responsible consumer effect*. In the empirical analyses, the specific importance of the socially responsible consumer effect has been defined in terms of weak and strong sustainability conditions for CSR firms. If only the weak (and not the strong) condition is shown to hold, then employee motivation is not sufficient to offset the expected higher costs implied by the CSR choice and the preferences of socially responsible consumers become crucial for the survival and success of socially responsible firms.

Our findings in fixed effect estimates on the determinants of net cash flow per worker on two subsamples of firms—one selling intermediate and the other final consumer goods—support the weak condition hypothesis. More generally, the significance of the socially responsible consumer effect on the determinants of net sales per worker is confirmed by additional fixed effects and GMM autoregressive approaches.

The robustness check utilizing two instrumental variables—the differential impact of KLD400 affiliation for the two subsamples and the evaluation of the relationship between CSR and corporate performance net of firm-idiosyncratic time-invariant characteristics—support the interpretation that reverse causation between CSR and corporate performance may not entirely explain the findings.

Finally, a test of the structural stability of the socially responsible consumer effect clearly shows that its impact occurred mainly during the second part of the time interval examined, supporting the hypothesis that the role of socially responsible consumers may be increasing.

Table 10.3c The effect of corporate social responsibility choice on net sales per employee (fixed effect estimates)

	Log (Net sales per employee)			
	1990/1996	1997/2001	1990/1996	1997/2001
KLD400	0.15 (2.10)	0.01 (0.18)	-0.01 (-0.10)	0.14 (3.99)
KLD400consumer	-0.16 (-1.89)	0.13 (2.40)	—	-0.16 (-2.80)
KLD400intermediate	—	—	—	0.03 (0.73)
Entry	0.05 (0.70)	0.03 (0.77)	0.17 (1.95)	-0.16 (-2.63)
Log(Postexit)	-0.11 (-1.01)	-0.15 (-2.55)	0.04 (0.66)	0.22 (0.94)
Military	0.15 (0.91)	0.23 (1.01)	-0.13 (-1.12)	0.14 (0.74)
Environment	-0.22 (-0.76)	0.15 (0.80)	0.15 (0.92)	0.12 (0.85)
Productquality	-0.02 (-0.10)	0.13 (0.85)	-0.19 (-0.68)	0.09 (0.68)
Badgovernance	—	0.08 (0.60)	-0.01 (-0.04)	0.19 (1.08)
Badlabour	0.09 (0.55)	0.19 (1.09)	0.10 (0.60)	0.19 (1.08)
Log (Size)	-0.70 (-43.99)	-0.75 (-56.97)	-0.70 (-43.99)	-0.75 (-56.97)
Constant	10.96 (80.94)	12.45 (104.00)	10.97 (80.94)	12.45 (104.01)
R-sq: Within	0.42	0.36	0.42	0.36
R-sq: Between	0.36	0.41	0.36	0.41
R-sq: Overall	0.35	0.41	0.35	0.41
Observations	4,174	7,827	4,174	7,827
Groups	751	1,076	751	1,076
Overall regression significance (F-test)	162.54	226.63	162.57	226.83
Significance of fixed effects (F test)	153.99	86.03	155.40	86.48
Fixed effect ±				
KLD400	0.07826*	0.05943*	0.07857*	0.05960*
NonKLD400	-0.31247*	-0.13027*	0.31373*	-0.13065*
Fixed effect net of Industry and Size ±±				
KLD400	0.03868*	0.03009*	0.03892*	0.03035*
NonKLD400	-0.15446*	-0.06596*	-0.15538*	-0.06653*

Notes
Legend
The table reports results of panel fixed effect estimates for the impact of social responsibility (affiliation to the KLD400 index) on net sales per employee by sub-period sample. For details about the estimates see Table 10.3a.
± subgroup means ±± subgroup mean residuals after regressing fixed effects on size and industry dummies.
T-stats in parentheses. *significant at 5 per cent level **significant at 1 per cent level.

Appendix: Criteria of the FTSE KLD400 Social Index*

Social issue ratings

Community

STRENGTHS *Charitable Giving.* The company has consistently given over 1.5% of trailing three-year net earnings before taxes (NEBT) to charity, or has otherwise been notably generous in its giving. *Innovative Giving.* The company has a notably innovative giving program that supports nonprofit organizations, particularly those promoting self-sufficiency among the economically disadvantaged. Companies that permit non-traditional federated charitable giving drives in the workplace are often noted in this section as well. *Non-US Charitable Giving.* The company has made a substantial effort to make charitable contributions abroad, as well as in the U.S. To qualify, a company must make at least 20% of its giving, or have taken notably innovative initiatives in its giving program, outside the U.S. *Support for Housing.* The company is a prominent participant in public/private partnerships that support housing initiatives for the economically disadvantaged, *e.g.*, the National Equity Fund or the Enterprise Foundation. *Support for Education.* The company has either been notably innovative in its support for primary or secondary school education, particularly for those programs that benefit the economically disadvantaged, or the company has prominently supported job-training programs for youth. *Other Strength.* The company has either an exceptionally strong volunteer program, in-kind giving program, or engages in other notably positive community activities.

CONCERNS *Investment Controversies.* The company is a financial institution whose lending or investment practices have led to controversies, particularly ones related to the Community Reinvestment Act. *Negative Economic Impact.* The company's actions have resulted in major controversies concerning its economic impact on the community. These controversies can include issues related to environmental contamination, water rights disputes, plant closings, "put-or-pay" contracts with trash incinerators, or other company actions that adversely affect the quality of life, tax base, or property values in the community. *Other Concern.* The company is involved with a controversy that has mobilized community opposition, or is engaged in other noteworthy community controversies.

Corporate governance

STRENGTHS *Limited Compensation.* The company has recently awarded notably low levels of compensation to its top management or its board members. The limit for a rating is total compensation of less than $500,000 per year for a CEO or $30,000 per year for outside directors. *Ownership Strength.* The company owns between 20% and 50% of another company KLD has cited as having an area of social strength, or is more than 20% owned by a firm that KLD has rated as having social strengths. When a company owns more than 50% of another firm, it has a controlling interest, and KLD treats the second firm as if it is a division of the first. *Other Strength.* The company has an innovative compensation plan for its board or executives, a unique and positive corporate culture, or some other initiative not covered by other KLD ratings.

CONCERNS *High Compensation.* The company has recently awarded notably high levels of compensation to its top management or its board members. The limit for a rating is total compensation of more than $10 million per year for a CEO or $100,000 per year for outside directors. *Tax Disputes.* The company has recently been involved in major tax disputes involving more than $100 million with the Federal, state, or local authorities. *Ownership Concern.* The company owns between 20% and 50% of a company KLD has cited as having an area of social concern, or is more than 20% owned by a firm KLD has rated as having areas of concern. When a company owns more than 50% of another firm, it has a controlling interest, and KLD treats the second firm as if it is a division of the first. *Other Concern.* The company restated its earnings over an accounting controversy, has other accounting problems, or is involved with some other controversy not covered by other KLD ratings.

Diversity

STRENGTHS *CEO.* The company's chief executive officer is a woman or a member of a minority group. *Promotion.* The company has made notable progress in the promotion of women and minorities, particularly to line positions with profit-and-loss responsibilities in the corporation. *Board of Directors.* Women, minorities, and/or the disabled hold four seats or more (with no double counting) on the board of directors, or one-third or more of the board seats if the board numbers less than 12. *Work/Life Benefits.* The company has outstanding employee benefits or other programs addressing work/life concerns, *e.g.*, childcare, elder care, or flextime. *Women & Minority Contracting.* The company does at least 5% of its subcontracting, or otherwise has a demonstrably strong record on purchasing or contracting, with women- and/or minority-owned businesses. *Employment of the Disabled.* The company has implemented innovative hiring programs, other innovative human resource programs for the disabled, or otherwise has a superior reputation as an employer of the disabled. *Gay & Lesbian Policies.* The company has implemented notably progressive policies toward its gay and lesbian employees. In particular, it provides benefits to the domestic partners of its employees. *Other Strength.* The company has made a notable commitment to diversity that is not covered by other KLD ratings.

CONCERNS *Controversies.* The company has either paid substantial fines or civil penalties as a result of affirmative action controversies, or has otherwise been involved in major controversies related to affirmative action issues. *Non-Representation.* The company has no women on its board of directors or among its senior line managers. *Other Concern*. The company is involved in diversity controversies not covered by other KLD ratings.

Employee relations

STRENGTHS *Cash Profit Sharing*. The company has a cash profit-sharing program through which it has recently made distributions to a majority of its workforce. *Employee Involvement*. The company strongly encourages worker involvement and/or ownership through stock options available to a majority of its employees, gain sharing, stock ownership, sharing of financial information, or participation in management decision-making. *Health and Safety Strength*. The company is noted by the US Occupational Health and Safety Administration for its safety programs. *Retirement Benefits Strength*. The company has a notably strong retirement benefits program. *Union Relations*. The company has a history of notably strong union relations. *Other Strength*. The company has strong employee relations initiatives not covered by other KLD ratings.

CONCERNS *Union Relations*. The company has a history of notably poor union relations. *Health and Safety Concern*. The company recently has either paid substantial fines or civil penalties for wilful violations of employee health and safety standards, or has been otherwise involved in major health and safety controversies. *Workforce Reductions*. The company has reduced its workforce by 15% in the most recent year or by 25% during the past two years, or it has announced plans for such reductions. *Retirement Benefits Concern*. The company has either a substantially underfunded defined benefit pension plan, or an inadequate retirement benefits program. *Other Concern*. The company is involved in an employee relations controversy that is not covered by other KLD ratings.

Environment

STRENGTHS *Beneficial Products and Services*. The company derives substantial revenues from innovative remediation products, environmental services, or products that promote the efficient use of energy, or it has developed innovative products with environmental benefits. (The term 'environmental service' does not include services with questionable environmental effects, such as landfills, incinerators, waste-to-energy plants, and deep injection wells.) *Clean Energy*. The company has taken significant measures to reduce its impact on climate change and air pollution through use of renewable energy and clean fuels or through energy efficiency. The company has demonstrated a commitment to promoting climate-friendly policies and practices outside its own operations. *Communications*. The company is a signatory to the CERES Principles, publishes a notably substantive environmental report, or has notably effective internal communications systems in place for environmental best practices. *Pollution Prevention*. The company has notably strong pollution prevention programs including both emissions reductions and toxic-use reduction programs. *Recycling*. The company either is a substantial user of recycled materials as raw materials in its manufacturing processes, or a major factor in the recycling industry. *Other Strength.* The company has demonstrated a superior commitment to management systems, voluntary programs, or other environmentally proactive activities.

CONCERNS *Hazardous Waste.* The company's liabilities for hazardous waste sites exceed $50 million, or the company has recently paid substantial fines or civil penalties for waste management violations. *Regulatory Problems.* The company has recently paid substantial fines or civil penalties for violations of air, water, or other environmental regulations, or it has a pattern of regulatory controversies under the Clean Air Act, Clean Water Act or other major environmental regulations. *Ozone Depleting Chemicals.* The company is among the top manufacturers of ozone depleting chemicals such as HCFCs, methyl chloroform, methylene chloride, or bromines. *Substantial Emissions.* The company's legal emissions of toxic chemicals (as defined by and reported to the EPA) from individual plants into the air and water are among the highest of the companies followed by KLD.

Agricultural Chemicals. The company is a substantial producer of agricultural chemicals, *i.e.*, pesticides or chemical fertilizers. *Climate Change.* The company derives substantial revenues from the sale of coal or oil and its derivative fuel products, or the company derives substantial revenues indirectly from the combustion of coal or oil and its derivative fuel products. Such companies include electric utilities, transportation companies with fleets of vehicles, auto and truck manufacturers, and other transportation equipment companies. *Other Concern.* The company has been involved in an environmental controversy that is not covered by other KLD ratings.

Human rights

STRENGTHS *Indigenous Peoples Relations Strength.* The company has established relations with indigenous peoples near its proposed or current operations (either in or outside the U.S.) that respect the sovereignty, land, culture, human rights, and intellectual property of the indigenous peoples. *Labor Rights Strength.* The company has outstanding transparency on overseas sourcing disclosure and monitoring, or has particularly good union relations outside the U.S. *Other Strength.* The company has undertaken exceptional human rights initiatives, including outstanding transparency or disclosure on human rights issues, or has otherwise shown industry leadership on human rights issues not covered by other KLD human rights ratings.

CONCERNS *Burma Concern.* The company has operations or investment in, or sourcing from, Burma. *Labor Rights Concern.* The company's operations outside the U.S. have had major recent controversies related to employee relations and labor standards or its U.S. operations have had major recent controversies involving sweatshop conditions or child labor. *Indigenous Peoples Relations*

Concern. The company has been involved in serious controversies with indigenous peoples (either in or outside the U.S.) that indicate the company has not respected the sovereignty, land, culture, human rights, and intellectual property of indigenous peoples. *Other Concern.* The company's operations outside the U.S. have been the subject of major recent human rights controversies not covered by other KLD ratings.

Product

STRENGTHS *Quality.* The company has a long-term, well-developed, company-wide quality program, or it has a quality program recognized as exceptional in U.S. industry. *R&D/Innovation.* The company is a leader in its industry for research and development (R&D), particularly by bringing notably innovative products to market. *Benefits to Economically Disadvantaged.* The company has as part of its basic mission the provision of products or services for the economically disadvantaged. *Other Strength.* The company's products have notable social benefits that are highly unusual or unique for its industry.

CONCERNS *Product Safety.* The company has recently paid substantial fines or civil penalties, or is involved in major recent controversies or regulatory actions, relating to the safety of its products and services. *Marketing/Contracting Controversy.* The company has recently been involved in major marketing or contracting controversies, or has paid substantial fines or civil penalties relating to advertising practices, consumer fraud, or government contracting. *Antitrust.* The company has recently paid substantial fines or civil penalties for antitrust violations such as price fixing, collusion, or predatory pricing, or is involved in recent major controversies or regulatory actions relating to antitrust allegations. *Other Concern.* The company has major controversies with its franchises, is an electric utility with nuclear safety problems, defective product issues, or is involved in other product-related controversies not covered by other KLD ratings.

Controversial business issues

Adult entertainment

Distributors. The report includes publicly traded U.S. companies that derive 15% or more of total revenues from the *rental, sale, or distribution* (wholesale or retail) of adult entertainment media products. *Owners and Operators.* The report includes publicly traded U.S. companies that own and/or operate adult entertainment establishment. *Producers.* The report includes publicly traded U.S. companies that produce adult media products including movies, magazines, books, calendars, and websites. *Providers.* The report includes publicly traded U.S. companies that offer pay-per-view adult entertainment. *Ownership of an Adult Entertainment Company.* The company owns more than 20% of another company with adult entertainment involvement. (When a company owns more than 50% of company with adult entertainment involvement, KLD treats the adult entertainment company as a consolidated subsidiary.) *Ownership by an Adult Entertainment Company.* The company is more than 50% owned by a company with adult entertainment involvement.

Alcohol

Licensing. The company licenses its company or brand name to alcohol products. *Manufacturers.* Companies that are involved in the manufacture of alcoholic beverages including beer, distilled spirits, or wine. *Manufacturers of Products Necessary for Production of Alcoholic Beverages.* Companies that derive 15% or more of total revenues from the supply of raw materials and other products necessary for the production of alcoholic beverages. *Retailers.* Companies that derive 15% or more of total revenues from the distribution (wholesale or retail) of alcoholic beverages. *Ownership of an Alcohol Company.* The company owns more than 20% of another company with alcohol involvement. (When a company owns more than 50% of company with alcohol involvement, KLD treats the alcohol company as a consolidated subsidiary.) *Ownership by an Alcohol Company.* The company is more than 50% owned by a company with alcohol involvement.

Firearms

Manufacturers. The company is engaged in the production of small arms ammunition or firearms, including, pistols, revolvers, rifles, shotguns, or sub-machine guns. *Retailers.* The company derives 15% or more of total revenues from the distribution (wholesale or retail) of firearms and small arms ammunition. *Ownership of a Firearms Company.* The company owns more than 20% of another company with firearms involvement. (When a company owns more than 50% of company with firearms involvement, KLD treats the firearms company as a consolidated subsidiary.) *Ownership by a Firearms Company.* The company is more than 50% owned by a company with firearms involvement.

Gambling

Licensing. The company licenses its company or brand name to gambling products. *Manufacturers.* Companies that produce goods used exclusively for gambling, such as slot machines, roulette wheels, or lottery terminals. *Owners and Operators.* Companies that own and/or operate casinos, racetracks, bingo parlors, or other betting establishments, including casinos; horse, dog, or other race tracks that permit wagering; lottery operations; on-line gambling; pari-mutuel wagering facilities; bingo; Jai-alai; and other sporting events that permit wagering. *Supporting Products or Services.* Companies that provide services in casinos that are fundamental to gambling operations, such as credit lines, consulting services, or gambling technology and technology support. *Ownership of a Gambling Company.* The company owns more than 20% of another company with gambling involvement. (When a company owns more than 50% of company with gambling involvement, KLD treats the gambling company as a consolidated subsidiary.) *Ownership by a Gambling Company.* The company is more than 50% owned by a company with gambling involvement.

Military

Manufacturers of Weapons or Weapons Systems. Companies that derive more than 2% of revenues from the sale of conventional weapons or weapons systems, or earned $50 million or more from the sale of conventional weapons or weapons systems, or earned $10 million or more from the sale of nuclear weapons or weapons systems. *Manufacturers of Components for Weapons or Weapons Systems.* Companies that derive more than 2% of revenues from the sale of customized components for conventional weapons or weapons systems, or earned $50 million or more from the sale of customized components for conventional weapons or weapons systems, or earned $10 million or more from the sale of customized components for nuclear weapons or weapons systems. *Ownership of a Military Company.* The company owns more than 20% of another company with military involvement. (When a company owns more than 50% of company with military involvement, KLD treats the military company as a consolidated subsidiary.) *Ownership by a Military Company.* The company is more than 50% owned by a company with military involvement.

Nuclear power

Ownership of Nuclear Power Plants. Companies that own nuclear power plants. *Ownership of a Nuclear Power Company.* The company owns more than 20% of another company with nuclear power involvement. (When a company owns more than 50% of company with nuclear power involvement, KLD treats the nuclear power company as a consolidated subsidiary.) *Ownership by a Nuclear Power Company.* The company is more than 50% owned by a company with nuclear power involvement.

Tobacco

Licensing. The company licenses its company name or brand name to tobacco products. *Manufacturers.* The company produces tobacco products, including cigarettes, cigars, pipe tobacco, and smokeless tobacco products. *Manufacturers of Products Necessary for Production of Tobacco Products.* The company derives 15% or more of total revenues from the production and supply of raw materials and other products necessary for the production of tobacco products. *Retailers.* The company derives 15% or more of total revenues from the distribution (wholesale or retail) of tobacco products. *Ownership of a Tobacco*

Company. The company owns more than 20% of another company with tobacco involvement. (When a company owns more than 50% of company with tobacco involvement, KLD treats the tobacco company as a consolidated subsidiary.) *Ownership by a Tobacco Company.* The company is more than 50% owned by a company with tobacco involvement.

(KLD Research and Analytics 2009a)

Notes

* Prior to July 2009 the KLD400 was known as the Domini Social Index; in November 2009KLD became part of the RiskMetrics Group.
1 The authors thank Helen Alford, Michele Bagella, Laura Boccardelli, Saverio De Santo, Iftekhar Hasan, James Lothian, Ferruccio Marzano, Francesco Nucci, Alberto Pozzolo, Lorenzo Sacconi, and Stefano Zamagni for their useful suggestions and Osea Giuntella for his valuable research assistance. Support from *Econometrica* and the Veritatis Splendor's Research Project on Social Responsibility is acknowledged. The usual disclaimer applies.
2 According to the Social Investment Forum (2007), socially responsible investments involve around 11 per cent of assets under professional management in the US. These investments grew 324 per cent (from \$639 billion to \$2.71 trillion) between 1995 and 2007 compared to a general growth in professionally managed assets of 260 per cent during the same period. A demonstration of the high sensitivity of shareholders for CSR is that support for resolutions on social and environmental issues increased from 9.8 per cent in 2005 to 15.4 per cent in 2007.
3 There is both a price and quantity effect under the assumption of a non-zero and less than infinite price-elastic aggregate supply curve for the given good. The assumption is that a positive demand shock has a positive effect on prices that is consistent with different market structures. This assumption is compatible with short-run equilibrium in perfect competition, with forms of monopolistic competition, and with monopoly.
4 For convenience, the only effects considered here are second order (i.e. due to a reduction of prices caused by an increase in firm supply), negligible, and dominated by the main effect.
5 For convenience, the only second-order effects considered here are those generated by an upward-sloping labour supply curve (i.e. a reduction of workers hired due to higher wage costs), negligible, and dominated by the main effect.
6 Consider that the first order condition of Equation (10.1) is

$$\frac{\partial \pi(sr)}{\partial sr} = \frac{\partial p(sr)}{\partial sr} F[.] + p(sr)\frac{\partial F[.]}{\partial sr} - \frac{\partial w(sr)}{\partial sr} x(sr) - \frac{\partial x(sr)}{\partial sr} w(sr)$$

where $\frac{\partial F[.]}{\partial sr} = \left[\frac{\partial x(sr)}{\partial sr} e(sr) + \frac{\partial e(sr)}{\partial sr} x(sr)\right]$. The same expression may be obtained

by summing equations (10.2), (10.3), and (10.4).
7 According to a standard definition, individuals have social preferences when what matters for them is not just what is allocated to them but also to other agents who are relevant to them (Fehr and Falk 2002).
8 A preliminary industry-based classification of firms selling to final consumers and firms selling intermediate goods revealed several fallacies and industries of dubious

classification. Thus, a firm-specific taxonomy was developed by looking at each firm's product portfolio. Firms were assigned to the KLD400consumer subgroup if they had at least one important final product or portfolio of products (accounting for more than 30 per cent of their sales) for which consumer demand is sufficiently elastic and therefore consumers may exercise without costs their option to 'vote' (buy) the product (i.e. firms selling medical goods for which demand is inelastic were excluded from this group). Firms that did not possess these characteristics were included in the alternative KLD400intermediate subgroup.

9 These results were omitted for reasons of space but are available from the authors upon request.

10 The test does not require model estimates because it is based on the rank of the covariance matrix of the disturbances driving the multivariate random walk. If this rank is equal to a certain number of common trends, this implies the presence of cointegration and vice versa. If the rank is equal to zero, as in the null hypothesis, then there are no common trends among the variables. Thus, failure to reject the null hypothesis of zero common trends is also an indication that the variables do not form a cointegrated combination.

References

Accion USA (2009) *2007 Annual Report*, Washington, DC: Accion USA. Online. Available at www.accionusa.org/Uploads/FileManager/Annual%20Report/AR_2007.pdf (accessed 6 October 2009).

Acemoglu, D., Johnson, S., and Robinson, J.A. (2001) 'The colonial origins of comparative development: an empirical investigation', *American Economic Review*, 91(5): 1369–401.

Adriani, F. and Becchetti, L. (2002) 'Fair trade: a "third generation welfare" mechanism to make globalisation sustainable', CEIS Working Paper no. 170, Rome: Centre for Economic and International Studies, Università degli studi di Roma 'Tor Vergata'.

Agell, J. and Lundborg, P. (2003) 'Survey evidence on wage rigidity and unemployment: Sweden in the 1990s', *Scandinavian Journal of Economics*, 105(1): 15–29.

Aghion, P., Caroli, E., and Garcia-Peñalosa, C. (1999) 'Inequality and economic growth: the perspective of the new growth theories', *Journal of Economic Literature*, 37(4): 1615–60.

Aiken, M. and Spear, R. (2005) 'Work integration social enterprises in the United Kingdom', EMES Working Paper no. 05/01, Liège: EMES European Research Network.

Akerlof, G.A. (1982) 'Labor contracts as partial gift exchange', *The Quarterly Journal of Economics*, 97(4): 543–69.

Akerlof, G.A. and Kranton, R.E. (2000) 'Economics and identity', *Quarterly Journal of Economics*, 115(3): 715–53.

Akerlof, G.A., Rose, A.K., Yellen, J.L., Hessenius, H., Dornbusch, R., and Guitian, M. (1991) 'East Germany in from the cold: the economic aftermath of Currency Union', *Brookings Papers on Economic Activity*, 1991(1): 1–105.

Alesina, A. and Glaeser, E.L. (2004) *Fighting Poverty in the US and Europe: a world of difference*, Oxford: Oxford University Press.

Alesina, A. and Perotti, R. (1994) 'The political economy of growth: a critical survey of the recent literature', *World Bank Economic Review*, 8(3): 351–71.

Alesina, A., Di Tella, R., and MacCulloch, R. (2001) 'Inequality and happiness: are Europeans and Americans different?', NBER Working Paper no. 8198, Cambridge, MA: National Bureau of Economic Research.

Almond, S. and Kendall, J. (2001) 'Low pay in the UK: the case for a three sector comparative approach', *Annals of Public and Cooperative Economics*, 72(1): 45–76.

Amin, A., Cameron, A., and Hudson, R. (2002) *Placing the Social Economy*, Oxford: Routledge.

Anderson, J.C. and Frankle, A.W. (1980) 'Voluntary social reporting: an Iso-Beta portfolio analysis', *Accounting Review*, 55(3): 467–79.

Andreoni, J. (1989) 'Giving with impure altruism: applications to charity and Ricardian equivalence', *Journal of Political Economy*, 97(6): 1447–58.

Andreoni, J. (1990) 'Impure altruism and donations to public goods: a theory of warm-glow giving', *Economic Journal*, 100(401): 464–77.

Anheier, H.K. (1991) 'Employment and earnings in the West German nonprofit sector: structures and trends 1970–1987', *Annals of Public and Cooperative Economics*, 62(4): 673–94.

Anheier, H.K. and Ben-Ner, A. (eds) (2003) *The Study of the Nonprofit Enterprise: theories and approaches*, New York: Kluwer Academic.

Anheier, H.K. and Salamon, L.M. (1992) 'In search of the nonprofit sector, I: the question of definitions', *Voluntas*, 3(2): 125–61.

Anselin, L. (1998) *Spatial Econometrics: methods and models*, Dordecht: Kluwer Academic.

Aoki, M. (2001) *Toward a Comparative Institutional Analysis*, Cambridge, MA: MIT Press.

Archambault, E. (2001) 'Historical roots of the nonprofit sector in France', *Nonprofit and Voluntary Sector Quarterly*, 30(2): 204–30.

Arellano, M. and Bover, O. (1995) 'Another look at the instrumental variable estimation of error-components models', *Journal of Econometrics*, 68(1): 29–51.

Armendáriz de Aghion, B. (1999) 'On the design of a credit agreement with peer monitoring', *Journal of Development Economics*, 60(1): 79–104.

Armendáriz de Aghion, B. and Morduch, J. (2005) *The Economics of Microfinance*, Cambridge, MA: MIT Press.

Arrow, K.J. (1974) *The Limits of Organization*, New York: Norton.

Ascoli, U. and Ranci, C. (2002) 'Changes in the welfare mix: the European path', in U. Ascoli and C. Ranci (eds) *Dilemmas of the Welfare Mix: the new structure of welfare in an era of privatization*, New York: Kluwer Academic, pp. 225–44.

Aupperle, K.E., Carroll, A.B., and Hatfield, J.D. (1985) 'An empirical examination of the relationship between corporate social responsibility and profitability', *Academy of Management Journal*, 28(2): 446–63.

Autor, D.H., Katz, L.F., and Krueger, A.B. (1998) 'Computing inequality: have computers changed the labor market?', *Quarterly Journal of Economics*, 113(4): 1169–213.

Bacchiega, A. and Borzaga, C. (2001) 'Social enterprises as incentive structures', in C. Borzaga and J. Defourny (eds) *The Emergence of Social Enterprise*, London: Routledge, pp. 273–95.

Bacchiega, A. and Borzaga, C. (2003) 'The economics of the third sector: toward a more comprehensive approach', in H.K. Anheier and A. Ben-Ner (eds) *The Study of the Nonprofit Enterprise: theories and approaches*, New York: Kluwer Academic/Plenum Publishers, pp. 27–48.

Bacon, C. (2005) 'Confronting the coffee crisis: can fair trade, organic, and specialty coffees reduce small-scale farmer vulnerability in northern Nicaragua?', *World Development*, 33(3): 497–511.

Badelt, C. and Weiss, P. (1990) 'Non-profit, for-profit and government organisations in social service provision: comparison of behavioural patterns for Austria', *Voluntas*, 1(1): 77–96.

Bagella, M., Becchetti, L., and Hasan, I. (2004) 'The anticipated and concurring effects of the EMU: exchange rate volatility, institutions and growth', *Journal of International Money and Finance*, 23(7–8): 1053–80.

Bahle, T. (2003) 'The changing institutionalization of social services in England and

Wales, France and Germany: is the welfare state on the retreat?', *Journal of European Social Policy*, 13(1): 5–20.

BancoSol (2009) *2008 Annual Report*, La Paz: BancoSol. Online. Available at www. bancosol.com.bo/archivos/memorias/report2008.pdf (accessed 29 September 2009).

Banerjee, A.W., Besley, T. and Guinnane, T.W. (1994) 'Thy neighbor's keeper: the design of a credit cooperative with theory and a test', *Quarterly Journal of Economics* 109(2): 491–515.

Barro, R.J. and Becker, G.S. (1989) 'Fertility choice in a model of economic growth', *Econometrica*, 57(2): 481–501.

Barro, R.J. and Sala-i-Martin, X. (1992) 'Convergence', *Journal of Political Economy*, 100(2): 223–51.

Basu, K. (1999) 'Child labor: cause, consequence and cure, with remarks on international labor standards', *Journal of Economic Literature*, 37(3): 1083–119.

Basu, K. (2000) 'The intriguing relation between minimum adult wage and child labour', *Economic Journal*, 110(462): 50–61.

Basu, K. and Van, P.H. (1998) 'The economics of child labor', *American Economic Review*, 88(3): 412–27.

Baumol, W.J. (1993) 'Social wants and dismal science: the curious case of the climbing costs of health and teaching', *Proceedings of the American Philosophical Society*, 137(4): 612–37.

Becchetti, L. and Adriani, F. (2005) 'Does the digital divide matter? The role of information and communication technology in cross-country level and growth estimates', *Economics of Innovation and New Technology*, 14(6): 435–53.

Becchetti, L. and Costantino, M. (2008) 'The effects of fair trade on affiliated producers: an impact analysis on Kenyan farmers', *World Development*, 36(5): 823–42.

Becchetti, L. and Fucito, L. (2000) 'La finanza etica: valutazioni teoriche e simulazioni empiriche', *Rivista di Politica Economica*, 90(5): 29–67.

Becchetti, L. and Di Giacomo, S. (2004) 'The unequalizing effects of ICT on economic growth', *Metroeconomica*, 58(1): 155–94.

Becchetti, L. and Gianfreda, G. (2007) 'Contagious "social market enterprises": the role of Fair Traders', *Rivista di Politica Economica*, 97(3): 51–84.

Becchetti, L. and Huybrechts, B. (2008) 'The dynamics of fair trade as a mixed-form market', *Journal of Business Ethics*, 81(4): 733–50.

Becchetti, L. and Mastromatteo, G. (2006) 'The quest for growth: theoretical and empirical findings and the rise of a bottom-up approach to sustainable development', *Economia Internazionale*, 59(4): 437–66.

Becchetti, L. and Michetti, M. (2008) 'When consumption generates social capital: creating room for manoeuvre for pro-poor policies', ECINEQ Working Paper no. 88, Palma de Mallorca: Society for the Study of Economic Equality.

Becchetti, L. and Pisani, F. (2007) 'Promoting access to credit for small uncollateralized producers: moral hazard, subsidies and local externalities under different group lending market structures', CEIS Departmental Working Paper no. 249, Rome: Centre for Economic and International Studies, Università degli studi di Roma 'Tor Vergata'.

Becchetti, L. and Rosati, F.C. (2007) 'Global social preferences and the demand for socially responsible products: empirical evidence from a pilot study on fair trade consumers', *World Economy*, 30(5): 807–36.

Becchetti, L. and Solferino, N. (2005) 'The dynamics of ethical product differentiation and the habit formation of socially responsible consumers', Working Paper no. 8,

Corso di Laurea in Economia delle Imprese Cooperative e delle Organizzazioni Non-profit, Facoltà di Economia, Università di Bologna, Sede di Forlì. Online. Available at www.aiccon.it/working_paper.cfm (accessed 6 July 2009).

Becchetti, L. and Trovato, G. (2005) 'The determinants of child labour: the role of primary product specialization', *Labour*, 19(2): 237–71.

Becchetti, L., Costantino, M., and Portale, E. (2007a) 'Human capital, externalities and tourism: three unexplored sides of the impact of FT affiliation on primary producers', CEIS Working Paper no. 262, Rome: Centre for Economic and International Studies, Università degli studi di Roma 'Tor Vergata'.

Becchetti, L., Di Giacomo, S., and Pinnacchio, D. (2007b) 'Corporate social responsibility and corporate performance: evidence from a panel of US listed companies', *Applied Economics*, 40(5): 541–67.

Becchetti, L., Durante, R., and Sambataro, S. (2006) 'A matching of two promises: microfinance and social responsibility', CEIS Departmental Working Paper no. 225, Rome: Centre for Economic and International Studies, Università degli studi di Roma 'Tor Vergata'.

Becchetti, L., Federico, G., and Solferino, N. (2005a) 'The game of social responsibility: pioneers, imitators and social welfare', Working Paper no.15, Corso di Laurea in Economia delle Imprese Cooperative e delle Organizzazioni Nonprofit, Facoltà di Economia, Università di Bologna, Sede di Forlì. Online. Available at www.aiccon.it/working_paper.cfm (accessed 6 July 2009).

Becchetti, L., Giallonardo, L., and Tessitore, M.E. (2005b) 'Corporate social responsibility and profit maximizing behaviour', CEIS Working Paper no. 219, Rome: Centre for Economic and International Studies, Università degli studi di Roma 'Tor Vergata'.

Becchetti, L., Hasan, I., and Wachtel, P. (2008) 'The anticipated effects of EU enlargement: exchange rate volatility, institutions and conditional convergence', *Transition Studies Review*, 15(3): 431–46.

Becchetti, L., Paganetto, L., and Solferino, N. (2003) 'A virtuous interaction between pressure groups, firms and institutions: a subsidiarity principle in a horizontal differentiation model', CEIS Working Paper no. 194, Rome: Centre for Economic and International Studies, Università degli studi di Roma 'Tor Vergata'.

Becker, G.S., Murphy, K.M., and Tamura, R. (1990) 'Human capital, fertility, and economic growth', *Journal of Political Economy*, 98(5): S12–37.

Bender, D.H. (1986) 'Financial impact of information processing', *Journal of Management Information Systems*, 3(2): 22–32.

Ben-Ner, A. (1994) 'Who benefits from the nonprofit sector? Reforming law and public policy towards nonprofit organizations', *Yale Law Journal*, 104(3): 731–62.

Ben-Ner, A. (2002) 'The shifting boundaries of the mixed economy and the future of the nonprofit sector', *Annals of Public and Cooperative Economics*, 73(1): 5–40.

Ben-Ner, A. and Putterman, L. (1998) 'Values and institutions in economic analysis', in A. Ben-Ner and L. Putterman (eds) *Economics, Values, and Organization*, Cambridge: Cambridge University Press, pp. 3–72.

Ben-Ner, A. and Van Hoomissen, T. (1991) 'Nonprofit organizations in the mixed economy: a demand and supply analysis', *Annals of Public and Cooperative Economics*, 62(4): 519–50.

Bennett, J., Iossa, E., and Legrenzi, G. (2003) 'The role of commercial non-profit organizations in the provision of public services', *Oxford Review of Economic Policy*, 19(2): 335–47.

Benz, M. (2005) 'Not for the profit, but for the satisfaction? Evidence on worker well-being in non-profit firms', *Kyklos*, 58(2): 155–76.

Besley, T. and Ghatak, M. (2005) 'Competition and incentives with motivated agents', *American Economic Review*, 95(3): 616–36.

Beutler, F. and Brackmann, J. (1999) *Neue Mobilitätskonzepte in Deutschland: ökologische, soziale und wirtschaftliche Perspektiven*, Discussion Paper P 99–503, Berlin: Wissenschaftszentrum Berlin für Sozialforschung.

Bewley, T.F. (1999) *Why Wages Don't Fall during a Recession*, Cambridge, MA: Harvard University Press.

Bhagwati, J. and Hudec, R.E. (eds) (1996) *Fair Trade and Harmonization: prerequisites for free trade? Volume 1: economic analysis*, Cambridge, MA: MIT Press.

Bird, K. and Hughes, D.R. (1997) 'Ethical consumerism: the case of "fairly-traded" coffee', *Business Ethics: a European Review*, 6(3): 59–167.

Blakemore, K. (2003) *Social Policy: an introduction*, 2nd edn, New York: Open University Press.

Blinkert, B. and Klie, T. (1999) *Pflege im sozialen Wandel: eine Untersuchung über die Situation von häuslich versorgten Pflegebedürftigen nach Einführung der Pflegeversicherung*, Hannover: Vincentz.

Blundell, R. and Bond, S. (1998) 'Initial conditions and moment restrictions in dynamic panel data models', *Journal of Econometrics*, 87(1): 115–43.

Boessenecker, K.H. and Trube, A. (2000) *Privatisierung im Sozialsekto: Rahmenbedingungen, Verlaufsformen und Probleme der Ausgliederung sozialer Dienste*, Münster: Votum Verlag.

Bonatti, L., Borzaga, C., and Mittone, L. (2001) 'Profit versus non-profit firms in the service sector: an analysis of the employment and welfare implications', Discussion Paper 2, Trento: Dipartimento di economia, Università di Trento.

Bond, P. and Rai, A.S. (2009) 'Borrower runs', *Journal of Development Economics*, 88(2): 185–91.

Bond, S., Hoeffler, A., and Temple, J. (2001) 'GMM estimation of empirical growth models', CEPR Discussion Paper no. 3048, London: Centre for Economic Policy Research.

Bonin, J.P., Jones, D.C., and Putterman, L. (1987) *Economics of Co-operation and the Labour Managed Economy*, London: Harwood Academic.

Bonin, J.P., Jones, D.C., and Putterman, L. (1993) 'Theoretical and empirical studies of producer cooperatives: will ever the twain meet?', *Journal of Economic Literature*, 31(3): 1290–320.

Borzaga, C. (2003) 'L'analisi economica delle organizzazioni nonprofit: teorie, limiti e possibili sviluppi', in C. Borzaga and M. Musella (eds) *Produttività ed Efficienza nelle Organizzazioni Non Profit: il ruolo dei lavoratori e delle relazioni di lavoro*, Trento: Edizioni 31, pp. 23–48.

Borzaga, C. (2006) 'Cooperazione sociale e inserimento lavorativo: il contributo dell'analisi economica', *Giornale di Diritto del Lavoro e di Relazioni Industriali*, 28(109): 101–29.

Borzaga, C. (2007) 'Evoluzione recente, stato e prospettive della cooperazione sociale', *Impresa Sociale*, 76(3): 53–68.

Borzaga, C. and Defourny, J. (eds) (2001) *The Emergence of Social Enterprise*, London: Routledge.

Borzaga, C. and Depedri, S. (2005) 'Interpersonal relations and job satisfaction: some empirical results in social and community care services', in B. Gui and R. Sugden (eds) *Economics and Social Interaction: accounting for interpersonal relations*, Cambridge: Cambridge University Press, pp. 132–53.

Borzaga, C. and Depedri, S. (2009) 'Does it make a difference working for social cooperatives in Italy?', in A. Amin (ed.) *The Social Economy: international perspectives on economic solidarity*, London: Zed Press, pp. 82–114.

Borzaga, C. and Ianes, A. (2006) *L'Economia della Solidarietà: storia e prospettive della cooperazione sociale*, Roma: Donzelli.

Borzaga, C. and Mittone, L. (1997) 'The multi-stakeholder versus the nonprofit organisation', Discussion Paper 7, Trento: Dipartimento di economia, Università di Trento.

Borzaga, C. and Mori, A. (2008) 'Il settore nonprofit e la responsabilità sociale delle imprese: un'analisi per la Lombardia', *Impresa Sociale*, 77(2): 245–74.

Borzaga, C. and Musella, M. (eds) (2003) *Produttività ed Efficienza nelle Organizzazioni Nonprofit: il ruolo dei lavoratori e delle relazioni di lavoro*, Trento: Edizioni 31.

Borzaga, C. and Santuari, A. (2001) 'Italy: from traditional co-operatives to innovative social enterprises', in C. Borzaga and J. Defourny (eds) *The Emergence of Social Enterprise*, London: Routledge, pp. 166–81.

Borzaga, C. and Spear, R. (eds) (2004) *Trends and Challenges for Co-operatives and Social Enterprises in Developed and Transition Countries*, Trento: Edizioni 31.

Borzaga, C. and Tortia, E. (2005) 'Dalla cooperazione mutualistica alla cooperazione per la produzione di beni di interesse collettivo', in E. Mazzoli and S. Zamagni (eds) *Verso una Nuova Teoria della Cooperazione*, Bologna: Il Mulino, pp. 225–68.

Borzaga, C. and Tortia, E. (2006) 'Worker motivations, job satisfaction, and loyalty in public and non-profit social services', *Nonprofit and Voluntary Sector Quarterly*, 35(2): 225–48.

Borzaga, C. and Tortia, E. (2007) 'Social economy organisations in the theory of the firm', in A. Noya and E. Clarence (eds) *The Social Economy: building inclusive communities*, Paris: OECD Publishing, pp. 23–60.

Borzaga, C. and Tortia, E. (2009) 'Social enterprises and local economic development', in A. Noya (ed.) *The Changing Boundaries of Social Enterprises*, Paris: OECD Publishing, pp. 195–228.

Borzaga, C., Depedri, S., and Tortia, E. (forthcoming) 'Testing the distributive effects of social enterprises: the case of Italy', in G. Degli Antoni and L. Sacconi (eds) *Social Capital, Corporate Social Responsibility, Economic Behaviour and Performance*, Basingstoke: Palgrave Macmillan.

Borzaga, C., Galera, G., and Nogales, R. (2008) *Social Enterprise: a new model for poverty reduction and employment generation*, Bratislava: UNDP Regional Bureau for Europe and the Commonwealth of Independent States.

Borzaga, C., Gui, B., and Povinelli, F. (2001) 'The specific role of non-profit organizations in the integration of disadvantaged people: insights from economic analysis', in R. Spear, J. Defourny, L. Favreau, and J-L. Laville (eds) *Tackling Social Exclusion in Europe: the contribution of the social economy*, Aldershot: Ashgate, pp. 267–86.

Borzaga, C., Mongera, M., and Giovannini, M. (2009) 'Work integration in the open labour market: lessons from Italian social co-operatives', paper presented at the 2nd EMES International Conference on Social Enterprise, Trento, 1–4 July 2009.

Bouchard, M.J., Ferraton, C., and Michaud, V. (2006) 'Base de données sur les organisations d'économie sociale, les critères de qualification des organisations', Chaire de recherche du Canada en économie sociale no. R-2006–02, Montréal: Université du Québec.

Bowles, S. (1998) 'Endogenous preferences: the cultural consequences of markets and other economic institutions', *Journal of Economic Literature*, 36(1): 75–111.

Bowles, S. (2004) *Microeconomics. Behaviour, Institutions, and Evolution*, Princeton, NJ: Russel Sage Foundation/Princeton University Press.

Bracci, A. (2009) 'Il rapporto tra impresa sociale in Svizzera e Italia: analisi di due case studies', *Impresa Sociale*, 78(1): 287–306.

Brandsen, T., van de Donk, W., and Putters, K. (2005) 'Griffins or chameleons? Hybridity as a permanent and inevitable characteristic of the third sector', *International Journal of Public Administration*, 28(9–10): 749–65.

Brown, T.L., Potoski, M., and Van Slyke, D.M. (2007) 'Trust and contract completeness in the public sector', *Local Government Studies*, 33(4): 607–23.

Brynjolfsson, E. and Hitt, L.M. (1996) 'Paradox lost? Firm-level evidence on the returns to information systems spending', *Management Science*, 42(4): 541–58.

Brynjolfsson, E. and Hitt, L.M. (2000) 'Beyond computation: information technology, organizational transformation and business performance', *Journal of Economic Perspectives*, 14(4): 23–48.

Buckley, G. (1996) 'Rural and agricultural credit in Malawi: a study of the Malawi Mudzi Fund and the smallholder agricultural credit administration', in D. Hulme and P. Mosley (eds) *Finance against Poverty*, vol. 2, London: Routledge, pp. 302–72.

Burger, A. and Dekker, P. (2001) *The Nonprofit Sector in the Netherlands*, Working Document no. 70, Den Haag: Sociaal en Cultureel Planbureau.

Burger, A. and Veldheer, V. (2001) 'The growth of the nonprofit sector in the Netherlands', *Nonprofit and Voluntary Sector Quarterly*, 30(2): 221–46.

Busse, R. and Riesberg, A. (2004) *Health Care Systems in Transition: Germany*, Copenhagen: European Observatory on Health Care Systems and Policies.

Campbell, C. M. and Kamlani, K. S. (1997) 'The reasons for wage rigidity: evidence from a survey of firms', *Quarterly Journal of Economics*, 112(3): 759–89.

Campos Franco, R. (2005) 'Defining the Nonprofit Sector: Portugal', Working Papers of the Johns Hopkins Comparative Nonprofit Sector Project no. 43, Baltimore, MD: Johns Hopkins Center for Civil Society Studies.

Card, D. (1999) 'The causal effects of education on earnings', in O. Ashenfelter and D. Card (eds) *Handbook of Labor Economics*, vol. 3A, Amsterdam: Elsevier, pp. 1801–63.

Card, D. and Krueger, A.B. (2000) 'Minimum wages and employment: a case study of the fast-food industry in New Jersey and Pennsylvania: comment', *American Economic Review*, 90(5): 1397–420.

Castro, J.E. (2001a) 'Impact assessment of Oxfam's fair trade activities: The case of the Cooperativa Integral de producciòn de vidrio soplado Cantel, R.L. (COPAVIC)', mimeo, Oxford: Oxfam.

Castro, J.E. (2001b) 'Impact assessment of Oxfam's fair trade activities: the case of Productores de Miel Flor de Campanilla', mimeo, Oxford: Oxfam.

Clotfelter, C.T. (ed.) (1992) *Who Benefits from the Nonprofit Sector?*, Chicago: University of Chicago Press.

Coleman, B.E. (1999) 'The impact of group lending in Northeast Thailand', *Journal of Development Economics*, 60(1): 105–41.

Collier, P. (2007) *The Bottom Billion: why the poorest countries are failing and what can be done about it*, Oxford: Oxford University Press.

Commission of the European Communities (2009) 'Contributing to Sustainable Development: the role of Fair Trade and nongovernmental trade-related sustainability assurance schemes', Communication from the Commission to the Council, the European Parliament and the European Economic and Social Committee, Brussels, 5 May 2009, COM (2009) 215 final.

Conférence permanente des coordinations associatives (2008) *Les Secteurs Associatifs et leurs Relations avec l'Etat dans l'Europe des 27: Essai d'analysee comparee*, Etudes et Documents no. 4, Paris: Conférence permanente des coordinations associatives.

Cowe, R. and Williams, S. (2000) *Who Are the Ethical Consumers?*, Manchester: Co-operative Bank.

Cremer, H., Marchand, M., and Thisse, J.F. (1991) 'Mixed oligopoly with differentiated products', *International Journal of Industrial Organization*, 9(1): 43–53.

Cutler, D.M. and Berndt, E.R. (2001) *Medical Care Productivity and Output*, Chicago: University of Chicago Press.

Daley-Harris, S. (2009) *State of the Microcredit Summit Campaign, Report 2009*, Washington, DC: Microcredit Summit Campaign.

Dasgupta, P. and Maskin, E. (1986) 'The existence of equilibrium in discontinous economic games, II: applications', *Review of Economic Studies*, 53(1): 27–41.

d'Aspremont, C., Gabszewicz, J.J., and Thisse, J.F. (1979) 'On Hotelling's "stability in competition"', *Econometrica*, 47(5):1145–50.

David, P.A. (1990) 'The dynamo and the computer: an historical perspective of the modern productivity paradox', *American Economic Review*, 80(2): 355–61.

Davies, S. (2008) 'Contracting out employment services to the third and private sectors: a critique', *Critical Social Policiy*, 28(2): 136–64.

Davister, C., Defourny, J., and Gregoire, O. (2004) 'Work integration social enterprises in the European Union: an overview of existing models', EMES Working Paper no. 04/04, Liège: EMES European Research Network.

Deardorff, A.V. (2000) 'Policy implications of the trade and wages debate', *Review of International Economics*, 8(3): 478–96.

Deavers, K.L. and Hattiangadi, A.U. (1998) 'Welfare to work: building a better path to private employment opportunities', *Journal of Labor Research*, 19(2): 205–28.

De Charms, R. (1968) *Personal Causation: the internal affective determinants of behavior*, New York: Academic Press.

Deci, E.L. (1975) *Intrinsic Motivation*, New York: Plenum Press.

Defourny, J. and Nyssens, M. (eds) (2008) 'Social enterprise in Europe: recent trends and developments', EMES Working Paper no. 08/01, Liège: EMES European Research Network.

De Grauwe, P. and Schnabl, G. (2008) 'Exchange rate stability, inflation, and growth in (south) eastern and central Europe', *Review of Development Economics*, 12(3): 530–49.

Dehne, A., Friedrich, P., Woon Nam, C., and Parsche, R. (2008) 'Taxation of nonprofit associations in an international comparison', *Nonprofit and Voluntary Sector Quarterly*, 37(4): 709–29.

Delacroix, J. (1995) 'Review of K. Samuelsson "Religion and Economic Action: the Protestant ethic, the rise of capitalism and the abuses of scholarship" (Toronto: University of Toronto Press, 1993)', *Journal for the Scientific Study of Religion*, 34(1): 126–7.

de Melo, M., Denizer, C., and Gelb, A. (1996) 'Patterns of transition from plan to market', *World Bank Economic Review*, 10(3): 397–424.

Demos & Pi (2004) 'Osservatorio sul capitale sociale degli italiani: l'Italia "solidale"', Vicenza: Demos & Pi. Online. Available at www.demos.it/2004/pdf/capitale_sociale_04.pdf (accessed 13 July 2009).

De Pelsmacker, P., Driesen, L., and Rayp, G. (2003) 'Are fair trade labels good business? Ethics and coffee buying intentions', Working Papers of Faculty of Economics and Business Administration no. 03/165, Ghent: Ghent University.

DiMaggio, P. and Powell, W.W. (1988) 'The iron cage revisited: institutional isomorphism and collective rationality in organizational fields', in C. Milofsky (ed.) *Community Organizations: studies in resource mobilization and exchange*, New York: Oxford University Press.

Di Tella, R., MacCulloch, R.J., and Oswald, A.J. (2001) 'Preferences over inflation and unemployment: evidence from surveys of happiness', *American Economic Review*, 91(1): 335–41.

Dixit, A. and Norman, V. (1986) 'Gains from trade without lump-sum compensation', *Journal of International Economics*, 21(1–2): 111–22.

Domar, E.D. (1966) 'The soviet collective farm as a producer cooperative', *American Economic Review*, 56 (3): 734–57.

Dopfer, K. (ed.) (2005) *The Evolutionary Foundations of Economics*, Cambridge: Cambridge University Press.

Dow, G.K. (1986) 'Control rights, competitive markets, and the labor management debate', *Journal of Comparative Economics*, 10(1): 48–61.

Dow, G.K. (2003) *Governing the Firm: workers' control in theory and practice*, Cambridge: Cambridge University Press.

Durlauf, S.N. and Fafchamps, M. (2005) 'Social capital', in S.N. Durlauf and P. Aghion (eds) *Handbook of Economic Growth*, vol. 1B, Amsterdam: Elsevier, pp. 1639–93.

Durlauf, S.N. and Johnson, P.A. (1995) 'Multiple regimes and cross-country growth behaviour', *Journal of Applied Econometrics* 10(4): 365–84.

Durlauf, S.N. and Quah, D.T. (1999) 'The new empirics of economic growth', in J.B. Taylor and M. Woodford (eds) *Handbook of Macroeconomics*, vol. 1A, Amsterdam: Elsevier, pp. 235–308.

Easterlin, R.A. (2001) 'Income and happiness: towards a unified theory', *Economic Journal*, 111(473): 465–84.

Easterlin, R.A. (2005) 'Building a better theory of well-being', in L. Bruni and P. Porta (eds) *Economics and Happiness: framing the analysis*, Oxford: Oxford University Press, pp. 29–64.

Easterly, W. (2003) 'Can foreign aid buy growth?', *Journal of Economic Perspectives*, 17(3): 23–48.

Easterly, W. and Levine, R. (1997) 'Africa's growth tragedy: policies and ethnic divisions', *Quarterly Journal of Economics*, 112(4): 1203–50.

Easterly, W., Ritzen, J., and Woolcock, M. (2000) 'On "good" politicians and "bad" policies: social cohesion, institutions, and growth', Policy Research Working Paper no. 2448, Washington, DC: World Bank.

Economides, N. (1986) 'Minimal and maximal product differentiation in Hotelling's duopoly', *Economic Letters*, 21(1): 67–71.

Economist (2005) 'The good company', 22–28 January, 374(8410): 11.

Ekman, P., Davidson, R.J., and Friesen, W.V. (1990) 'The Duchenne smile: emotional expression and brain physiology II', *Journal of Personality and Social Psychology*, 58(2): 342–53.

Elstub, S. (2006) 'Towards an inclusive social policy for the UK: the need for democratic deliberation in voluntary and community associations', *Voluntas* 17(1): 17–39.

Encyclopedia Britannica Online (2009) s.v. 'Capitalism'. Online. Available at www.britannica.com/EBchecked/topic/93927/capitalism (accessed 7 July 2009).

Esfahani, H.S. and Ramírez, M.T. (2003) 'Institutions, infrastructure, and economic growth', *Journal of Development Economics*, 70(2): 443–77.

Esping-Andersen, G. (1999) *Social Foundations of Postindustrial Economies*, Oxford: Oxford University Press.

Evers, A. and Laville, J-L. (2004) *The Third Sector in Europe*, Cheltenham: Edward Elgar.

Fairtrade Foundation (2008) 'Fairtrade Foundation Annual Review 2007/2008', London: Fairtrade Foundation.

Fairtrade Labelling Organizations International (FLO) (2009) 'Fairtrade labelling initiatives', Bonn: Fairtrade Labelling Organizations International. Online. Available at www.fairtrade.net/labelling_initiatives1.html (accessed 10 July 2009).

Fazzi, L. (1996) 'Social policies and the non-profit sector in Italy: a critique of the ideologies of contracting-out', *Economic and Industrial Democracy*, 17(1): 75–97.

Feenstra, R.C. (1998) 'Integration of trade and disintegration of production in the global economy', *Journal of Economic Perspectives*, 12(4): 31–50.

Feenstra, R.C. and Hanson, G.H. (2003) 'Global production sharing and rising inequality: a survey of trade and wages', in E.K. Choi and J. Harrigan (eds) *Handbook of International Trade*, Oxford: Basil Blackwell, pp. 146–85.

Fehr, E. and Falk, A. (2002) 'Psychological foundations of incentives', *European Economic Review*, 46(4–5): 687–724.

Fehr, E. and Gächter, S. (2000) 'Fairness and retaliation: the economics of reciprocity', *Journal of Economic Perspectives*, 14(3): 159–81.

Fehr, E. and Schmidt, K.M. (1999) 'A theory of fairness, competition and cooperation', *Quarterly Journal of Economics*, 114(3): 817–68.

Fehr, E. and Schmidt, K.M. (2001) 'Theories of fairness and reciprocity: evidence and economic applications', Working Paper no. 75, Zurich: Institute for Empirical Research in Economics, University of Zurich.

Fehr, E. and Schmidt, K.M. (2002) 'The economics of fairness and reciprocity: evidence and economic applications', in M. Dewatripont, L.P. Hansen, and S.J. Turnovsky (eds) *Advances in Economics and Econometrics: theory and applications, Eighth World Congress*, vol. 1, Cambridge: Cambridge University Press, pp. 208–57.

Feldstein, M. and Horioka, C. (1980) 'Domestic saving and international capital flows', *Economic Journal*, 90(358): 314–29.

Ferrera, M. and Rhodes, M. (eds) (2000) *Recasting European Welfare States*, London: Frank Cass.

Finca International (2009) *2008 Annual Report*, Washington, DC: Finca International. Online. Available at www.villagebanking.org/atf/cf/%7BF69F69E6–275A-4FA1-BC75–649E1EDCD1A4%7D/Annual%20Report%202008.pdf (accessed 27 September 2009).

Fingleton, B. (2000) 'Convergence: international comparisons based on a simultaneous equation model with regional effects', *International Review of Applied Economics*, 14(3): 285–305.

Fingleton, B. (2001) 'Equilibrium and economic growth: spatial econometric models and simulations', *Journal of Regional Science*, 41(1): 117–48.

Fischer, S., Sahay, R., and Vegh, C.A. (1996) 'Stabilization and growth in transition economies: the early experience', *Journal of Economic Perspectives*, 10(2): 45–66.

Flynn, P. and Hodgkinson, V.A. (2001) 'Introduction', in P. Flynn and V.A. Hodgkinson (eds) *Measuring the Impact of the Nonprofit Sector*, New York: Kluwer Academic/ Plenum Publishers.

Folbre, N. (2008) 'Reforming care', *Politics and Society*, 36(3): 373–87.

Foster, W. and Bradach, J. (2005) 'Should nonprofits seek profits?', *Harvard Business Review*, 83(2): 92–100.

Frankel, J.A. (2002) 'Promoting better national institutions: the role of the IMF', paper presented at the Third Annual IMF Research Conference, Washington, DC, 7–8 November.

Freedman, M. and Jaggi, B. (1986) 'An analysis of the impact of corporate pollution disclosures included in Annual Financial Statements on investors' decisions', in M. Neimark (ed.) *Advances in Public Interest Accounting*, Vol. 1, Greenwich, CT: JAI, pp. 193–212.

Freeman, R.E. (1984) *Strategic Management: a stakeholder approach*, Boston: Pitman.

Freise, M. and Zimmer, A. (2004) 'Der dritte Sektor im wohlfahrtsstaatlichen Arrangement der post-sozialistischen Visegrád-Staaten', in H. Kötz, P. Rawert, K. Schmidt, and R.W. Walz (eds) *Non Profit Law Yearbook, 2003*, Köln: Carl Heymanns, pp. 175–94.

Freud, D. (2007) *Reducing Dependency, Increasing Opportunity: options for the future of welfare to work*, London: Department of Work and Pensions.

Frey, B.S. (1997) *Not Just for the Money: an economic theory of personal motivation*, Cheltenham, UK: Edward Elgar.

Frey, B.S. and Osterloh, M. (1999) 'Yes, managers should be paid like bureaucrats', *Journal of Management Inquiry*, 14(1): 96–111.

Frey, B.S. and Stutzer, A. (2000) 'Happiness, economy and institutions', *Economic Journal*, 110(466): 918–38.

Friedman, M. (1962) *Capitalism and Freedom*, Chicago: IL: University of Chicago Press.

Frumkin, P. and Andrè-Clark, A. (2000) 'When missions, markets and politics collide: values and strategy in the nonprofit human services', *Nonprofit and Voluntary Sector Quarterly*, 29(1): 141–163.

Furubotn, E.G. (1976) 'The long run analysis of the labour managed firm: an alternative interpretation', *American Economic Review*, 66(1): 104–23.

Furubotn, E.G. and Pejovich, S. (1970) 'Property rights and the behaviour of the firm in a socialist state: the example of Yugoslavia', *Zeitschrift für Nationalökonomie*, 30(5): 431–54.

Gagliardi, F. (2008) 'Financial development and the growth of cooperative firms', *Small Business Economics*, 32(2): 231–45.

Galera, G. (2008) 'The impact of cooperatives and social enterprises on socio-economic development in Poland', in A. Giza-Poleszczuk and J. Hausner (eds) *The Social Economy in Poland: achievements, barriers to growth and potential in light of research results*, Warsaw: Foundation for Social and Economic Initiatives, pp. 135–62.

Galor, O. and Moav, O. (2004) 'From physical to human capital accumulation: inequality in the process of development', *Review of Economic Studies*, 71(4): 1001–26.

Gangopadhyay, S., Ghatak, M. and Lensink, R. (2005) 'On joint liability and the peer selection effect', *Economic Journal* 115(506): 1005–15.

Ghatak, M. and Guinnane, T.W. (1999) 'The economics of lending with joint liability: theory and practice', *Journal of Development Economics*, 60(1): 195–228.

Glaeser, E.L. and Shleifer, A. (2001) 'Not-for-profit entrepreneurs', *Journal of Public Economics*, 81(1): 99–115.

Glendinning, C. and Kemp, P.A. (eds) (2006) *Cash and Care: policy challenges in the welfare state*, Bristol: Policy Press.

Globescan (2007) *Corporate Social Responsibility Monitor, 2007*, Toronto: Globescan. Online. Available at www.globescan.com/csrm_overview.htm (accessed 3 March 2009).

Goddeeris, J.H. (1988) 'Compensating differentials and self-selection: an application to lawyers', *Journal of Political Economy*, 96(2): 411–28.

Gowdy, G. and Seidl, G. (2004) 'Economic man and selfish genes: the implications of group selection for economic valuation and policy', *Journal of Socio-Economics*, 33(3): 343–58.

Grameen Bank (2009) *2008 Annual Report*, Dacca: Grameen Bank. Online. Available at www.grameen-info.org/index.php?option=com_content&task=view&id=687&Itemid= 693 (accessed 6 October 2009).

Granovetter, M. (1985) 'Economic action and social structure: the problem of embeddedness', *American Journal of Sociology*, 91(3): 481–510.

Gray, B.H. and Schlesinger, M. (2002) 'Health', in L.M. Salamon (ed.) *The State of Nonprofit America*, Washington, DC: Brookings Institution Press, pp. 65–106.

Green, C. and Heywood, J.S. (2008) 'Does performance pay increase job satisfaction?', *Economica*, 75(300): 710–18.

Greene, W.H. (2000) *Econometric Analysis*, 4th edn, Upper Saddle River, NJ: Prentice-Hall.

Grillo, M. (1992) 'Cooperative di consumatori e produzione di beni sociali', in E. Granaglia and L. Sacconi (eds) *Cooperazione, Benessere e Organizzazione Economica*, Milano: Franco Angeli, pp. 95–138.

Grilo, I. (1994) 'Mixed duopoly under vertical differentiation', *Annales d'Économie et de Statistique*, 33: 91–112.

Grimalda, G. and Sacconi, L. (2005) 'The constitution of the not-for-profit organisation: reciprocal conformity to morality', *Constitutional Political Economy*, 16(3): 249–76.

Gui, B. and Sugden, R. (eds) (2005) *Economics and Social Interaction: accounting for interpersonal relations*, Cambridge: Cambridge University Press.

Gumkowska, M., Herbst, J., and Wygnanski, K. (2008) 'Promoting the Role of Social Enterprises in Poland', in C. Borzaga, G. Galera, and R. Nogales, *Social Enterprise: a new model for poverty reduction and employment generation*, Bratislava: UNDP Regional Bureau for Europe and the Commonwealth of Independent States, pp. 78–103.

Gwartney, J. and Lawson, R. (2003) *Economic Freedom of the World: 2003 annual report*, Vancouver, BC: Fraser Institute. Online. Available at www.freetheworld.com/release_2003.html (accessed 16 April 2009).

Hall, R.E. and Jones, C.I. (1997) 'Levels of economic activity across countries', *American Economic Review*, 87(2): 173–7.

Handy, F. and Katz, E. (1998) 'The wage differential between nonprofit institutions and corporations: getting more by paying less?', *Journal of Comparative Economics*, 26(2): 246–61.

Hansmann, H. (1980) 'The role of nonprofit enterprises', *Yale Law Journal*, 89(5): 835–901.

Hansmann, H. (1988) 'Ownership of the firm', *Journal of Law, Economics and Organisation*, 4(2): 267–304.

Hansmann, H. (1996) *The Ownership of Enterprise*, Cambridge, MA: Harvard University Press.

Hansmann, H. (2000) 'Response to review essay of "The Ownership of Enterprise"', *Non-Profit and Voluntary Sector Quarterly*, 29(1): 179–84.

Haugh, H. and Kitson, M. (2007) 'The third way and the third sector: New Labour's economic policy and the social economy', *Cambridge Journal of Economics*, 31(6): 973–94.

Hayes, M.G. (2006) 'On the efficiency of fair trade', *Review of Social Economy*, 64 (4): 447–68.

Hebb, T., Wortsman, A., Mendell, A., Neamtan, N., and Rouzier, R. (2006) *Financing Social Economy Enterprises*, final report, Ottawa: Carleton Centre for Community Innovation.

Helliwell, J.F. and Huang, H. (2005) 'How's the job? Well-being and social capital in the workplace', NBER Working Paper no. 11759, Cambridge, MA: National Bureau of Economic Research.

Helliwell, J.F. and Putnam, R.D. (2000) 'Economic growth and social capital in Italy', in P. Dasgupta and I. Serageldin (eds) *Social Capital: a multifaceted perspective*, Washington, DC: World Bank, pp. 253–68.

Herman, R.D. and Renz, D.O. (2008) 'Advancing nonprofit organizational effectiveness research and theory: nine theses', *Nonprofit Management and Leadership*, 18(4): 399–415.

HM Treasury and Cabinet Office (2007) 'The Future Role of the Third Sector in Social and Economic Regeneration: final report', Cm 7189, London: Stationery Office. Online. Available at www.cabinetoffice.gov.uk/media/cabinetoffice/third_sector/assets/the_future_role_of_the_third_sector_in_economic_and_social_regeneration.pdf (accessed 13 July 2009).

Hodgson, G.M. (1993) *Economics and Evolution: bringing life back into economics*, Cambridge: Polity Press.

Hodgson, G.M. (1998) 'Competence and contract in the theory of the firm', *Journal of Economic Behavior and Organization*, 35(2): 179–201.

Hodgson, G.M. (2006) *Economics in the Shadows of Darwin and Marx: essays on institutional and evolutionary themes*, Cheltenham, UK: Edward Elgar.

Hombach, B. (2000) *The Politics of the New Centre*, Cambridge: Polity Press.

Hopkins, R. (2000) *Impact Assessment Study of Oxfam Fair Trade: final report*, Oxford: Oxfam Fair Trade Programme.

Hulgård, L. (2006) 'Danish social enterprises: a public-third sector partnership', in M. Nyssens (ed.) *Social Enterprise: at the crossroads of market, public policies and civil society*, London: Routledge.

Hulme, D. and Mosley, P. (1996) *Finance Against Poverty*, vols 1–2, London: Routledge.

Hupe, P.L., Meijs, L.C.P.M., and Vorthoren, M.H. (2000) *Hybrid Governance: the impact of the nonprofit sector in the Netherlands*, The Hague: Social and Cultural Planning Office.

Ianes, A. and Tortia, E. (forthcoming) 'Creativity and institutional building: the case of Italian social cooperatives', in S. Sacchetti and R. Sugden (eds) *Knowledge in the Development of Economies: institutional choices under globalisation*, Cheltenham, UK: Edward Elgar, pp. 158–80.

IFF Research (2005) *A Survey of Social Services across the UK*, London: IFF Research. Online. Available at www.cabinetoffice.gov.uk/media/cabinetoffice/third_sector/assets/survey_social_enterprise_across_uk.pdf (accessed 13 July 2009).

Im, K.S., Pesaran, M.H., and Shin, Y. (2003) 'Testing for unit roots in heterogeneous panels', *Journal of Econometrics*, 115(1): 53–74.

Independent Sector (2005) *The Nonprofit Almanac*, Washington, DC: Urban Institute Press.

Ingram, R.W. and Frazier, K.B. (1980) 'Environmental performance and corporate disclosure', *Journal of Accounting Research*, 18(2): 614–22.

Iqbal, M. (2001) 'Islamic and conventional banking in the nineties: a comparative study', *Islamic Economic Studies*, 8(2): 1–27.

Islam, N. (1995) 'Growth empirics: a panel data approach', *Quarterly Journal of Economics*, 110(4): 1127–70.

Israel, D. and Levinson, A. (2004) 'Willingness to pay for environmental quality: testable empirical implications of the growth and environment literature', *Contributions to Economic Analysis and Policy*, 3(1): Art 2.

James, E. (1983) 'How nonprofits grow: a model', *Journal of Policy Analysis and Management*, 2(3): 350–65.

James, E. and Rose-Ackerman, S. (1985) 'The nonprofit enterprise in market economies', PONPO Working Paper no. 95, New Haven, CT: Program on Nonprofit Organizations, Yale University.

Jensen, M.C. (1986) 'Agency costs of free cash flow, corporate finance, and takeovers', *American Economic Review*, 76(2): 323–9.

Johnson, S. (2000) 'Literature review on social entrepreneurship', Edmonton: Canadian Centre for Social Entrepreneurship, University of Alberta School of Business. Online. Available at www.business.ualberta.ca/CCSE/publications/publications/Lit.%20 Review%20SE%20November%202000.rtf (accessed 13 July 2009).

Jones, D. and Keogh, W. (2006) 'Social enterprise: a case of terminological ambiguity and complexity', *Social Enterprise Journal*, 2(1): 11–26.

Jones, D.C. and Kato, T. (2007) 'The impact of teams on output, quality and downtime: an empirical analysis using individual panel data', IZA Discussion Paper no. 2917, Bonn: Institute for the Study of Labor (IZA).

Jones, M.K. (2006) 'Is there employment discrimination against the disabled?', *Economic Letters*, 92(1): 32–7.

Jones, M.K. (2008) 'Disability and the labour market: a review of the empirical evidence', *Journal of Economic Studies*, 35(5): 405–24.

Jorgenson, D.W. and Stiroh, K.J. (2000) 'Raising the speed limit: U.S. economic growth in the information age', *Brookings Papers on Economic Activity*, 2000(1): 125–211.

Jorgenson, D.W., Ho, M.S., and Stiroh, K.J. (2002) 'Projecting productivity growth: lessons from the U.S. growth resurgence', *Federal Reserve Bank of Atlanta Economic Review*, 87(3): 1–13.

Kalaitzidakis, P., Mamuneas, T.P., Savvides, A., and Stengos, T. (2001) 'Measures of human capital and nonlinearities in economic growth', *Journal of Economic Growth*, 6(3): 229–54.

Karlan, D.S. (2005) 'Social connections and group banking', *Economic Journal* 117(517): F52–F84.

Katz, L.F. and Murphy, K.M. (1992) 'Changes in relative wages, 1963–1987: supply and demand factors', *Quarterly Journal of Economics*, 107(1): 37–78.

Kaushal, N. and Kaestner, R. (2001) 'From welfare to work: has welfare reform worked?', *Journal for Policy Analysis and Management*, 20(4): 699–719.

Kendall, J. (2000) 'The mainstreaming of the third sector into public policy in England in the late 1990s: whys and wherefores', *Policy and Politics*, 28(4): 541–62.

Kendall, J. and Anheier, H.K. (2001) 'Conclusion: the third sector at the crossroads? Social, political and economic dynamics', in H.K. Anheier and J. Kendall (eds) *Third Sector Policy at the Crossroads: an international nonprofit analysis*, London: Routledge.

Kerlin, J.A. (2006) 'Social Enterprise in the United States and Europe: understanding and learning from the differences', *Voluntas*, 17(3): 246–62.

Kidd, M.P., Sloane, P.J., and Ferko, I. (2000) 'Disability and the labour market: an analysis of British males', *Journal of Health Economics*, 19(6): 961–81.

King, R.G. and Levine, R. (1993) 'Finance and growth: Schumpeter might be right', *The Quarterly Journal of Economics*, 108(3): 717–37.

KLD Research and Analytics (2009a) *Environmental, Social and Governance (ESG)*

Ratings. Online. Available at www.kld.com/research/ratings_indicators.html (accessed 21 September 2009).

KLD Research and Analytics (2009b) *FTSE KLD 400 Social Index*. Online. Available at www.kld.com/indexes/ds400index/index.html (accessed 31 July 2009).

Klein, P.G. and Luu, H. (2003) 'Politics and productivity', *Economic Inquiry*, 41(3): 433–47.

Kluve, J. (2006) 'The effectiveness of European active labor market policy', IZA Discussion Paper no. 2018, Bonn: Institute for the Study of Labor (IZA).

Knapp, M. (2002) 'The mixed economy of care: critical issues and developments in England since 1990', in Institut für Sozialarbeit und Sozialpädagogik (ed.) *Social Services in Transition: towards a European social services information system*, Frankfurt: Institut für Sozialarbeit und Sozialpädagogik, pp. 43–58.

Kodner, D.L. (2003) 'Consumer-directed services: lessons and implications for integrated systems of care', *International Journal of Integrated Care*, 3 (June): 1–7.

Kohler, P. (2007) 'The economics of fair trade: for whose benefit? An investigation into the limits of fair trade as a development tool and the risk of clean-washing', HEI Working Papers no. 06–2007, Geneva: Graduate Institute of International Studies.

Koivumaa-Honkanen, H., Honkanen, R., Viinamäki, H., Heikkilä, K., Kaprio, J., and Koskenvuo, M. (2000) 'Self-reported life satisfaction and 20-year mortality in healthy Finnish adults', *American Journal of Epidemiology*, 152(10): 983–91.

KPMG Global Sustainability Services (2005) *KPMG International Survey of Corporate Responsibility Reporting, 2005*, Amsterdam: KPMG Global Sustainability Services.

Kramer, R.M. (1981) *Voluntary Agencies in the Welfare State*, Berkeley, CA: University of California Press.

Kreps, D.M. (1990) 'Corporate culture and economic theory', in J.E. Alt and K.A. Shepsle (eds) *Perspectives on Positive Political Economy*, Cambridge: Cambridge University Press, pp. 90–143.

Krueger, A.B. and Malečková, J. (2003) 'Education, poverty, and terrorism: is there a casual connection?', *Journal of Economic Perspectives*, 17(4): 119–44.

Lamothe, M. and Lamothe, S. (2009) 'Beyond the search for competition in social service contracting: procurement, consolidation, and accountability', *American Review of Public Administration*, 39(2): 164–88.

Laville, J.L. (2001) 'France: social enterprises developing proximity services', in C. Borzaga and J. Defourny (eds) *The Emergence of Social Enterprise*, London: Routledge, pp. 100–19.

LeClair, M.S. (2002) 'Fighting the tide: alternative trade organizations in the era of global free trade', *World Development*, 30(6): 949–58.

Leete, L. (2000) 'Wage equity and employment motivation in nonprofit and for-profit organizations', *Journal of Economic Behavior and Organization*, 43(4): 423–46.

Le Grand, J. (1991) 'Quasi-markets and social policy', *Economic Journal*, 101(408): 1256–67.

Le Grand, J. and Bartlett, W. (eds) (1993) *Quasi Markets and Social Policy*, London: Macmillan.

Lehr, B. and Lichtenberg, F. (1999) 'Information technology and its impact on productivity: firm-level evidence from government and private data sources, 1977–1993', *Canadian Journal of Economics*, 32(2): 335–62.

Leibenstein, H. (1966) 'Allocative efficiency vs. "X-efficiency"', *American Economic Review*, 56(3): 392–415.

Leś, E. (2009) 'The third sector in post-transition Poland', *Revista Española del Tercer Sector*, no. 10 (September): 171–87.

Leś, E. and Jeliazkova, M. (2007) 'The social economy in Central East and South East Europe', in A. Noya and E. Clarence (eds) *The Social Economy: building inclusive economies*, Paris: OECD Publishing, pp. 189–210.

Levine, D.I. (1991) 'Cohesiveness, productivity, and wage dispersion', *Journal of Economic Behavior and Organization*, 15(2): 237–55.

Link, B.G. and Phelan, J.C. (2001) 'Conceptualizing stigma', *Annual Review of Sociology*, vol. 27: 363–85.

Liu, Z. and Stengos, T. (1999) 'Non-linearities in cross-country growth regressions: a semiparametric approach', *Journal of Applied Econometrics*, 14(5): 527–38.

Locke, E.A. (1969) 'What is job satisfaction?', *Organizational Behavior and Human Performance*, 4(4): 309–36.

Loss, M. (2003) 'National profiles of work integration social enterprises: Italy', EMES Working Paper no. 03/04, Liège: EMES European Research Network.

Lucas, R.E. (1988) 'On the mechanics of economic development', *Journal of Monetary Economics*, 22(1): 3–42.

McCabe, A. and Hahn, S. (2006) 'Promoting social enterprise in Korea and the UK: community economic development, alternative welfare provision, or a means to welfare to work?', *Social Policy and Society*, 5(3): 387–98.

McIntosh, C., Villaran, G., and Wydick, B. (2008) 'Microfinance and home improvement: using retrospective panel data to measure program effects on fundamental events', San Francisco: Department of Economics, University of San Francisco. Online. Available at www.usfca.edu/fac_staff/wydick/mf&hi.pdf (accessed 22 September 2009).

McWilliams, A. and Siegel, D. (2000) 'Corporate social responsibility and financial performance: correlation or misspecification?', *Strategic Management Journal*, 21(5): 603–9.

Maddala, G.S. (1983) *Limited-Dependent and Qualitative Variables in Econometrics*, Cambridge: Cambridge University Press.

Maddala, G.S. and Wu, S. (1999) 'A comparative study of unit root tests with panel data and a new simple test', *Oxford Bulletin of Economics and Statistics*, 61(S1): 631–52.

Mair, J. and Martí, I. (2006) 'Social entrepreneurship research: a source of explanation, prediction, and delight', *Journal of World Business*, 41(1): 36–44.

Malcomson, J.M. (1981) 'Unemployment and the efficiency wage hypothesis', *Economic Journal*, 91(364): 848–66.

Mankiw, N.G., Romer, D., and Weil, D.N. (1992) 'A contribution to the empirics of economic growth', *Quarterly Journal of Economics*, 107(2): 407–37.

Manning, A. (2003) 'The real thin theory: monopsony in modern labour markets', *Labour Economics*, 10(2): 105–31.

Margolis, J.D. and Walsh J.P. (2001) 'Misery loves companies: whither social initiatives by business?', Social Enterprise Series no. 19, Harvard Business School Working Paper no. 01–058, Cambridge, MA: Harvard Business School.

Marshall, A. (1890) *Principles of Economics*, London: Macmillan.

Marshall, A. (1919) *Industry and Trade: a study of industrial technique and business organization; and of their influence on the conditions of various classes and nations*, London: Macmillan.

Masanjala, W.H. and Papageorgiou, C. (2004) 'The Solow model with CES technology: nonlinearities and parameter heterogeneity', *Journal of Applied Econometrics*, 19(2): 171–201.

Maseland, R. and de Vaal, A. (2002) 'How fair is fair trade?', *De Economist*, 150(3): 251–72.

Mauro, P. (1995) 'Corruption and growth', *Quarterly Journal of Economics*, 110(3): 681–712.

Mendell, M. and Nogales, R. (2009) 'Social enterprises in OECD member countries: what are the financial streams?', in A. Noya (ed.) *The Changing Boundaries of Social Enterprises*, Paris: OECD Publishing, pp. 89–138.

Mendoza, R. and Bahadur, C. (2002) 'Toward free and fair trade: a global public good perspective', *Challenge*, 45(5): 21–62.

Michie, J. and Sheehan, M. (1999) 'No innovation without representation? An analysis of participation, representation, R&D and innovation', *Economic Analysis*, 2(2): 85–97.

Microfinance Information Exchange (2008) *Trend Lines 2005–2007 MFI Benchmarks*. Online. Available at www.themix.org/publications/trend-lines-2005–2007-mfi-benchmarks (accessed 22 September 2009).

Mill, J.S. (1848) *Principles of Political Economy, with some of their applications to social philosophy*, London: John W. Parker.

Mirvis, P.H. (1992) 'The quality of employment in the nonprofit sector: an update on employee attitudes in nonprofits versus business and government', *Nonprofit Management and Leadership*, 3(1): 23–41.

Mirvis, P.H. and Hackett, E.J. (1983) 'Work and workforce characteristics in the nonprofit sector', *Monthly Labor Review*, 106(4): 3–12.

Mitchell, R.C. and Carson, R.T. (1989) *Using Surveys to Value Public Goods: the contingent valuation method*, Washington, DC: Resources for the Future.

Mocan, N.H. and Viola, D. (1997) 'The determinants of child care workers' wages compensation: sectoral difference, human capital, race, insiders and outsiders', NBER Working Paper no. 6328, Cambridge, MA: National Bureau of Economic Research.

Monsma, S.V. and Soper, J.C. (1997) *The Challenge of Pluralism: church and state in five democracies*, Lanham: Rowman and Littlefield.

Montemurro, F. (2008) 'Il rapporto tra enti locali e terzo settore: un'indagine Auser', *Autonomie locali e servizi sociali*, 1(aprile): 47–60.

Monzon, J.L. and Chaves, R. (2008) 'The European social economy: concept and dimensions of the third sector', *Annals of Public and Cooperative Economics*, 79(3–4): 549–77.

Moore, G. (2004) 'The fair trade movement: parameters, issues and future research', *Journal of Business Ethics*, 53(1–2): 73–86.

Morduch, J. (1999) 'The microfinance promise', *Journal of Economic Literature*, 37(4): 1569–614.

Mori, N. and Fulgence, K. (2009) 'Social entrepreneurship in Tanzania: assessment of enabling environment', paper presented at the 2nd EMES International Conference of Social Enterprises, Trento, Italy, 1–4 July 2009. Online. Available at www.euricse.eu/sites/default/files/Neema_Mori_1_.pdf (accessed 23 August 2009).

Mori, P. (2007) 'Motivazioni e funzioni dell'impresa sociale di tipo capitalistico: un'analisi economica', paper presented at the Conference for Law and Economics, Milan: Bocconi University, 9 November.

Mosca, M., Musella, M., and Pastore, F. (2007) 'Relational goods, monitoring and non-pecuniary compensations in the nonprofit sector: The case of the Italian social services', *Annals of Public and Cooperative Economics*, 78(1): 57–86.

Murphy, K.M., Shleifer, A., and Vishny, R.W. (1991) 'The allocation of talent: the implications for growth', *Quarterly Journal of Economics*, 106(2): 503–30.

Nelson, R.R. and Winter, S.G. (1982) *An Evolutionary Theory of Economic Change*, Cambridge, MA: Harvard University Press.

Nelson, V. and Galvez, M. (2000) 'Social impact of ethical and conventional cocoa trading on forest-dependent people in Ecuador', Kent: Natural Resources and Ethical Trade Programme, Natural Resources Institute, University of Greenwich. Online. Available at www.nri.org/projects/NRET/SocialImpact.pdf (accessed 12 April 2009).

Nicholls, A. (2008) 'Introduction: the changing landscape of social entrepreneurship', in A. Nicholls (ed.) *Social Entrepreneurship: new models of sustainable social change*, Oxford: Oxford University Press, pp. 1–36.

Nyblom, J. and Harvey, A. (2000) 'Tests of common stochastic trends', *Econometric Theory*, 16(2): 176–99.

Nyssens, M. (ed.) (2006) *Social Enterprise: at the crossroads of markets, public policies and civil society*, London: Routledge.

Oliner, S.D. and Sichel, D.E. (2002) 'Information technology and productivity: where are we now and where are we going?', *Federal Reserve Bank of Atlanta Economic Review*, 87(3): 15–44.

O'Reilly, A. (2003) 'The right to decent work of persons with disabilities', IFP/Skills Working Paper no. 14, Geneva: International Labour Organization.

Organisation for Economic Co-operation and Development (2008) *OECD Health Data 2008: statistics and indicators for 30 countries*, Paris: OECD.

Oxfam (2002) *Rigged Rules and Double Standards: trade, globalisation and the fight against poverty*, by K. Watkins and P. Fowler, Oxford: Oxfam International.

Oxford Policy Management and International Institute for Environment and Development (2000) 'Fair Trade: overview, impact, challenges', Oxford: Oxford Policy Management. Online. Available at www.opml.co.uk/publications/client_reports/fair_trade_over.html (accessed 10 July 2009).

Pagano, M. (1997) 'Financial markets and growth: an overview', *European Economic Review*, 37(2–3): 613–22.

Pagano, U. (1992) 'Property rights equilibria and institutional stability', *Economic Notes*, 20(2): 189–228.

Page, S. (ed.) (2006) *Trade and Aid: partners or rivals in the development policy*, London: Cameron May.

Pariente, W. (2000) 'The impact of fair trade on a coffee cooperative in Costa Rica: a producer's behaviour approach', Paris: DEA d'Economie du Développement Université Paris I Panthéon Sorbonne.

Paton, R. (2003) *Managing and Measuring Social Enterprises*, London: Sage.

Pättiniemi, P. (2001) 'Finland: labour cooperatives as an innovative response to unemployment', in C. Borzaga and J. Defourny (eds) *The Emergence of Social Enterprise*, London: Routledge, pp. 82–99.

Pättiniemi, P. (2006) 'Case Finland: development of legal framework for social enterprises in Finland', paper presented at the seminar 'Emerging models of social entrepreneurship: possible paths for social enterprise development in Central East and South East Europe', Zagreb, 28–29 September 2006. Online. Available at www.oecd.org/dataoecd/8/51/37508850.pdf (27 August 2009).

Paul, C.J.M. and Siegel, D.S. (2006) 'Corporate social responsibility and economic performance', *Journal of Productivity Analysis*, 26(3): 207–11.

Pava, M.L. and Krausz, J. (1996) 'The association between corporate social-responsibility and financial performance: the paradox of social cost', *Journal of Business Ethics*, 15(3): 321–57.

Pavot, W., Diener, E., Colvin, C.R., and Sandvik, E. (1991) 'Further validation of the satisfaction with life scale: evidence for the cross-method convergence of well-being measures', *Journal of Personality Assessment*, 57(1): 149–61.

Penrose E. (1959) *The Theory of the Growth of the Firm*, Oxford: Oxford University Press.

Perista, H. and Nogueira, S. (2002) 'National profiles of work integration social enterprises: Portugal', EMES Working Paper no. 02/09, Liège: EMES European Research Network.

Perista, H. and Nogueira, S. (2006) 'Work integration social enterprises in Portugal: a tool for work integration?', in M. Nyssens (ed.) *Social Enterprise: at the crossroads of market, public policies and civil society*, London: Routledge, pp. 195–205.

Pestoff, V.A. (1992) 'Third sector and co-operative services: an alternative to privatization', *Journal of Consumer Policy*, 15(1): 21–45.

Pestoff, V.A. (2004) 'The development and future of the social economy in Sweden', in A. Evers and J.L. Laville (eds) *The Third Sector in Europe*, Cheltenham: Edward Elgar, pp. 55–72.

Pfenning, A. and Bahle, T. (2002) 'Structures of social services in Germany', in Institut für Sozialarbeit und Sozialpädagogik (ed.) *Social Services in Transition: towards a European social services information system*, Frankfurt: Institut für Sozialarbeit und Sozialpädagogik, pp. 68–91.

Phelps, E.S. (1997) *Rewarding Work: how to restore participation and self-support to free enterprise*, Cambridge, MA: Harvard University Press.

Pitt, M.M. and Khandker, S.R. (1998) 'The impact of group-based credit programs on poor households in Bangladesh: does the gender of participants matter?' *Journal of Political Economy*, 106(5), 958–96.

Podivinsky, J.M. and Steward, G. (2006) 'Why is labour-managed firm entry so rare? An analysis of UK manufacturing data', *Journal of Economic Behavior and Organization*, 63(1): 177–92.

Polanyi, M. (1958) *Personal Knowledge. Towards a post critical philosophy*, Chicago: University of Chicago Press.

Prescott, E.S. (1997) 'Group lending and financial intermediation: an example', *Federal Reserve of Bank Richmond Economic Quarterly*, 83(4): 23–48.

Preston, A.E. (1989) 'The nonprofit worker in a for-profit world', *Journal of Labor Economics*, 7(4): 438–63.

Preston, L.E. and O'Bannon, D.P. (1997) 'The corporate social–financial performance relationship: a typology and analysis', *Business and Society*, 36(4): 419–29.

Provasi, G. (2004) *Lo Sviluppo Locale: una nuova frontiera per il nonprofit*, Milano: Franco Angeli.

Psacharopoulos, G. (1994) 'Returns to investment in education: a global update', *World Development*, 22(9): 1325–43.

Putnam, R. (1993) *Making Democracy Work: civic traditions in modern Italy*, Princeton: Princeton University Press.

Quah, D. (1999) 'The weightless economy in economic development', CEP Discussion Paper no. 417, London: Centre for Economic Performance, London School of Economics and Political Science.

Rawls, J. (1974) 'Some reasons for the maximin criterion', *American Economic Review*, 64(2): 141–6.

Ray, D. (1998) *Development Economics*, Princeton, NJ: Princeton University Press.

Regulator of Community Interest Companies (2007) *Report to the Secretary of State for Trade and Industry*, London: Regulator of Community Interest Companies. Online. Available at www.cicregulator.gov.uk/news/Annual%20Report/CIC%20Annual%20 Report%202005–06.pdf (accessed 17 July 2009).

Roach, S.S. (1991) 'Services under siege: the restructuring imperative', *Harvard Business Review*, 69(5): 82–91.

Rodrik, D. (1998) 'Globalisation, social conflict and economic growth', *World Economy*, 21(2): 143–58.

Rodrik, D. (1999) 'Where did all the growth go? External shocks, social conflict, and growth collapses', *Journal of Economic Growth*, 4(4): 385–412.

Rodrik, D. (2000) 'Institutions for high-quality growth: what they are and how to acquire them', *Studies in Comparative International Development*, 35(3): 3–31.

Rodrik, D. (2002) 'Trade policy reform as institutional reform', in B.M. Hoekman, A. Mattoo, and P. English (eds) *Development, Trade, and the WTO: a handbook*, Washington, DC: World Bank, pp. 3–10.

Rodrik, D. (2004) 'Rethinking growth policies in the developing world', Luca d'Agliano Lecture. Torino, 8 October. Online. Available at http://ksghome.harvard.edu/~drodrik/Luca_d_Agliano_Lecture_Oct_2004.pdf (accessed 14 August 2009).

Romer, P.M. (1990) 'Endogenous technological change', *Journal of Political Economy*, 98(5): S71–102.

Ronchi, L. (2002) 'The impact of fair trade on producers and their organizations: a case study with Coocafé in Costa Rica', PRUS Working Paper no. 11, Sussex: Poverty Research Unit at Sussex, University of Sussex.

Roper, J. and Cheney, G. (2005) 'The meanings of social entrepreneurship today', *Corporate Governance*, 5(3): 95–104.

Rose-Ackerman, S. (1996) 'Altruism, nonprofits, and economic theory', *Journal of Economic Literature*, 34(2): 701–28.

Ruf, B.M., Muralidhar, K., Brown, R.M., Janney, J.J., and Paul, K. (2001) 'An empirical investigation of the relationship between change in corporate social performance and financial performance: a stakeholder theory perspective', *Journal of Business Ethics*, 32(2): 143–56.

Ruhm, C. and Borkoski, C. (2003) 'Compensation in the nonprofit sector', *Journal of Human Resources*, 38(4): 992–1021.

Ruiz Olabuénaga, J.I. (2000) *El sector no lucrativo en España*, Bilbao: Fundaciòn BBVA.

Sacchetti, S. and Sugden, R. (2003) 'The governance of networks and economic power: the nature and impact of subcontracting relationships', *Journal of Economic Surveys*, 17(5): 669–91.

Sacchetti, S. and Sugden, R. (2009) 'The organization of production and its publics: mental proximity, markets and hierarchies', *Review of Social Economy*, 67(3): 289–311.

Sacconi, L. (2000) *The Social Contract of the Firm: economics, ethics, and organisation*, Berlin: Springer-Verlag.

Sachs, J.D. and Warner, A.M. (1997) 'Fundamental sources of long-run growth', *American Economic Review*, 87(2): 184–8.

Sachs, J.D. and Warner, A.M. (2001) 'The curse of natural resources', *European Economic Review*, 45(4–6): 827–38.

Sala-i-Martin, X. (1997) 'I just ran two million regressions', *American Economic Review*, 87(2): 178–83.

Sala-i-Martin, X. (2002) '15 years of new growth economics: what have we learnt?', Working Paper no. 172, Santiago: Central Bank of Chile.

Salamon, L.M. (1987) 'Of market failure, voluntary failure, and third-party government: toward a theory of government-nonprofit relations in the modern welfare state', *Nonprofit and Voluntary Sector Quarterly*, 16(1): 29–49.

Salamon, L.M. (1990), *Struttura e finanziamento del nonprofit sector negli Usa*, Milano: Giuffrè Editore.

Salamon, L.M. (1993) 'The marketization of welfare: changing nonprofit and for-profit roles in the American welfare', *Social Service Review*, 67(1): 16–39.

Salamon, L.M. and Anheier, H.K. (1998) 'Social origins of civil society: explaining the nonprofit sector cross-nationally', *Voluntas*, 9(3): 213–48.

Salamon, L.M., Lems, L.C., and Chinnock, K. (2000) 'The Nonprofit Sector: for what and for whom?', Working Papers of the Johns Hopkins University Comparative Nonprofit Sector Project no. 37, Baltimore, MD: Johns Hopkins Center for Civil Society Studies.

Salamon, L.M., Anheier, H.K., List, R., Toepler, S., Sokolowski, S.W., and Associates (1999) *Global Civil Society: dimensions of the nonprofit sector*, Baltimore, MD: Johns Hopkins Center for Civil Society Studies.

Salop, S.C. (1979) 'A model of the natural rate of unemployment', *American Economic Review*, 69(1): 117–25.

Savas, E.S. (2000) *Privatization and Public–Private Partnership*, New York: Chatham House.

Savedoff, W.D. (2006) *Public Policy for People with Disabilities in Chile: learning from international experiences*, report submitted to the Inter-American Development Bank, Portland, ME: Social Insight.

Schmid, G. (1998) 'Transitional labour markets: a new European employment strategy', WZB Discussion Paper FS I 98–206, Berlin: Wissenschaftszentrum Berlin für Sozialforschung.

Schmitter, P.C. and Trechsel, A.H. (2004) *The Future of Democracy in Europe: trends, analyses and reforms*, Strasbourg: Council of Europe.

Screpanti, E. and Zamagni, S. (2004) *Profilo di Storia del Pensiero Economico*, Roma: Carocci Editore.

Sen, A.K. (1977) 'Rational fools: a critique of the behavioural foundations of economic theory', *Philosophy and Public Affairs*, 6(4): 317–44.

Sen, A.K. (1993) 'Internal consistency of choice', *Econometrica*, 61(3): 495–521.

Sen, A.K. (2006) 'Giustizia e libertà', *Impresa Sociale* 75(1): 11–21.

Shapiro, C. and Stiglitz, J.E. (1984) 'Equilibrium unemployment as a worker discipline device', *American Economic Review*, 74(3): 433–44.

Shedler, J., Mayman, M., and Manis, M. (1993) 'The illusion of mental health', *American Psychologist*, 48(11): 1117–31.

Shepherd, A.R. (2000) 'Minimum wages and the Card-Krueger paradox', *Southern Economic Journal*, 67(2): 469–78.

Sichel, D.E. (1997) *The Computer Revolution: an economic perspective*, Washington, DC: Brookings Institution.

Sivesind, K.H., Lorentzen, H., Selle, P., and Wollebaek, D. (2002) *The Voluntary Sector in Norway: composition, changes, and causes*, ISF Report no. 2002–02, Oslo: Institutt for Samfunnsforskning.

Smith, A. and Twomey, B. (2002) 'Labour market experiences of people with disabilities', *Labour Market Trends*, 110(8): 415–27.

Sobel, J. (2005) 'Interdependent preferences and reciprocity', *Journal of Economic Literature*, 43(2): 392–436.

Social Investment Forum (2007) 'Executive summary' of *2007 Report on Socially Responsible Investment Trends in the United States*, Washington, DC: Social Investment Forum. Online. Available at www.socialinvest.org/resources/pubs/documents/FINALExecSummary_2007_SIF_Trends_wlinks.pdf (accessed 24 August 2009).

Solomon, R.C. and Hanson, K.R. (1985) *It's Good Business*, New York: Atheneum.

Solow, R.M. (1956) 'A contribution to the theory of economic growth', *Quarterly Journal of Economics*, 70(1): 65–94.

Spear, R. and Bidet, E. (2005) 'Social enterprise for work integration in 12 European countries: a descriptive analysis', *Annals of Public and Cooperative Economics*, 76(2): 195–231.

Stanwick, P.A. and Stanwick, S.D. (1998) 'The relationship between corporate social performance, and organizational size, financial performance, and environmental performance: an empirical examination', *Journal of Business Ethics*, 17(2): 195–204.

Statistics Canada (2004) *Cornerstones of Community Highlights of the National Survey of Nonprofit and Voluntary Organizations*, Ottawa: Statistics Canada.

Steinberg, R. (1990) 'Labor economics and the non-profit sector: a literature review', *Non-profit and Voluntary Sector Quarterly*, 19(2): 151–69.

Stewart, D.M., Kane, P.R., and Scruggs, L. (2002) 'Education and training', in L.M. Salamon (ed.) *The State of Nonprofit America*, Washington, DC: Brookings Institution, pp. 107–48.

Stiglitz, J.E. (2002) *Globalization and Its Discontents*, New York: W.W. Norton.

Stiglitz, J.E. and Weiss, A. (1981) 'Credit rationing in markets with imperfect information', *American Economic Review*, 71(3): 393–410.

Stiglitz, J.E., Sen, A., and Fitoussi, J-P. (2009) *Report of the Commission on the Measurement of Economic Performance and Social Progress*. Online. Available at www.aedd.fr/public/frmedias/docutheque/document/aedd/2009/359_rapport_stiglitz1.pdf (accessed 11 February 2009).

Strassmann, P.A. (1990) *The Business Value of Computers: an executive's guide*, New Canaan, CT: Information Economics Press.

Stryjan, Y. (2004) 'Sistema di sviluppo della cooperazione in Svezia: sviluppo del sistema e "embeddedness" locale', *Impresa Sociale*, 73(4): 140–59.

Stryjan, Y. and Wijkström, F. (1996) 'Cooperatives and nonprofit organizations in Swedish social welfare', *Annals of Public and Cooperative Economics*, 67(1): 5–27.

Stultz, R.M. and Williamson, R. (2003) 'Culture, openness and finance', *Journal of Financial Economics*, 70(3): 313–39.

Sugden, R. (1991) 'Rational choice: a survey of contributions from economics and philosophy', *Economic Journal*, 101(407): 751–85.

Suranovic, S. (2002) 'International labour and environmental standards agreements: is this fair trade?', *World Economy*, 25(2): 231–45.

Taylor-Gooby, P. (1996) 'Paying for welfare: the view from Europe', *Political Quarterly*, 67(2): 116–26.

Thamm, D. (1995) 'Geld statt guter Worte: Zur Finanzierung freier Wohlfhartspflege', in T. Rauschenbach, C. Sachsse, and T. Olk (eds) *Von der Wertgemeinschaft zum Dienstleistungsunternehmen*, Frankfurt am Main: Suhrkamp, pp. 356–76.

Thompson, J. and Doherty, B. (2006) 'The diverse world of social enterprise: a collection of social enterprise stories', *International Journal of Social Economics*, 33(5–6): 361–75.

Torgler, B. and Garcia-Valinas, M.A. (2005) 'The willingness to pay for preventing environmental damage', CREMAS Working Paper 2005–22, Basel: Center for Research in Economics, Management and the Arts.

Tortia, E.C. (2003) 'Property rights, distribution of value added, and accumulation of capital in labour managed firms', *Economia Politica*, 20(2): 251–86.

Tortia, E.C. (2006) 'Self-financing in labour-managed firms (LMFs): individual capital accounts and bonds advances', in S. Novkovic and V. Sena (eds) *Cooperative Firms in Global Markets*, Kidlington, Oxford: JAI Press/Elsevier, pp. 233–61.

Tortia, E.C. (2008) 'Worker well-being and perceived fairness: survey-based findings from Italy', *Journal of Socio-Economics*, 37(5): 2080–94.

Trevor-Roper, H.R. (1969) 'Religion, the Reformation and social change', in H.R. Trevor-Roper, *The European Witch-Craze of the Sixteenth and Seventeenth Centuries and Other Essays*, New York: Harper & Row, pp. 1–45.

Trukeschitz, B. (2004) '*Soziale Dienste in Österreich—Beschäftigungsstudie 2002. Trägerstruktur, Angebotsstruktur und Beschäftigung. Stichprobenbeschreibung*, mimeo, Wien: Abteilung für Sozialpolitik, Wirtschaftsuniversität Wien.

United Nations Development Programme (2008) *Social Enterprise: a new model for poverty reduction and employment generation*, Bratislava: UNDP Regional Centre for Europe and the Commonwealth of Independent States.

Valentinov, V. (2007) 'The property rights approach to nonprofit organisations: the role of intrinsic motivation', *Public Organisation Review*, 7(1): 41–55.

Valentinov, V. (2008) 'The economics of the non-distribution constraint: a critical reappraisal', *Annals of Public and Cooperative Economics*, 79(1): 35–52.

Vanek, J. (1970) *The General Theory of Labour Managed Market Economies*, Ithaca, NY: Cornell University Press.

Vanek, J. (1977) *The Labor-managed Economy: essays by J. Vanek*, Ithaca, NY: Cornell University Press.

Vantomme, D., Geuens, M., De Houwer, J., and De Pelsmacker, P. (2006) 'Explicit and implicit determinants of ethical consumerism', in C. Pechmann and L. Price (eds), *Advances in Consumer Research*, no. 33, Duluth, MN: Association for Consumer Research, pp. 699–703.

Verschoor, C.C. (1998) 'A study of the link between a corporation's financial performance and its commitment to ethics', *Journal of Business Ethics*, 17(13): 1509–16.

Vick, N., Tobin, R., Swift, P., Spandler, H., Hill, M., Coldham, T., Towers, C., and Waldock, H. (2006) *An Evaluation of the Impact of the Social Care Modernisation Programme on the Implementation of Direct Payments*, London: Health and Social Care Advisory Service. Online. Available at www.masc.bham.ac.uk/pdfs/DP%20 Final%20Report.pdf (accessed 13 July 2009).

Waddock, S.A. and Graves, S.B. (1997) 'The corporate social performance–financial performance link', *Strategic Management Journal*, 18(4): 303–19.

Walras, L. (1865) *Les Associations populaires de consommation, de production et de crédit*, Paris: Dentu.

Ward, B. (1958) 'The firm in Illyria: market syndicalism', *American Economic Review*, 44(4): 566–89.

Weisbrod, B.A. (1977) *The Voluntary Nonprofit Sector: an economic analysis*, Lexington, MA: Lexington Books.

Weisbrod, B.A. (1983) 'Nonprofit and proprietary sector behavior: wage differentials among lawyers', *Journal of Labor Economics*, 1(3): 246–63.

Weisbrod, B.A. (1988) *The Nonprofit Economy*, Cambridge, MA: Harvard University Press.

Weisbrod, B.A. (1989) 'Rewarding performance that is hard to measure: the private nonprofit sector', *Science*, 244(4904): 541–6.

Weisbrod, B.A. (ed.) (1998) *To Profit or Not to Profit: the commercial transformation of the nonprofit sector*, Cambridge: Cambridge University Press.

Wijkström, F., Einarsson, S., and Larsson, O. (2004) *Staten och det civila samhället. Idétraditioner och tankemodeller i den statliga bidragsgivningen till ideella organisationer*,

Working Paper series in Business Administration no. 2004:21, Stockholm: Socialstyrelsen koch EFI, Ekonomiska Forskningsinstitutet, Handelshögskolan i Stockholm.

Wilding, K., Clark, J., Griffith, M., Jochum, V., and Wainwright, S. (2006) *The UK Voluntary Sector Almanac*, London: National Council for Voluntary Organisations.

Wing, K.T., Pollak, T.H., and Blackwood, A. (2008) *The Nonprofit Almanac 2008*, Washington, DC: Urban Institute Press.

Wolch, J.R. (1990) *The Shadow State: government and voluntary sector in transition*, New York: The Foundation Center.

World Bank (2003) *World Development Report 2003. Sustainable development in a dynamic world: transforming institutions, growth, and quality of life*, Washington, DC: World Bank and Oxford University Press.

World Fair Trade Organization (2009) *10 Principles of Fair Trade*. Online. Available at www.wfto.com/index.php?option=com_content&task=view&id=2&Itemid=14 (accessed 6 July 2009).

World Trade Organization (2008) *International Trade Statistics, 2008*, Geneva: WTO Publications. Online. Available at www.wto.org/english/res_e/statis_e/its2008_e/its08_toc_e.htm (accessed 19 July 2009).

World Values Survey Association (2006) *European and World Values Surveys: four-wave integrated data file, 1981–2004, v.20060423, 2006*. Surveys designed and executed by the European Values Study Group and World Values Survey Association. File Producers: ASEP/JDS, Madrid, Spain and Tilburg University, Tilburg, the Netherlands. File Distributors: ASEP/JDS and GESIS, Cologne, Germany.

Wydick, B. (1999). 'Can social cohesion be harnessed to repair market failures? Evidence from group lending in Guatemala', *Economic Journal* 109(457): 463–75.

Yellen, J.L. (1984) 'Efficiency wage models of unemployment', *American Economic Review*, 74(2): 200–5.

Yeo, R. and Moore, K. (2003) 'Including disabled people in poverty reduction work: "nothing about us, nothing without us"', *World Development*, 31(3): 571–90.

Young, D.R. (1983) *If Not for Profit, for What? A behavioral theory of the nonprofit sector based on entrepreneurship*, Lexington, MA: Lexington Books.

Young, D.R. (2005) 'Mission-market tension in managing nonprofit organizations', Nonprofit Studies Program Working Paper no. 05–02, Atlanta, GA: Andrew Young School of Policy Studies, Georgia State University.

Zamagni, S. (2005) 'Per una teoria civile dell'impresa cooperativa', in E. Mazzoli and S. Zamagni (eds) *Verso una Nuova Teoria della Cooperazione*, Bologna: Il Mulino, pp. 15–56.

Zhao, L., Develtere, P., Cui, Z., and Wang, D. (2009) 'New co-operatives in China: the emergence of an indigenous model of social enterprises', paper presented at the 2nd EMES International Conference of Social Enterprises, Trento, Italy, 1–4 July 2009. Online. Available at www.euricse.eu/sites/default/files/Li_Zhao-Delvetere_1_.pdf (accessed 27 August 2009).

Zick Varul, M. (2009) 'Ethical selving in cultural contexts: fairtrade consumption as an everyday ethical practice in the UK and in Germany', *International Journal of Consumer Studies*, 33(2): 183–9.

Zimmer, A., Appel, A., Dittrich, C., Lange, C., Sittermann, B., Stalmann, F., and Kendall, J. (2005) *The Third Sector and the Policy Process in Germany*, TSEP Working Paper no. 9, London: Third Sector European Policy Network, Centre for Civil Society, London School of Economics and Political Science. Online. Available at www.npm-online.de/download/Zimmer_ThirdSector_PolicyProcess.pdf (accessed 13 July 2009).

Index

Note: Page numbers in *italics* denote tables, those in **bold** denote figures.